NEW DOCUMENTS ILLUSTRATING EARLY CHRISTIANITY

A Review of the
Greek Inscriptions and Papyri
published in 1978

by

G. H. R. Horsley

The Ancient History Documentary Research Centre
Macquarie University
1983

The Ancient History Documentary Research Centre (Director: E. A. Judge, Professor of History) has been formed within the School of History, Philosophy & Politics at Macquarie University to focus staff effort in research and professional development and to coordinate it with the work of other organisations interested in the documentation of the ancient world.

Committee for *New Documents illustrating Early Christianity*

Chairman: P. W. Barnett, Master of Robert Menzies College, Macquarie University.
Secretary: P. T. O'Brien, Head, New Testament Department, Moore Theological College, Sydney.
Members: P. Geidans, D. M. Knox, J. Lawler.

Editorial Consultants

F. I. Andersen, Professor of Studies in Religion, University of Queensland.
G. W. Clarke, Deputy Director, Humanities Research Centre, Australian National University.
W. J. Dumbrell, Vice-Principal, Moore Theological College, Sydney.
J. A. L. Lee, Senior Lecturer in Greek, University of Sydney.
K. L. McKay, Reader in Classics, Australian National University.

This volume has been produced with the support of the Australian Institute of Archaeology (N.S.W. Branch), Buxworth Pty. Ltd., National Panasonic (Aust.) Pty. Ltd., the Macquarie University Greek Summer School, the Macquarie University Research Grant, and the following individual donors:— J. Deakin, P. Geidans, P.E. Hollingdale, J.A.L. Lee, A.F. and M. Pennington, J. and P. Reay-Young, G.K. Riethmuller, W. Ritchie, and G. Sperling.

Editorial correspondence should be addressed to Mr G. H. R. Horsley, School of History, Philosophy & Politics, Macquarie University, North Ryde, N.S.W. 2113, Australia.

Business address: The Ancient History Documentary Research Centre, Macquarie University, North Ryde, N.S.W. 2113, Australia.

SUGGESTED CATALOGUING DATA:

Horsley, G. H. R.
    New Documents illustrating early Christianity. A review of the Greek inscriptions and papyri published in 1978.

Bibliography.
Includes index.
ISBN 0 85837 546 X
ISBN 0 85837 545 1 (pbk)

1. Bible. New Testament — Language, style. 2. Inscriptions, Greek. 3. Manuscripts (Papyri). 4. Greek language, Biblical. 5. Church History — Primitive and early church. I. Macquarie University. Ancient History Documentary Research Centre. II. Title.

PA 810   1983   487.4

Typeset by Essay Composition, 225 Miller Street, North Sydney, Australia
Printed by J. Bell and Company Pty. Ltd., 15 McCauley Street, Alexandria, Australia.

CONTENTS

LIST OF ENTRIES

A. New Testament Context

B. Minor Philological Notes

C. Biblical and Related Citations

D. Judaica

E. Ecclesiastica

F. Varia

INTRODUCTION

This Review is primarily a reporting service, designed to make more widely known especially to biblical scholars published texts of philological and historical interest. Those who follow up the bibliographies to particular items will therefore find that much in these pages is derivative, although independent suggestions and comments are also offered. Entries in MM and BAGD are again supplemented/qualified considerably. The character and objectives of the Macquarie-based project to rework MM, for which *New Docs* is intended to serve as a preliminary contribution, is explained in the Preface to *New Docs 1976*. See also C.J. Hemer, 'Towards a new Moulton and Milligan', *Novum Testamentum* 24 (1982) 97–123.

The reader who has been mainly kept in mind during the writing of entries has been the NT researcher, teacher, or student. Readers should be clear that the Review does not aim to provide definitive statements about any text treated. Undoubtedly some of the suggestions put forward in these pages will need correction or supplementation, and so **short notes** in reply (following the format of this volume) will be considered for inclusion. At present, the offer of long articles cannot be entertained.

While the main focus is upon the NT and the first four centuries, texts of later date have been included if it is judged that they may be of interest to students of that era (e.g., liturgical and homiletical texts; biblical citations). Some texts (e.g. **4,9,19,95**) have been covered simply because they are representative of the times in some way, and make a general contribution to understanding NT background. It is envisaged that, as the Review proceeds over a number of years, it will gradually form a *Chrestomathie* for those whose main focus of interest is the NT and Early Church History but who do not have ready access to the epigraphic and papyrological documents.

This volume treats texts published during 1978, either for the first time or as re-editions, in corpora and 'conspectus' volumes (such as *AE, BE, SEG*). Occasionally such a text will render necessary more-than-passing discussion of texts published at some earlier date, which were not re-published in 1978. Following the practice of *SEG*, we have not refrained from including occasional references to texts and discussions published after 1978, where they are relevant. The emphasis is heavily upon Greek texts, although Latin documents and occasionally ones including Semitic words are noticed. Corpora consisting entirely of, e.g., Latin inscriptions, or hieroglyphic, demotic or Coptic papyri have not been taken into account.

Listed below are all collections for the year 1978 which have been read, arranged according to the abbreviations used in this volume. Where the abbreviation is bracketed, the work was read, but no texts were selected for noting in this volume. Unless otherwise specified, all references to texts throughout this Review are to item numbers in the work whose abbreviation precedes it, not to page numbers. Volume number and date are provided throughout the Review for all texts from non-1978 corpora. Where no volume number and date are given, the reference is to a publication of 1978 as listed below. Occasional publications from 1976 and 1977 which were missed have been included. It is our aim to keep to the five-year lag between the year whose publications are being culled and the appearance of this Review.

1

List of works read

AE	— *L'Année épigraphique 1978* [1981]
Assuan	— *Assuan*, by E. Bresciani/S. Pernigotti (Biblioteca di studi antichi 16; Pisa, 1978)
Bagnall/Worp, *CSBE*	— *The Chronological Systems of Byzantine Egypt*, by R. S. Bagnall and K. A. Worp (*Studia Amstelodamensia* 8; Zutphen, 1978)
BE	— *Bulletin épigraphique*, by J. and L. Robert, in *Revue des études grecques* 91 (1978) 385–510
Carthage	— *Excavations at Carthage 1975, 1976, 1977 conducted by the University of Michigan*, ed. J. H. Humphrey (5 vols, 1976–1980; [Tunis, vol. 1; Ann Arbor, vols. 2–5])
CMRDM	— *Corpus Monumentorum Religionis Dei Menis* (*CMRDM*), by E. N. Lane (4 vols., *EPRO* 19; Leiden 1971-1978)
[Cohen, et al., *Coin-Inscriptions*]	— *The Coin-Inscriptions and Epigraphical Abbreviations of Imperial Rome*, by H. Cohen/J. C. Egbert/R. Cagnat (Chicago, 1978)
CPR	— *Corpus Papyrorum Raineri* VI. *Griechische Texte* III.1, edd. H. Harrauer and S. M. E. van Lith (2 vols; Vienna, 1978)
CSIR	— *Corpus Signorum Imperii Romani* (*Great Britain*) I.1. *Corbridge, Hadrian's Wall East of the North Tyne*, by E. J. Phillips (Oxford, 1977)
Durrbach, *Choix*	— *Choix d'Inscriptions de Délos*, by F. Durrbach (Paris, 1921–1922; repr. *Subsidia Epigraphica* 6; Hildesheim, 1976)
Eretria	— *Eretria* VI. *Ausgrabungen und Forschungen*, by J.-P. Descoeudres et al. (Bern, 1978) [includes publication of funerary inscriptions, pp. 21–61]
Fest. Dörner	— *Studien zur Religion und Kultur Kleinasiens. Festschrift für F. K. Dörner zum 65. Geburtstag am 28. Feb. 1976*, edd. S. Şahin/E. Schwertheim/J. Wagner (2 vols, *EPRO* 66; Leiden, 1978)
[Gawantka]	— *Aktualisierende Konkordanzen zu Dittenbergers Orientis Graeci Inscriptiones Selectae* (*OGIS*) *und zur dritten Auflage der von ihm begründeten Sylloge Inscriptionum Graecarum* (*Syll.³*), by W. Gawantka (*Subsidia Epigraphica* 8; Hildesheim, 1977)
Gibson, 'Christians for Christians'	— *The 'Christians for Christians' Inscriptions of Phrygia*, by E. P. Gibson (*Harvard Theol. Studies* 32; Missoula, 1978)
Grenier, *Anubis*	— *Anubis alexandrin et romain*, by J.-C. Grenier (*EPRO* 57; Leiden, 1977)
Grenier, *Fabia Stratonice*	— *L'Autel funéraire isiaque de Fabia Stratonice*, by J.-C. Grenier (*EPRO* 71; Leiden, 1978)
[Gschnitzer, *Staatsvertrag*]	— *Ein neuer spartanischer Staatsvertrag und die Verfassung des Peloponnesischen Bundes*, by F. Gschnitzer (*Beiträge zur kl. Philologie* 93; Meisenheim am Glan, 1978)
Holbl, *Zeugnisse*	— *Zeugnisse ägyptischer Religionsvorstellungen für Ephesus*, by G. Holbl (*EPRO* 73; Leiden, 1978)
Homm. Vermaseren	— *Hommages à Maarten J. Vermaseren*, edd. M. B. de Boer/T. A. Edridge (3 vols; *EPRO* 68; Leiden, 1978)
I. Bithynia	— *Inschriften griechischer Städte aus Kleinasien* VII. *Bithynische Studien*, by S. Şahin (Bonn, 1978)
IG IV².1	— *Inscriptiones Graecae* IV². *Inscriptiones Argolidis* 1. *Inscriptiones Epidauri*, ed. F. Hiller von Gaertringen (Berlin, 1929; repr. Chicago, 1977)
IGA 2	— *Inscriptiones Graecae Aegypti* II. *Inscriptiones nunc Alexandriae in Museo*, ed. E. Breccia (Cairo, 1911; repr. Chicago, 1978)
IGA 3	— *Inscriptiones Graecae Aegypti* III. *Inscriptiones 'Memnonii' sive Besae oraculi ad Abydum Thebaidis*, edd. P. Pedrizet/G. Lefebvre (Nancy, 1919; repr. Chicago, 1978)
IGA 4	— *Inscriptiones Graecae Aegypti* IV. *Inscriptiones nominum graecorum et aegyptiacorum aetatis romanae incisae sive scriptae in tabellis. 'Mummy Labels'*, ed. W. Spiegelberg (Leipzig, 1901; repr. Chicago, 1978)
IGA 5	— *Inscriptiones Graecae Aegypti* V. *Inscriptiones Christianae Aegypti*, ed. G. Lefebvre (Cairo, 1907; repr. Chicago, 1978)
IGCB	— *Inscriptiones Graecae Christianae veteres et Byzantinae* 1. *Peloponnesus. Isthmos-Korinthos*, ed. N. A. Bees (privately printed, Athens, 1941; repr. Chicago, 1978)

I. Lampsakos	— *Inschriften griechischer Städte aus Kleinasien* VI. *Die Inschriften von Lampsakos*, ed. P. Frisch (Bonn, 1978)
I. Magnesia Sip.	— *Inschriften griechischer Städte aus Kleinasien* VIII. *Die Inschriften von Magnesia am Sipylos*, ed. T. Ihnken (Bonn, 1978)
Kenchreai	— *Kenchreai, Eastern Port of Corinth* III. *The Coins*, by R. L. Hohlfelder (Leiden, 1978)
Kenyon, *Class. Texts*	— *Classical Texts from Papyri in the British Museum*, ed. F. G. Kenyon (London, 1891; repr. Milan, 1977)
NIP	— *Nouvelles inscriptions de Phrygie*, ed. T. Drew-Bear (*Studia Amstelodamensia* 16; Zutphen, 1978)
P. Carlini lett.	— *Papiri letterari greci* edd. A. Carlini et al. (*Biblioteca degli studi classici e orientali* 13; Pisa, 1978)
P. Chester Beatty IV/V	— *Chester Beatty Biblical Papyri IV and V. A New Edition with text-critical Analysis*, ed. A. Pietersma (*American Studies in Papyrology* 16; Toronto, 1977)
P. Chester Beatty XIII/XIV	— *Two Manuscripts of the Greek Psalter in the Chester Beatty Library, Dublin*, ed. A. Pietersma (*Analecta Biblica* 77; Rome, 1978)
[*P. Hercul.* 2]	— *I Papyri Ercolanesi 2. Indice topografico e sistematico*, ed. V. Litta (Naples, 1977)
P.L. Bat.	— *Textes grecs, démotiques et bilingues*, edd. E. Boswinkel, P. W. Pestman et al. (*Papyrologica Lugduno-Batava* 19; Leiden, 1978)
P. Landl.	— *Zwei Landlisten aus dem Hermupolites*, edd. P. J. Sijpesteijn/K. A. Worp (*Studia Amstelodamensia* 7; Zutphen, 1978)
P. Oxy.	— *The Oxyrhynchus Papyri* XLVI, ed. J. R. Rea (London, 1978)
P. Sakaon	— *The Archive of Aurelius Sakaon. Papers of an Egyptian Farmer in the Last Century of Theadelphia*, re-ed. G. M. Parássoglou (*Papyrologische Texte und Abhandlungen* 23; Bonn, 1978)
P. Strasb.	— *Papyrus grecs de la Bibliothèque Nationale et Universitaire de Strasbourg* V, 4, edd. J. Schwartz et al. (Strasburg, 1978)
[*Pap. Flor.* 3]	— *Euripide, Eretteo*, ed. P. Carrara (*Papyrologica Florentina* 3; Florence, 1977)
[*Pap. Flor.* 4, 8]	— *Demosthenis fragmenta in papyris et membranis servata* ed. B. Housmann (2 vols; *Papyrologica Florentina* 4, 8; Florence, 1978, 1981)
SEG	— *Supplementum Epigraphicum Graecum* 28 (1978 [1982])
Shear, Kallias	— *Kallias of Sphettos and the Revolt of Athens in 286B.C.*, by T.L. Shear (*Hesperia Suppl.* 17; Princeton, 1978)
TAM	— *Tituli Asiae Minoris* IV. *Tituli Bithyniae* 1. *Paeninsula Bithynica praeter Calchedonem*, ed. F.K. Dörner (Vienna, 1978)
Walbank, *Proxenies*	— *Athenian Proxenies in the Fifth Century B.C.*, by M. B. Walbank (Toronto, 1978)
Wiseman, *Corinthians*	— *The Land of the Ancient Corinthians*, by J. Wiseman (*Studies in Mediterranean Archaeology* 50; Göteborg, 1978)
Wistrand	— *The so-called Laudatio Turiae. Introduction, Text, Translation, Commentary*, by E. Wistrand (*Studia Graeca et Latina Gothoburgensia* 34; Göteborg, 1976)

[M. Guarducci, *Epigrafia greca* IV. *Epigrafi sacre pagane e cristiane* (Rome, 1978), has been held over to the next Review, apart from occasional references.]

Abbreviations

Other abbreviations follow standard conventions, except where altered for clarity.

Journals — as in *L'Année philologique* (but note, e.g., *RAC = Reallexikon für Antike und Christentum*, not *Riv(ista) di Ant(ichità) Crist(iana)*).

Papyrological works — as in S. R. Pickering, *Papyrus Editions* (North Ryde, N.S.W., 1984).

Epigraphical works (for which no standard guide exists) — according to generally used conventions (see LSJ), preceded where necessary by *I.* (e.g. *I.Bithynia*).

Ancient authors, biblical and patristic works — generally as in LSJ, BAGD, and Lampe (see below).

Some other abbreviations used, occasionally frequently, in this volume:

Aland, *Repertorium*	— K. Aland, *Repertorium der griechischen christlichen Papyri*, I. *Biblische Papyri* (Berlin, 1976)
BAGD	— Bauer/Arndt/Gingrich/Danker, *A Greek-English Lexicon of the New Testament and other Early Christian Literature* (Chicago, 1979²)
BDF	— Blass/Debrunner/Funk, *A Greek Grammar of the New Testament and other Early Christian Literature* (Chicago, 1961)
Bib.Pat.	— *Biblia Patristica. Index des citations et allusions bibliques dans la littérature patristique* (Centre d'analyse et de documentation patristiques; 3 vols; Paris, 1975-81)
CIJ	— J. B. Frey, *Corpus Inscriptionum Judaicarum* (2 vols; Rome, 1936, 1952); vol. 1 repr. with Prolegomenon by B. Lifshitz (New York, 1975)
CPJ	— V. A. Tcherikover, A. Fuks, et al., *Corpus Papyrorum Judaicarum* (3 vols; Cambridge [Mass.], 1957–64)
DACL	— Cabrol/Leclercq, et al., *Dictionnaire d'archéologie chrétienne et de liturgie* (15 vols; Paris, 1907–1953)
Deissmann, *Bible Studies*	— G. A. Deissmann, *Bible Studies* (ET: Edinburgh, 1923; repr. Winona Lake, 1979)
Deissmann, *LAE*	— G. A. Deissmann, *Light from the Ancient East* (Grand Rapids, 1980⁴)
ECL	— Early Christian Literature
Foraboschi	— D. Foraboschi, *Onomasticon Alterum Papyrologicum* (4 vols; Milan, 1966–71)
Gignac, I/II	— F. T. Gignac, *A Grammar of the Greek Papyri of the Roman and Byzantine periods* I, *Phonology;* II, *Morphology* (Milan, 1976, 1982)
Hatch and Redpath	— Hatch and Redpath, *A Concordance to the Septuagint and other Greek Versions of the Old Testament* (Oxford, 1897; 2 vols. repr. Graz, 1954)
Lampe	— Lampe, *A Patristic Greek Lexicon* (Oxford, 1961, repr.)
LSJ/LSJ Suppl.	— Liddell/Scott/Jones, *A Greek-English Lexicon* (Oxford, 1940⁹, repr. with supplement ed. E. A. Barber, 1968)
LXX	— Septuagint (Rahlfs' edition)
Migne, *PG/PL*	— Migne, *Patrologia Graeca/Patrologia Latina* (Paris, 1857-87/1844-64)
MM	— Moulton and Milligan, *The Vocabulary of the Greek Testament* (London, 1930; repr.)
Naldini	— M. Naldini, *Il Cristianesimo in Egitto. Lettere private nei papiri dei secoli II-IV* (Florence, 1968)
N/A²⁶	— Nestle/Aland, *Novum Testamentum Graece* (Stuttgart, 1979²⁶)
NB	— F. Preisigke, *Namenbuch ... enthaltend alle ... Menschennamen ... in griechischen Urkunden ... Ägyptens ...* (Heidelberg, 1922)
Peek, *GVI*	— W. Peek, *Griechische Vers-Inschriften* I (Berlin, 1955)
Solin, *GPR*	— H. Solin, *Die griechischen Personennamen in Rom. Ein Namenbuch* (3 vols; Berlin, 1982)
Spoglio	— S. Daris, *Spoglio lessicale papirologico* (3 vols; Milan, 1968)
UBS³	— *The Greek New Testament* (New York: United Bible Societies, 1975³)
Turner, *Typology*	— E. G. Turner, *The Typology of the Early Codex* (Pennsylvania, 1977)
van Haelst	— J. van Haelst, *Catalogue des papyrus littéraires juifs et chrétiens* (Paris, 1976)
WB	— F. Preisigke, et al., *Wörterbuch der griechischen Papyrusurkunden* (Heidelberg, et alibi, 1924-)

An asterisk (*) beside a reference in the bibliography for an entry signifies, where more than one edition exists, which has been reprinted; otherwise the *editio princeps* has been followed.

Dates are AD unless otherwise marked. IV¹ = 'first half IVth century', IV² = 'second half IVth century'; etc.

Textual sigla used are as follows:—

αβ̣	— letters not completely legible
. . . .	— 4 letters missing
– – – –	— indeterminate number of letters missing
[αβ]	— letters lost from document and restored by editor
[± 8]	— about 8 letters lost
⟨αβ⟩	— letters omitted by scribe and added by editor
(αβ)	— editor has resolved an abbreviation in the text
{αβ}	— letters wrongly added by scribe and cancelled by editor
[[αβ]]	— a (still legible) erasure made by scribe
ʽαβʼ	— letters written above the line
α´ or α̅	— letter stands for a numerical equivalent
v., vv., vac.	— one, two, several letter spaces left blank (*vacat*) on document
m.1, m.2	— first hand (*manus*), second hand
recto, verso	— the conventional front and back of a papyrus sheet.

The **Format of most entries** is as follows:—

Item no. Short title
Provenance   Date
editio princeps
Text
Brief descriptive comment
Bibliography (very selective, normally including only actual references to the text)
Translation
Comment

Where a text is not quoted in full or at all this format is somewhat modified, but should still be clear (e.g. Section B, *Minor Philological Notes*). Within the larger subdivisions of the Review items have usually been arranged chiefly by genre (e.g. letters, epitaphs), and within that, chronologically. This arrangement does not apply to Section B, where entries are alphabetical; nor, of course, to Section F (*Varia*). In Section C entries follow canonical book order with liturgical/credal material at the end. Where an entry deals with a diversity of texts, it is placed in the genre grouping to which the first, usually the main, text belongs.

The **indexes** are to be regarded as an integral element in the Review. They will usually provide the easiest means of discovering which biblical words and passages are discussed, what ideas and institutions, etc.

Item numbers are in bold type throughout the Review, for cross-referencing.

The following individuals have contributed separate entries to this volume: C.J. Hemer (**17**), C.A. Hope/M. Riddle (**106**), J.A.L. Lee (**83**), W. Tabbernee (**98**). All other entries are by the undersigned. Translations have been made by the author of the entry.

For those wishing to refer to this Review, the **abbreviation** *New Docs, 1978* is suggested.

Acknowledgements

Advice from colleagues on specific matters is acknowledged in the appropriate entry. Detailed responses to draft entries by G.W. Clarke, E.A. Judge, J.A.L. Lee and K.L. McKay have been particularly valued. The ever-cheerful help of A.L. Connolly, J. Elder, P. Geidans and P. Hollingdale with typing and proof-reading has eased my burden greatly. The multitude of services provided efficiently and with constant good-will by staff of the Macquarie University Library should be placed on public record. D. Surtees' combination of enthusiastic good will and professionalism in his craft has again ensured the rapid yet accurate typesetting of the volume. My wife's parents have given me much over the last eight years, above all an example of generous-heartedness; and it is to them that *New Docs, 1978* is dedicated with affection.

G.H.R. HORSLEY

A. NEW TESTAMENT CONTEXT

1. Joining the household of Caesar

Oxyrhynchos II

ed.pr. — J. R. Rea, *P.Oxy.* 3312, pp.99-100 (pl.5)

```
        c. 12 letters ] [ c. 8 letters
        c. 10 letters ]  υιο [ 2-4 letters
        . . .] τὰ ἀβάσκαντα ἀυτ´οῦ τέ-
        κνα καὶ Ἰσιδώραν τὴν
    5   ἀδελφήν σου καὶ Ἀθηναΐδα.
        καὶ γράψον μοι ἀσπαλῶς
        περὶ Διονυσαρίου ὅτι πόσων
        μηνῶν ἐστιν. ἀσπάζετ[αί
        σε Γαῖ⟨α⟩ καὶ τὰ τέκνα αὐτ[ῆς
   10   καὶ ὁ σύμβιος. γίνωσ⟨κε⟩ οὖ[ν
        ὅτι Ἑρμῖνος ἀπῆλθεν ἰς Ῥώμ[ην
        καὶ ἀπελεύθερος ἐγένετ[ο
        Καίσαρος ἵνα ὀπίκια λάβ[ῃ.
        ἀσπάζου πάντας τοὺς
   15   σοὺς κατ' ὄνομα καὶ οἱ ⟨ἐ⟩μοὶ
        πάντες σε ἀσπάζονται.
               ἐρρῶσθαί σε εὔχομαι.
        verso (downwards) ] ου Ὀξυρυγχ( )
        (at foot, upside down in relation to the front, m. 2) . ιστη.
```

The ending of a private letter; read φ for π at *ll.*6,13.

Bib. — O. Montevecchi, *ZPE* 34 (1979) 113-17; E.A. Judge, *Rank and Status in the World of the Caesars and St Paul* (*Broadhead Lecture* 4; Christchurch, 1982) 18-20.

5 ... [Greet] ... his children — may the evil eye not touch them! — and Isidora |your sister and Athenais. And be sure you write to me about Dionysarion, how many months 10 (pregnant) she is. Gaia greets you as do her children |and her husband. Know, then, that Herminos went off to Rome and became a freedman of Caesar in order to take 15 appointments. Greet all |your family individually just as all mine greet you. I pray you are well. (*verso*) ... Oxyrhynchos (?)

The comment about Herminos is included quite casually in this letter, yet it provides a hint about service in the *familia Caesaris* which the three monographs of the mid-1960s/early 1970s on the subject did not envisage. The most recent is P.R.C. Weaver, *Familia Caesaris. A Social Study of the Emperor's Freedmen and Slaves* (Cambridge, 1972). A person might be born into Caesar's household as a slave, or his master might sell him into imperial service; but until this fragmentary letter came to light there had been nothing in our sources to suggest that an outsider could take the initiative of gaining access for a career. The lure of *officia* — the letter uses the technical term (13); on which see R. P. Saller, *Personal Patronage Under the Early Empire* (Cambridge, 1982) 15-17 — is what impels Herminos, according to the writer; but that he was prepared to relinquish a free status for this is hard to imagine. It is equally difficult to envisage a slave being as mobile as this letter implies, even if he had saved sufficient money. Weaver mentions (36) the cases of several freedmen who made unauthorized attempts, motivated by the desire for *potentia*, to become *Augusti liberti;* and perhaps Herminos belongs in this category. Money alone would not open the door to such a career, of course: patronage would be needed. Saller provides useful discussion of the importance of mediators for provincials seeking advancement (168-87). *P.Oxy.* 3312 thus raises the question whether access to the Roman civil service was more open than has been thought hitherto. A solution to this question will have to await the emergence of further evidence. In the meantime attention may be drawn to Epiktetos, *Discourse* 4.1.95, where the 'wise man' tries to decide how he can travel most safely: τί ποιήσω; φίλος ἔσομαι Καίσαρος· ἐκείνου με ὄντα ἑταῖρον οὐδεὶς ἀδικήσει, 'what shall I do? I will become a friend of Caesar; no one will harm me if I am his companion'. The allusion here is to the notion of *amicitia Caesaris*, discussed at **75**.

P.R.C. Weaver (*per litt.*) suggests to me two possibilities about Herminos' status. The first is 'that he is already an Imperial slave without status indication, and without a post in the administration. As a resident in Egypt, his opportunities for being recruited into the Imperial service would be far more limited than those of Imperial slaves in Rome and Italy, who would have easier access to the necessary patronage. But the implication of *ll.*11-13 is that his *first* appointment *followed* on his manumission, whereas normal recruitment would be *before* manumission, and at the junior level. Variations from this would be more likely in the earlier part of I or later in III'. Does the suggested dating of this papyrus merit reconsideration, then? Alternatively, though less preferred by Weaver, is the possibility 'that he is a slave of a non-imperial owner and, having the right qualifications and patronage, was transferred to the emperor's ownership as an Imperial slave and then manumitted. None of this is apparent in the text of the papyrus, so it must be conjecture.'

In the light of Montevecchi's explanation that Dionysarion is pregnant (and not a baby a few months old, as *ed.pr.* translates; for the terminology, being so many 'months' cf. Lk. 1.36, of Elizabeth), Judge suggests (19) that the writer of our letter may have been the father of the expected child. But Montevecchi's intuition that the writer was probably a woman is preferable. The focus of interest in the letter is upon women; Herminos is mentioned at the end, before the concluding greeting, simply because he provides a snippet of particular news to send back to Oxyrhynchos. The greeting sent by 'Gaia and her children and husband' (9-10) contrasts with the standard order in Classical Greek writers where family members are mentioned in the order: husband (named), children, wife (often unnamed). While there are exceptions to this pattern, examples abound in the fourth-century orators. Even if the letter emanates from a male mind the writer cannot have been Dionysarion's husband, unless we suppose that he is sending his letter to someone else and asks incidentally how his own wife's pregnancy is proceeding.

For generalized κατ' ὄνομα greetings (15) see **52**. MM lack a separate entry for ἀσφαλῶς, although three papyrus attestations of the adverb are listed, s.v. ἀσφαλής, ad fin., where its common frequency is noted. BAGD takes over these three references, s.v. ἀσφαλῶς, but lacks the usual indication 'MM' at the end of their entry. A revised MM will need a separate entry for each NT word in order to avert the potential for confusion which may otherwise occur. The figurative usage in this particular letter provides a parallel to illustrate Acts 2.36, ἀσφαλῶς οὖν γινωσκέτω πᾶς οἶκος Ἰσραήλ, κτλ.; and the reference could therefore be added to BAGD, s.v., 2.

With mention of the *familia Caesaris* it is pertinent to ask whether the word οἰκιακός may occasionally be used to refer to members of this group. One such candidate is Marcus Valerius Junianus, οἰκιακός μου, named by Claudius in a letter to the guild of Dionysiac artists: T. Wiegand, *Milet* 1.3(1914) 156.10-11; text repr. in E.M. Smallwood, *Documents Illustrating the Principates of Gaius, Claudius and Nero* (Cambridge, 1967) 373b. P.R.C. Weaver (*per litt.*) thinks that in view of the cognomen Junianus, this man is more likely to be an *ingenuus* than a freedman; it is unlikely that οἰκιακός refers to the *familia Caesaris*; he is to be thought of as a *familiaris*, an *amicus Caesaris* (cf. **75**). In the NT the noun is found twice, Mt. 10.25 (of members of a household, with the implication strong — in view of the contrast being made with οἰκοδεσπότης — that they are the house-slaves), and 10.36 (probably of a man's relatives — they are his ἐχθροί — rather than those in his household; though this sense cannot certainly be ruled out here). To illustrate the NT usage MM quoted two papyri: *P.Oxy.* 2(1899) 294 (22AD), a letter in which a man says he is under pressure to become someone's οἰκιακός, here a member of his household; and *P.Giss.* (1912, repr. 1973) 88, a letter of recommendation (Heptakomia,II) in which the writer says that Ἀπολλωνοῦν τὴν ἀναδιδοῦσάν σοι | τὸ ἐπιστόλιον οἰκιακήν μου οὖσαν (here it us unclear whether the woman is a relative or is connected in some other way with the writer's *oikos*). These two references are the only two cited by BAGD. In addition to the Miletos text noted above, the following attestations may be listed: *P. Mil. Vogl.* 1 (1937) 25 (Tebtynis, 126/7), a court speech in which the *rhetor* mentions that the plaintiff is an οἰκιακός of the accused (*col. 2, l.*14; *col. 3, l.*7; a relative, or someone of inferior status? — perhaps the latter here); *PSI* 5(1917) 463 (Arsinoite nome, 157-60), a complaint to a *strategos* by a woman concerning her husband, who has removed various items from their house, including gold, bronze vases, clothing and σκεύη οἰκιακά, 'household items' (22). One other thing removed was [κ]οσ|μάρια γυναικεῖα (11-12), for which cf. 1 Pet. 3.3. On κοσμάριον and related words see W. Croenert's n. on *P. Oxy.* 3.494.10 at *Stud. Pal.* 4 (1905, repr. 1965) p.93, and add as a further example *P. Hamb.* 1 (1911, repr. 1973) 10.41 (Theadelphia, II). The presence of οἰκιακός is not easy to comprehend at *P. Ant.* 2(1960) 94 (Antinoopolis, VI), 'I write to you via the boatman(?) of the monastery,' διὰ τοῦ οἰκιακοῦ | τοῦ σκάφους τοῦ μοναστηρίου (8-9; cf. οἰ]κιακοῦ τοῦ σκάφους, 21, where the context is fragmentary). See the editors' n. on the word, ad loc. *Stud.Pal.* 20 (1921) 85, page 2, *recto l.*4 has the phrase εἰς οἰκιακὴν ὑπηρεσίαν, which recurs later in the same text, page 2, *verso l.*13. Finally, *CPR* 35 (Pesla, before 322 (?); this re-edition supersedes *Stud. Pal.* 8 [1908, repr. 1965] 1018) is an instruction by Hyperechios to Apollonios the wine-receiver, οἰν[οπα]ραλημπτῇ: 'Provide for my household retinue (*or* domestic requirements) 20 knidia of new wine', δὸς | εἰς οἰκιακὴν ὑπη[ρε]σίαν οἴνου νέου | κνίδια εἴκοσι (2-4). For ὑπηρεσία in the sense 'retinue' cf. Job 1.3.

2. The 'good news' of a wedding

Oxyrhynchos   II

ed.pr. — J. R. Rea, *P.Oxy.* 3313, pp.100–03 (pl. 6)

Ἀπολ[λώνι]ος καὶ Σαραπιὰς Διονυσίᾳ
      (*vac.*)   χαίρειν.
χαρ[ᾶς ἡμ]ᾶς ἐπλήρωσας εὐαγγελισαμένη
τὸν γ[άμον] τοῦ κρατίστου Σαραπίωνος καὶ εὐθέως
5 ἂν ἤλθ[ομε]ν διακονήσοντες αὐτῷ ὡς ἐν εὐκταιοτάτῃ
ἡμῖν ἡμ[έ]ρᾳ καὶ συνευφρανθησόμενοι, ἀλλὰ διὰ τὸν
δι[αλο]γισμὸν καὶ ὅτι ἀναλαμβάνομεν ἀπὸ νωθρείας
οὐκ ἠδυνήθημεν ἐλθεῖν. ῥόδα πολλὰ οὔπω γέγο-
νεν ἐνθάδε, ἀλλὰ σπανίζει, καὶ ἐκ πάντων
10 τῶν κτημάτων καὶ παρὰ πάντων τῶν στεφανη-
πλόκων μόλις ἠδυνήθημεν συλλέξαι ἃ ἐπέμ-
ψαμέν σοι διὰ Σαραπᾶ χείλια, τρυγηθέντων καὶ
ὧν ἔδει αὔριον τρυγηθῆναι. νάρκισσον ὅσην ἤθελες εἴχομ'εν', ὅθεν ἀντὶ ὧν ἔγραψας δισχειλίων
15 τετρακισχειλίαν ἐπέμψαμεν'. οὐ βουλόμε'θα'δέ σε
οὕτως κ[ατ]αγεινώσκειν ἡμῶν ὡς μεικρολόγων
ὥστε καταγελῶσαν γράψαι πεπομφέναι τὴν
τιμήν, ὁπότε καὶ ἡμεῖς ἔχομεν τὰ παιδία
ὡς ἴδια τέκνα καὶ πλέον τῶν ἡμῶν τιμῶμεν
20 καὶ ἀγαπῶμεν αὐτὰ καὶ οὕτως χαίρομεν ἴσα
σοι καὶ [τ]ῷ πατρὶ αὐτῶν. περὶ ὧν ἄλλων θέλεις
γρ[ά]ψο[ν ἡμ]ῖν. ἄσπασα[ι] Ἀλέξανδρον τὸν
κράτιστον καὶ τοὺς ἀβασκάντους 'αὐτοῦ' Σαραπίωνα
καὶ Θέωνα καὶ Ἀριστόκλειαν καὶ τὰ τέκνα
25 Ἀριστοκλείας. μαρτυρήσει σοι Σαραπᾶς περὶ τῶν ῥόδων ὅτι πάντα πεποίηκα εἰς τὸ
ὅσα ἤθελες πέμψαι σοι, ἀλλὰ οὐχ εὖρο[[ν]]μεν.
    (*m. 2*) ἐρρῶσθαί σε εὐχόμεθα, κυρία.
  verso (*m. 1*) Διονυσίᾳ γυναικὶ (*vac.*) Ἀλεξάνδρου.

A complete papyrus (18B × 31H cm.) with wide margins top, bottom and on the left side, written in very clear script. The series of corrections to verb forms from singular to plural (14, 15, 27) suggests to *ed.pr.* that one of the senders dictated the letter but occasionally lapsed into forgetting that the letter was coming from two people.

Bib. — E. A. Judge, *Rank and Status in the World of the Caesars and St Paul* (*Broadhead Lecture* 4; Christchurch, 1982) 24–26.

**Apollonios and Sarapias to Dionysia, greetings. You filled us with joy when you
5 announced the good news of most noble Sarapion's marriage; and |we would have
come straightaway to give him our support on a day most prayed for by us, and to join
in the rejoicing. But in view of the judicial circuit and the fact that we are recovering**

from sickness we were not able to come. There are not yet many roses in bloom here,
10 **rather, they are hard to come by; and from all | the properties and from all the garland-**
weavers we were scarcely able to get together the thousand which we sent to you via
Sarapas, although we even picked blooms which ought to have been picked tomorrow.
As for narcissi, we had as much as you wanted, hence in place of the two thousand
15 **you wrote for | we sent four thousand. But we do not want you so to condemn us as**
penny-pinchers that you write in mockery that you have sent the money, when we too
20 **hold the youngsters as our own children and have greater regard for them | and love**
them more than our own, and thus our joy is equal to yours and their father's. Write
to us about other things you want. Greet most noble Alexandros, and his Sarapion and
Theon and Aristokleia — may the evil eye not touch them! — and Aristokleia's
25 **children. | Sarapas will confirm to you that about the roses I have done all I could to**
send you as many as you wanted, but we could not locate them. (*m.2*) We pray that
you are well, lady. (*Verso, m.1*) To Dionysia, wife of Alexandros.

The warm tone which permeates this memorable letter reveals that we are privy to a circle
of close friends; and they are people of considerable means. It seems to be of no consequence
whether 2000 or 4000 flowers are sent (*ll.*14–15). The impression of the wealth of the senders
is further confirmed by the almost off-hand reference to 'all the estates' (9–10), while the use
of κράτιστος (4, 23) as an epithet attached to personal names helps us locate the family of
the recipient of this letter as one of considerable status. *WB* Suppl. 1.3 Abschn. 9, col. 385
and *Spoglio* provide a wealth of other references to the use of this epithet, whose true NT
parallel is the polite address to Theophilos at Lk. 1.3; for the occurrences at Acts 23.26; 24.3,
and 26.25, where they are used as a title for officials of high rank, are different (for this
application cf. *P.Oxy.* 3275.11, dated 14–23/6/103–117). Together with such texts as
P.Brem. (1936, repr. 1970) 65.10, and *P.Giss.*1 (1910) 26.4 (both early II) — noted by *ed.pr.*
— the examples in this new letter could well be included in a revised MM entry and added
to BAGD, s.v., 2. Something of the status of the people involved in this letter may also be
inferred from the banter about miserliness and the sending of money (15–18): see, briefly,
Judge, 26. What lays bare the warmth of the friendship above all is the sentiment at *ll.*18–21,
for although the letter then proceeds to a conventional list of greetings, what we have there
is distinctive.

Ed.pr. suggests that Dionysia, the recipient, is the second wife of Alexander and step-
mother of Sarapion, the bridegroom. The wording [τ]ῷ πατρὶ αὐτῶν(21) and τοὺς
ἀβασκάντους ʼαὐτοῦʼ(23) suggests this, when taken together with the address on the back. The
one further possibility to consider about Rea's reconstruction of the family links is whether
'Aristokleia and the children of Aristokleia' (24–25) allows the inference that she is widowed
or divorced: on this cf. *New Docs 1977*, 3, pp.31–32.

Egypt's climate made it the 'nursery' of the Roman world: flowers could be grown year-
round, and were exported widely. On this see A. C. Johnson, *Roman Egypt*, vol. 2 in
T. Frank (ed.), *An Economic Survey of Ancient Rome* (1936; repr. New Jersey, 1959) 4,
where the fame of its garland industry is mentioned (cf. *ll.*10–11 in our letter). Rea mentions
(n. to *ll.*8–9) the existence of a festival in early February, the Rhodophoria, from which he
deduces that this letter was possibly written just prior to it, since ready-to-pick roses were
not yet available in abundance. For the cultivation of flowers one may note such texts as
BGU 4 (1912) 1119 (Alexandria, 5BC), a lease document for land in which there are presently
being grown vineyards, a rose garden, and beans (*ll.*10–11). *P.Ross.Georg.* 2 (1929, repr.
1966) 18 (Arsinoite nome, 141) summarizes details of the lease of a narcissus garden
(*ll.*249–52).

Judge is right to dismiss the hypothesis that this letter is Christian. The presence of a number of words and phrases prominent in the NT may make this idea attractive at first glance, but in view of the date of our letter such philological affinities are not sufficient for the notion to be entertained. Rather, these parallels with NT vocabulary and usage illustrate how normal is the language employed in the NT. Thus, with χαρ[ᾶς ἡμ]ᾶς ἐπλήρωσας (3) note Rom. 15.13, where Paul prays that the God of hope πληρῶσαι ὑμᾶς πάσης χαρᾶς καὶ εἰρήνης; and cf. Jn. 3.29; 15.11; 16.24; 17.13; Acts 13.52; Phil. 2.2; 2 Tim. 1.4; 1 Jn. 1.4; 2 Jn. 12.

From the point of view of NT vocabulary the verb εὐαγγελίζομαι (3) is the most arresting item, yet an investigation of the usage of εὐαγγελ- words only serves to confirm the claim advanced in the previous paragraph. At Longus, *Daphnis and Chloe* 3.33, the shepherd approaches Chloe, τόν τε γάμον εὐηγγελίζετο, and the context is certainly one of joy and happiness; it therefore provides an excellent parallel to *ll*.3–4 of our text. But just as it is a coincidence of wording and is not to be thought of as an allusion to that romance — if it were, *P.Oxy.* 3313 would provide our first papyrus reference to Longus and would establish a *terminus ante quem* for this writer who has been dated anywhere between II–VI; for the most recent discussion of the date see R. L. Hunter, *A Study of Daphnis and Chloe* (Cambridge, 1983) 3–15, who narrows the range down to late II or early III (15) — so also the use of the verb holds out no suggestion of a Christian milieu for this letter. For a useful catalogue of εὐαγγελ- words in the novel *Chaireas and Callirhoe* by Chariton (c. 50BC–150AD) see P. W. van der Horst, *NovT* 25 (1983) 349. Documentary examples of this word and related forms may be reviewed here briefly.

εὐαγγελίζω
— *P.Giss.*27 = *CPJ* 2 (1960) 439 (Hermopolis, beginning of 117(?)), a private letter in which reference is made to τιν[ὶ] παι|δαρίῳ ἐρχομένῳ εὐαγγελίζοντι τὰ τῆς νείκης | αὐτοῦ καὶ προκοπῆς 'a slave coming to bring the good news of his victory and success'. This example (cited by MM) is still the only attestation of the active to parallel Rev. 10.7 and 14.6; and the usage is unequivocally secular.

εὐαγγελίζομαι
— *IGRR* 4 (1927, repr. 1964) 1756 (= Buckler/Robinson, *Sardis* VII. *The Inscriptions* [Leyden, 1932], 8), a decree in which it is said that on the day that a son of Augustus took the *toga virilis* εὐανγελίσθη ἡ πόλις (*l*.14).
— *P.Oxy.* 3313.3, the letter under discussion.
— *P.Oxy.* 16 (1924) 1830.3–6 (VI), a very interesting letter concerning the inundation:

> εὐαγγελίζομαι καὶ νῦν τῇ ὑμετέρᾳ
>
> εὐδοκίμησιν τὸν εὐλογιμένον γόνιμ(ον)
>
> 5 τῆς Αἰγύπτου ποταμὸν προσβεβηκ(έναι)
>
> τῇ δυνάμει τοῦ Χριστοῦ.

'I again bring the good news to your honour that the blessed fertilizing river of Egypt has risen by the power of Christ'.

The last of these is a Christian text, yet even there the verb reflects the ordinary usage found in secular documents.

εὐαγγέλιον
— *SB* 1 (1915) 421.2 (provenance unknown, soon after 238) a letter which begins ἐπεὶ γν[ώ]στ[ης ἐγενόμην τοῦ] | εὐαγγελ[ίο]υ περὶ τοῦ ἀνη|γορεῦσθαι Καίσαρα . . ., 'since I have become aware of the good news about the proclamation as Caesar (of Gaius Julius Verus Maximus Augustus) . . .' This text already discussed in Deissmann, *LAE*, 367.
— *SB* 6.4 (1962) 9401.4 (Fayum, IV–VI), a letter which introduces a NT quotation with the formula τὸ τοῦ ἁγίου [εὐαγγελίου . . ., 'the saying of the holy gospel'. The restoration here is by analogy with texts like the next item.
— *P.Princ.* 3 (1942, repr. 1975) 180.8 (provenance unknown, VI(?)), a lease which employs the words τὸ ἅγιον εὐαγγέλιον.

— *IGA* 5.741 (provenance unknown, n.d.) a (book(?)) container with the words Μάρκου εὐαγγελίου written on it.

The last three examples register the Christian specialization of the word, and may be noted at BAGD, s.v., 3; but *SB* 421 indicates that the singular noun, like other words in this group, has its quite expected, ordinary use. This text should not be forgotten, therefore, when the NT usage, singular everywhere, is being considered.

εὐαγγέλια
— *OGIS* 1 (1903, repr. 1970) 4.41–42 (323BC), a decree of Nesos for Thersippas in which the *damos* καὶ εὐαγγέλια | καὶ σωτήρια ἔ[θ]υσε.
— *SEG* 1 (1923) 362.7–8 (Samos, c.306BC), honorific decree in which the *demos* votes ἄγειν ἡμᾶς ἐπὶ τοῖς εὐαγγελίοις | Ἀντιγόνεια καὶ Δημητρίεια.
— *IG* XII Suppl. (1939) 168 (Ios, c.306–301BC), decree to honour Antigonos in which it is decided to institute εὐα]γγέλια.
— *IG* II² (1913, repr. 1974) 1224 (c.166BC), in which Myrina, a town on Lemnos, offers [εὐ]αγγελίων θυσία (*l.*15).
— *IG* VII (1892) 417.68 (Amphiaraia on the Oropos, IBC), mentions εὐαγγέλια τῆς Ῥω[μαίων νίκης].
— *IGRR* 4 (1927, repr. 1964) 860 (re-ed. by L. Robert in J. des Gagniers et al., *Laodicée du Lycos. Le Nymphée* [Quebec, 1969] 265-77), an honorific inscription (IAD) which praises an individual for, among other things, 'giving (largesse) magnanimously at the festival for "good news"', ἐπιδίδοντα ἐν εὐανγελίοις εὐψύχω[ς] (*l.*12).
— *IG* II².1081 (Athens, III init.), an inscription where it is used of Geta, though heavily restored: βουλὴ συνήχθη ἐπὶ τοῖς [εὐαγγ]ελίοις . . .
— L. Moretti, *Archeologia Classica* 5 (1953) 255-59 (*non vidi*; cf. *BE* [1955] 95), restores an inscription for the Peloponnese to mention a festival instituted for good news concerning the imperial family, [τὰ δὲ] εὐαγγέ[λια ὑπὲρ] οἴκο[υ παντὸς] τ[ῶ]ν Σεβ[β. θύσαντα. The previous reading for the third word was συαγγε[.
— *PSI* 7 (1925) 768.8 (Hermopolis Magna, 24/7/465), a fragmentary text with mention of τῶν εὐαγγελίων.

The usage of the neuter plural noun is clear: it refers to good news (often emanating from a monarch), such as news of their victories or benefactions; and in particular the word is employed of the sacrifices celebrated on such an occasion. The occurrences are nearly all Hellenistic in date. Robert, *Laodicée du Lycos*, 273, where εὐαγγελ- words are discussed, notes that such phrases as εὐαγγέλια θύειν go back to VBC (e.g., Aristoph., *Knights* 656). He notes further (274 nn.2, 3) two examples of ἡ ἀγγελία = τὰ εὐαγγέλια. For an earlier list of epigraphical references collected by Robert see *BCH* (1936) 184-89; repr. in his *Opera Minora Selecta* 1 (Amsterdam, 1969) 195-200, at 198 n.2. The tabulation here is not complete; several more examples can be derived from Robert. BAGD's entry, *ad init.*, quotes *OGIS* 458, and refers to *IG* II².1081 and *SB* 421: the first two are plural, the last is singular. In view of the specialized meaning that τὰ ἐ. may carry, such usages deserve more careful differentiation, with references added to Robert's two discussions.

J.A.L. Lee has drawn my attention to Cicero's use of εὐαγγέλια three times in letters written to Atticus, and they are worth passing notice here in view of their date: 2.3.1, *primum, ut opinor*, εὐαγγέλια. *Valerius absolutus est Hortensio defendente* (shortly after Dec. 60BC); 2.12.1, *quibus* εὐαγγέλια *quae reddam nescio* (19/4/59BC); 13.40.1, *itane? nuntiat Brutus illum ad bonos viros?* εὐαγγέλια (17/8/45BC).

εὐαγγέλιος
— *IGRR* 4 (1927, repr. 1964) 996 = 1708 (Samos, time of Augustus), re-ed. with new frag. by P. Herrmann, *AM* 75 (1960) 70-82 no.1.; at *l.*6 the broken text is restored to read [εὐα]νγέλιον ἡμέραν, referring to a festival on the occasion of certain news coming from Rome. The usage is thus fairly similar to that of the neuter plural noun.

εὐάγγελμα
— *IG Bulg.* 2.659 (Nikopolis on the Ister, 197) a letter of Septimius Severus to Caracalla after the

Parthian victory, which mentions instituting a festival ἐπὶ τοῖς τῶν ἡμετέρων ἀγαθῶν [εὐ]ανγέλμασι — *non vidi;* cf. Robert, *Laodicée du Lycos*, 273 n.ll.

εὐαγγελιστής

— *IG* XII.1 (1895) 675 (Rhodes, n.d.), Δάφνας καὶ θεοῦ | ἀρχιερεὺς . . . | ΟΗΡΟC (ὁ ἥρως ?; or ὁ [ἱε]ρὸς ?) εὐαγγελιστής (*ll.*2–6).

— *P.Oxy*. 8 (1911) 1151.45 (V(?)), a Christian amulet which offers a prayer through John 'the evangelist', and others.

— *P.Lond*. 5 (1917, repr. 1973) 1708.166 (Antinoopolis, May–Nov. 567(?)), mention of τοῦ ἁγίου εὐαγγελιστοῦ of this city.

— *PSI* 8 (1927) 953.82 (Oxyrhynchos, VI), a reference to John 'the evangelist'.

— *CPR* 1 (1895, repr. 1974) 30, I.4 (VI), John 'apostle (εὐλόγου) and evangelist'.

— *SB* 3.1 (1926, repr. 1974) 6087.18 (provenance unknown, VII), mention of Mark 'the evangelist'.

These examples are all distinctively Christian, except for the problematic inscription from Rhodes, whose Christian link can nevertheless not be ruled out entirely. For turn-of-the century bibliography on this see BAGD, s.v., or MM, s.v. The text is orthographically poor elsewhere than in *l.*6, and to have some rough idea of its date might help establish whether we have here a pre- or non-Christian use or one that is potentially Christian. I incline to think that it is non-Christian, 'proclaimer of oracular messages' (so LSJ, s.v., 2).

προευαγγελίζομαι

— No documentary occurrences are known to me to illustrate the NT *hapax* at Gal. 3.8. But that it is not distinctively a Pauline coinage is clear from three occurrences in Philo (listed by G. Friedrich, *TDNT* 2 (1964) 737; only two of these are noted in MM and BAGD); while the fact that it is used by a scholiast to Soph. *Trach.* (see Friedrich) indicates that it is not confined to Jewish writers either.

Εὐάγγελος

— G. Petzl, *ZPE* 30(1978) 253–55 no.1 (Saittai in Lydia, 194/5; repr. as *SEG* 914; *TAM* 5.1[1981] 179b): confession text set up by Stratoneikos son of Evangelos; clearly non-Christian.

— *SEG* 1517 (Terenouthis in Egypt, II/IV), funerary stele for Εὐάγγελος φιλότεκνος (for the epithet see **11** below).

— *AE* (1977) 33, epitaph for Octavia Evangelis (Rome, n.d.).

Further examples are noted at *New Docs 1976*, **53**.

What may be concluded from this survey of εὐαγγελ- words in the documentary texts? In the case of those forms also found in the NT there are documentary examples which are either prior to IAD, or if later have no Christian theological import. *P.Oxy.* 1830 is particularly to be noted in this connection, since it is an explicitly Christian letter. The fact that the NT employs universally the singular of the neuter noun is certainly remarkable, and it cannot be doubted that this specialized usage was the result of conscious choice. Yet we should not lose sight of the relatively widespread occurrence in the Hellenistic period of the neuter plural, again with a specialized meaning whereby it is related to news frequently connected with royalty. For such distinctive phraseology found in Matthew as τὸ ἐ. τῆς βασιλείας (4.23; 9.35; 24.14), and elsewhere in the NT — in view of the theological attribution of kingship to Christ/God — τὸ ἐ. τοῦ Χριστοῦ/τοῦ κυρίου/τοῦ θεοῦ (Mk. 1.1, 14; Rom. 1.3; 15.16, 19; 1 Cor. 9.12; 2 Cor. 2.12; 9.13; 10.14; 11.7; Gal. 1.7; Phil. 1.27; 1 Thes. 2.2, 8, 9; 3.2; 2 Thes. 1.8; 1 Pet. 4.17), is not likely to have been coined without regard to the special appropriateness it is accorded by the Hellenistic usage. Of course, this latter does not halt abruptly at the turn of the era as the tabulation above shows: it continues contemporaneously with and beyond the period when the NT books were composed. While the NT usage is distinctive, therefore, it cannot be divorced from the larger context of the *koine*, within which one other equally distinctive application was widespread, one which provides the stem from which the NT usage took root. Whether or not the theological basis for the phraseology can be traced to the OT, philologically and socially it would have been perfectly comprehensible to those living in Graeco-Roman cities in the Roman period. Even the word εὐαγγελιστής which became entirely monopolized for Christian use may have had a 'previous existence' in an oracular context, if the evidence of *IG* XII.1.675 is to be admitted as secular.

Other philological items must be noted more briefly. The use of διακονέω τινί (5) provides a further example of this construction to be noted in MM and BAGD, s.v.; cf. Mt. 25.44; Lk. 8.3; Heb. 6.10; Rev. 15.25. For the legal technical term διαλογισμός (7) cf. *ed.pr.*'s note ad.loc.; in the NT it is perhaps most nearly approached at Jas. 2.4 κριταὶ διαλογισμῶν, though it is not a true parallel. The noun νωθρεία (7) does not occur in the NT, although its related adjective is found at Heb. 5.11 and 6.12. MM, s.v., provide one example of the noun (to which we may add *SB* 5.1 [1934] 7571.4, in addition to the new letter), four of the verb (to which several may be added from *WB* 2.1 [1925] 142-43), but none of the adjective. Three instances are known to me, all of which may be added to a revised MM entry (the first is recorded in BAGD): *P.Brem.* (1936, repr. 1970) 61.13-15 (Hermopolis, early II(?)), ἐγὼ δὲ | ἀγωνι[ῶι κα]θ᾿ ἡμέραν, μὴ πάλιν | νωθ[ρ]ὸ[ς ἦς 'I worry daily lest you are sick again'; *PSI* 14 (1957) 1386, *verso l.*6 (Oxyrhynchos, III; letter on back of an epic fragment dated IBC/ IAD), νωθρὸς ὢν σοὶ αὐτὸ ἔδωσα (in view of the end of *l.*5 being hard to read the context of *l.*6 is difficult to reconstruct); *UPZ* 1 (1922-27) 110.95, where Wilcken read ἢ νωθρός above the line (164BC). For the form ἠδυνήθημεν (11) see Gignac 2.230-31, and Mandilaras, § 246, 247; while for ἤθελες (13-14) see Gignac 2.228-29, and Mandilaras, § 291. There are numerous examples of τρυγάω in *WB* and *Spoglio* and along with the new examples in this papyrus (*ll.*12, 13) they could be added to MM, and to BAGD (which notes specifically only *P.Oslo.* 21.13 for documentary attestations): for the NT note Lk. 6.44; Rev. 14.18, 19. With the use of καταγινώσκω here (16) cf. Gal. 2.11; 1 Jn. 3.20, 21. The date of this letter makes the occurrence in it of καταγελάω (17) earlier by more than a century than MM's attestation; for the NT cf. Mt. 9.24 = Mk. 5.40 = Lk. 8.53. For the perfect πεπομφέναι (17) note generally K. L. McKay, *BICS* 27 (1980) 23-49, which examines perfect aspect in documentary papyri. Lk. 6.3 is the only place where ὁπότε is found (significantly for the stylistic pretensions of the letter writer, it is Lk. which provides the parallel); cf. BDF § 105, 381, 455(1). BAGD and MM have only a couple of documentary examples, to which this one (*l.*18) may now be added. The future participles expressing purpose (*ll.*5,6) may well be another indication of more pretentious Greek.

Like εὐαγγελίζομαι the presence of the verb ἀγαπάω (20) ought not to make us wonder whether the text may be Christian simply because the verb and noun have a notable frequency in the NT. The verb is in fact well on the way to replacing φιλέω in the *koine*. In fact, the prevalence of ἀγαπάω and its related forms in the LXX and NT marks a distinct change from Classical Greek usage where φιλέω is the usual word, although ἀγαπάω is already coming in strongly (see Joly, noted below). There is no reason to suppose that Jewish (and Christian) usage deliberately selected the less common classical word for some specific reason; it is simply that the LXX/NT reflects very largely the actual usage of the time. An additional reason why φιλέω may have been replaced by ἀγαπάω as the general word for 'love' could well be the specialized use of φιλέω in sexual contexts, as a euphemism for βινέω. On this see G.P. Shipp, *Modern Greek Evidence for the Ancient Greek Vocabulary* (Sydney, 1979) 126-27. I am grateful to S.P. Swinn who has allowed me to read an unpublished study of ἀγαπ- words in the LXX. A discussion of the verb which deserves wide notice is R. Joly, *Le vocabulaire chrétien de l'amour est-il original?* φιλεῖν *et* ἀγαπᾶν *dans le grec antique* (Brussels, 1968).

Finally, BAGD, s.v. μαρτυρέω, 1, b, makes no mention of papyrus examples for the sense 'confirm, attest', as here (*l.*25), to illustrate the two occurrences in the NT: Jn. 5.32; 1 Jn. 5.10.

3. Petition to a prefect

Oxyrhynchos   c.47-54
ed.pr. — J. R. Rea, *P.Oxy.* 3271, pp.8-9 (pl.3)

Γναίωι Οὐεργιλίωι Καπίτωνι δι(ὰ) δύο υἱ(ῶν)
Κλαυδίων Ποτάμωνος καὶ Ἀπολλ( )
   παρὰ Ἰσιδώρας τῆς Ἀπολλωνίο(υ) [
δε κατὰ δὲ τεκνοθεσίαν Διονυσίο(υ)
5   ᾽τοῦ καὶ ... ωνίου῾ Ἀλεξανδρ ... σταθμούχου
οἰκίας τῆς οὔσης ἐν τῷ γ̅
...].....[

Top portion of a papyrus sheet; the back is blank.
Bib. — E. A. Judge, *Rank and Status in the World of the Caesars and St Paul* (*Broadhead
      Lecture* 4; Christchurch, 1982) 10-14.

**To Gnaeus Vergilius Capito through her two sons Claudius Potamon and Claudius
Apoll(onios?) from Isidora daughter of Apollonios, but by adoption daughter of
5 Dionysios, |also called . . .onios, Alexandrian (citizen), proprietor of a house which is
in the Gamma (district) . . .**

Brief as it is this fragment contains a couple of features deserving of mention. Isidora
presents her petition through her two sons, and the certainty that they are Roman citizens
— as may be inferred from their nomenclature; Judge's discussion focuses primarily upon
the value of studying names for evidence about the social rank and status of individuals —
may be the reason why their names precede hers, even at the cost of the lack of clarity of
*l.*1: whose sons they are does not emerge until two lines later. On the rarity of special grants
of citizenship in this period see the comment at **4**. Though the subject of her petition is
entirely lost, from what survives she is intent upon identifying herself with some exactitude;
we are provided with her father's name, her adoptive father's name, the latter's by-name (on
such double names cf. *New Docs 1976*, **55**; for a less common by-name formula note *P.Oxy.*
3295 [24-28/8/285], a document registering a child whose mother is Aurelia Nike ἤτοι Taias,
*l.*11), her claim to Alexandrian citizenship (at *P.Oxy.* 47 [1980] p.xix Rea provides parallels
to show that 'Alexandrian' in this document refers to Isidora), and the fact that she owns
property in one of the five 'letter' districts (alpha to epsilon) of Alexandria. Such a full
identification is unexceptional in quasi-official documents like this, of course, and draws
attention to the importance in antiquity of self-documentation for individuals. For women
owning property see the brief list covering 1976 and 1977 publications in *New Docs 1977*,
3, pp.28-29. From 1978 publications mentioning women who do not need to act through their
male next of kin, in virtue of the *ius liberorum*, note the following texts as a supplement to
those listed at *New Docs 1977*, **3**, pp.30-31: *P.Strasb.* 671 (dated 272); *P.Oxy.* 3302.3 (300/1);
P.Sakaon 60 (= *P.Thead.* 1; dated 306) records the sale of a house between two women in
this category (*ll.* 5,7), both illiterate; one of them figures in another house sale, *P.Sakaon*
59.5 (= *P.Thead.* 2, dated 305). For *matronae stolatae* (cf.*New Docs*, ibid.) we may add *IGA*
2.130 (Kom Khanziri in Egypt, II fin./III init.); and *AE* 715 (Tomis, III fin.), an epitaph for
a child whose mother is described as *stolata femina*.

The petitioner is the adoptive daughter of Dionysios, κατὰ τεκνοθεσίαν. This word is here attested for the first time in Greek; Rea notes that τεκνόθεσις (attributed by *Spoglio*, s.v., to *P.Col.Zen.* 1 = *P.Col.* 3 (1934) 58.9) is in fact a 'ghost' word. For the NT the obvious parallel to the new word is υἱοθεσία: Rom. 8.15, 23; 9.4; Gal. 4.5; Eph. 1.5. F. Lyall, *JBL* 88 (1969) 458-66, argues that Paul's use of adoption terminology was 'a deliberate, considered, and appropriate reference to Roman law'. But why Roman law? Paul would be referring to Greek law; and given the date of the text Isidora in *P.Oxy.* 3271 would not have been adopted under Roman law (E.A. Judge in a note to me). MM provide references to several inscriptions and two papyri to illustrate the use; the latter two, *P.Oxy.* 9 (1912) 1206 (335AD; by this time Roman law had become universal) *ll*.8, 14, 16-17, [20], and *P.Lips.* (1906) 28 (Hermopolis, 381) *ll*.12, 14, 17, 22, 24, 27 (and cf. the verb υἱοθετέω at *l*.22, for which Lampe has some patristic examples), are adoption documents, and therefore naturally full of such terminology. To these we may add *P.Oslo* 3 (1936) 114.4 (Oxyrhynchos, I/early II), and *P.Erlangen* (1942) 28.6 (Arsinoe, II¹), both of which predate MM's texts by over two centuries. Probably in neither of these texts is Roman law in view, given their date. Deissmann mentions (*Bible Studies*, 239) that in contrast to καθ' υἱοθεσίαν δέ 'the corresponding formula for the adoption of females is κατὰ θυγατροποΐαν δέ'. Since the gender distinction is observed here, perhaps the use of the word τεκνοθεσία in the new petition may reflect the inappropriateness of υἱοθεσία applied to a woman. On every occasion where Paul employs the noun the context is a generalizing plural, 'we' or 'you'; and it is therefore entirely to be expected as normal Greek usage that the form used has a masculine weighting (υἱο-) when reference is made to males and females together.

4. Fishing lease
Oxyrhynchos   III
ed.pr — J. R. Rea, *P.Oxy.* 3269, pp.4-5 (pl.1)

```
       .    .    .    .    .
......] ἄγραν ἰχθύ[ων 6-8 letters ἀνα-]
βάσεως τοῦ ἐνεστῶτος α (ἔτους)'' ἀπό τε ὑπο-
χέων πρὸς ταῖς περὶ Πέλα θύραις Τα(ν)-
ύρεως καλουμέναις ἐπὶ τῷ σὲ καὶ χα-
5 ρυβδεύειν κατὰ τὸ τέταρτον μέ-
ρος ἐν ταῖς αὐταῖς θύραις πρὸς τὸ ἔ-
χειν τοὺς μεμισθωκότας τὰ λοι-
πὰ τέταρτα τρία παρέχοντας λί-
να καὶ σκάφας καὶ ἁλιέας ὧν πάντω(ν)
10 τὸν συνφωνηθέντα φόρον αὐτόθι
ἀπεσχήκαμεν διὰ χειρὸς ἐκ πλήρους
πρὸς τὸ τὴν ἄγραν αὐτὸν ποιήσασθαι
ἀ]κωλύτως ἐφ' ὃν προσήκι χρόνο(ν)
...].....ιας οὔσης τῷ [Ζ]ωίλῳ δια
15 ........] ποιήσασθαι .....τ' ταις
       .    .    .    .    .
```

Both beginning and ending are lost of this nearly square papyrus (8B × 9H cm.); the back is blank.

> . . . **catch of fish [during the] inundation of the current first year, from the fish traps(?)**
> **to the (sluice-)gates near Pela, called the gates of Tanyris, subject to your also fishing**
> 5 **the pool | in accordance with your quarter-share (in the catch) at the same gates, so that**
> **the lessors may have the remaining three-quarters (since) they are providing the nets,**
> 10 **boats and fishermen, for all of which | we have received on the spot the agreed rent by**
> **hand in full, so that he may make his catch unhindered for the time which is**
> 15 **appropriate . . . being for Zoilos | . . . to make . . .**

This fishing lease is one of four documents published as *P.Oxy.* 3267–3270 which adds to the meagre examples hitherto known: *P.Wisconsin* 1(= *P.L.Bat.* 16) (1967) 6 (Oxyrhynchos, 210/11), re-ed. J.R Rea, *ZPE* 12 (1973) 262–264; and possibly *P.Strasb.* 4.4 (1973) 569 (provenance unknown, 27/7/162), though the text is too damaged for certainty. The most recently-published, and best-preserved, such lease is *P.Turner* (1981) 25 (Oxyrhynchos, 28/12/161). Rea also provides references (*P.Oxy.*, p.1) to a few other documents in which fishing rights are mentioned as part of a lease agreement about property. The four new texts range from c.37–41 to IV, and reflect the basic continuity of these agreements over three centuries, allowing for increasing wordiness over time. *P.Oxy.* 3267 belongs to the time of Gaius (Caligula) but has not been reprinted here because it is too fragmentary. The text above has been reproduced to give some idea of the type of agreement and the form of words used; but some particulars from the other three new leases will also be noted briefly below. On fishing regulations see R. Taubenschlag, *The Law of Greco-Roman Egypt in the Light of the Papyri* (Warsaw, 1955²) 664–66.

At *l*.1 the phrase ἄγραν ἰχθύ[ων provides an exact parallel to Lk. 5.9 where Simon Peter was amazed ἐπὶ τῇ ἄγρᾳ τῶν ἰχθύων. *P.Wisconsin* 1.6 has [ἐπὶ] | τῇ ἄγρᾳ at *ll*.18–19, and in that particular context Rea (n. in *ZPE* article, p.264; cf. his n. to *P.Oxy.* 3270.19, p.7) thinks that the noun may be referring to 'the whole period of the right to fish'. Earlier in the same chapter, Lk. 5.4, the fishermen are told to let down their nets εἰς ἄγραν. MM have no entry for this noun at all, so the following occurrences would be needed for an entry: *P.Wisconsin* 1.6. 3–4 ([εἰς ἄ]|γραν ἰχθύω[ν), 18–19 (quoted above); *P.Oxy.* 3268.7–9 (II), ἐπιδέχομαι τὴν | ἄγραν τοῦ ἐκβησομένου | ἰχθύος διώρυχος, 'I undertake the catching of fish which will be forthcoming from the canal'; *P.Oxy.* 3269.1, 12; *P.Oxy.* 3270.9 (14/9 — 15/10/309), ἄγραν εἰχθύων; in *P.Turner* 25 Sarapion leases to three men 'the catching of every fish (τὴν ἄγραν τοῦ παντὸς | εἰχθύος, 10–11) which is in the ponds he owns', and the lessees acknowledge: με|μισθώμεθα τὴν ἄ|γραν (34–36). Related to this noun is the verb ἀγρεύειν: the occurrence at *P.Oxy.* 3270.11 may be added to the two other literal examples noted by MM, s.v., though they do not exactly parallel the figurative use of the verb at Mk. 12.13, ἵνα αὐτὸν ἀγρεύωσιν λόγῳ.

In their entry for ἁλιεύς, MM discuss contracted and other variant spellings; cf. Moulton/ Howard, *Grammar of NT Greek*, 2.89–90. In the new group of texts note ἁλιέας at *l*.9 of the text reprinted above, and ἁλεῖς (also acc. pl.) at *P.Oxy.* 3267.11. While still on the subject of fishing we may note further the use of κοινωνοί at *P.Oxy.* 3270.5, 8: Aurelius Lucius 'and his partners' make an offer to lease a fishing area to Aurelius Sarapion 'and his partners'; the latter are 'contractors of the fishing concession' (μισθωταῖς | εἰχθυηρᾶς, 5–6) of Oxyrhynchos. E.A. Judge has drawn my attention to H. Wankel, *Die Inschriften von*

Ephesos Ia (Bonn, 1979) 20, a lengthy inscription dated 54–59AD, 'which shows that half the fishermen/fish dealers of Ephesos were Roman citizens, at a time when citizenship was still a rare privilege'. Texts like this provide support for his theory (cf. *New Docs 1977*, **84**) that relatively low-status people obtained citizenship (from army service or manumission), and thereby high formal rank, in spite of its rarity among those of high status, and that this was a feature of NT church circles. P.J. Sijpesteijn, n. ad *P.Wisconsin* 1.6, suggests that someone must have written this document for the person involved 'as the style of writing is far too skilled for a fisherman'; but the *a priori* assumption may be questionable.

Given the mention of κοινωνός here, some brief comment should be made about a recent monograph, J. P. Sampley, *Pauline Partnership in Christ. Christian Community and Commitment in Light of Roman Law* (Philadelphia, 1980). Sampley argues that certain Pauline passages, most notably Gal. 2.9 (James, Kephas and John δεξιὰς ἔδωκαν ... κοινωνίας to Paul and Barnabas), and Phil. 4.15 (the Philippian *ekklesia* was the only one which ἐκοινώνησεν with Paul in the matter of giving and receiving), reflect the Roman legal notion of consensual *societas*. The most fundamental problem with this hypothesis is that Sampley fails to demonstrate that κοινων- words are the normal equivalent of Latin *societas* and its related forms. While there are some points of overlap, undoubtedly, the true equivalent for κοινων- is *communis/communitas* and the like. See W. Popkes, 'Gemeinschaft', *RAC* 9 (1976) 1100–1145, esp. 1119. F. Hauck, *koinos*, *TDNT* 3 (1965) 798, regards κοινωνός as a 'technical term for a business partner or associate', but even within a commercial context this circumscribes the word too much: see *New Docs 1976*, **40**, p.85, where Lk. 5.7, 10 are discussed. Sampley's argument, attributing to κοινωνία and related words the same force as *societas* in its technical Roman legal context, is philologically unsound. Further, even granting Sampley's case, he goes too far in arguing (e.g., 51, 71, 103) for an actual *societas* between Paul and the Jerusalem leaders, and between Paul and the Philippian believers; surely Paul is applying a metaphor. Evidence would be needed for a *societas* between one individual partner and one collective partner if the relationship between Paul and the Philippians envisaged by Sampley is to begin to be credible. It is too readily assumed that because Paul is a Roman citizen he will be well-acquainted with technicalities of Roman law; and further that those to whom Paul writes will be similarly conversant with such terminology merely because they live in a Roman *colonia* (Sampley, 61, 105). That Paul's injunction at Phil. 4.2 to τὸ αὐτὸ φρονεῖν would be readily equated by his readers with the legal phrase *in eodem sensu* is not a convincing suggestion.

Three other words may be mentioned in passing: with ἀκωλύτως at *P.Oxy.* 3269.13 cf. Acts 28.31, sufficiently documented in MM. The occurrence of σκάφη at *l*.9 in the same text could be added to MM's examples; although in the NT it is not used of fishing skiffs, at Acts 27.16, 30, 32 it refers to a life-boat. Finally, at *P.Oxy.* 3268.6–7 and *P.Oxy.* 3270.8 we may note ἑκουσίως in the standard formula for undertaking the lease; cf. Heb. 10.26 and 1 Pet. 5.2. MM, s.v., provide a number of examples ranging across several centuries, and draw attention to its use in legal contexts such as these new leases illustrate.

Finally, mention should be made here of L. Robert, *BCH* 102 (1978) 522–33, in which the fragmentary *IG* XII.9 (1915) 1260 is re-evaluated, and a new inscription published (both from Byzantion, time of Hadrian; cf. *SEG* 561,562). Both are dedications, the first making mention of Διον[υ]σοβολειτῶν (2 — Robert's new reading), while the second includes the words οἱ θιασῖται Διονύσῳ Παραβόλῳ (2). The βολ- stem in both these words provides a link with *CIJ* 2.945 (Joppa, II), discussed briefly at *New Docs 1976*, **40** — on συγγενική in that text see now H. W. Pleket, *VC* 37 (1983) 201. In the Byzantion inscriptions Dionysos is presiding over associations — or the same one? — of fishermen.

5. A widow's plight

P. Sakaon 36 (a re-edition of *P.Ryl.* 2 [1915] 114) is a petition to a prefect (Theadelphia, c.280) by Aurelia Artemis, whose husband had looked after the flock of sheep of a certain Syrion, a *dekaprotos* of their village of Thraso. No sooner had her husband died — his body was still laid out, *l.*17 — than Syrion burst into the house aiming to seize (ἀφαρπάζειν, 15) the property of her infant children (νηπίων τέκνων, 16, 22, 26, 31), and removed 60 sheep and goats belonging to her husband which, despite appeals, he refused to return. In his note appended to the end of the petition (34–36) the prefect orders the *epistrategos* to investigate the matter. A portion of the latter's proceedings in 280/1 survives as *P.Sakaon* 31 (*ed.pr.* — *P. Thead.* 15). Though the widow and her two sons presented themselves, Syrion was able to evade giving an account of himself, it being represented that he had been sent off 'on pressing business affecting the treasury', εἰς τὰ ἀναγκαιότερα τὰ τῷ ταμείῳ διαφέ|ροντα (17–18).

We ought not to expect that any such particular incident will parallel exactly the generalizing situations evoked by the gospel parables; for the latter, while drawing upon everyday events, do not claim to reflect specific instances but to typify the general circumstances, and are a vehicle by which some point can be taught vividly. The particular incident from which these two documents survive must have proved a continuing wrangle; and at a general level it illustrates the parable of the persistent widow in Lk. 18.1–8, although that story is told to convey a very different notion (18.1). One might also think of the censure at Mk. 12.40 against οἱ κατέσθοντες τὰς οἰκίας τῶν χηρῶν. In its context this graphic comment is directed against a particular group (12.38); but it will undoubtedly have struck a chord in other situations.

6. Expiation and the cult of Men
Sounion (Attika)   II/III
ed. — *IG* II².1366

> Ξάνθος Λύκιος Γαίου Ὀρβίου καθειδρύσατο ἱερ[ὸν τοῦ Μηνὸς]
> Τυράννου, αἱρετίσαντος τοῦ θεοῦ, ἐπ' ἀγαθῇ τύχῃ. καὶ [μηθένα]
> ἀκάθαρτον προσάγειν. καθαριζέστω δὲ ἀπὸ σκόρδων κα[ὶ χοιρέων]
> καὶ γυναικός. λουσαμένους δὲ κατακέφαλα αὐθήμερον εἰσ[πορεύ-]
> 5 εσθα(ι). καὶ ἐκ τῶν γυναικέων διὰ ἑπτὰ ἡμερῶν λουσαμένην κ[ατα-]
> κέφαλα εἰσπορεύεσθαι αὐθήμερον. καὶ ἀπὸ νεκροῦ διὰ ἡμερῶν δ[έκα]
> καὶ ἀπὸ φθορᾶς ἡμερῶν τεσσαράκοντα, καὶ μηθένα θυσιάζειν ἄνε[υ]
> τοῦ καθειδρυσαμένου τὸ ἱερόν. ἐὰν δέ τις βιάσηται, ἀπρόσδεκτος
> ἡ θυσία παρὰ τοῦ θεοῦ. παρέχειν δὲ τῶι θεῶι τὸ καθῆκον, δεξιὸν
> 10 σκέλος καὶ δορὰν καὶ κεφαλὴν καὶ πόδας καὶ στηθύνιον καὶ ἔλαιον
> ἐπὶ βωμὸν καὶ λύχνον καὶ σχίζας καὶ σπονδήν, καὶ εὐείλατος
> γένοιτο ὁ θεὸς τοῖς θεραπεύουσιν ἁπλῇ τῇ ψυχῇ. ἐὰν δέ τινα

ἀνθρώπινα πάσχη ἢ ἀσθενήσῃ ἢ ἀποδημήσῃ που, μηθένα ἀνθρώπων ἐξουσίαν ἔχειν, ἐὰν μὴ ὧι ἂν αὐτὸς παραδῶι. ὃς ἂν δὲ πολυ-
15 πραγμονήσῃ τὰ τοῦ θεοῦ ἢ περιεργάσηται, ἁμαρτίαν ὀφειλέτω Μηνὶ
Τυράννωι, ἣν οὐ μὴ δύναται ἐξειλάσασθαι. ὁ δὲ θυσιάζων τῇ ἑβδόμῃ
τὰ καθήκοντα πάντα ποιείτω{ι} τῶι θεῶι. λαμβανέτω{ι} τῆς θυσίας ἧς
ἂν φέρη σκέλος καὶ ὦμον, τὰ δὲ λοιπὰ κατακοπτέτω (ἐν τῷ) ἱερῶι. εἰ δέ τις
{εἰ δέ τις} προσφέρει θυσίαν τῶι θεῶι, ἐγ νουμηνίας μέχρι πεντεκαι-
20 δεκάτης. ἐὰν δέ τις τράπεζαν πληρῶι τῶι θεῶι, λαμβανέτω τὸ ἥμισ[υ].
τοὺς δὲ βουλομένους ἔρανον συνάγειν Μηνὶ Τυράννῳ, ἐπ' ἀγαθῆι τύ[χηι].
ὁμοίως δὲ παρέξουσιν οἱ ἐρανισταὶ τὰ καθήκοντα τῶι θεῶι, δε[ξιὸν]
σκέλος καὶ δορὰν καὶ κοτύλην ἐλαίου καὶ χοῦν οἴνου καὶ να[στὸν χοινι-]
κιαῖον καὶ ἐφίερα τρία καὶ κολλύβων χοίνικες δύο καὶ ἀκρό[δρυα, ἐ-]
25 ἂν κατακλιθῶσιν οἱ ἐρανισταὶ καὶ στέφανον καὶ λημνίσ[κον].
καὶ εὐείλατος γένοιτο ὁ θεὸς τοῖς ἁπλῶς προσπορευομένοις.

A nearly-complete inscription, above which is carved a large crescent (the omnipresent sign of Men), here shaped more like a horseshoe. Variations here from the text in *CMRDM* are: the two hypercorrections in *l*.17 have been bracketed out, as have the duplicate first three words of *l*.19; and at the end of *l*.24 Sokolowski's restoration has been included in place of ἀκρό[αμα].

Bib. — **CMRDM* 1.13, pp.8-10 (pl.10); discussed in *CMRDM* 3, pp.7-16.

Xanthos the Lykian, slave (?) of Gaius Orbius, set up the temple of Men Tyrannos — the god having chosen him — for good fortune. And no-one impure is to draw near; but let him be purified from garlic and swine and woman. When members have bathed
5 **from head to foot, on the same day they are to enter. |And a woman, having washed from head to foot seven days after menstruation, is to enter on the same day. And (likewise) for ten days after (contact with) a corpse, and forty days after a miscarriage; nor is anyone to offer sacrifice without the founder of the temple (being present). If anyone violates (these provisions) his sacrifice will be unacceptable to the god. He is**
10 **to provide what is appropriate for the god, a right |leg, hide, head, feet, chest, oil for the altar, a lamp, kindling and a libation; and may the god be very merciful to those who serve in simpleness of soul. But if he (i.e., the founder) dies, or is sick or travelling abroad no person is to have authority except him to whom he transmits it. Anyone who**
15 **interferes |with the god's possessions or is meddlesome, let him incur sin against Men Tyrannos which he certainly cannot expiate. And let him who sacrifices on the seventh (day of the month) perform all that is appropriate for the god; let him receive a leg and shoulder of the sacrifice which he brings, and as for the rest let him cut it up at the temple. And if anyone offers a sacrifice to the god, let it be from new moon till the**
20 **fifteenth. |If anyone fills a table for the god, let him receive half (its contents). Those who wish may form a club for Men Tyrannos, for good fortune. Likewise, the club members shall provide what is appropriate for the god, a right leg, hide, a *kotyle* of oil, twelve *kotylai* of wine, a measure's worth of well-kneaded cake, three sacrificial**
25 **cakes, two measures of small cakes, and hard-shelled fruits, |as well as a wreath and a woollen ribbon, whenever the club members banquet. And may the god be very merciful to those who approach in simplicity.**

Methodological questions

The assembling by E. Lane in *CMRDM* of the epigraphical, visual, numismatic, and (very sparse) literary evidence for the cult of the god Men raises acutely two methodological issues for the study of ancient religion. First, by focusing upon the cult in Attika, Lydia, central Asia Minor, and Pisidian Antioch — it is elsewhere attested only a little in the Greek islands and Italy, with one or two small finds in other regions (Dacia, Syria) — Lane has been able to draw attention effectively to the variety which may exist between different local expressions of such a cult. This should act as an important warning against assuming that features of a cult in one place must be normative for that cult elsewhere. Cultural factors, and the personalities of individual founders of localized groups, will be elements contributing to the diversity, although naturally certain aspects must be sufficiently fundamental and standard so that the cult could be recognized for what it is. Yet, secondly, the haphazard nature of the finds always means that there is a risk of getting out of perspective what a private cult may be like in a certain place. For all we know, the sole inscription testifying to Men from city X may be extremely idiosyncratic. Taken together with two other inscriptions set up at Sounion by Xanthos, the text printed above may be an example of this risk: being by far the longest surviving document devoted specifically to the cult of Men — *CMRDM* 1.28, from Smyrna, is longer but Men figures only incidentally in it — there is the temptation to see it as setting the pattern for Men in II/III Attika. Related to these issues of local diversity and potential eccentricity in the information conveyed by documentary sources about cult groups is the question, what constitutes a cult of Men? While Lane deals with the association of various other gods with Men, it is a weakness in his treatment that this question is not addressed. It is clear from a good number of the inscriptions in *CMRDM* that Men is subordinate to other deities. *CMRDM* 1.75 (Damara in Lydia, n.d.) illustrates the problem, for this is claimed to be the only inscription in the corpus where mysteries are alluded to (*CMRDM* 3, p.83). But Men is on the periphery of this particular cult which is concerned particularly with Demeter, the mystery-goddess *par excellence*. In fact, the fragmentary *CMRDM* 1.79 (Sardis, n.d.) also refers to mysteries, though here too Men seems not to be the main focus. A collection like *CMRDM* may thus inadvertently convey a misleading impression that Men had a higher profile in antiquity than was in fact the case.

The Sounion inscription

By origin Men appears to have been an Iranian male moon god, who became so assimilated to a Hellenic milieu by IIIBC that the Greek name Men (or Meis) became the one by which he was known. (In this respect we may compare the inscription from Sardis [I/II] concerning the cult of Ahura Mazda/Zeus, discussed at *New Docs 1976*, **3**.) The earliest evidence for his cult, from Attika, is in III² BC (unless the title of a play by Menander, *Menagyrtai*, refers to mendicant priests of the god, as Lane suggests in *Berytus* 17 [1968] 99), while the other terminus comes from the very few late-IV items attesting his worship from Italy (*CMRDM* 1.22-27). With the three Sounion inscriptions dated II/III Attika thus testifies to a continuity of Men-cult of at least half a millenium. Like Isis, Sarapis, and Dionysos, with each of whom he is occasionally associated, Men was a foreign divinity who gained a wide popular appeal, although his cult does not appear to have been promoted as aggressively as theirs. Links exist also with other more traditionally Greek gods (Apollo, Hermes, Zeus), as well as with the Anatolian Mother goddess and Attis.

Turning to the Sounion inscriptions the two not printed above may be dealt with briefly. *CMRDM* 1.11 (now lost) is a laconic dedication, Ξά[ν]θος Μ[ηνὶ Τυράννῳ], restored by analogy — and, presumably, proximity of the find — with 1.12 and 13. No.12 itself is a very abbreviated version of no.13 (printed above): the only information it includes which is not found in no.13 comes at *ll*.21-22, where among the purity provisions concerning contact with corpses and miscarriage there is inserted the prohibition ἀνδροφόνον μηδὲ περὶ τὸν τόπον. Lane regards no.13 as a later copy of no.12, providing fuller details about the regulation of the cult which could not be fitted on to no.12. For references to some other pairs of documents which reflect the process of redaction and which thus may usefully be drawn into NT debate on redaction criticism see *New Docs 1976*, **26**, pp.76-77.

The founder of this cult in Attika was a slave from Lykia, whose master was a Roman citizen, as may be discerned from the *duo nomina* of Gaius Orbius. Xanthos was selected by Men (*l*.2) to establish the temple. Similar authorizations are mentioned in other cults: for example, the Agdistis inscription from Philadelphia in Lydia (II²/1¹BC) set up by Dionysios mentions that it was to him that Zeus gave the instructions concerning purifications and other matters (*SIG*³ 985.12; for discussion of this inscription and some analogies it offers for the early Christian churches see S.C. Barton/G.H.R. Horsley, *JbAC* 24 [1981] 7-41). Another way to demonstrate one's divine authority for establishing a cult is to mention a dream in which the god appears: see *New Docs 1976*, **6** with the discussion on p.31. Only one κατ' ὄναρ dedication is known for Men, *CMRDM* 4.137 (Pisidian Antioch): Μηνὶ εὐ|χαριστήρι|ον |[κα]τὰ ὄναρ, which thus corrects Lane's comment at *CMRDM* 3, p.24; note also his brief comment (3, p.122) on Mt. 2.12 where the Magoi are warned κατ' ὄναρ not to return to Herod. Nevertheless, behind at least some of the several κατ' ἐπιταγήν dedications to Men from Lydia (*CMRDM* 1.33, 49, 53, 54, 61, 85 [re-ed. respectively as *TAM* 5.1 (1981) 342, 458, 536, 537, 255, 524]; cf. 76, ἐπέταξεν θεός; 93, ἐξ ἐπιταγῆς, is from N. Phrygia; add *TAM* 5.1.51) there may have been a dream experience (so Lane, *CMRDM* 4 , p.46). On the phrase κατ' ἐπιταγήν, cf. *New Docs 1977*, **49**. From other 1978 publications E. Schwertheim, *Fest. Dörner* 2.796, no. 1A5 (pl. 187), records the κατ' ὄναρ dedication of an altar to θεᾷ Μα|νετηνῇ (Hocaköy in Bithynia, 155/6). *TAM* 67 (environs of Nikomedeia, 155/6) is another κατ' ὄναρ dedication, of an altar to the goddess Manetene; the phrase occurs also in the very fragmentary *TAM* 101. From Epidauros the following occurrences in *IG* IV².1 range in date from pre-IAD to 304(?): 266, 386, 396, 426, 427, 430, 438, 459, 470, 475, 495, 511, 513, 516, 527, 537, 544, 549, 565.

The purity provisions require not abstinence from certain foods and sexual continence so much as bathing to remove their taint (*ll*.3-5). A set number of days is prescribed if ceremonial uncleanness has been incurred before devotees of Men may re-enter the temple (5-7). With this we may compare G.-J.-M.-J. Te Riele's publication, *BCH* 102(1978) 325-31, of a fragmentary sacred law (Megalopolis in Arkadia, c.200BC; cf. *SEG* 421), which records similar provisions including the requirement of washing from head to foot, ἐκ κεφαλᾶς | λουσάμενον (12-13). This text is of more than passing interest since it provides our earliest attestation from mainland Greece of the official establishment of a cult — as opposed to dedications arising out of private piety — of the Egyptian gods Isis, Sarapis and Anoubis. With the prohibitions introduced by ἀπό in the Sounion inscription and in the Megalopolis text cf. the comments of Te Riele (328-29), with a collection of other examples at 328 n.11). Among other 1978 publications of relevance to the subject of purification are *IGA* 2.163 (Ptolemais, a little before I[BC?]; = *SB* 1.3451), a fragmentary text which prescribes a certain number of days' delay after abortion or childbirth before entry into the temple. From Marib in the Yemen may be mentioned *CIASA* (for bibliographical details of this work see **110**)1, pp.87-89, an inscription recording the penitential offering of a statue because a woman entered the god's sanctuary with unclean clothes.

Returning to the Sounion inscription, implicit in its first half-dozen lines is that anyone may become an adherent: sex and status are irrelevant. *SIG*³ 985, mentioned above, is explicit about this question: access to Dionysios' *oikos* is granted to 'men and women, free people and slaves' (*ll*.5-6, 53-54; cf. Barton/Horsley, 16-17). Ceremonial purity is not the only concern, however, and the hope is twice expressed that Men may be beneficent to those who approach him ἁπλῇ τῇ ψυχῇ (12; cf. 26). MM, s.v. ἁπλοῦς, quote this inscription, but certain occurrences of the noun provide the best NT parallels to the sentiment here: ἐν ἁπλότητι τῆς καρδίας ὑμῶν (Eph. 6.5); ἐν ἁ. τῆς καρδίας φοβούμενοι τὸν κύριον (Col. 3.22); cf. 2 Cor. 11.3 where Paul fears his readers' thoughts may be diverted ἀπὸ τῆς ἁπλότητος ... τῆς εἰς τὸν Χρίστον. The same sentiment is to be seen behind Mt. 5.8, οἱ καθαροὶ τῇ καρδίᾳ ... τὸν θεὸν ὄψονται. The literary tradition provides parallels to the requirement of a pure soul; some references are given in R. Turcan's review of *CMRDM* 3, at *Gnomon* 51 (1979) 282.

While certain taboos can be removed with time and washing, interference with τὰ τοῦ θεοῦ (sacred utensils, perhaps?) constitutes *hamartia* against Men, which cannot be expiated (14-16). As MM note, s.v. ἱλάσκομαι, this passage provides an exact verbal parallel for Heb. 2.17, εἰς τὸ ἱλάσκεσθαι τὰς ἁμαρτίας τοῦ λαοῦ. The verb occurs also at *CMRDM* 1.35 (Gyölde in Lydia, 236/7; re-ed. as *TAM* 5.1 [1981] 322), where several people had to propitiate (εἰλασάμενυ [*sic*], 6) Meter Anaeitis on behalf of their children; 1.43 (Koresa(?) in Lydia, 114/5; *TAM* 5.1.317), where people who have done wrong propitiate the goddess (ἱλάσαντο αὐτήν, 19); 1.51 (Aivatlar in Lydia 118/9; *TAM* 5.1.440), which records that a cheating banker was punished with death and it was left to his daughter to propitiate Meter Atimis and Men Tiamou (εἰλα|σαμένη, 18-19); 1.58 (Koloe in Lydia, n.d.; *TAM* 5.1.251), in which a certain Hermogenes ἱλάσετο τὸν θεόν (9-10) after being punished for slandering someone concerning some wine. The verb is entirely restored at 1.67 (*TAM* 5.1.499). (In passing, we may note that in addition to the Sounion inscription ἁμαρτία and related words appear in several Men texts from Lydia: *CMRDM* 1.42 [Koresa(?), 143/4; *TAM* 5.1.461]; nos. 70 and 71 [*TAM* 5.1.173, 172] two funerary stelai from Tarsi(?), dated 98/9 and 93/4 respectively, each using the verb προσαμαρτάνω of doing harm to the tomb; 1.77 [Sardis, n.d.], a very heavily restored text in which the dedicator says (*ll*.2-6), ἁμ[αρ]|[τήσας κα]ταπίπτω εἰς ἀ[σ]|[θένειαν] καὶ ὁμολογῶ τ[ὸ] | [ἁμάρτημ]α Μηνὶ Ἀξιω[τ]|τηνῷ ... For discussion whether public confession of sins as a response to illness is basically a Near Eastern, not a Graeco-Roman phenomenon, see F. Kudlien, *MHJ* 13[1978] 1-14; cf. *SEG* 1620). For the simple verb we may also note *SB* 3 (1926, repr. 1974) 6934 (El-Bagawat, Byzantine(?)), an inscription from the necropolis invoking Χριστὲ πάτερ and using the form ἵλαθ(ε); in this instance the term reflects Biblical usage. The compound verb ἐξιλάσκομαι occurs in ECL (the Sounion inscription is noted in BAGD, s.v.), not NT. Two further documentary instances of this verb may be noted. *P.Tebt.* 3.1 (1933) 750 is a letter (187BC(?)) in which the writer says, εἰμὲν ἔτι | οἱ θεοὶ εἴλως αὐτοῖς ἐστιν (*sic*), παραστησάτωσαν καὶ ἐξαρά|τωσαν τὰ ἐν τῶι θησαυρῶι | σιτάρια, μόλις γὰρ ἐξιλάσαντι (*sic*) |[τ]ὸν ἄνθρωπον, 'If the gods are still propitious to them, let them provide (100 transport animals) and carry away the corn in the store, for they will hardly appease the fellow' (12-17, trans. *ed.pr.*). In a letter of a much later date, *P.Strasb.* (1963) 233 (provenance unknown, III²), a man mentions that he was attacked by brigands on a journey ([πε]|πτώκαμεν εἰς λῃστήριον, 1-2; cf. Lk.10.30, λῃσταῖς περιέπεσεν), but θεοῖς χάρις ὅτι ἐξίλησα ἐγὼ γυμνός (3), 'Thanks be to the gods, because I appeased them since I was destitute (*or*, unarmed ?)'. These two examples make plain that the word is not confined to a strict religious sense, even if the latter provides the primary context.

Two related nouns may also be mentioned. C. Mango/E.J.W. Hawkins, *DOP* 18 (1964) 335-40, report two painted inscriptions from the north church in the monastery of St Chrysostom, Mt Kyrenia, Cyprus. One, nearly complete (dated early XII; pl.41), comprises seven trimeters in which the *dux* of Cyprus, Eumathios Philokales, is said to have built the church 'for the expiation of the evil acts he committed', πρὸς ἐξιλασμὸν ὧν κακῶς παρεσφάλη

(7). Mango/Hawkins suggest (339) that he built this church 'to repair his own bad standing' with the ecclesiastical hierarchy. For ἱλασμός we may note the Christian use in a will and two petitions all probably from Antinoe in the 520s. *P.Cairo Masp.*´1 (1911, repr. 1973) 67003.21, a petition concerning land under dispute bequeathed to a monastery by a widow εἰς πρόσφοραν καὶ ἀγαπήν, ὑπὲρ ἱλασμō ψυχῆς αὐτῆς; 67004.3, a petition in which it is said, ἔγνωσται . . . ὁ πρ[ὸ]ς θν καὶ σωτῆρα Χν ἱλασμὸς ἡμῶν . . . *P.Cairo Masp.* 2 (1913, repr. 1973) 67151.123, a will in which something is bequeathed ὑπὲρ ἱλασμοῦ ψυχῆς μου καὶ ἁγίας |προσφορᾶς . . . (at *l*.259 the noun is almost entirely restored).

Now, at *NTS* 27 (1981) 640-56 K. Grayston has examined the LXX usage of the ἱλάσκομαι group of words, four of which occur twice each in the NT. While such a study with a consciously limited scope has value (see below), the assumption which appears to be the foundation of the article is questionable, namely that the LXX undoubtedly provides *the* locus for NT usage. False conclusions are inevitable. For example, when it is claimed (652-53) that the absence of ἐξιλάσκομαι from the NT shows how little the latter is influenced by cultic terminology, documentary evidence which is not necessarily cultic at all, and which is certainly unrelated to Jewish cult, is being ignored. From where, one may ask, did the LXX translators get this group of words? The only answer which is philologically satisfactory is, from vernacular *koine*, particularly (though not solely) as found in Ptolemaic Egypt. Thus a text like *P.Tebt.* 750 (quoted above) is especially instructive in view of its date and the decidedly non-cultic context in which ἐξιλάσκομαι occurs. For further consideration of this general issue see my review article on the nature of the Greek of the Bible, forthcoming in *Biblica*. D. Hill, *Greek Words and Hebrew Meanings* (Cambridge, 1967), acknowledges the existence of the Sounion inscription (24 n.2), but the seeking out of further documentary attestations would have added weight to his general conclusion (47) from studying ἱλάσκομαι words, that 'the meaning of a Hebrew word is not a reliable guide to the meaning of every Greek word which may render it'. Finally on this word group we may note Grayston's useful insight that they imply an apotropaic function. He points to 1 Kgdms 3.14 as a good example: the wickedness of Eli's family will never be expiated (ἐξιλασθήσεται). This parallels well the sentiment given expression in the Men inscription under discussion (*ll*.14-16).

The detailed provisions about sacrifices are accompanied by the important rider that anyone who performs his dues without Xanthos or his nominee being present (12-14) will find his sacrifice unacceptable to Men. This warning clause provides our only information about officials in the cult: the founder has the place of pre-eminence and he has sole right to nominate his successor. (For the wording 'transmit authority' at *l*.14 cf. Jn. 1.12, ἔδωκεν . . . ἐξουσίαν). The Philadelphian group mentioned above also largely lacks any reference to officials in the cult (Barton/Horsley, 22). The egalitarian tone of that inscription may be paralleled in the Sounion inscription with the mention of an *eranos* whose members will meet under the patronage of Men Tyrannos (22). When they do come together appropriate sacrifices are expected, and when they share in a meal together the god's statue (presumably) is to be garlanded as an indication that he is sharing in their banquet (25). On this notion of the god himself sharing in the banquet cf. *New Docs 1976*, 1.

Brief comments follow on some words not already discussed above. MM's entry on αἱρετίζω is the briefest in their entire dictionary (barring cross-references like s.v. ἄγγος): this text (*l*.2) alone is quoted. As a further documentary attestation we may add *UPZ* 1 (1927, repr. 1977) 109 (provenance unknown, 98BC), a copy of a letter in which it is said ἐπεὶ ἐν τῆι πόλει αἱρετίζω | αὐτοὺς ὡς [ποι]ῶσί [μο]ι [τ]ὸ πρ[ο]σκύνημα αὐτῶν, κτλ. Mt. 12.18 is the sole NT occurrence, ὁ παῖς μου ὃν ἡρέτισα. The use of λούομαι (4) may be worth adding to MM where a couple of pertinent inscriptions and several papyri are already listed; in the NT 2 Pet.

2.22 is the only example of the middle. For γυναικεῖος (5) MM offer only papyrus attestations, but this Men inscription provides a meaning which, while not particularly applicable to the sole NT occurrence (1 Pet. 3.7) may serve to add a wider dimension to a revised MM entry. MM, s.v. ἀνθρώπινος, draw attention to the somewhat unexpected present tense (for the more usual πάθη) in the clause ἐὰν δέ τινα | ἀνθρώπινα πάσχῃ (12-13). For the noun τράπεζα cf. *New Docs 1977*, **7**, and add B. Levick, *JHS* 91 (1971) 80-84; cf. *BE* (1972) 486. The final word to merit comment here is περιεργάζομαι (15) for which MM supply a few documentary parallels, including this inscription. (Of these, note that in *PSI* 5[1917] 494 the context of the letter is irrecoverable because the papyrus is split down the centre.) Two further texts may be added to MM's collection. *P.Cair.Zen.* 3(1928, repr. 1971) 393 is a letter (provenance unknown, n.d.) in which a certain Apollonios writes to Zenon with news that someone wants to buy the big horse, 'but I cannot haggle about the price unless I hear from you', ἐγὼ δὲ οὐ δύνα|μαι περιεργάσασθαι περὶ τῆς | τιμῆς, κτλ (4-6). *P.Princ.* 3 (1942, repr. 1975) 119 is an effusive petition (provenance unknown, early IV) which begins τοὺς περιεργαζομένους τὰς ἀλλοτρίας κτήσεις καὶ ἐνδίξιν | [ἐ]πιχιροῦντας μισοῦσιν μὲν οἱ νόμοι μισεῖ δὲ καὶ ἡ σὴ μισο|πονηρία, κτλ, 'Both the laws and your own hatred of wickedness hate those who meddle with the property of others and attempt an indictment . . .' (trans. *ed.pr.*).

The preceding paragraph will convey the fact that MM (followed by BAGD) drew heavily and effectively upon the Sounion inscription. But it is sobering to realise the different guises under which those two dictionaries have recorded it. In MM it is called *Syll.* [= *SIG*; i.e. 2nd edn] 633 and dated II, svv. αἱρετίζω, ἀκάθαρτος, ἁπλοῦς; dated 'Rom.', s.v. ἀνθρώπινος, and 'Imperial Period' , s.v. ἱλάσκομαι. Under φθορά we get *Syll.*633 = '*Syll.*³ 1042' where the date offered is II; both second and third edition numbers are also provided s.v. πληρόω, but the date is II/III; while for περιεργάζομαι only the third edition number is given, dated II/III. BAGD largely recorded the inscription as *Syll.*³ 1042, but provide a date only s.v. φθορά. A reader could easily be forgiven for thinking that *CIA* III.74.16 (*BAGD*, s.v. ἐξιλάσκομαι) refers to quite another text. By no means are the NT dictionaries alone in such inconsistency. For example, LSJ mentions IAD as the date for *SIG*³ 985, svv. μύσος and παράγγελμα III, although it is elsewhere recorded as IBC (e.g., φθορεῖον, φύλαξ III.1). Until agreed abbreviations for epigraphical works are settled the process of weeding out inconsistencies can only be haphazard. Such agreement is much needed to avoid conveying false impressions about the number of times a rare word (for example) may occur.

Lydia and central Asia Minor

As in Attika and the Islands so in Lydia the cult of Men found expression in various small sanctuaries. In the area around Kula it seems clear that the cult was very popular and that there was not one focal sanctuary, but several; and it is observed at *BE* (1978) 434 that the existence of a number of these small, localized shrines — a far remove from the great Greek temples — provides evidence for belief in the power of a god like Men. The great majority of texts concerned with Men in the Kula district — dated inscriptions range from 66/7 to (probably) 269/70 (*CMRDM* 1.56 and 65 [*TAM* 5.1.577, 252] respectively) — are dedications set up as the result of a vow, to record thanks to the god concerning matters as diverse as health restored or finding a wife. As an example of the former note *CMRDM* 1.59 (Kula, n.d.; *TAM* 5.1.323), where the dedicatee gives thanks [ὑ]πὲρ τῆς ὁλοκληρίας | [τῶν] ποδῶν, an example worth adding to MM s.v. ὁλοκληρία, where only papyrus attestations are provided. *CMRDM* 1.80 (Sardis, 160/1) instances the god's help in the search for a wife:

[Μην]ὶ Ἀξιοτηνῷ Ἐ[πα-]   ποδῶν τὴν εὐχήν,
[φρόδ]ειτος οἰκο[νό-]   κολασθεὶς ἀνέθη-
[μος Κλαυ]δίο[υ Στρα-]   10 κεν καὶ ἀπὸ νῦν εὐλο-
[τ]ονείκου εὐξά[με-]   γεῖ μετὰ τῶν ἰδίων
5 νος ἐὰν λήψεται   πάντων. Ἔτους σμε΄,
γυναῖκαν ἣν θέλω   μη(νὸς) Δείου βι΄.
καὶ λαβὼν καὶ μὴ ἀ-

To Men Axiotenos Epaphrodeitos, steward of Claudius Stratonicus, having made a
5 **vow | if he should get the wife which I want, and getting her but not paying his vow,**
10 **after being punished he set up (the inscription), | and from now on he blesses (the god)**
with all his family. In the year 245, month Deios, 12th(?).

There are numerous other such texts where Men punishes an individual for a wrong act or sin of omission whether committed against the god or against other people. A selection of half a dozen is provided here to give some idea of the god's involvement with ordinary domestic life. All are II, the first five from Ayazviran (ancient Koresa?), and the sixth from Tarsi, not far away.

1. 1.43 (114/5; *TAM* 5.1.317), pigs allowed to wander.
2. 1.47 (118/9; *TAM* 5.1.460):

Ἔτους σγ΄, μη(νὸς) Ἀρτεμεισίου ς΄, ἐ-   τέρα Ταρσηνὴν καὶ Ἀπόλλωνα Τάρσι-
πὶ Τροφίμη Ἀρτεμιδώρου Κι-   ον καὶ Μῆνα Ἀρτεμιδώρου Ἀξι-
κιννάδος κληθεῖσα ὑπὸ τοῦ   10 οττηνὸν Κόρεσα κατέχοντα
θεοῦ ἰς ὑπηρεσίας χάριν μὴ   καὶ ἐκέλευσεν στηλλογραφ-
5 βουληθοῦσα ταχέος προσελ-   ηθῆναι νέμεσιν καὶ καταγρά-
θεῖν ἐκολάσετο αὐτὴν καὶ μα-   ψαι ἐμαυτὴν ἰς ὑπηρεσίαν
νῆναι ἐποίησεν. ἠρώτησε οὖν Μη-   τοῖς θεοῖς.

In the year 203, month Artemisios, the sixth, when Trophime, daughter of
Artemidoros, son of Kikinnas, was called by the god into the favour of service she was
5 **not | willing to come quickly; the god punished her and made her mad. So she asked**
10 **Meter Tarsene and Apollo Tarsios and Men Artemidorou Axiottenos | who possessed**
Koresa, and he ordered the revenge to be written on a stone and to enroll myself in
service to the gods.

As frequently in Lydia Men has a name in the genitive case attached to him, which is taken to refer to the founder of the localized sanctuary (cf. *CMRDM* 3, pp.67-68). P. Herrmann, *Fest.Dörner* 1.415-23, points out that there are 26 known bynames accorded to Men, all confined to Lydia.

    The notion of being called into service by the god provides a suggestive parallel for NT ideas on this subject; although the noun ὑπηρεσία occurs in ECL (*1 Clement*; Diognetus), not NT, we may note, e.g., Acts 13.36, ὑπηρετήσας τῇ τοῦ θεοῦ βουλῇ; 1 Cor. 4.1, ὡς ὑπηρέτας Χριστοῦ. Certainly the more general idea of being 'called' by God is pervasive in the NT. At *CMRDM* 3, pp. 32-33, 43, Lane suggests that the mention of Men possessing (κατέχων) a place refers to a spiritual dimension, not to political control. Whether ὁ κατέχων at 2 Thes. 2.7 is used of the Emperor or of Paul (cf. BAGD, s.v., 1γ) this usage in this and several other Men inscriptions provides a parallel which may be of some relevance. As an alternative to κατέχων the participle βασιλεύων also occurs with reference to the spiritual realm, e.g., *CMRDM* 1.42 (Koresa(?), 143/4; *TAM* 5.1.461), which may also be of interest for the βασιλ- word group in the NT, pervasive in the Gospels (e.g., Jn. 18.36).

3. 1.51 (118/9; *TAM* 5.1.440), a cheating banker is punished with death.
4. 1.42 (143/4; *TAM* 5.1.461), a woman has committed *hamartia* (unspecified; text breaks off).
5. 1.44 (156/7; *TAM* 5.1.318), a woman sends her son-in-law mad by means of poison. The god's punishment is directed not only at her, but her son suffers a severe accident as well.
6. 1.69 (164/5; *TAM* 5.1.159), a *himation* was stolen from the baths. Men made the culprit return it and admit his theft. The owner could not be found, 'so the god ordered through an *angelos* that the cloak was to be sold and to record on a stele his powers', ὁ θεὸς οὖν ἐκέλευ|σε δι' ἀγγέλου πραθῆναι τὸ εἶμα|τὶν καὶ στηλλογραφῆσαι τὰς δυ|νάμεις (8-11). For *angeloi* in Asia Minor see L. Robert, *Opera Minora Selecta* (Amsterdam, 1969) 1.419-23, dealing with a fragmentary dedication (Lydia, II or III) to Ἀγγέλῳ Ὁσίῳ | [Δικ]αίῳ set up δι' προφητο[ῦ], 'by the mediation of the prophet' Alexander of Saittai. Is the *angelos* in *CMRDM* 1.69 an apparition in a dream, or perhaps a human intermediary (cf. Gal. 3.19, διαταγεὶς δι' ἀγγέλων)? This text is well worth drawing into a revised MM entry for that noun.

One feature of some of these texts provides a parallel at a general level to the story of Ananias and Sapphira in Acts 5.1-11: to act wrongly against others will set the god against the culprit, and it is the god who will expose and punish him. In the LXX we might compare more specifically the warning at Mal. 1.14, καὶ ἐπικατάρατος ὃς ἦν δυνατὸς καὶ ὑπῆρχεν ἐν τῷ ποιμνίῳ αὐτοῦ ἄρσεν καὶ εὐχὴ αὐτοῦ ἐπ' αὐτῷ καὶ θύει διεφθαρμένον τῷ κυρίῳ. For another example of a Christian fulfilling his vow (cf. *New Docs 1976*, **4**) note G. Dagron/J. Marcillet-Jaubert, *Belleten* 42(1978) 411-12 no.37 (Korykos in Cilicia, V(?); cf. *SEG* 1279).

Several other features may receive briefer attention. From Lydia and Phrygia a number of dedications on behalf of others (particularly family members, including *threptoi*) are attested (*CMRDM* 1.33, 35, 39, 40, 41, 50, 63, 65, 68, 72, 86, A2 [respectively, *TAM* 5.1.342, 322, 348, 452, 457, 453, 319, 252, 500, 442, 526, 253], all from Lydia; 91, 92 [= *NIP* II.2; cf. *SEG* 1174], from Phrygia; 4.18 attests this practice at Pisidian Antioch. To these we may add an example not known to Lane, published in S. Mitchell, *Regional Epigraphical Catalogues of Asia Minor*, II. *The Ankara District. The Inscriptions of North Galatia* [*BIAA Monograph* 4 = *BAR Internat. Series* 135; Oxford, 1982] 393 [pl.14]). At *CMRDM* 2.A6 (Comana in Cappadocia, n.d.) a *neokoros* makes a dedication to Lord Men ὑπὲρ τῆς Διοδώρου | Γορδίου τοῦ ἱερέως | σωτηρίας. This text brings before us another term deserving brief comment. Twice among the Lydian texts (*CMRDM* 1.41, 72 = *TAM* 5.1.457, 442) and several times from Phrygia and central Asia Minor (1.88, 91, 92 [= *NIP* II.2; cf. *SEG* 1174], 105 [= *NIP* II.3], 107, 142) dedications are made for the *soteria* of individuals, or even of whole village communities (for the latter note 1.88, 105). One such dedication to Men on behalf of a *threpte* is set up by a couple who describe themselves as φιλόθεοι (*CMRDM* 1.41 [*TAM* 5.1.457], printed with brief discussion at *New Docs 1977*, **79**). One further text is printed here by way of example, *CMRDM* 1.72 (Karaoba in Lydia, n.d.; *TAM* 5.1.442):

Εὔτυχος Ἰου-   ὑπὲρ υἱοῦ Νεική-
λίας Ταβίλλης   [τ]ου Μηνὶ Ἀξι-
δοῦλος πραγμα-   εττηνῷ διὰ
τευτὴς σὺν   10 τὸ σ⟨ω⟩θῆναι αὐ-
5 καὶ τῇ γυναικὶ   τὸν ὑπὸ τοῦ θε-
Ἐπιγόνῃ εὐχὴν   οῦ ἀσθενοῦντα.

5 Eutychos, slave of Julia Tabille, her manager, along with | his wife Epigone, made a
10 dedication on behalf of their son Niketos to Men Axiettenos because | he was saved by
the god when he was sick.

On πραγματευτής see the brief comment in *New Docs 1977*, **19**. In these inscriptions σωτηρία
normally refers to preservation from some physical illness or danger.

Lane adduces one inscription, *CMRDM* 1.50 (Koresa(?) in Lydia, 235/6; *TAM* 5.1.453),
in which he holds that Men appears as 'a compassionate and forgiving god' (*CMRDM* 3,
p.31, cf. 20); but this phraseology is an exaggeration and may give a misleading impression.
In this text a woman found herself unable to provide the bull she had vowed to Men for
hearing her prayers on behalf of her brothers, and the god accepted a stele instead.

CMRDM 2.A8 (Kula in Lydia(?), 161/2) certainly deserves notice:

Κατ' ἐπίπνοιαν Διὸς Κιλ-
λαμενηνοῦ Ἀρχελάου
κώμη Μηνὸς τεκοῦσαν
καὶ Μῆναν Τύραννον καθι-
5 έρωσαν ἔτους σμς΄ μη(νὸς)
Πανήμου.

In accordance with the inspiration of Zeus Killamenenos the village of Archelaos
5 dedicated (the temple of) the mother of Men and Men Tyrannos | in the year 246, month
Panemos.

In commenting on this cult of Men and his (unnamed) mother set up by a community Lane
speaks of the 'striking parallelism to Christianity, which Men-cult was competing with'
(*CMRDM* 3, p.81). Concerning the first part of this statement the caveat should be noted
that analogous situations (if that is even the case here) by no means always bespeak influence.
Specifically (as E.A. Judge points out to me), *villages* did not dedicate buildings or cults to
Christ in II (did they ever?). As to Lane's second clause something more than
contemporaneous existence in similar geographical areas needs to be posited to allow the
claim of rivalry in any conscious form between such groups. There is nothing from the Men
side which might undergird such a claim, nor is there any anti-Men polemic in the Fathers.
Were both seeking adherents from the same social groups? Undoubtedly there may have been
some overlap here; but unlike Christianity or the religion of Isis no evidence has come to light
so far which suggests that devotees of Men actively proselytised to win new adherents. *Pace*
Lane, *Berytus* 15 (1964) 22, conscious rivalry with Christianity need not be read into the sole
dogmatic statement of monotheism in the Men inscriptions (*CMRDM* 1.83 [*TAM* 5.1.75];
see **7**).

The notion of divine inspiration attested in this inscription is paralleled once elsewhere, as noted by E. Schwertheim, who first edited the text above, *MDAI* 25 (1975) 357-65. At *SIG³* 695 (Magnesia on the Maeander, II¹ BC; re-ed. F. Sokolowski, *Lois sacrées de l'Asie Mineure* [Paris, 1955] 33) a divine injunction is being conveyed to a whole town: θείας ἐπιπνοίας καὶ παραστάσεως γενομένης τῶι σύνπαντι πλήθει | τοῦ πολιτεύματος εἰς τὴν ἀποκατάστασιν τοῦ ναοῦ συντέλειαν, κτλ (12-13), 'after divine inspiration and manifestation occurred to the whole body of the citizenry for the complete restoration of the shrine . . .' These two epigraphical passages deserve to be built into future discussion of θεόπνευστος at 2 Tim. 3.16.

Pisidian Antioch

Beside the evidence for private cult associations involving the god Men, and small sanctuaries where Men exercised influence over those living in the vicinity, we need to balance the numismatic finds which incorporate iconography of Men. For in those cities where such coins were struck, we may usually — though not always — infer the existence of a public, state-sponsored cult. While in Attika and W. Asia Minor the religion of Men found largely personal expression through local sanctuaries and private dedications, the further east one goes the more public is the cult. This was pre-eminently the case at Pisidian Antioch, where Men was the tutelary deity of the city. Yet the private/public distinction based on geographical regions should not be pressed too hard. Thus *CMRDM* 1.127 (Plouristra(?) in Pisidia, n.d.) records a dedication to Men made by a phratry: οἱ περὶ Αὐρ. | Ἀρτέμωνα Ἑρμοκλ[έ]|ους φράτρα Μηνὶ | Πλουριστρέων εὐχήν. (For other phratries and groups devoted to Men, note *CMRDM* 1.16, 17, 34, 53, 54, 57 [these last four, respectively, *TAM* 5.1.351, 536, 537, 576] 87, A3 [*TAM* 5.1.490], in addition to the *eranos* mentioned in the Sounion inscription printed at the beginning of this entry.)

Antioch was already established as the major centre for the cult of Men well before the city became a Roman *colonia* in 25BC. From Strabo 12.8.14 we know that the cult owned slaves and lands, which were distributed among the Roman colonists. The cult went into decline during IAD, though it appears from coin issues to have been regenerated under Antoninus Pius (*CMRDM* 3, p.56). Decline did not mean obliteration, however; the only temple of Men so far found at Antioch (actually on a hill outside the city) includes many inscriptions, the earliest of which is a dedication by a freedman of Claudius (*CMRDM* 1.160). This temple has yielded well over 100 inscriptions, mostly brief and formulaic, and dated III².

Even though the scale is very different Men was to Antioch what Artemis was to Ephesos. The opposition to the spread of Christianity in the latter was a result of a perceived threat to the worship of Artemis and to the business it generated (Acts 19.27). Paul and other companions stayed at Ephesos for a lengthy period and the city was seen by them as particularly strategic for their mission. In contrast, Acts' account of the stay in Antioch appears to cover little more than a week (13.14, 44, 50-51), with a (probably) brief return visit later (14.21). Here the preaching was specifically to Jews and gentile sympathizers (13.16, 43). But when on the second sabbath the listeners included many non-Jews (13.44) the Jews stirred up τὰς σεβομένας γυναῖκας τὰς εὐσχήμονας καὶ τοὺς πρώτους τῆς πόλεως to expel them (13.50). These leading men we should infer to be the Roman magistrates of the city, by analogy with Philippi which was also a *colonia* (Acts 16.19-23, 35-39). Now, the epigraphical evidence suggests that certain leading Roman families at Antioch were associated with the Men-cult there (see *CMRDM* 3, pp.112-13 for references and discussion). It is not too speculative to suggest that the sort of argument which could have been brought against Paul and Barnabas to have them expelled was that their message was a threat to the city's main god and his cult, and would draw adherents away from the worship of Men. (If it is doubted that such an argument might be used by Jews, the pragmatism of the accusation about kingship at the trial of Jesus — Jn. 19.12, 15 — might offer an analogy.) Acts is quite silent about the god, but this attempt to read between the lines may be worth further reflection.

Further Men texts

TAM 5.1 (1981) 51, 345, 347, 490a (cf. *SEG* 903), 525 (*ed.pr.* — P.Herrmann, *Fest. Dörner* 1.418-23; cf. *SEG* 910; *BE* [1979] 434), and 597 are further Lydian inscriptions concerning Men not in *CMRDM*. Mitchell, *RECAM* 2 (noted above) includes a very brief Men inscription (28b) not found in *CMRDM*; his 230 = *CMRDM* 1.157; 356 = *CMRDM* 1.110. *NIP* publishes the following Men monuments from Phrygia not already noted above: II.1 (Nakoleia, n.d.; pl. 8), anepigraphic votive relief; II. 4 (Kadoi, n.d.; pl. 9), bust of Men with very fragmentary inscription; II. 5 = *SEG* 1168 (Kotiaion, n.d.; pl. 9), dedication in fulfilment of a vow inscribed on what is probably a statue base; III.22 = *SEG* 1199 (Nakoleia, n.d.; pl. 15) fragmentary dedication in which S. Mitchell, *JRS* 70 (1980) 223, restores [M]ηνί at *l.*3 (*SEG* 1194 mistakenly refers this restoration to another text in *NIP*). C. Naour, *Tyriaion en Cabalide: épigraphie et géographie historique* (*Studia Amstelodamensia* 20; Zutphen, 1980) 18 (= *SEG* 1232; pl. 10) and 30 both mention Men in curse formulae on epitaphs; neither of these Lykian texts is included in *CMRDM*. For a bibliographic note on the Men material from Attika cf. *SEG* 233.

7. The great power of God

Saittai (Lydia) n.d.

ed.pr. — J. Keil/A. von Premerstein, *Bericht über eine zweite Reise in Lydien* (*Öst. Akad. der Wiss.*, *ph.-hist. Kl.*, 54.2; Vienna, 1911) 109-10, no.211.

Εἷς θεὸς ἐ-
ν οὐρανοῖς,
μέγας Μὴν
Οὐράνιος,
5 μεγάλη δύ-
ναμις τοῦ ἀ-
θανάτου θε-
οῦ.

Altar, with this text on the top half of one face as its only decoration.

Bib. — *CMRDM* 1.83, p.55 (pl.35); cf. *CMRDM* 3.79; *TAM* 5.1 (1981) 75 (includes bibliography).

One god in the skies, great Men of the sky, great power of the immortal god.

This tripartite acclamation of Men calls for brief comment. The monotheistic formula — discussed in other contexts at *New Docs 1976*, **5, 68** (where the inscription is quoted without comment), **69**; *New Docs 1977*, **116** — is unique to the cult of Men. The fact that it occurs in this isolated example is indicative of syncretism. With the phrase here cf. the dedication (*TAM* 5.1.246; Kula in Lydia, 256/7) made by Stratoneikos Kakoleis τοῦ ἑνὸς | καὶ μόνου θεοῦ ⟨ἱ⟩ερεὺς καὶ τοῦ Ὁ|σίου καὶ Δικαίου (1-3). The phrase ἐν οὐρανοῖς in this context provides a useful parallel to those NT occurrences where the plural occurs, commonly (though not invariably) of the place where God dwells, e.g., ὁ κύριος ἐν οὐρανοῖς (Eph. 6.9): further examples at BAGD, s.v. οὐρανός, 2a. MM's entry for this noun could be expanded usefully by the addition of such parallels. For Christian examples of the εἷς θεός acclamation from the 1978 culling note *SEG* 1389 (Eboda in Palestine, Byzantine), *IGA* 5.492 (Herment(?), n.d.), and 5.224 (Deir Abu Hennis, n.d.); this last reads εἷς ὁ θεὸς [ὁ βοηθῶν] καὶ ὁ Χ(ριστὸ)ς αὐτοῦ καὶ [τὸ] πνε[ῦμα] αὐτοῦ. ἰχθύς. The ἰχθύς acrostic may also occur in *IGA* 5.225, where the text reads Φηβά[μμ]ων Ἰ(ησοῦ)ς ιχις (= ἰχθύς, or Χριστός?). At *IGA* 5.20 (Gabbary, IV) a painted inscription on a funerary chapel reads Χ(ριστὸ)ς. Ἰη(σοῦ)ς. θ(εοῦ). υ(ἱὸ)ς. σωτήρ [. This may be an attempt to reflect the 'fish' acrostic which has gone awry by the use of *nomina sacra*.

At *New Docs 1976*, **68** Acts' reported description (8.10) of Simon Magos as ἡ δύναμις τοῦ θεοῦ ἡ καλουμένη Μεγάλη was discussed. This Men inscription shows, first, that ἡ δύναμις as a synonym for God was not restricted to Jewish thought; and second it may work against Haenchen's deletion of τοῦ θεοῦ (Comm. ad loc.). No remains of the Men cult are attested in Samaria. Men coins survive from Laodicea ad Libanum in Syria (cf. *CMRDM* 3, p.100), but attestation of the cult is otherwise confined to Greece, the Islands and Asia Minor. So the possibility that Simon had contact with the Men cult is most unlikely. The converse, that the person who set up this altar to Men in Lydia had contact with Simon's writings, is equally remote. Coincidences of wording and thought do occur, and the temptation to detect influence from one to the other should be resisted where so much is unknown.

CMRDM 4.159, p.50 (pl.41.5) reprints a dedication to great Men from Pisidian Antioch, which takes the form of a letter-game. A *nu* is presumably to be restored at the top of the main column.

```
                    [N]
                     H
                     M
                     Σ
            N        A
            H        Γ
            M        E
            ΣΑΓΕΜ
                     E
                     Γ
                     A
                    NHMΣ
                    εὐχ[ήν]
```

Relevant here, too, is the confession text published by P. Herrmann in *Fest. Dörner*, 1.418-21 (Maionia in Lydia, n.d.; cf. *BE* 434), which concerns an appeal made to Men when a loan of money was not repaid. *Ll*.1-3 read: Μέγας Μὶς Ἀρτεμιδώρου Ἀξ[ι]|[ο]ττα κατέχων καὶ ἡ δύνα|[μ]ις αὐτοῦ... For a survey of cryptic letter games, both pagan and Christian, see M. Guarducci, *ANRW* II.16.2 (Berlin, 1978) 1736-73.

8. A more than perfect wife

Rome   c.18–2BC

ed. — E. Wistrand, *The so-called Laudatio Turiae* (Göteborg, 1976) 18–31 (pls. 1–7)

(*col.* 1)

Rara sunt tam diuturna matrimonia, finita morte, non divertio in[terrupta; nam contigit]
nobis ut ad annum XXXXI sine offensa perduceretur. utinam vetust[a consortio habu-]
isset mutationem vice m[e]a, qua iustius erat cedere fato maiorem.
30 *domestica bona pudici[t]iae, opsequi, comitatis, facilitatis, lanificii stud[i, religionis]*
sine superstitione, o[r]natus non conspiciendi, cultus modici cur [memorem? cur dicam
de tuorum cari-]
tate, familiae pietate, [c]um aeque matrem meam ac tuos parentes col[ueris eandemque
quietem]
illi quam tuis curaveris, cetera innumerabilia habueris commun[ia cum omnibus]
matronis dignam f[a]mam colentibus? propria sunt tua quae vindico ac [perpaucae in
tempora]
35 *similia inciderunt, ut talia paterentur et praestarent, quae rara ut essent [mulierum]*
fortuna cavit.

(*col.* 2)

25 *Pacato orbe terrarum, res[titut]a re publica, quieta deinde n[obis et felicia]*
tempora contigerunt. fue[ru]nt optati liberi, quos aliqua[mdiu sors invi-]
derat. si fortuna procede[re e]sset passa sollemnis inservie[ns, quid utrique no-]
strum defuit? procedens a[li]as spem finiebat. quid agitav[eris propter hoc quae-]
que ingredi conata sis, f[ors] sit an in quibusdam feminis [conspicua et admirabi-]
30 *lia, in te quidem minime a[dmi]randa conlata virtutibu[s tuis reliquis praetereo.]*
diffidens fecunditati tuae [et do]lens orbitate mea, ne tenen[do in matrimonio]
te spem habendi liberos [dep]onerem atque eius caussa ess[em infelix, de divertio]
elocuta es, vocuamque [do]mum alterius fecunditati t[e tradituram non alia]
mente nisi ut nota con[co]rdia nostra tu ipsa mihi di[gnam et aptam con-]
35 *dicionem quaereres p[ara]resque, ac futuros liberos t[e communes pro-]*
que tuis habituram adf[irm]ares, neque patrimoni nos[tri, quod adhuc]
fuerat commune, separa[ti]onem facturam, sed in eodem [arbitrio meo id]
et si vellem tuo ministerio [fu]turum: nihil seiunctum ni[hil separatum te]
habituram, sororis soc[rusve] officia pietatemque mihi d[einceps praestituram.]
. . .
48 *Tibi vero quid memorabi[lius] quam inserviendo mihi o[peram dedisse te]*
ut quom ex te liberos ha[b]ere non possem, per te tamen [haberem et diffi-]
50 *dentia partus tui alteriu[s c]oniugio parares fecunditat[em?]*

A selection from the extant portion (parts of c.120*ll.* survive) of a very large inscription (two adjacent slabs, each originally 84B x 295H cm., containing perhaps 180–90*ll.*), possibly built originally into the structure of a tomb. What survives is in several fragments, the most recent find being published by A.E. Gordon, *AJA* 54 (1950) 223–26 (pls. 26–27). Wistrand provides the only complete English translation which incorporates Gordon's fragment.

Bib. — E.A. Judge in *Polis and Imperium* (Festschrift E.T. Salmon), ed. J.A.S. Evans
(Toronto, 1974) 298–301; A.E. Gordon, *Epigraphica* 39 (1977) 7–12; *AE* 14;
W. Kierdorf, *Laudatio Funebris. Interpretationen und Untersuchungen zur Ent-
wicklung der römischen Leichenrede* (*Beitr. zur kl. Phil.*106; Meisenheim am Glan,
1980) 33–48 (complete text, with some differences from Wistrand's, at 139–45);
N.M. Horsfall, *BICS* 30 (1983) 85–98 (pls. 9–15 — identical to those in Wistrand,
but considerably larger; fig.1 on p.86 sets out the relative arrangement of the
surviving fragments).

(*col.*1)

**Uncommon are marriages which last so long, brought to an end by death, not broken
apart by divorce; for it was our happy lot that it should be prolonged to the 41st year
without estrangement. Would that our venerable association had been dissolved by
something happening to me rather than to you, by which it would have been fairer that**
30 **I as the older surrendered to fate! |As for your domestic virtues, loyalty (to our
marriage), obedience, courteousness, easy good-nature, your assiduous wool-working,
reverence (for the gods) without superstition, attire not designed for attracting
attention, modest refinement — what need have I to make mention of these? Why
should I speak of your love for your own, your devotion to your family, since you have
treated with equal honour my mother and your own parents, and provided for her the
same peace (in retirement) as for your own family; and other virtues too many to count
you possess in common with all other married women who cherish a good name.**
35 **Distinctive of you are these features which I am declaring, and very few women |have
met with similar circumstances so that they should suffer such experiences and manifest
such achievements, matters which the Fortune of women has taken care to ensure are
seldom their lot.**

(*col.*2)

25 **When the world was at peace, and our homeland restored, then we attained to restful
and happy times. Children had been our hope, which for some considerable time Fate
had begrudged us. If Fortune had borne to continue taking care of us in her established
way, what would either of us have failed to obtain? But by continuing in another
direction Fortune was putting an end to our hope. What you did because of this, and
the steps you attempted, may perhaps be striking and astonishing in certain other**
30 **women, |yet in you they are scarcely to be wondered at when compared to your other
virtues; and I pass over them. When you despaired of your fertility, and lamented my
childlessness lest, by retaining you in marriage, I might resign my hope of having
children and as a result suffer misfortune, you spoke plainly about divorce. You would
hand over our house freely to the fertility of another woman, with no other intention**
35 **than that, depending on our harmonious relationship, you yourself would |seek and
provide for me a match that was fitting and appropriate. And you affirmed that you
would treat the children-to-be as ours in common, and as though they were your own;
and that you would not make division of our inheritance which was still held in
common, but that it would remain under my authority and — if I wished it — under
your management. You would have nothing divided, nothing separated, and thereafter
you would manifest the functions and devotion of a sister and a mother-in-law. . . (*l.*48)
But as for you, what is more worthy of remembrance than that you made it your
business, in service of my interests, that when I could not have children by you yet**

50 **through you I should have them, and because of your despair | of having children you would provide offspring by my marriage to another woman?**

Has this inscription ever been picked up and drawn upon by Biblical Studies for the light it has to shed upon the marriage relationship of a wealthy Roman couple of I²BC? Certainly it deserves attention, and the fact of its being in Latin rather than Greek should not diminish its interest for NT work.

The husband and his wife are both anonymous; earlier attempts to identify them with Q. Lucretius Vespillo (*cos*.19BC) and his wife Turia — whence the popular modern title for the inscription — founder in view of the decidedly apolitical outlook of the husband, and his failure to mention the previous achievements of his family and that of his wife (cf. Horsfall, 91–92). That they were a couple of considerable means is most immediately obvious from the size of the inscription, even in its extant form 'the longest Latin inscription erected by a private individual' (ibid., 85).

In form, this text is a funeral oration, perhaps read by the husband at his wife's grave; a list of nearly 50 (partly) extant members of this rhetorical genre is tabulated by Kierdorf, 137–49 (his nos. 42 and 43 are two complete Christian examples, by Ambrose). Frequently compared with the *laudatio 'Turiae'* is the contemporary *laudatio Murdiae, CIL* VI.10230 = *ILS* 8394 (Rome, time of Augustus), for which full translations are also rare: for the most recent see N.M. Horsfall, *Ancient Society: Resources for Teachers* 12.2 (1982) 29–31. Because they gave the opportunity for rhetorical display well-known orators were used to write and deliver them; and it should not be a matter for surprise that they may occasionally have served a political end. A likely example of this would have been Augustus' oration for Agrippa, now known in small part through a Greek translation of the original Latin, preserved on a papyrus fragment, *P. Köln* 1 (1976) 10 (Fayum, time of Augustus): *ed.pr.* — L. Koenen, *ZPE* 5(1970) 217–83 (pl.8a): to the bibliography in *P. Köln* add M.W. Haslam, *CJ* 75 (1980) 193–99, who offers another Latin back-translation from the Greek; and E. Badian, *CJ* 76 (1981) 97–107, who includes further notes on the Latin original.

Yet our *laudiato*, like that for Murdia, is far removed from that sphere: it belongs to the genre of public oration, yet it turns its back on politics except insofar as the virtues of the deceased are highlighted. She was forced to move beyond the domestic sphere to block the attempt of others to invalidate her father's will while her husband was absent in Macedonia (1.3–26); and she endured physical and verbal humiliation at the hands of politicians in her attempts to get her husband recalled from exile (2.11–21). The writer of this *laudatio* employs certain rhetorical features (anaphora, chiasmus, *occultatio*), but judged by stylistic criteria the speech is not a success (cf. Horsfall, 90–91). Yet overriding these formal aspects is the depth of personal feeling and sense of loss of his life-partner of so many years (at 1.28 the correct reading for the length of their marriage may be *XXXI*, not *XXXXI*; cf. Horsfall, 93). This inscription gives us the single most impressive personal statement of the depth of the marriage-bond known to me in the later Graeco-Roman world.

The mention of wool-working in the list of virtues should not deflect us from the importance of such a list simply because *domum servavit, lanam fecit* is such a cliché in epitaphs. Of biblical passages 1 Pet. 3.1–10 and 1 Tim. 2.9 are relevant especially for their common attitude to modesty of dress; cf. Prov. 31.10–31 where the wife is praised because of her ability in running her household, just as in this inscription where service-words like *custodia* and *ministerium* occur (1.39 and 2.38 respectively; cf. Wistrand's note on 1.37–40). For testimony from the Greek heritage note in general Xen., *Oec.* 7.3-10.13, and also *ll.*83-93 from Semonides' poem on the different kinds of women (text in, e.g., H. Lloyd-Jones,

Females of the Species. Semonides on Women [London, 1975] 56-59). For discussion of each of the terms in the catalogue of virtues (1.30-36) see Wistrand's notes, particularly that on *pudicitia* (Wistrand, 36-37). As for the relationship between husband and wife, his precedence is taken for granted, as the presence of words like *obsequium* in the list indicates (1.30). Yet it is apparent throughout that her initiative is certainly not stifled. T.E.V. Pearce, *Eranos* 77 (1974) 16-33, collects a useful selection of inscriptions and literary sources to illustrate the Roman wife's standing as *custos* of the house (his examples extend back to the Greek world); he draws attention to 'the close association of the obedience of the wife with her position as mistress of the house' (21).

The extent to which the wife lived for her husband and his well-being is emphasized not only by her activity during the civil war in which she ran personal risks for him and came to harm; it is highlighted by the offer she made to resolve their personal sorrow at being childless. Sterility is simply assumed to lie with the woman (2.31-32). Her proposed way out of the dilemma provides a number of interesting parallels to such a Near Eastern incident as the story of Abram and Sarai (Gen. 16.1-15), though the differences should not be minimized. The fact that the husband preferred his marriage to the continuation of his family is an attitude 'starkly and irreconcilably anti-Augustan' (Horsfall, 93). If the form of their marriage was *cum manu* (as Horsfall suggests [92] may possibly be inferred from the reference to *obsequium* at 1.30) rather than by *coemptio*, then they held a conservative view of Roman marriage. The stated purpose of Augustus' marriage legislation in 18BC was to encourage an increase in the birthrate thereby ensuring a continuing supply of military manpower for the state. In a recent discussion of this legislation, A. Wallace-Hadrill argues (*PCPS* 27 [1981] 58-80) that, behind the official purpose lay the real goal, namely to stabilize the transmission of property, and hence of status, from generation to generation (59). While this legislation was not the first attempt in this area, it was distinguished by its endeavour to intervene in the pattern of inheritance (60). For other recent study of this Augustan legislation see P. Csillag, *The Augustan Laws and Family Relations* (Budapest, 1976); L.F. Raditsa, *ANRW* II.13 (1980) 278-339; G.K. Galinsky, *Philologus* 125 (1981) 126-144 (kindly drawn to my attention by N.M. Horsfall, *per litt.*). As the husband presents the matter, his wife is not submitting to the pressure of the legislation in her request that he remarry: her reason is the much more private one of sacrificial love for him. It may be that by 28BC both were already beyond the age for which the marriage legislation was applicable; and Horsfall calculates (93) that, if so, she may have been c. 20 years old upon her marriage in the 40s, an age far more mature than that for most Roman brides. Was it, then, a first marriage for her? For what the comparison is worth, *TAM* 124 (Nikomedeia, n.d.) records on an epitaph for Damostrata that she lived for 32 years, and was married for 12.

Yet it is clear from the section dealing with the husband's recall from exile that they were not out of step with Augustus in everything. For as Judge has pointed out (301) we have in this inscription two references to the *clementia Caesaris* (2.7a, 19; cf. 2.2) about which neither cynicism nor reserve is implied. Furthermore, 2.25 reflects a genuine relief at the end of the turmoil of the Civil War.

How typical was this marriage for Romans of means at the time? This question can only be resolved by detailed study of the literary and documentary sources. It is a *desideratum* not least for NT studies, in order that Pauline and other comments about marriage and the position of the wife vis-à-vis her husband may be examined within the wider context of contemporary society. M.R. Lefkowitz/M.B. Fant, *Women's Life in Greece and Rome* (London, 1982) collects in translation literary and documentary sources relating to women; on Roman wives, mothers and daughters see particularly their pp. 133-56 (which includes a translation of the *laudatio Murdiae*).

9. A tribute from a *syntrophos*, and others

Ayazviran in Lydia 96/7

ed.pr. — G. Petzl, *Fest.Dörner* 2.752-55, no.2 (pl.78)

Ἔτους ρπαʹ, μη(νὸς) Ἀπελλαίου ιβʹ· Ἀπφῦς
Μενάνδρου καὶ Μελτίνη Ἀπολλώ-
νιον τὸν υἱὸν ἐτίμησαν. *vacat*
Χάρμος καὶ Ἄπφιον καὶ Ἀσκληπιάδη[ς]
5 οἱ ἀδελφοὶ καὶ Ἀπολλώνιος ὁ γαμ-
βρὸς καὶ ἡ γυνὴ αὐτοῦ καὶ ἡ πενθε-
ρὰ καὶ ἡ σύντροφος Τρυφῶσα κ[αὶ]
ὁ ἀνὴρ αὐτῆς Θεόφιλος καὶ ὁ δο[ῦ-]
μος ὁ ἱερὸς καὶ ἡ φράτρα αὐτοῦ ν
10 στεφάνοις χρυσέοις ἐτείμησαν.

A crown is depicted above the wording on the stele.
Bib. — *SEG* 893; *TAM* 5.1 (1981) 470a

In the year 181, month Apellaios, the 12th. Appios son of Menander and Meltine
5 honoured their son Apollonios. Charmos, Appion and Asklepiades │his brothers, and
Apollonios his brother-in-law together with his wife, his (the deceased Apollonios')
mother-in-law, his foster-sister Tryphosa and her husband Theophilos, the holy
10 association, and his brotherhood │honoured him with gold crowns.

The use of the verb τιμάω helps us identify this text as a posthumous honorific one for Apollonios. Several distinct groups have shared in the dedication: immediate family members, relatives by marriage, and fellow-members of a religious association and a brotherhood. These two elements, a collaborative dedication of honours to a dead man, are found in another, longer though incomplete inscription published by Petzl, ibid, 746-52, no.1 (pl.177; Ayazviran, n.d.; *SEG* 899; *TAM* 5.1.483a).

The women mentioned here warrant passing comment: only the deceased's mother and foster-sister are named. His mother-in-law and his sister-in-law are both anonymous; in contrast, no mention is made of the dead man's wife, so we should infer that she had predeceased him. The noun πενθερά is not commonly found in documentary texts. MM note one papyrus in illustration of the NT's Mt. 8.13 = Mk. 1.30 = Lk. 4.38; Mt. 10.35 = Lk. 12.53; no others are known to me. In addition to the epigraphical attestation here we may note *NIP* IV.36, pp.99-100 (Uğurlu, near Eumeneia in Phrygia, n.d.; *SEG* 1158), a (re-edited) tombstone for a man, his wife and τῇ π[εν]│θερᾳ Ἰουλία (5-6). Tryphosa is described as a σύντροφος, but the meaning here is certainly to be distinguished from that at its sole NT occurrence (Acts 13.1), where Manaen is described as Ἡρώδου τοῦ τετραάρχου σύντροφος. These two uses may be differentiated in the non-literary sources by the following examples:

1. foster-brother/sister
   — *BGU* 4 (1912) 1058 (provenance unknown, 13BC), which mentions at the conclusion of the document an 'agreement', συνχώρησιν περὶ δουλικοῦ παιδίου │ συντ[ρ]όφου (49-50; though the reading of the final word is very uncertain);

— *P.Ryl.* 2 (1915) 106.3 (Arsinoe, 158), notification of a death forwarded from Capito συντρόφου ἀπε|λευθέρου of the deceased Ptolema (3);

— G. Petzl, *ZPE* 30 (1978) 275, no.24.7 (pl.14; Ayazviran in Lydia, 193/4; = *SEG* 895; TAM 5.1 [1981] 473b), epitaph for Trophime;

— ibid., 261 no.6 (pl.11; Saittai in Lydia, n.d.; = *SEG* 920; *TAM* 5.1.167d), epitaph in which one of the dedicatees is Eutychis ἡ σ. (8-9);

— ibid., 262 no.8 (pl.11; Saittai in Lydia, n.d.; = *SEG* 921; *TAM* 5.1.168a) epitaph in which τὸν | σ. occurs (6-7);

— ibid., 268 no.13 (pl.12; Hamidiye in Lydia, n.d.; = *SEG* 903; *TAM* 5.1.490a; cf. *BE* [1979] 439), a fragmentary Men dedication ὑ|[π]ὲρ τῶν συντρό|[φων--- (3-5);

— *P.Oxy.* 7 (1910) 1034 (II), a σ. is one of three heirs mentioned in a draft will (*ll.*3, 7);

— *SB* 1 (1915) 1735.9 (provenance unknown, n.d.), mummy label on which a woman is called σύντρωφος (*sic*) of Paniskos;

2. comrade (of some superior person; client relationship implied?)

— *PSI* 6 (1920) 584.5-6 (Philadelphia, 240s BC), a letter from the Zenon archive in which it is mentioned that 'Ammonios who gives you this letter' τυγχά|νει ὢν βιαίον σύντρο|φος (4-6);

— *OGIS* 247.2 (Delos, 187-175BC), inscription which speaks of Heliodoros as τὸν σ. τοῦ βασιλέως (i.e. Seleukos IV Philopator); see Dittenberger's n., where references to this phrase in Polybios are given;

— *OGIS* 323.2 (Pergamon, 156/5BC; *IGRR* 4 [1927] 288), largely but with probability restored, ὁ σύντρο]φος τοῦ β.;

— *OGIS* 331.6, 28 (Pergamon) comprising two letters (Attalos II to Athenaios, 25/12/142BC; Attalos III to Kyzikos, 8/10/135BC) in which Sosander is spoken of as τοῦ σ. ἡμῶν (6), and σ. τοῦ πατρός μου (28). These texts reappear in C.B. Welles, *Royal Correspondence in the Hellenistic Period* (New Haven, 1934; repr. Rome, 1966) nos. 65, 66.

— *OGIS* 334.3 (Pergamon, 159-133BC), the demos honours Apollonides τὸν σ. τοῦ βασιλ[έως];

— *OGIS* 372.2 (Delos, 86BC (?)), honours for Dorylaios τὸν σ. of Mithridates Eupator;

— *BGU* 8 (1933) 1847.24 (Herakleopolite nome, 51/50BC at earliest), petition in which the writer mentions sending Chairesion τὸν σ. ἡμῶν 'whom you don't know' to hand over the document (this text could illustrate the other meaning instead);

— *SIG*³ 798.6 (Kyzikos, 37AD), honorific decree in which the sons of Kotys are called συντρόφους καὶ ἑταίρους ἑαυτῶι (i.e., Gaius (Caligula)).

A few further attestations occur in MM, s.v. To these examples we may add two instances of the noun, in both of which the usage is less specific: J. G. Milne, *Inscriptiones Graecae Aegypti* I. *Inscriptiones nunc Cairo in Museo* (Oxford, 1905; repr. Chicago, 1976) 9203 = *SB* 5.2 (1938) 8230 (el-Assayah near Edfu, II²BC), a grave epigram in which the deceased speaks of leaving his brother's συντροφίην (14); and *P.Tebt.* 2 (1907) 407 (199(?)), where it is mentioned that some slaves could be freed 'because of the fellowship and solicitude existing between us' (edd. trans.), --- διὰ] τὴν συνο[ῦ]σάν μοι [πρὸς αὐ]τοὺς [σ]υντροφίαν καὶ κηδεμονίαν (6).

Returning to the inscription with which this entry began, two of the names merit brief comment. The name Theophilos is frequently attested in papyri from IIIBC-VII/VIII: for references see *NB* and Foraboschi. Solin, *GPR* 1.81-82, attests 66 examples known from Rome, ranging in date from II/I-IV/V: nearly ⅔ are IAD. Of the 33 whose status can be determined only one is of senatorial standing (IV²), and one other is free-born (IAD); the remainder are freed or of servile status. *New Docs 1977*, **18** reprinted a posthumous honorific inscription for Theophilos son of Thynites, clearly a man of some position at Iulia Gordos (75/6). The Theophilos addressed at Lk. 1.3 (cf. Acts 1.1) is called κράτιστε, which perhaps implies some social standing: cf. the discussion of the term in *P.Oxy.* 3313 at **2**. As for

Tryphosa, no papyrus attestations are known to me, though there are a good number of inscriptions. MM, s.v., note several from Magnesia, and the new text printed here provides a further Asia Minor example. Solin, *GPR* 2.787-88, collects 33 from Rome (including the NT Tryphosa, Rom. 16.12); nearly all of the 13 for whom status can reasonably be determined (freed or servile) occur within the period I-II.

Finally, we may note that the phrase ὁ δοῦμος ὁ ἱερός (8-9) which is not particularly common — see Petzl, *Fest.Dörner* 2.748-49, for discussion; his inscription no.1 published in that article also attests the phrase (*ll.*5-6) — refers to a religious association, though in this particular case the deity/deities which provides its focus cannot be identified.

10. A faithful slave

Elbeyli (Bithynia)   1[2]
ed.pr. — S. Şahin, *I.Bithynia* III.12, pp.60–61 (pl.12)

> Ἐνθάδε γηράσαντ' Ἰταλὸν
> κατέθαψε δακρύσας
> οἰκονόμον πιστὸν
> Χρῆστος ἀποφθίμενον
> 5 ἀντ' ἀγαθοῦ δὲ βίου καὶ
> δουλοσύνης φιλοεργοῦ
> τὴν ὁσίαν αὐτῷ
> τήνδ' ἀπέτεισε χάριν.

Stele originally from the necropolis of Nikaia.
Bib. — *SEG* 1033

In this place Chrestos buried aged Italos; he wept for his faithful slave when he died.
5 **|In return for (Italos') good life and industrious servitude (Chrestos) fulfilled these sacred rites for him as a favour.**

This brief epigram illustrates well what was said at *New Docs 1977*, **15**, p.53 about the master's humane relationship with his slave being a matter for advertisement by means of the erection of a tombstone. The emphasis here is no less upon the master's ὁσιότης than upon Italos' faithfulness and industriousness. Given his name, Chrestos must himself have been previously of servile status.

In that 1977 entry MM's reference to Πίστος as a personal name was mentioned; from 1978 publications we may note Πίστη, the sole word on a tombstone, *Eretria*, p.40 no.79 (IIIBC). The editor refers to another example from Eretria, *IG* XII.9.459. On the noun πίστις note T.C. Gilmour, *The use of πίστις and its cognates in the Apostolic Fathers* (Diss. Auckland, 1983) — *non vidi*.

11. A woman's virtues

Cairo   late I/early II
ed.pr. — P. J. Sijpesteijn, *Mnem.* 31 (1978) 418-20

side 1

    Οὐαλερίαν · Μάρκου · θυγατέρα · ἰνγένουαν
    ἀπὸ Καισαρείας · τῆς Μαυρειτανίας εὔνουν
    φιλόστοργον · σεμνὴν · ἄμωμον ·

side 2

    φίλανδρον · φιλότεκνον εὐνοῦχον
5 εὐσεβείας καὶ φιλαγαθίας εἵνεκε ὁ ἀνὴρ
    Λούκιος Δέξιος Ἡρκουληειανὸς ἐκήδευσε.

Inscription written on two sides of a coffin cartonnage.
Bib. — *AE* 828; *SEG* 1536

Here lies Valeria, daughter of Marcus, of free-born status from Caesarea in
Mauritania. She was kind, affectionate, dignified, blameless; (*side 2*) she loved her
5 **husband and her children, and was faithful to her marriage. | Out of respect and love**
for what is good her husband, Lucius Dexios from Herculaneum, buried her.

As *ed.pr.* notes there is nothing unusual about the presence of foreigners in Egypt; but if
Ἡρκουληειανός is a reference to the husband's town of origin — an alternative is that it is
intended to represent the cognomen *Herc(u)lianus* — then, in view of the destruction of
Herculaneum in 79 and the average life expectancy in Egypt of c.30 years, a terminus of c.110
can be inferred for the death of Valeria (Sijpesteijn, 420). Yet too exact a terminus should
not be posited since Herculaneum was not Valeria's town of origin, and we should expect
her to have been younger — perhaps considerably so — than her husband. Furthermore, an
average life expectancy of 30 years does not mean that people died typically at age 30, and
infant mortality figures — to the extent they are included — would distort the figure.
B. Boyaval has paid considerable attention recently to problems of demography in Graeco-
Roman Egypt. He draws upon mummy-labels as well as funerary inscriptions from five
necropoleis (pagan and Christian) for his investigations. For the former see his *Corpus des
étiquettes de momies grecques* (Lille, 1976). It emerges clearly that the use of inscriptions for
demographic questions about Egypt, at least, leads to very vulnerable conclusions. The main
thing these texts can tell us is the subjective reaction of the living to the dead; they cannot
be expected to yield answers to our demographic questions. The following publications by
Boyaval may be noted: *ZPE* 18 (1975) 49-74 (on age indications in mummy-labels); *ZPE* 21
(1976) 217-43 (age indications on Greek funerary inscriptions from Egypt); *CE* 52 (1977)
345-51 (evidence of age at death in Egypt); *ZPE* 26 (1977) 262-66 (on the impossibility of
applying 'differential' demography — i.e., whether age at death varies according to social
position, wealth of the family, etc. — to the study of Graeco-Roman Egypt); *ZPE* 28 (1978)
193-200 (on the relationship between female 'surmortalité' — i.e., the proportion of female
to male deaths being markedly higher (in certain age-groups) — and their child-bearing age);
Revue du Nord 59 (1977) 163-91 (note here especially his comprehensive list of inscriptions
and mummy-labels by provenance and with some indication whether they are Christian or

not). It is relevant to mention here, too, M.Clauss, *Chiron* 3 (1973) 395-417 (useful bibliography, 412-14).

The inscription is notable for the first attested example of *ingenuus* transcribed in Greek letters; and in particular for the use of εὐνοῦχος of a woman. *Ed.pr.* suggests that the word here reflects its actual etymology (εὐνή + ἔχειν, 'one who keeps, i.e. guards, the marriage bed'). Now while the meaning 'chaste' is clearly the idea behind the word in this text, J.A.L. Lee points out to me that a more likely semantic development would be from 'eunuch' in the literal, physical, sense to one who (like a eunuch) refrains from sexual activity. While the plethora of adjectives in this list encourages us to see this word as adjectival, too — *ed.pr.* notes that only one other such instance is known (Sophokles) — the line between noun and adjective may be rather thin (so, too, at Mt. 19.12). Lampe, s.v. εὐνουχία, notes that this — and, we may infer, the other εὐνουχ- words — is used only of men: παρθενία is the equivalent expression for sexual abstention in women. For Latin examples of *eunuchus*, 'chaste, continent', see A. Blaise, *Dictionnaire latin-français des auteurs chrétiens* (Turnhout, 1954), s.v. The meaning here is different from those in the NT: court chamberlain (Acts 8.27,34,36,38,39), and those who choose abstinence *from* marriage (Mt. 19.12 (*ter*); εὐνουχίζω occurs twice in the same verse). Though the adjective in this new inscription does not illustrate NT usage, it certainly deserves inclusion in a revised MM entry; their current discussion offers only one late papyrus attestation.

The list of virtues is entirely unembroidered — what a contrast it makes with an extended funerary eulogy like the *laudatio 'Turiae'* (see **8**)! Its very spare character offers general affinities — *mutatis mutandis* — with those lists of virtues and vices found in the NT and elsewhere. However, the specific virtues enumerated here overlap only marginally with NT moral vocabulary (cf. *New Docs 1977*, **83**): only one (ἄμωμος) forms part of the regular vocabulary of the epistles, two others are found once each in the Pauline letters, and another two appear once each in the Pastorals. Of the seven terms here (the nouns in the ἕνεκα phrase have reference to the husband) εὔνους is not found in the NT, but cf. εὔνοια, only at Eph. 6.7; σεμνός is largely confined to the Pastorals (1 Tim. 3.8,11; Tit. 2.2; so too σεμνότης), although it is employed at Phil. 4.8. The privative ἄμωμος occurs several times of believers generally as of the Church (Eph. 1.4; 5.27; Phil. 2.15; etc.), and twice in a more specialized sense of Christ's sacrifice (Heb. 9.14; 1 Pet. 1.19); none of these passages parallels exactly the rather undefined use in this epitaph.

This leaves us with three adjectives, φιλόστοργος, φίλανδρος, φιλότεκνος; all were discussed together — the first in detail — at *New Docs 1977*, **80**. Some further attestations (along with the related nouns) from the 1978 culling may be listed here as a supplement.

φιλόστοργος (NT — Rom. 12.10 only)

— *I. Magnesia Sip.* 1, a lengthy inscription concerned with the establishment of *sympoliteia* between Smyrna and Magnesia (Smyrna, 245BC; = *OGIS* 229); at *l.*6 king Seleukos is said to be εὐσεβῶς τὰ πρὸς τοὺς θεοὺς διακειμένους καὶ φιλοστόργως τὰ πρὸς τοὺς γονεῖς, 'settling piously matters relating to the gods and treating affectionately matters relating to his parents'.

— Durrbach, *Choix* 72 (Delos, 187-175BC), honorific inscription on a statue-base for Heliodoros of Antioch εὐνοίας ἕνεκεν καὶ φιλοστο[ργίας] | [τ]ῆς εἰς τὸν βασιλέα (i.e., Seleukos; *ll.*6-7); familial relations are not in view here.

— ibid., 110 (Delos, 130-117BC), decree honouring Krateros of Antioch for his *arete, eunoia* and *philostorgia* towards Antiochos Philopator, since he acted as the latter's *tropheus*.

— E. Schwertheim, *Fest. Dörner* 2.809, no.II, A.1 (Kyzikos, I fin.), φιλοστοργία occurs (*ll.*14-15) in a decree, used of priestesses in relation to gods and goddesses. This appears to provide an exception to the conclusion at *New Docs 1977*, **80**, p.103 that in the Asia Minor examples familial ties are always in view.

— *IGA* 2.135 (Alexandria, I), φιλ[οστοργίας] | χάριν in an epitaph.

— *IGA* 2.154 (Alexandria, I/II), Τι(βέριον) Κλαύδιον Ἀπίωνα | τὸν πάντα ἄριστον | καὶ φιλοστοργότατον | ἀδελφὸν | Κλαυδία Φιλορώμαια.

— C. Naour, *ZPΣ* 29 (1978) 97-100, no.1 (pl.3) = *SEG* 1232 (Tyriaion in Lykia, n.d.), an epitaph which uses the formula φιλοστοργίας καὶ μνήμης | ἕνεκα (5-6) with reference to the deceased, several males and one female.

— ibid., 104-05, no.6 (pl.4) = *SEG* 1237 (Tyriaion, n.d.), same formula in an epitaph.

— ibid., 107, no.8 (pl.4) = *SEG* 1239 (Tyriaion, n.d.), an epitaph which Euanthos set up for his wife Helene φιλοστοργία[ς] (*sic* — for the lack of χάριν or ἕνεκα see Naour's n., ad loc.).

These last three items re-appear in C. Naour, *Tyriaion en Cabalide: épigraphie et géographie historique* [*Studia Amstelodamensia* 20; Zutphen, 1980] as nos. 18,20,14 respectively.

— *I.Bithynia* III.20 = *SEG* 1070 (provenance unknown within Bithynia, early Empire), a fragmentary funerary epigram which at *l.*6 reads φιλ' ἄνερ, γλυκύτατε πάντων, φιλόστοργε, φι[λο———. Here the term is used of a man (by his wife?).

φίλανδρος (NT — Tit. 2.4 only)

— *SEG* 953.25 (Kyzikos, second quarter IAD; see *SEG* for bibliog. details, and note *BE* 393), ---γυναῖκ]α οὐ μόνον φιλανδρότατον | [ἀλλὰ καὶ---, in a lengthy honorific decree for Apollonis.

— Gibson, *Christians for Christians* 31 (region of Kotyaion in N. Phrygia, III; = *SEG* 1110), brief epitaph for a wife, made διὰ φιλανδρία|ν μνίας χάριν (4-5). The *chi* in the last word is in the shape of a cross: see discussion at **98**.

— *TAM* 124 (Nikomedeia, n.d.), a woman praised in an epitaph by her husband for her σωφροσύνης ἀγαθῆς | φιλανδρίας δὲ μάλιστα (4-5).

— *TAM* 130 (Nikomedeia, n.d.), metrical epitaph for a wife described as ἡ ἀκατάγνωστος | [κὲ] φίλανδρος (10-11). On the former adjective (NT: only Tit. 2.8) cf. *BE* (1974) 573, p.296.

— *IGA* 2.375 (provenance unknown within Egypt, n.d.) σω|φροσύνη καὶ φιλαν|δρία (3-5) in an epitaph for a woman.

— *IGA* 2.383 (provenance unknown within Egypt, n.d.), vocative φίλανδρε in an epitaph.

φιλότεκνος (NT — Tit. 2.4 only)

— *IGA* 2.342 (Tel el-Iahudieh, no later than IAD), epitaph for Glaukias φ.

— *SEG* 1493 (Terenouthis in Egypt, I/II), funerary stele for Herenios, described as ποιητὴς | καὶ ἐπει|γραματό|γραφος φιλότεκν|ος.

— *SEG* 1517 (Terenouthis in Egypt, III/IV), funerary stele for Εὐάγγελος φ. (for the name cf. **2**).

— *SEG* 1518 (Terenouthis in Egypt, III/IV), funerary stele for Achillas φ.

— *SEG* 1522 (Terenouthis in Egypt, III/IV), funerary stele for Didyme φ.

— *SEG* 1523 (Terenouthis in Egypt, III/IV), funerary stele for Serapias πιλότεκνος (a spelling not unique: see *SEG* 20 [1964] 552, noted below).

— *SEG* 1526 (Terenouthis in Egypt, III/IV), funerary stele for Διονυσάριν φιλότεκνος.

— *IGA* 2.371 (= *SB* 1 (1915) 411; Lower Egypt, III/IV), epitaph for the gymnasiarch Sarapion, addressed with a string of adjectives: φιλότε|κνε, φιλογύναιε, φιλόφιλε, εὐφρόσυνε, ἄλυπε, | χρηστέ, χαῖρε (2-4).

— *IGA* 2.369 (Kom-el-Qadi, n.d.), epitaph for Σάμβ|υ(?) φ.

— *IGA* 2.386 (Alexandria, n.d.), φιλότεκνε in a very fragmentary epitaph.

— *NIP* IV.18 (Eumeneia, n.d.), φιλότε[as an epithet (*l.*4) for a father in an epitaph set up by his sons; restored by *ed.pr.* as φιλότεκνον or φιλοτεκνίας χάριν.

— *IGA* 5.50 (Alexandria, n.d.), φ. as a proper name suggested by Lefebvre; cf. the name Eustorgia at *I.Tyre* (1977) 176, noted at *New Docs 1977*, **80**, p.103. A certain Aurelios Eustorgios is named at *IGA* 2.129 (Alexandria, II).

Terenouthis figures well in the new attestations of φιλότεκνος; it was one of the necropoleis analysed by Boyaval in the articles noted above. A group of 126 brief texts from there (all III/IV) is listed at *SEG* 20 (1964) 512-637 = *SB* 8.2 (1967) 10162/512-637 (though the latter fails to provide the information whether a male or a female figure is carved on the stone).

In these epitaphs the following epithets occur (a female is in view if the number is italicised): φίλανδρος, *536*; φιλάδελφος (cf. **74**), 524, *536*; φιλότεκνος, 524, *525*, *526*, 527, *534*, 535, 542, *543*, 546, 549, 552 (πιλότεκνος), *554*, 571, 600, 601, 608, *619*, *623*, 632, 634, *636*; φιλόφιλος, 546, 600 (φιλόπιλο⟨ς⟩). Two further texts from the group deserve quoting for their accumulation of epithets: Σαραποῦς Εὐάνθου ἄωρος ἄτεκνος | φιλόανδρος φιλάδελφος φιλόφιλος | ὡς ἐτῶν ιδ΄ (ἔτους) ϛ΄ Φαῶφι η΄ (522); and Ἀθηνάριν φιλότεκνος φίλανδρ[ος] |[φιλά]δελφος ἀγαθω[τ]άτη ὡς (ἐτῶν) ιβ΄, | Ἐπεὶφ β΄. εὐψύχι (628). Boyaval (1978: 194 n.3) notes these texts as evidence of marriage and child-bearing by the age of twelve (no. 628); but his inference from 522 that sterility by the age of fourteen was thought worthy of record, is by no means a necessary one. Sarapous may simply have died before she bore any children. Epitaphs were not set up to 'point the finger' so bluntly, even granted that it was universally accepted that childlessness was due to the woman, not the man (cf. **8**). Ἄτεκνος here expresses commiseration that she has no descendants to keep her memory alive. Two further examples of φιλόφιλος may be noted from the 1978 culling: *IGA* 2.312 (Alexandria, II), and 353 (Alexandria(?), n.d.), the latter an epitaph for Theudas Peteautos described as both νύμφιος and ἄγαμος (for the name cf. Acts 5.36; this attestation should be noted for MM, s.v.). The notion of 'friend of all' discussed briefly at *New Docs 1977*, **15**, p.54 may be supplemented here by a not dissimilar phrase in *I.Bithynia* III.6, pp.55-56 (Bölcekova in Bithynia, Imperial period; = *SEG* 1020), a funerary epigram for Lucius in which the deceased speaks for himself as πιστὸς | ἐν φίλοις φίλος (5-6). At *TAM* 132 (Yenidoğan in Bithynia, n.d.) the deceased is described as παρὰ πᾶσιν φίλοις φίλον (9).

Finally, we may note the noun φιλαγαθία in the inscription for Valeria (not itself NT, though the adjective occurs once, at Tit. 1.8). For the verb note the text republished by E. Schwertheim, *Fest. Dörner* 2.819, no.13 (Kyzikos, 119BC or 94AD, depending on the era in use), in which οἱ θιασῖται καὶ θιασίτιδες (1) of a cult of Meter Kybele and Apollo crown a certain Stratonike who served as priestess and acted benevolently, φ[ι]λ[α]γαθήσασ[αν] (7). The proclamation of this honour took place ἐν τῇ τοῦ Διὸς συναγωγῇ (7): this non-Jewish use of συναγωγή is worth noting for a revised MM entry on that noun (cf. **94**). For another example see *SB* 5.2 [1938] 7835.12 (reprinted at *New Docs 1976*, **5**, pp.28-29).

12. A wealthy devotee of Isis

Bari (Apulia)?   c.132-40

ed.pr. — J.-C. Grenier, *Fabia Stratonice*, 6 (pls.1, 3)

> D   M
> *Fabiae.Q f.Stratonice*
> *optimae.ac.piissimae.coniugi*
> *L.Plutius.Hermes*

Text on a stone altar, three sides of which contain sculpted low-reliefs.

To the divine spirits. For Fabia Stratonike, daughter of Quintus, best and most reverent wife, Lucius Plutius Hermes (set this up).

The text on this altar is a common type of funeral tribute, with conventional epithets. Above the Latin is a bust of the deceased; a *sistrum* (rattle) and a *situla* (jar for lustral water) are depicted nearby on either side. Above Stratonike is a carved bird, probably a peacock. On the right and left faces of the altar are depicted respectively Anoubis and an Egyptian figure whom Grenier interprets as Osiris-Antinous.

The presence of the *sistrum* and the *situla* are the strongest indication that Stratonike — and her husband? — was a devotee of Isis. The peacock, together with the bas-relief figures on the side faces of the stone, are included as symbols of eternal life (see below). The fine quality of the monument suggests that Plutius and his wife, who from their names were Greeks who had inherited Roman citizenship from freedmen parents — for the rare name Plutius see Grenier, 8-10 — belonged to a wealthy, perhaps high-status, level of society.

It has often been thought that women more than men became involved in the cult of Isis, and that its appeal lay particularly with the *demi-monde;* the Roman elegiac poets have conveyed the latter idea, though their evidence on its own distorts the picture somewhat. However, S.K. Heyob, *The Cult of Isis among Women in the Graeco-Roman World* (*EPRO* 51; Leiden, 1975), has drawn attention to the fact that women are attested as participating in the worship of Isis rather less than men. As for hierarchical positions within the cult, while women could hold priesthoods in the imperial period, these largely appear to be at subordinate levels. The only cultic role reserved exclusively for women was that of *kanephoros*, basket-carrier, in the festival processions honouring the goddess. A similar viewpoint about women as cult officials was presented just prior to Heyob's book by F. Dunand, *Le culte d'Isis dans le bassin oriental de la Méditerranée* (*EPRO* 56; Leiden, 1973) 3.163-67, where it is suggested (167) that the predominance of a male hierarchy points to the persistence of Egyptian traditions when the cult moved into the Graeco-Roman world. Heyob provides a convenient survey (18-36) of official Roman anti-Isis actions from mid-IBC, culminating in Tiberius' edict of 19AD, and the responses of later emperors until the cult's demise in IV.

In arguing for the identification of the Egyptian figure on the left face with Osiris-Antinous, Grenier suggests (27) that the monument is to be dated within the decade following Hadrian's return to Rome in 132/3 (Antinous drowned in the Nile in 130; Hadrian died in 138). The altar and this hypothetical identification is not discussed in G. Hölbl's general survey of several Egyptian gods in M.J. Vermaseren (ed.), *Die orientalischen Religionen im Römerreich* (*EPRO* 93; Leiden, 1981) 167-74 (on Osiris-Antinous); nor is it mentioned in L. Vidman's excellent survey of Isis and Sarapis in ibid., 121-56. More surprisingly, no attention is paid to it in R. Lambert, *Beloved and God. The story of Hadrian and Antinous* (London, 1984), a work in which the link between Osiris and Antinous is discussed (see index, s.v. Osiris). Lambert's Appendix 1 (224-37) lists all known sculptures of Antinous of Hadrianic date; 10 of the 115 in his catalogue are taken to represent Antinous as Osiris (though no. 24, a head, is described as A. *or* O., the link with Osiris in no.53 is not certain, and no.63 is a bust of A. as Dionysos–Osiris). Of these ten items five are from the Villa Adriana at Tibur, three emanated from Egypt, while the provenance of the other two is not given. No.53 is a small alabaster bust from Egypt which was 'collapsible into five pieces for travelling', which 'suggests the domestication and popularity of the cult of Antinous' (230). Whereas Grenier doubts (25) whether the cult of Antinous was popular in Italy (apart from the cult at Hadrian's villa) he suggests (27) that temples of Isis may have included statues of Osiris-Antinous and that the assimilation with Antinous provided a means of making the veneration of Osiris more acceptable to Romans otherwise repelled by the spectacle of a dismembered god. Yet Lambert argues (187-92) that the cult was popular among all strata of society in Italy: '. . . Antinous, as a god of salvation in his own right, or as identified with

Dionysos or Hermes, with the gods of Egypt or of fertility, found many devotees at all social levels in Italy and . . . their loyalty proved some of the most intense and persistent of all' (189).

The cult of Isis and its dispersion throughout the Graeco-Roman world has received a great deal of attention since the later 1960s. Fundamental to this renewed interest is L. Vidman, *Sylloge inscriptionum religionis Isiacae et Sarapiacae* (Berlin, 1969). Among the most significant documents which have recently come to light the Isis-aretalogy from Maroneia in Macedonia (II²/1¹BC) should perhaps take pride of place: see L. Grandjean, *Une nouvelle arétalogie d'Isis à Maronée* (*EPRO* 49; Leiden, 1975); cf. *New Docs 1976*, **2**. From 1978 publications note Hölbl, *Zeugnisse*, a study of the documentary and literary evidence for Egyptian religious cults at (mainly) Hellenistic and Roman Ephesos. For other gods — Artemis apart — from this city see also D. Knibbe in *Fest. Dörner* 2.489-503 (cf. *SEG* 853), to which C. Borker has provided some supplementary references, *ZPE* 41 (1981) 187 n.30. For Italy, see Hölbl, *Beziehungen der ägyptischen Kultur zu Altitalien* (*EPRO* 62; Leiden, 1978).

L. Vidman, *Homm. Vermaseren* 3.1296-99 (cf. *AE* 614), discusses a sarcophagus lid (Salonae in Dalmatia, IV¹), long known but only in the 1960s recognized as belonging to an Isis devotee. Although it does not affect the link with Isis for this item, he rejects as unconvincing the attempt to interpret an abbreviated portion of the Latin inscription as an explicit reference to Isis and Sarapis.

In the same volume (997-98, pls. 215-16; cf. *SEG* 1585) S. Şahin has published a metrical epitaph for a man who was an initiate of the cult of Isis (S. Propontis, n.d.):

Οὐ δνοφερὰν Ἀχέροντος ἔβαν νεκυο-
στόλον οἶμον | Μηνικέτης, μακάρων
δ’ ἔδραμον εἰς λιμένας· | δέμνια γὰρ λινόπε-
πλα θεᾶς ἄρρητα βεβήλοις | Αἰγύπτου τρα-
5 φεροῖς δώμασιν ἁρμοσάμαν· | τιμήεις δὲ βρο-
τοῖσι θανών, ξένε, τὰν ἐπίσαμον | φάμαν Ἰσια-
κῶν μάρτυρ’ ἐπεσπασάμαν· | πατρὶ δὲ κῦδος
ἔθηκα Μενεσθεῖ, τρισσὰ λελοιπὼς | τέκνα·
τὺ δὲ στείχοις τάνδε ὁδὸν ἀβλαβέως.

It was not the murky route bearing the dead over Acheron which I, Meniketes, travelled, but I ran to the harbours of the blessed. For I assembled for her rich home the linen-draped bed of the goddess of Egypt, a secret to be kept from the uninitiated.
5 **|Honoured among men I died, stranger, and gained this famous reputation among Isis devotees as a witness. To my father Menestheus I have given glory, leaving him three children. But as for you (stranger), go on your way unharmed.**

For the haven of the blessed other examples are noted by Şahin, 998. At 2 Cor. 12.4 ἄρρητα ῥήματα refers to verbal secrets; in this epigram something visible is indicated by the adjective. While the word is common enough, MM's entry could benefit from a few more examples, such as this one.

Macrobius (*Sat.* 1.20.17) preserves the text of an oracle given by Sarapis to the Ptolemaic king of Cyprus, Nikokreon, who died in 311. R. van den Broek, *Homm. Vermaseren* 1.123-41, re-examines this text, in which Sarapis is conceived as a huge cosmic man (*makranthropos*). He draws attention to parallels in pre-Hellenistic Greek thought (especially Orphism), and in Egyptian and Indian literature. Orphism is to be seen as the particular source for the 'pantheistic monism which became current in Roman times' (139). Among the statements in the oracle occurs the phrase οὐράνιος κόσμος κεφαλή (2), 'the heavenly creation is my head . . .'. In relation to this another 'head' metaphor comes to mind, where Christ is ἡ κεφαλὴ τοῦ σώματος, τῆς ἐκκλησίας (Col. 1.18; cf. 2.19). MM offer no parallels to this NT passage, and Plut. *Galba* 4.3 (noted in BAGD, s.v. 1b) approximates to the language, but not to the idea. E. Lohse's excellent discussion in his Commentary (*Hermeneia* series; ET: Philadelphia, 1971) 52-55 mentions Macrobius and the Orphic fragments, which van den Broek has now discussed in more detail.

The inclusion of a peacock on Stratonike's altar makes it apposite to mention here that these birds are included in some Christian mosaics from Northern Euphratesia (on the border of modern Turkey and Syria), published by H. Candemir/J. Wagner, *Fest. Dörner*, 1.192-231 (pls. 74-99). The basilica mosaic from Hülümen (223-25, text fig. 6 facing p. 220; dated end IV/early V) includes many animals: elephants, tigers, a hyena, fish, and birds — among the latter are a pair of peacocks on either side of an amphora (pls. 91-92), and another in a nearby medallion (pl. 96). From Aşaği Çardak a martyrion (V/VI) includes a mosaic part of which portrays a peacock (pl. 81; Candemir/Wagner, 210-11; cf. *SEG* 1319). The inscriptions surviving on these mosaics (cf. *SEG* 1319-1325) hold little interest, although an instance of ἐλευθέρα, 'wife', occurs in a church mosaic dated 447 from Kürdülü Kersentaş (ibid., 227-28; pl. 44; cf. *SEG* 1324, and *BE* [1979] 603):

> Πρωτέας ἅμα Αὐγούστῃ
> ἐλευθέρᾳ σαυτοῦ εὐξάμενοι
> ὑπὲρ ἀφέσεως ἁμαρτίων
> αὐτῶν κὲ σωτερίας Κανδίδο⟨υ⟩
>
> 5　υἱοῦ αὐτῶν τὸν ἅγιον τόπον
> ἐψήφωσαν, ἔτους ἐνάτου
> νψʹ μηνὸς Δίου εἰνδικτίο-
> νος πρώτης. Μαρᾶς ψηφοθέτης.

Proteas together with your (*sic*) wife Auguste, having prayed for the forgiveness of their sins and the salvation of Kandidos their son, paved the holy place in the year 759, in the month Dios, first indiction. Maras was the mosaic-maker.

For other attestations of ἐλευθέρα with this meaning see S.C. Barton/G.H.R. Horsley, *JbAC* 24 (1981) 20 n.62. Churches and monasteries in the region are discussed by H. Hellenkamper, *Fest. Dörner*, 1.389-414.

13. 'Wise beyond her years . . .'

Caesarea (Mauretania)　　　　　　　　　　　　　　　　　　　　　　　　　　　　　II[1]
ed.pr. — P. Leveau, *Karthago* 18 (1975/76) 127-31 (pl.30a)

> Marcia Roga[ta---]
> Cyt[i]sis annor(um) XV, [men]s(ium) [---]
> h[aec f]uit pia et sapiens
> ultramodum aetatis, velut
> 5　contendente sensu cum
> celeritate fatorum.

A funerary *mensa* from a burial in a necropolis.
Bib. — *AE* 896

Marcia Rogata . . . Cytisis, aged 15 years, . . . months. She was pious and wise beyond
5 **her age, as though her mind was competing with | the swift onset of death.**

Whether *Rogata* is Marcia's cognomen — in which case she is a Roman citizen — or serves
as a by-name formula, 'Marcia, called . . . Cytisis', is uncertain. This text is memorable for
its attribution to the deceased of the process of maturation quickened up in competition with
the speed of fate. At *New Docs 1976*, **74**, p.116, a number of inscriptions (mostly Jewish)
were discussed amongst which were epitaphs for children which accorded to them adult titles
and functions, such as *grammateus*, or gymnasiarch. L. Robert, *BCH* 102 (1978) 402 n.57
(cf. *SEG* 849), offers a reworking of portions of *CIG* 2720 (Stratonikeia in Karia, II), reading
at *l.*17 τοὺς καθ' ἡλικίαν υἱοὺς (*sic*) φιλοσόφους. In this honorific inscription, therefore, the two
adolescent sons are being represented as (adult) philosophers.

The main interest afforded by this monument is that similar funerary offering tables are
not normally found until IV: they are well-attested in a nearby Christian necropolis dated
to that century. Yet the other items recovered from this burial (among them pitchers, lamps,
glassware and a bronze *as* of Nerva) secure a date of II[1]. It is therefore the earliest known
example of this type of funerary monument in Africa (Leveau, 131), and provides a useful
illustration of a burial feature which Christians of a later age adopted in a distinctive fashion.

14. God the giver of wisdom
Eumeneia   III[1]
ed.pr. — T. Drew-Bear, *NIP* IV.8, pp.75-78 (pls. 21-22)

Ζμύρνα τὰν περίσαμο-
ν ἐγείνατο, Γελλία σεμνή, |
Εὐμενέων δ' ὑπέδεκτο
κλυτὸν πέδον ·
5 ἀλλὰ σὺ μοῦνα |
καλλοσ{σ}ύνᾳ προ-
φέρεσκες (*leaf*) ἐϋκλέ-
α φῦλ{λ}α γυναικῶν · |
δῶκε δέ σοι σοφί-
10 ην θεὸς οὐρανῷ ἐνβα[σιλεύων], |
ὄφρα τεὸν φιλέουσα πόσ[ιν κλέος]
ἄφθιτον ἕξεις · | κιρναμέ[νη κάλ-]
λει σοφίην ἀρετήν τε τ[ελείαν?] . |
Φλ· Πωλλίων τὸ μν[ημεῖον ἐποίησε ἑ-]
αυτῷ καὶ Κλα · Γελλί[ᾳ τῇ γυναικί] ·
15 εἰ δέ τις ἕτερον θήσ[ει, δώσει τῷ]
[φί]σκῳ ✶ ´γ · τὸ ἀν[τίγραφον ἀπετέθη εἰς]
[—————————————]

Six hexameters followed by standard ownership details on a marble altar, clearly purchased ready-carved in view of the difficulty which the mason had to fit the wording in properly. *Bib.* — *SEG* 1126; *BE* (1979) 520; A.-M. Vérilhac, *Epigraphica* 42 (1980) 236; S. Mitchell, *JRS* 70 (1980) 224.

Smyrna gave birth to you the most distinguished lady, stately Gellia, and the famous
5 **earth of Eumeneia received you. |But you alone surpass in beauty the renowned race**
10 **of women, and |God reigning in heaven gave you wisdom in order that, loving your**
husband, you will have immortal renown, blending with your beauty wisdom and
perfect (?) virtue. Flavius Pollio made the tomb for himself and his wife Claudia Gellia.
15 **|If anyone inters another he will give to the treasury 3000 dr. The copy has been placed**
in [the archives (?) . . .].

This epitaph — metrical ones are rare at Eumeneia, according to *ed.pr.* — testifies to the trend towards monotheism in the II/III Roman world; cf. Mitchell, who in his brief comment on this text draws attention to the popularity in Phrygia during this period of cults of the 'Highest' god (on *theos hypsistos* see *New Docs 1976*, **5**; *1977*, **12, 116,** p.208). *Ed.pr.* is right to emphasize (78) that, along with such motifs as surpassing beauty and eternal fame, *l.*10 — with which he compares the statement in Hes. *Theog.* 71 that Zeus is the one ὃ δ' οὐρανῷ ἐμβασιλεύει — is 'characteristic of the pagan mentality'. Although this compound verb does not occur in the NT, we may note of βασιλεύω that the notion of God/Christ reigning *in heaven* is at best only implicit: Lk. 1.33; 1 Cor. 15.25; Rev. 11.15, 17; 19.6. The striking use and frequency of the verb with an abstract subject in Rom. 5 and 6 is noteworthy: ἁμαρτία (5.21; 6.12), θάνατος (5.14, 17), χάρις (5.21).

Wisdom as a gift of Zeus is not a common motif, according to Vérilhac; nor does σοφία figure often in epitaphs praising women. On this see J. Pircher, *Das Lob der Frau im vorchristlichen Grabepigramm der Griechen* (*Commentationes Aenipontanae* 26, *Philologie und Epigraphik* 4; Innsbruck, 1979) 54. He knows of two pre-Roman examples: Peek, *GVI* 81 (Athens, IVBC), and 1881 (= his no. 18; Sardis, II/I). At p.57 n.13 Pircher lists eight further instances, spanning the period I/II-IV; to these may be added the epitaph for Epiphania (Tomis, II/III; cf. *SEG* 27 [1977] 404), reprinted at *New Docs 1977*, **16,** *ll.*16-17. For wisdom as a divine gift in the NT note Jas. 3.17, ἡ δὲ ἄνωθεν σοφία; at 2 Pet. 3.15 Paul is said to have written κατά τὴν δοθεῖσαν αὐτῷ σοφίαν. Wisdom from God is more directly seen in Christ, e.g., 1 Cor. 1.30 of Christ ὃς ἐγενήθη σοφία ἡμῖν ἀπὸ θεοῦ (cf. 1.24 where he is spoken of as θεοῦ σοφίαν); at 1 Cor. 12.8 Paul notes ᾧ μὲν γὰρ διὰ τοῦ πνεύματος δίδοται λόγος σοφίας; and cf. the prayer at Eph. 1.17 that God δῴη ὑμῖν πνεῦμα σοφίας καὶ ἀποκαλύψεως. In Gellia's epitaph it is said that divinely-given wisdom evidenced itself in her love for her husband; the immortal renown she thereby won for herself is to be understood as people's memory of her, prompted and kept alive by the public record inscribed on this altar. Attractive as is this sentiment of a faithful marriage partnership it lacks the poignancy of the individual tribute of the *Laudatio 'Turiae'*, discussed at **8**. This personal 'remoteness' reflects the fact that the statements in the epigram are all *topoi*: *ed.pr.* gathers numerous parallels, many represented in Peek, *GVI*. To his collection may be added *GVI* 1471 (Pantikapaion, II/IBC — noted by Vérilhac) in which it is said of the dead husband, 'you alone were delineated as the yardstick of virtue', ὁ τῆς γὰρ ἀρετῆς μοῦνος ἐκλάσθης κανών (7); this provides an interesting alternative to the praise of Gellia's virtue in the new epigram (12), though whereas that man set the standard she excelled it.

15. Epigram for Apollonios of Tyana

Aigeai(?) (Cilicia)   III or IV

ed. pr. — G. Dagron/J. Marcillet-Jaubert, *Belleten* 42 (1978) 402–05, no. 33 (pl.6)

[οὖτο]ς Ἀπ[ό]λλωνος μὲν ἐπώνυμος, ἐκ Τυά‖[νων δ]ὲ

λάμψας ἀνθρώπων ἔσβεσεν ἀμπλακίας.‖

[γαῖα τρο]φὸς Τυάνων· τὸ δ' ἐτήτυμον οὐρανὸς αὐτὸν‖

[γείναθ' ὅ]πως θνητῶν ἐξελάσιε πόνους.

The stone was very possibly used as the architrave or lintel over a shrine in which was placed a statue of Apollonios. Numerous alternative restorations to those given above have been suggested by others.

Bib. — E. Bowie, *ANRW* II.16.2 (1978) 1687–88 (simultaneous, independent publication to *ed.pr.*); *SEG* 1251; *BE* (1979) 592; C.P. Jones, *JHS* 100 (1980) 190–94 (pl.1b); R. Merkelbach, *ZPE* 41 (1981) 270; *N.J. Richardson/P. Burian, *GRBS* 22 (1981) 283–85; W. Peek, *Philologus* 125 (1981) 297–98

This man called after Apollo and who came from Tyana gained fame by quelling the faults of men. The land of Tyana nursed him, but it was really heaven who bore him so that he might expel the sufferings of mortals.

The form of the stone and the obvious restoration οὖτος at the beginning of these elegiac verses suggest an adjacent statue; the text thus allows us to infer a cult of Apollonios (so Bowie) and thereby to confirm the tradition of his influential activity in Cilicia. Yet the inference of a cult is less than certain for, as E. A. Judge points out to me, statues could be displayed in niches around a cult place but those worshipped are *inside* the cella of a temple. While both *ed. pr.* and Bowie independently suggested Aigeai as the possible provenance of the stone, Jones advances several reasons why Tarsos cannot be ruled out (191). While the unusual letter styles make dating hard, Jones suggests late IV (though III is not ruled out), as against *ed. pr.*'s 'after 217 and before the Christianization of the Empire' (405). Apollonios was drawn into anti-Christian polemic in late IV by such writers as Eunapius, and Jones detects resonances (194) between the epigram and the way Apollonios is depicted in the *Historia Augusta*: 'it is tempting to place [the epigram] in the context of the struggle waged by paganism and Christianity in the fourth century' (ibid.).

Stylistically the verses are carefully composed, with certain words repeated, or contrasted, and a distinct parallelism between each couplet. The text given above speaks of Apollonios' ethical/philosophical work (1–2) as against his reputation for miraculous healing (3–4). Bowie's restoration δέξαθ' at the beginning of *l*.4 (accepted by Jones, who offers the restoration σῶμα τά]φος for *l*.3) points to a different contrast: the first couplet deals with Apollonios' work on earth, the second with his work in heaven, implying his more-than-human status. Jones conveniently assembles (193) the evidence for the development of his cult. Whether or not restorations implying divinity for Apollonios are accepted, the cult shrine which may possibly be inferred from the form of the stone (see above) has some parallels in the divine honours accorded in the early Empire by towns to its famous sons or benefactors: Jones (193, and n.32) notes several parallels, including one from IAD Herculaneum, and compares Acts 14.11–13 where Paul and Barnabas are identified with Hermes and Zeus; but this incident is not really analogous.

Several items of vocabulary are worth noting here. With the figurative use of ἐξελαύνω in connection with illness cf. the simple verb at Lk. 8.29, ἠλαύνετο ἀπὸ (or ὑπὸ) τοῦ δαιμονίου. With λάμπω used of a person cf. Mt. 17.2 (of the transfigured Jesus' face), and perhaps Mt. 5.16, λαμψάτω τὸ φῶς ὑμῖν . . . The epigram provides a clear-cut example of οὐρανός used as a periphrasis or euphemism for god/the gods, and is worth bearing in mind in relation to NT passages like Lk. 15.18, 21, ἥμαρτον εἰς τὸν οὐρανόν, κτλ, and the recurrent phrase βασιλεία τῶν οὐρανῶν (= β. τοῦ θεοῦ) — cf. BAGD, s.v., 3 — for the epigram shows that this usage is not exclusively a semitism. For σβέννυμι in a moral context cf. examples in BAGD s.v., 2, where 1 Thes. 5.19, τὸ πνεῦμα μὴ σβέννυτε, offers the nearest, though not an exact, parallel. MM's entries for these four words could therefore well include reference to the Apollonios epigram. Finally, in support of Bowie's restoration of the verb δέχομαι at *l.*4 of a person being 'received' into heaven (cf. Jones, 192) cf. Acts 3.21, . . . Ἰησοῦν, ὃν δεῖ οὐρανὸν μὲν δέξασθαι . . ., and 7.59 (Stephen's dying words), κύριε Ἰησοῦ, δέξαι τὸ πνεῦμά μου.

Bowie's lucid survey of Apollonios, in which this epigram is mentioned, *ANRW* II.16.2 (1978) 1652-99, includes a bibliography for the century preceding 1976. Two main issues are examined, the figure of Damis in Philostratos, *vita Ap.*, and the pre-Philostratos tradition concerning Apollonios. In the same volume of *ARNW* C.H. Talbert discusses (1619-51) ancient biographies as vehicles for religious propaganda: on Philostratos, *vita Ap.*, see especially 1621-22, 1635, 1638-39. For the Synoptic Gospels in relation to such biographies see 1647-50: '. . . the proper context in which to view the Synoptic Gospels is that of ancient cultic biographies of philosophers and rulers' (1649).

R. J. Penella has published a newly-collated text of Apollonios' *Letters*, along with translation and commentary: *The Letters of Apollonius of Tyana* (*Mnemosyne Suppl.* 56; Leiden, 1979). I have not seen F. Lo Cascio, *Sulla Autenticità delle Epistole di Apollonio Tianeo* (Palermo, 1978), a subject treated by Penella concisely and usefully (23-29): of the 115 letters preserved separately, together with a further 16 different ones in Philostratos, *vita Ap.*, Penella rejects or suspects nearly one-fifth. C.P. Jones, *Chiron* 12 (1982) 137-44, has recently examined Apollonius *Ep.*53, a testimonial letter for the philosopher written to the council of Tyana by a certain Claudius (not the emperor).

16. A ravening lion

In *Carthage* 1.199 M. Henig publishes a gemstone used in a signet ring (pl.31; I AD(?)), which has carved on it a lion leaping on the back of an antelope. This motif is known from other gems, and also from funerary sculpture. Examples of the latter from the year's culling are *CSIR* 79-83 (all from Corstopitum, modern Corbridge in England, and dated between II[1] and III; pls. 23-25). All but one (82) are very fragmentary pieces from grave monuments: no. 82 is excellently preserved, perhaps because it was subsequently adapted for use as a fountain. *CSIR* 253 (Condercum, modern Benwell, II or III; pl. 69) portrays a lion clutching a man's head in its forepaws.

It is clear that in funerary contexts this motif symbolizes 'the ravening power of death' (J.M.C. Toynbee, *Animals in Roman Life and Art* [London, 1973] 67). Henig suggests that this notion may not be confined to such portrayals, and that to have had it carved for a signet ring may have served as a *memento mori*. Alternatively, its function may have been magical, an apotropaic device 'against the powerful forces of destruction encompassing man' (ibid.).

This well-recognized symbolism is not always perceived to be behind two NT passages, ἐρρύσθην ἐκ στόματος λέοντος (2 Tim. 4.17), and ὁ ἀντίδικος ὑμῶν διάβολος ὡς λέων ὠρυόμενος περιπατεῖ ζητῶν τινα καταπιεῖν (1 Pet. 5.8). In the first the writer is saying 'I nearly died'; an allusion to Nero or 'the imperial power' (cf. Dibelius/Conzelmann, Comm. in the *Hermeneia* series, ad. loc.) is considerably less likely. In the second the simile is employed to refer vividly to 'spiritual' death, or apostasy. Merely to call it an 'obviously rural metaphor' (J.H. Elliott, *A Home for the Homeless. A Sociological Exegesis of 1 Peter, its Situation and Strategy* [Philadelphia, 1981] 63) falls well short of the mark. That both passages may recall phrases from the OT (Ps. 21.22 and 21.14, respectively) does not diminish the symbolic association, since it was a motif widely-used and perceived to have such force.

17. The Cities of the Revelation

In *Fest. Dörner* 2. 516-39, J. Lähnemann surveys the individual letters to the Seven Churches (Rev. 1.4-3.22) briefly in their historical setting, often following Lilje, and citing little independent primary evidence directly. The present entry takes occasion to mention some recently published documentary sources and modern discussions loosely grouped around the cities of Asia, and appends some brief notes on specific topics.

The scope of recent work on sites like Ephesos and Pergamon is vast, and no attempt to be systematic is made here. Pride of place must go to the very important repertorium, *Die Inschriften von Ephesos*, ed. H. Wankel *et.al.* (*Inschriften gr. Städte aus Kleinasien* 11-17; 7 vols so far; Bonn, 1979-81), which collects some 5000 texts, discussion of which will begin in the next volume of this Review.

Some previous entries in *New Docs* have touched on this group of cities. *New Docs 1976*, **3** reprints an inscription (I/II) which evidences the long continuity of a Zeus cult at Sardis since the Persian period. For Rev. 2.17 (Pergamon) cf. *New Docs 1976*, **39** on λευκός. The entry on Lydia and the purple trade (*New Docs 1977*, **3**), relates to Thyatira, and though of interest for Acts rather than Rev., will be taken up again below. For the view that the letters are modelled on imperial edicts (suggested by the formula λέγει) see *New Docs 1976*, **9**, p.40; W. Popkes, *ZNW* 74 (1983) 90-107, provides the most recent study of their function.

Many aspects of the background to the letters are discussed in my thesis, *A Study of the Letters to the Seven Churches of Asia with special reference to their local background* (Manchester, 1969), much of which will be incorporated in my forthcoming book, *The Letters to the Seven Churches of Asia in their Local Setting*.

Date

Some of the best recent studies of Rev. have reopened two questions which had previously commanded a measure of consensus. J.A.T. Robinson, *Redating the New Testament* (London, 1976), has championed an earlier dating of the book, and the commentaries of J.P.M. Sweet and P. Prigent, among others, have tended to play down the persecution element. For A.A. Bell, *NTS* 25 (1978/9) 93-102, the doubt about a Domitianic persecution further strengthens the argument against a Domitianic date. Whatever the solution, we have probably to see persecution not only in formal terms, but as working out through social pressures with which official policy might become identified almost accidentally. The few literary references may not be the most significant part of the evidence. For the suggestion that important hints may come from documentary sources see C.J. Hemer, *PEQ* 105 (1973) 6-12 (on the Jewish tax). See also A.Y. Collins, *BibRes* 26 (1981) 33-45 (holding to a Domitianic date despite caution over a Domitianic persecution). On aspects of the wider background see also B.F. Harris, *Prudentia* 11 (1979) 15-25; B.M. Levick, *Latomus* 41 (1982) 50-73; D.E. Aune, *BibRes* 26 (1981) 16-32; id., *BibRes* 28 (1983) 5-26; R. Syme, *Chiron* 13 (1983) 121-46 (on Domitian's last years).

Smyrna (cf. Rev. 2.8-11)

The newly available first volume of *Die Inschriften von Smyrna*, ed. G. Petzl (*Inschriften gr. Städte aus Kleinasien* 23; Bonn, 1982), contains 572 items, all sepulchral. A first glance gives promise of many illustrative gleanings, notably relating to the characteristic imagery and mythology of the city. More than a hundred texts of III-IBC at the beginning of the book incorporate the emblem of the wreath (cf. Rev. 2.10). A lament over a child (no. 549, I-II?) focuses on the local legend of Niobe weeping, together with the cry of the halcyon (cf. no.523.7-8, II or IBC). There is allusion to a ὑμνῳδὸς καὶ θεολόγος (no. 500 = *CIG* 3348; imperial cult, after 26 AD), and speculation about life after death (no.557, II?). Two Jewish inscriptions may be noted, additional to those in *CIJ* 2: no.296 gives the personal name Justus (= Zadok; cf. L. Robert, *Hellenica* 11-12 [1960] 259-62), γραμματεὺς τοῦ ἐν Ζμύρνῃ λαοῦ, and no. 297 the names Anna and Judas. Neither is dated. For inscriptions from Smyrna picked up in 1978 publications see *SEG* 883-886.

There is much else in the inscriptions worthy of study. There is the rare attestation of a woman ruler of the synagogue (ἀρχισυνάγωγος) who was also head of a household (*CIJ* 2. 741 = *IGRR* 4.1452, not earlier than III); J. B. Frey thinks that this inscription and the one from Myndos in Karia (*CIJ* 2. 756) use the term as a merely honorific title or as that of the wife of a male ruler. There is also a controversy over the interpretation of an enigmatic phrase in a Hadrianic inscription: οἱ ποτὲ Ἰουδαῖοι (*IGRR* 4.1431.29 = *CIJ* 2.742). A.T. Kraabel maintains (*JJS* 33 [1982] 455) that these are emigrants from Judaea rather than apostate Jews or the like.

One illustrative text is given here, published by L. Robert in *Hellenica* 5 (1948) 81, no.318 *bis* (pl. 13.1):

[Ἡ πρώτη τῆς Ἀσίας κάλλει καὶ μεγέθει καὶ λαμπροτάτη καὶ μητρόπολις καὶ γ΄ νεωκόρος τῶν Σεβαστῶν κατὰ τὰ δόγματα τῆς ἱερωτάτης συνκλήτου καὶ]

1   κόσμος τῆς Ἰωνίας, Σμυρναίων πόλις

           Ἰούλιον

           Μενεκλέα

           Διόφαντον

5   ἀσιάρχην

           ἐνδόξως φι-

           λοτειμησάμε-

           νον ἐξῆς ἡμε-

           ρῶν πέντε

10   τοῖς ὀξέσιν,

           ἡ γλυκυτάτη

           πατρίς.

[The first of Asia in beauty and greatness, the most splendid, the metropolis, three times temple-warden of the Augusti, according to the decrees of the most holy senate,] the ornament of Ionia, the city of the Smyrnaeans. To Julius Menekles Dio-
5 **phantos, | Asiarch, who has gloriously and zealously presented (a show of combat)**
10 **| with sharpened (weapons) five days successively, his dearest city (pays honour).**

The rivalry of the three principal cities of proconsular Asia, Ephesos, Smyrna and Pergamon, was proverbial (Dio Chrysost. 34.48; cf. *BMInscr* 489; Magie, *Roman Rule*, 636 n.1496). Smyrna received the third neocorate under Caracalla, and all three cities issued coins bearing their rival titles in extenso on the reverse (*BMCatalogue Ionia*, Eph. no.292; Sm. nos. 405-6; *BMC Mysia*, Perg. no.318; all of Caracalla). The array of formally sanctioned honours, here restored from the final phrase peculiar to this period, is characteristic of the inscriptions also. Robert explained the context of this difficult text (and of a parallel, *IGRR* 4.1230, of Thyatira) as gladiatorial, in the light of some words of an inscription of Sagalassos in Pisidia: ἡμερῶν δ᾽ ὁλοκλήρων ὀξέσι σιδήροις, 'four entire days with sharpened iron weapons' : *Rev. Arch.* 30 (1919) 31-32. All three then refer to gladiatorial shows presented by Asiarchs or imperial high priests, with sharpened blades to ensure the maximum bloodshed. 'Cet asiarque "a donné un *munus*, pendant cinq jours, avec des armes affilées". Cinq jours, cela témoigne d' une large libéralité '(Robert, 82). I hesitate to press the verbal parallel with ἡμερῶν δέκα (Rev. 2.10), seen as a period of violent suffering for the victim, though we may note the agonistic imagery of the 'crown', abundantly and variously illustrated from the Smyrna evidence.

Lydia and the Purple Trade

The account of the purple-trade in *New Docs 1977*, **3** does not raise the possibility that the purple in which Lydia dealt was not the Tyrian murex but a less expensive dye from the roots of the madder plant (*Rubia*), the so-called 'Turkey red', whose use has a very long history in Western Anatolia. M. Clerc, *de rebus Thyatirenorum* (Paris, 1896) 94, says it was still employed in his time, specifically at Akhisar (Thyatira). W.M. Ramsay, *The Historical Geography of Asia Minor* (London, 1890) 123, observes that the madder root was still then also produced abundantly in the Kara Taş district, 80km/50m E. of Akhisar, and was much in demand for the carpet-making of Kula until cheap European dyes replaced it.

The antiquity of dyeing in this region is well attested. The *Iliad* refers to the practice of purple-dyeing in Lydia and Karia (4.141-42), and it is even said that the dyeing of wool was invented by the Lydians at Sardis (Pliny, *NH* 7.56.195). Pliny also refers to a practice of colouring the fleeces even of living animals (*et viventium vellera purpura cocco, conchylio . . .* [text corrupt] *infecta*, '. . . with the kermes-gall, with the murex . . .', *NH* 8.74.197). Strabo (12.8.16/578) says that the wool of Kolossai was of the colour named from the city, Pliny's *colossinus*, the colour of the cyclamen flower (*NH* 21.27.51). Strabo further testifies (13.4.14/630) that the water at neighbouring Hierapolis was remarkably adapted to the dyeing of wool, ὥστε τὰ ἐκ τῶν ῥιζῶν βαπτόμενα ἐνάμιλλα εἶναι τοῖς ἐκ τῆς κόκκου καὶ τοῖς ἁλουργέσιν, 'so that wool dyed with the roots rivals that dyed with the kermes (*Quercus coccinea*) or the marine purple'. The focus of most of these references is on an *inland* area, of Lydia and the adjoining margin of Phrygia, an area including Thyatira. It has been said that the waters here too were specially suitable for dyeing, but Foucart's statement (*BCH* 11 [1887] 101) is not supported by his Strabo reference.

Altogether three sources of purple dye are widely attested. A full account of the shellfish dye is given in Pliny, *NH* 9.60.125ff. (cf. Vitruvius 7.13). For the kermes-oak and its dye see Pausanias 10.36.2-3 (describing the Mt. Parnassos district) and Theophrastus, *Hist.Plant.* 3.7.3; 3.16.1. For the madder root see also Pliny, *NH* 19.18.47 (*rubia tinguendis lanis et coriis necessaria*); Vitruvius 7.14.1 (*fiunt etiam purpurei colores infecta creta rubiae radice et hysgino*, where *hysginum* again probably denotes the kermes-oak, cf. Pliny, *NH* 9.65.140; in Greek ὕση is probably the kermes bush, and ὕσγινον and derivatives refer to the dye). Both these writers describe the making of specially prized shades and varieties by double-dyeing with tints of different types and origins. The use of the roots in Egypt is attested in *P.Oxy.* 7 (1910) 1051 (III) in a list of a woman's clothing and belongings: ἱμιλί|τριν πορφύρας ῥιζί|ου (12-14), 'half a pound of root-purple', the adjectival *hapax* ῥιζόσημος ('root-striped' = 'dyed with madder-purple stripes', 3), and ψευδοπόρφυρον (15), perhaps also referring to the madder. *P.Tebt.* 1 (1902) 8.30-31 (c.201BC) may refer to a state-controlled monopoly of the purple-trade already in the Lykian dependencies of the Ptolemies: τοὺ]ς ἐγλαβομένους τὴν κατὰ τὴν Λυκίαν | [πο]ρφυρικήν, 'those who have received the purple-trade contract for Lykia'; here presumably the murex is meant.

Though the term πορφυροπώλης/-ις is not known from Thyatira itself, the guild of βαφεῖς is mentioned at least seven times in the inscriptions, more than any other guild in a city notable for the number of such bodies (*CIG* 3406; *BCH* 11 [1887] 100-01, no.23; *CIG* 3497 = *IGRR* 4.1213; *CIG* 3498 = *IGRR* 4.1265; *IGRR* 4.1239, of possibly about 100AD; *IGRR* 4.1242, perhaps Augustan or shortly after; *IGRR* 4.1250).

Shifts of perspective here could affect our conception of Lydia's social status. If in fact her trade was separate from the imperial monopoly in the expensive marine dye, it does not support the attractive suggestion that she was a freedwoman of the imperial household. The possibility is of course not excluded (cf. Phil. 4.22). The name Lydia has sometimes been explained as an ethnic nickname ('the Lydian') or an ethnic slave name. There are, however, recently published attestations of women of apparent status: Julia Lydia of Sardis (L. Robert, *BCH* 102 [1978] 405; cf. *SEG* 928; after 17AD, μετὰ τὸν σεισμόν), and Julia Lydia Laterane of Ephesos, high priestess and daughter of Asia (*SEG* 869; cf. 857, where the name is restored; both dated I/II).

Lydia is described as σεβομένη τὸν θεόν (Acts 16.14). The traditional understanding of the 'Godfearers' has recently been challenged by M. Wilcox, *JSNT* 13 (1981) 102-22, and more radically by A.T. Kraabel, *Numen* 28 (1981) 113-26; cf. *JJS* 33 (1982) 445-62. This is not the place for detailed discussion of these views. Wilcox's cautions are salutary, though I think he tends to underplay the syntactical force of the article in designating separate groupings; he is certainly right in discounting here the Miletos theatre inscription (*CIJ* 2.748), the more so as it reads τῶν καί, not καὶ τῶν, and should be rendered accordingly. Kraabel's paper is essentially an *argumentum ex silentio*. The absence of reference in the inscriptions from six major Diaspora synagogues, only one of them of the first century, scarcely justifies a denial. 'Sympathisers' were presumably not accorded any status in Judaism, the Acts references may be less formal and more diversified than often assumed, and relations with the synagogues probably changed radically after 70. On 'Godfearers' see further **96**.

Examples of trade-guilds are particularly numerous in Lydia. *SEG* 29 (1979) cites a number of new texts from the city of Saittai, some 60km/35m NE of Sardis and a similar distance ESE of Thyatira: *ed.pr.* — S.Bakir-Barthel/H.Müller, *ZPE* 36 (1979) 163-94; others will be found in *TAM* 5.1 (1981) 79-93, which deals with a district of the hinterland of Lydia, and not directly with any of the cities of the Revelation. The trade-association in this city is usually termed συνεργασία, but also σύνοδος (*SEG* 29.1183). Examples from Saittai include the γναφεῖς (fullers, 1184), τέκτονες (carpenters/joiners, 1186; cf. the trade of Jesus, Mt. 13.55 = Mk. 6.3); λεινοργοί (linen-workers, 1191), πιλοποιοί (felt-makers/hatters, 1195) — all these are II — and ἐριοργοί (woolworkers, 1198, III). An association is also termed συμβίωσις, and its members συμβιωταί (1185; cf. 1188, II), a word recorded in this sense in inscriptions of Apamea (cf. LSJ Suppl.); *CMRDM* 1.54.1 uses the phrase ἱερὰ συμβίωσις of an association (Kula in Maionia, 171/2). For συμβιωταί see now *I.Smyrna* (noted above) 330 (n.d.), 331 (I or II?); for συμβίωσις, 218.3-4 (n.d.). But φίλοι (1188, 1195) seems not to be noted in this use in the lexica. We observe again the prominence of the clothing trades in Lydia.

On an honorary inscription from Thyatira (imperial period) cf. *SEG* 933.

Sardis (cf. Rev. 3.1-6)

There has been extensive study and excavation of Sardis in recent years. Two subjects of special interest are the discovery of gold-refining installations and the study of the great synagogue.

The early wealth of Lydian Sardis and of its last king Kroisos (c.560-46BC) were proverbial, and the oldest coinage has been attributed to the city. For the influence of the proverbial history of the fall of Kroisos in later literature cf. C.J. Hemer, *NTS* 19 (1972/3) 94-97, and see Rev. 3.2-3. Study of the installations found in the 'Pactolos North' area of the city suggests that gold-refining operations began there as early as 580BC (*AS* 20 [1970] 25). Production may have been controlled by the royal mint: among the gold specimens found are some bearing fragments of stamps of lions and incuse squares, the characteristic motifs of the prototype Lydian coinage (*AS* 26 [1976] 59).

The synagogue has attracted particular attention as the largest and most opulent yet known from the ancient world. In recent articles (including those cited above), A.T. Kraabel has argued that if this proves in any degree representative it will require radical rethinking of traditional images of Diaspora Judaism: *JJS* 33 (1982) 445-64, again raising the question of the 'God-fearers'; *JÖB* 32.2 (1981) 227-36, including scale plans; and especially 'Impact of the Discovery of the Sardis Synagogue', in G.M.A. Hanfmann (ed.), *Sardis from Prehistoric to Roman Times: Results of the Archaeological Exploration of Sardis 1958-1975* (Cambridge [Mass.] 1983) 178-90, 284 (notes). Cf. also Kraabel in *ANRW* II.19.1 (1979) 477-510. On the relations between Jews and pagans at Sardis see id., *Paganisme, Judaïsme, Christianisme. Mélanges offerts à M. Simon*, edd. A. Benoit et al. (Paris, 1978) 13-33 (cf. *SEG* 926).

Kraabel, 'Impact' (1983), in particular, is most stimulating for our rethinking of the relations of Jews, Christians and pagans at Sardis, both in the NT period and later: see for instance his account of Melito and his discussion of the lion symbol and of the tribe of the *Leontioi*. He draws on the very important group of synagogue inscriptions published by L. Robert, *Nouvelles inscriptions de Sardes* 1 (Paris, 1964). Robert rightly renders θεοσεβής (nos. 4,5) as 'pieux': in any case these later texts and their like are irrelevant to the 'God-fearer' question (see Robert's discussion, 41-45). It is also useful to notice the proud display by Jews of rank in the Gentile community, as instanced by Robert, no.14, p.55:

[Αὐρ. Ἑ]ρμογ[ένης Σ]αρδιανὸ[ς]
[βουλε]υτὴς [χρυσο]χόος *vacat*
[ἐπλήρ]ωσα τ[ὴν εὐχήν]. *(leaf)*

I, Aurelius Hermogenes, a Sardian councillor, goldsmith, have fulfilled my vow.

The *nomen* Aurelius (restored) points to a date between the Constitutio Antoniniana of 212 and mid-III, when its use died out. In response to the frequent doubt over the possibility of Jewish citizenship in a Gentile city we observe that several Jews in these inscriptions are designated Σαρδιανοί (citizens of Sardis, e.g. no.17), and others βουλευταί (members of the city council, e.g. nos. 13,16). The profession χρυσοχόος (partly restored here) is characteristic of Sardis, and the reading illustrated by the preservation of the first element of the word in no.13. On citizenship see further Robert, 56-57. Bodies of Jewish citizens seem to have been introduced in some cities under Seleucid constitutions. For Sardis see especially Jos., *Ant.* 14.10.24.259. For a contrary view see W.W. Tarn/G.T. Griffith, *Hellenistic Civilization* (London, 1952) 221. Another important (but late, probably after 429) inscription from the synagogue is the dedication by Samoe, 'priest and σοφοδιδάσκαλος' (cf. Kraabel [1983]: 183, 189). He was evidently the counterpart of a rabbi, but the term is Greek, and unrecorded in the lexica, and the language of Judaism as reflected in the epigraphy here and elsewhere in Asia Minor is nearly all Greek. *CIJ* 2.750, 751 are that collection's only entries for Sardis.

For epigraphical items from Sardis in 1978 publications not noted already cf. *SEG* 927, 929, 930.

Philadelphia (cf. Rev. 3.7-13)

See recent articles: S.C. Barton/G.H.R. Horsley, *JbAC* 24 (1981) 7-41 (on *SIG*³ 985); and, for the interesting later history of the city and its long resistance to Islam, H. Ahrweiler, *CRAI* (1983) 175-97. For republication of an epitaph from Christian Philadelphia (VI) cf. *SEG* 911.

Eyesalve (Rev. 3.18)

The evidence for Laodicea as a medical centre is discussed in my thesis (451-57) and in my forthcoming book. Many commentators have followed Ramsay (*Seven Churches*, 419, 429; cf. *Cities and Bishoprics of Phrygia* 1.52) in relating κολλύριον (cf. κολλουρίδιον at *New Docs 1977*, **56**) to the Laodicean medical school, and the 'Phrygian powder' which he connects with it as an ophthalmic agent (Ps.-Arist., *de mirab. auscult.* 58/834b). The school was established in Strabo's time in association with the temple of Karian Men (Strabo 12.8. 20/580), but located in the city. Its founder, Zeuxis Philalethes, a Herophilean, is named on Laodicean coinage (*BMC Phrygia*, Laod. no.153). His successors were Alexander and Demosthenes, both also surnamed Philalethes, and the latter is known as a renowned ophthalmologist, whose work was extant in translation in mediaeval times (M. Wellmann, *RE*, on Demosthenes no.11; *Hermes* 38 [1903] 546-66). There is no specific ascription of an eyesalve to Laodicea, though both Ps.-Arist. (above) and Galen (*de san. tuend.* 6.12, Kühn 6.439) ascribe ophthalmic materials to Phrygia in contexts where Laodicea in particular is probably in view. In fact, the evidence is circumstantial rather than explicit.

A recent publication discusses the collyrium stamps preserved from Roman times: H. Nielsen, *Ancient Ophthalmological Agents. A pharmaco-historical study of the collyria and seals for collyria used during Roman antiquity, as well as the most frequent components of the collyria* (Odense, 1974). The usual form is nearly always found west of the Rhine, often in military frontier posts, and bears Latin words written in reverse, for imprinting proprietary name, purpose and directions for use on a moist surface which hardened as a dry ointment-stick. This style of prescription seems to have been characteristic of the West, possibly even the Celtic West, whereas the fewer (less durable) finds from further east are of containers usually stamped or inscribed in Greek. Together the two types testify to a remarkable development of eye-medicine, and presumably to the great prevalence of ophthalmic diseases, throughout the Empire. The dating of the finds is in greater dispute.

It has been thought that most dated to the time of Augustus (Nielsen, 93). Nielsen notes, however, that the stamps are not mentioned in Pliny *NH* and, positively, that some are found in association with later coin-types. See, however, the lengthy series of recipes for eyesalves in the first-century medical writers Celsus (6.2-3, 30ff.) and Scribonius Largus (*Comp. Medic.* 18-37). The occurrence on the stamps of the recurring word *penicil(lus)* in very varied spellings and declensional forms (properly 'brush' or 'sponge') is not to be taken as indicating knowledge of the medicinal properties of a fungus or blue mould, but refers to an ointment distinguished by the mode of application, smearing with a soft brush or pad.

The types and ingredients (metal salts and the like) named on the stamps often correspond to those described in the medical writers. For recently found documentary texts see also L.C. Youtie, *ZPE* 51 (1983) 71-74. The inscribed texts of many of the stamps are collected in *CIL* 13.3.2 (1906) 10021.1-231. The following two examples will serve to illustrate. Both are square stones with details of one of the oculist's products cut in reverse on each of the four edges:

(i) 10021.60 (Augusta Treverorum [Trier]):
Eugeni diarhodon ad suppur(ationes) ex o(vo)
Eugeni diamisus ad asprit(udinem)
Eugeni chlor(on) ad dolores ex o(vo)
Eugeni penicille post impet(um)

Eugenius' *diarhodon* **for festering sores, with egg(-white); Eugenius'** *diamisus* **for roughness (trachoma); Eugenius'** *chloron* **for aches, with egg(-white); Eugenius'** *penicille* **after an attack.**

The names of the four types are written also on the upper surface of the stone, each above the relevant stamp.

(ii) 10021.112 (Nasium, Belgica [Naix]):
Iuni Tauri theodotium ad omnem lippitudi(nem)
Iuni Tauri authemerum ad epiphor(as) et omnem lippitud(inem)
Iuni Tauri penicillem ad omnem lippitud(inem)
Iuni Tauri diasmyrnes post impetum lippitu(dinis)

Junius Taurus' *theodotium* **for every kind of watering; Junius Taurus'** *authemerum* **for inflammations and every kind of watering; Junius Taurus'** *penicillem* **(sic) for every kind of watering; Junius Taurus'** *diasmyrnes* **after an attack of watering.**

The upper surface bears the name of the scribe and other graffiti.

Theodotium is paralleled in the literature by the *collyrium Theodoti* (Celsus 6.6.6). From its name, *authemerum* evidently claimed to be an instant remedy. The names *diarhodon*, *diasmyrnes* and *diamisus* are all unrecorded in *Oxford Latin Dictionary*, though the last may be the *diamisyos* of Marcellus Empiricus 9 (c.400). The three salves, then, presumably had as basic ingredients the products respectively of roses, myrrh and *misy* (μίσυ), a copper ore (? copper pyrites) or possibly a fungus. It will be noted that nearly all the proprietary names are Greek. For epigrams satirizing oculists' failures see *Anth.Pal.* 11.112,117,126.

The Rebuilding of Laodicea
In his defence of a Galban date for the Revelation, A.A. Bell, *NTS* 25 (1978/9) 100-01, makes interesting reference to the reconstruction of Laodicea after the earthquake of 60

(Tac., *Ann.*14.27). I concur with him in seeing possible allusion in Rev. 3.17 to the boasted self-sufficiency of the Laodiceans in rebuilding without imperial help, but the surviving building-inscriptions suggest a longer time-scale than he would allow. The well-known stadium inscription of Nikostratos (*CIG* 3935 = *IGRR* 4.845) is firmly dated to 79. Another document (*CIG* 3949 = *IGRR* 4.847) is available in *MAMA* 6 (1939) 2 in an improved form which permits more extensive restoration of the Latin heading and clearer evidence of date:

[*Imp. Domitiano Caesari Aug. Germ.*] *dedicante Sex.* [. . . . . . . *procos.*]

Διὶ μεγίστωι σωτῆρι καὶ Αὐτοκράτορι Δομιτιανῶι Καίσαρι Σεβαστῶ[ι Γερμανικῶι] ἀρχιερεῖ
μεγίστωι δημαρχικῆς ἐξο[υσίας τὸ . αὐτοκράτορ]ι τ[ὸ . ὑπάτωι τὸ .] πατρὶ [πατρίδος]
Τειβέριος Κλαύδιος Σεβαστοῦ ἀπελεύθερος Τρύφων τοὺς πύργ[ους καὶ τὰ περὶ] τοὺς πύργους
καὶ τὸ τρίπυλον σὺν [τῆι στρώσει(?) καὶ τῶι κόσμωι παντὶ] ἀνέ[θηκεν].

[To the emperor Domitianus Caesar Augustus Germanicus,] dedicated by Sextus [. . . proconsul].
To Zeus the greatest, the saviour, and to the emperor Domitianus (*name imperfectly erased*) Caesar Augustus [Germanicus], *pontifex maximus*, [in his . . . th year of] tribunician power, [. . . times acclaimed *imperator*, consul for the . . . th time,] father [of his country,] Tiberius Claudius Tryphon, freedman of (the) Augustus, erected the towers [and their surrounds] and the triple gate with [its paving(?) and all its adornment].

Tryphon's names show him to have been a freedman of Claudius (37-41), and he was still alive under Domitian, whose name is deleted as he suffered *damnatio memoriae*. The dedication to the emperor was evidently performed by the proconsul, as in the case of the Nikostratos inscription. Sextus is one of the less common Roman *praenomina*, and as one Sextus Julius Frontinus is known to have been proconsul of Asia about 88-90 his name should probably be restored here, for it is unlikely that another of the name could be assigned to this reign (see commentary in *MAMA*, ad loc.). If then this gate and its towers are of this date, they may represent the culmination of rebuilding, again through the donation of a wealthy individual, at a time near the traditional Domitianic date of the Rev. Cf. perhaps Rev. 3.20, and see M.J.S. Rudwick/E.M.B. Green in *ExpT* 69 (1957/8) 178. I have argued that other straws in the wind may be unobtrusively aligned in pointing to confirmation of the Domitianic date (thesis, 8-11).

(C.J. Hemer)

18. Travel risks

When Paul enumerates the things of which he can boast (2 Cor. 11.16–33) he is turning the conventional topics of self-praise on their head. On this see P. Marshall, *Enmity and other Social Conventions in Paul's Relations with the Corinthians* (Diss. Macquarie, 1980; forthcoming under the title *Enmity in Corinth: Social Conventions in Paul's Relations with the Corinthians*, in the series *Wissenschaftliche Untersuchungen zum Neuen Testament*) 553–63. At *v.*26 Paul mentions the various hazards he has encountered, risks attendant on any traveller. For his Graeco-Roman contemporaries a typical way to celebrate a safe return home after a journey was to make a thank-offering to the gods: Hor., *Odes* 1.5.12–16 is the *locus classicus* in the literary tradition, though there it is applied in a love-context with considerable wit. From 1978 documents the following representative inscriptions may be noted: *IGA* 2.109 (Koptos in Egypt, 247–221BC), in which Apollonios son of Sosibios makes a dedication to the great Samothracian gods, σωθεὶς | ἐγ μεγάλων κινδύνων ἐκ|πλεύσας ἐκ τῆς Ἐρυθρᾶς | θαλάσσης (4–7). Again, at *IGA* 2.121 (Alexandria, II(?)) Theano gives thanks to the great gods Boubastis and Arma on behalf of her daughter Theano, σωθεῖσα (emend to σωθείσης to refer to the daughter?) ἐγ μεγάλων κυνδύνων | ... (*ll*.4–5). In his note to the latter text, Breccia comments that the formula is common to maritime voyages (cf. κινδύνοις ἐν θαλάσσῃ in Paul's list, *v*.26). But it is not confined to such a context. G. Petzl, *ZPE* 30 (1978) 253–55 no.1 (pl.10.1), has published a confession text (region of Saittai in Lydia, 194/5) which relates to the cutting-down of a sacred oak tree. After acknowledging this and the consequent divine punishment which placed him near death (ἰσοθανάτους, 8), Stratoneikos son of Euangelos gives thanks that he was σωθεὶς ἐγ | μεγάλου κινδύνου (8–9). Petzl, ibid., 255–58, no.2 (pl.10.2) is another confession text (same provenance, 191/2), in which Menophilos acknowledges that he purchased sacred wood (ἱερὰ ξύ|λα, 4–5), and was divinely punished. These two inscriptions reappear as *SEG* 914 = *TAM* 5.1 (1981) 179b, and *SEG* 913 = *TAM* 5.1.179a, respectively; cf. *BE* (1979) 434.

19. The *Mimiamboi* of Herondas

The reissue of Kenyon, *Classical Texts*, may be noted here briefly since it includes as its main piece the Herondas papyrus roll, *P.Lit.Lond.* 96, dated most recently by P. J. Parsons to 'about AD 100' (*CR* 31 [1981] 110). On the orthography Herondas/Herodas see O. Masson, *RPh* 48 (1974) 89–91, where the former is preferred as the *lectio difficilior*. As a Hellenistic contemporary of Theokritos and Kallimachos, Herondas (*flor.* 270s/260s) wrote in a little-used genre, μιμίαμβοι, short verse dialogues dealing with aspects of ordinary life in a lively fashion. The major edition of his surviving poems, by W. Headlam/A.D. Knox (Cambridge, 1922), was reprinted in 1966; and more recently I.C. Cunningham has provided a more concise edition (Oxford, 1971), useful particularly for its survey of views about the poems. Cunningham's work shows, however, that there remain many matters of interpretation awaiting clarification and resolution. Among these is the question of Herondas' readership: were the poems intended for private readers, or for dramatic performance by one or several actors? This subject has been taken up — though not settled finally, judging from reviews — by G. Mastromarco, *Il pubblico di Eronda* (Padua, 1979) — *non vidi*.

Of the eight mimes surviving virtually complete all but no.8 (something of an *apologia* by the poet) have as their focus an urban, reasonably sophisticated citizenry of lower status. Subjects dealt with include a woman tempted to be unfaithful to her husband, a pimp's court-room speech indicting another man for assault, a mother's request to a teacher to punish her incorrigible son, and a visit to a temple of Asklepios to perform sacrifice and inspect its art works. While Herondas should not be removed from his proper context of Hellenistic (sub-)literature, the realism of his vignettes — questioned by Cunningham (14) on the basis of too narrow a view of realism — brings to life excellently aspects of the social milieu of ordinary people in Hellenistic Greek cities, whether in the eastern Aegean or in Alexandria. *Mutatis mutandis* such portrayals may be of general aid in helping us to envisage the hellenized urban context into which Christian groups made their mark somewhat later. In this connection see now W. Meeks, *The First Urban Christians* (New Haven, 1983).

20. Coins from Kenchreai

During several seasons of excavation in the 1960s at Kenchreai, which served as Corinth's eastern port opening into the Saronic gulf, over 1500 coins were recovered (nearly all bronze or copper), of which more than 1300 are included in Hohlfelder's publication, *Kenchreai* III. Not surprisingly, the finds parallel those made at Corinth and are nearly all from Greek and E. Mediterranean mints. One coin (a sextans?) from Palestine was found (no.297), to be dated 6–14AD; the mint presumably is Caesarea. The dearth of coins from the West 'confirms the eastern orientation of the port and the primary direction of its trade' (*Kenchreai*, 3). Acts 18.18 accords well with this: Kenchreai was the natural place to find a boat for a passage east (cf. Apuleius, *Met.* 10.35).

After being razed in 146BC the site of Corinth — and with it Kenchreai — was virtually abandoned for a century, until Julius Caesar refounded it in 44BC as a Roman *colonia* with the formal name *Laus Iulia Corinthiensis* (cf. Wiseman, *Corinthians*, 15 n.25). Its geographical position ensured it would again become of economic significance in the Eastern Mediterranean, and the second century saw it at its zenith. Corinth also provided a convenient political focus for Roman administration, and it became the capital of the province of Achaia, as Acts 18.12–17 reflects indirectly. Population is hard to gauge, but Wiseman estimates (12) that Corinth was larger in the first four centuries of its new existence than the classical or hellenistic city (c. 112–145,000 in 432 BC, and c. 130,000 in 323BC are Wiseman's figures). Economic and political instability during the third century set Corinth and interdependent towns like Kenchreai into decline, a decline hastened by earthquakes in IV[2] and the sack of the city in 396 by Alaric. Though this did not put a final end to Corinth the process of decline was not reversed (with one brief exception) for the next thousand years.

21. The pentagram (cf. *New Docs 1977*, 114)

In the brief comments offered in the previous Review on an epitaph (Tomis, VI) for a wineseller from Alexandria, Christian attribution was queried because of the presence of a five-pointed star at the end of the inscription: was the deceased a Jew? From the 1978 culling *IGA* 3.557 (Abydos, Ptolemaic period(?)) indicates that this symbol is not exclusive to Judaism. The Abydos graffito portrays a pyramid seen both in profile and from above, with a pentagram inscribed within the former's triangular shape. See the editors' n. ad loc. for discussion of this symbol, which they interpret as a prophylactic design often included on talismans used thus by the Pythagoreans. As for the Tomis epitaph, then, there is no internal evidence whether the deceased was Jewish, Christian, or pagan, but if Barnea's date (VI) is correct, we should lean to his view that the wineseller was Christian. The Tomis inscription also includes a palm branch: for two examples of this as a Christian symbol in epitaphs from the 1978 culling note *SEG* 1399 (with n.) and cf. 1394 (both from Eboda in Palestine, dated Byzantine and 550 respectively). In *SEG* 1394 the deceased man is said to be ἄγαμος. This adjective occurs several times in 1 Cor. 7 (*vv.* 8, 11, 32, 34) both of men and women; but this new attestation is too likely derived from Christian use to provide independent testimony.

B. MINOR PHILOLOGICAL NOTES

22. ἀκοή

E. Schwertheim, *Fest.Dörner* 2.821–22, no.17, republishes an inscription from Apollonia ad Rhyndacum in Mysia (n.d.):

<table>
<tr><td>Ἀγαθῇ τύχῃ·</td><td>εὐχαριστήριον</td></tr>
<tr><td>ταῖς ἀκοαῖς τῆς</td><td>τὰ ὦτα καὶ τὸν βω-</td></tr>
<tr><td>θεοῦ</td><td>μὸν ἐπὶ ἱερείας</td></tr>
<tr><td>Ἑ[ρ]μιανὸς ΟΚΙ--</td><td>ΠΡΟ . . . . . . ΥΤΗΣ.</td></tr>
<tr><td>5 ζήσας ἀπέδωκεν</td><td></td></tr>
</table>

5 To good fortune! For the hearing of the goddess Hermianos | having lived . . . rendered the ears and altar as a thank-offering when . . . was priestess.

The presence of both αἱ ἀκοαί and τὰ ὦτα in the same brief text suggest that the former is perhaps to be distinguished by the meaning 'hearing'. Hermianos recovered his hearing (by hearing the goddess speak? — E.A. Judge) and dedicates the (stone) ears. For this meaning of ἀκοή note 2 Pet. 2.8; and see BAGD, s.v., 1b (the example from *Ep.Barn.* quoted there has ἀκοή and ὠτίον in close conjunction), though the NT construction ἀκοῇ ἀκούω (Mt. 13.14; Acts 28.26) is translationese. In *IG* IV².126, a dedication at the Asklepieion at Epidauros (II), mention is made of αἱ Ἀκοαί at *ll*.10, 18; this may be the name of a shrine, so called perhaps because divine voices had been heard there (see ed. n. to *IG* IV¹ [1902] 955, the earlier edition of this text); more simply, perhaps, O. Weinreich (n. to this text in *SIG*³ 1170) suggests that the word refers to the stone ears attached to the temple wall as dedications. To the few citations of this noun in MM, papyrus finds can supply up to a dozen more attestations: see *WB* and *Spoglio*.

MM, s.v. εὐχαριστία, note one example only of εὐχαριστήριον (not NT).

23. ἀνανεόομαι

From the Hellenistic period additional to MM's citations note *I.Lampsakos* 4 — = *SIG*³ 591 — an honorific decree for Hegesias (196/5BC), which mentions that he went to Rome on an embassy and 'consulted with those members of the Senate who displayed good will

... and who renewed their existing friendship with them', χρηματίσας τῆι συνκλήτωι μετ[ὰ τούτων] | [τῶν δηλωσάν]των τὴν εὔνοιαν ... | ... καὶ ἀνανεωσαμένων τὴν ὑπάρχο[υσαν αὐ]|[τοῖς φιλίαν πρὸς] αὐτούς, κτλ (51-54). Similar wording occurs in an inscription mentioning the renewal of friendship between Delos and Rome, c.192BC, and in another in which a man is honoured by an association for renewing his εὔνοια towards it, c.153/2BC (Durrbach, *Choix*, 65 and 85 respectively).

Of much later date is a brief inscription (*IGA* 5.594) recording building renovations (Philai, n.d.) which includes the following wording: ἀ[ν]ενεώθη μέρος | [ἐ]κ λιβός (5-6), 'the part on the south-west was restored' (or 'the south-western side' may be possible here: for this meaning of μέρος see **47**). The verb (passive) occurs again in a similar building-renovations context, *IGA* 5.561.9 (Ombos, VI/VII), again at 597.5 (Philai, 785), and at 685.1 (provenance unknown, before mid-VII; = *SB* 5.3.8704). These attestations may be added to MM, late though they are, to modify their final sentence, ad loc.; NT, only Eph. 4.23.

In Bithynia, Aurelia Arria speaks of renovating a sarcophagus (ἀνανε[ω]σάμην τὴν πύελον) for the use of herself and her husband (*TAM* 249.1; III?). This usage of the verb is common in that region: *TAM* 231, 247, 251, 257, 258, 259, 263 (twice), 269, 272, 285, 294 (restored entirely), 355, 361, 366, 368 (the last four are Christian). In no.355 the work is done περὶ μνήμης Εὐγενίας διακόνου (*l*.1); on this text see further *BE* (1979) 559, and D. Feissel, *BCH* 104 (1980) 474-75, while for female deacons cf. *New Docs 1976*, **79**; *1977*, **109**. The compound ἐπανανεόομαι occurs in an identical context in *TAM* 352 (Christian), and has been restored by analogy at 266.

The noun ἀνανέωσις occurs at *IGA* 5.561.16, and a phrase from *P.Cairo Masp.* 2 (1913) 67151 which includes the word is quoted below at **26**; both references could be added to BAGD, s.v. (ECL, not NT).

24. ἀπαλλοτριόω

MM, s.v., note four Hellenistic inscriptions where this verb is used, to illustrate the three NT occurrences (all passive): Eph. 2.12; 4.18; Col. 1.21. To these may be added from 1978 publications *I.Magnesia Sip.* 19, an epitaph for Alexander set up in the proconsulship of Statius Quadratus (154/5), during whose governorship in Asia Polycarp was martyred (see ed.n. for references). The tombstone includes the following prohibition: μηδενὶ δὲ ἐξέστω ἀπαλλοτρι|ῶσαι αὐτὸ ἐκ τοῦ γένους μου (5-6), 'let no-one be permitted to alienate this (tomb) from my family'.

25. ἀπογίνομαι

To the documentary examples of this word (NT: only 1 Pet. 2.24) in the sense 'die' collected in MM (several more are listed in BAGD) we may add a fragmentary Christian epitaph for a woman (provenance unknown, V/VI), 'N, faithful in Christ, died (ἀπεγέ|νητο, 4-5) on 7 March, day 6 (i.e., Friday), indiction 11': *ed.pr.* — C. Mango/I. Ševčenko, *DOP* 32 (1978) 23 no. 30 (fig. 30): cf. *SEG* 1578.

26. ἄρρωστος

MM knew of no papyrus examples of this adjective (NT — Mt. 14.14; Mk. 6.5, 13; 16.[18]; 1 Cor. 11.30), and only one inscription, *SIG*² 858.17 (Delphi, IIBC; not repr. in *SIG*³). Since this entry was in their first fascicule which was incorporated unchanged into the complete one-volume work in 1930, *P.Cairo Masp.* 2 (1913, repr. 1973) 67151 (Antinoe, 15/11/570) could not be taken into account. This very lengthy will by Flavius Phoibammon, who like his father was *archiatros* of Antinoe (on this term see *New Docs 1977*, **2**), employs the adjective twice, at *l*.185 where he speaks of wishing 'all care and diligence and maintenance for the sick', τὴν πᾶσαν τῶ(ν) ἀρρώστων φιλοκαλίαν τε καὶ ἐπιμέλειαν | καὶ διαιτοχορηγίαν, to be accomplished by his brother John, who will have 'general responsibility for the complete renewal of attention to the sick', εἰς ἀνανέωσιν δίολου [τῆς] τ[ῶν] | ἀρρώστων φροντίδος (*ll*.191–92). While this last phrase is before us note the occurrence of διόλου, a further example — though late — to add to BAGD, s.v. ὅλος, 4, and MM, s.v. ὅλος, in illustration of Jn. 19.23.

In addition to the *SIG* inscription noted by MM, BAGD list one papyrus, *P.Cair.Zen.* 1 (1925, repr. 1971) 59018.5 (Philadelphia, c.5/4/258BC), a letter in which the speaker writes that ἐγὼ μὲν [ο]ὖν | [ἄρρωστ]ος ἐτύγχανον ἐ[[χ̲ͅ]] φαρμακείας ὤν . . . It is quoted here so that users of BAGD may be aware that the entire stem of the relevant word is restored here, even though it is an appropriate restoration for the context. This papyrus is reprinted as *SB* 3 (1926, repr. 1974) 6710, and *CPJ* 1 (1957) 6 (where Palestine is the provenance given). Note that in the listing by *Spoglio* the line reference is given incorrectly.

Given the dearth of documentary attestation for the adjective MM's entry concentrates heavily upon the related nouns and verb. For examples to update these see *WB* and *Spoglio*; we may add *P.Carlini lett.* 32 (for details about this papyrus see **55**), *l*.11, --- μεγάλαις πάνυ ἀρρωστ[ίαις.

27. ἀρχιδιάκονος

New Docs 1976, **91** reprinted a bronze slave collar (Sardinia, V²/VI¹) which carried the Latin inscription s[eruus sum] *Felicis arc*(hi)*diac*(oni): *tene me ne fugiam*. Of the 11 papyrus attestations listed in *WB* 3 (1931) Abschn. 21 (eight) and *Spoglio* (three), the earliest is dated V/VI. The slave collar must then be among the earliest documentary attestations of this title. *CPR* 10 provides a new example, in a certificate (Fayum (?), July/August 584 or 599 (?)) addressed to τῷ κυρ[   ] | ἀρχιδιακ[όνῳ (2–3). Attestation in the literary sources antedates considerably the slave collar: for example Caecilian of Carthage was elevated to the bishopric in 311 from his position as archdeacon (cf. W.H.C. Frend, in *Carthage* 3.22). Eulogius Alexandrinus, *fr. Novat.* (Migne, *PG* 104.353c, quoted by Lampe, s.v., C.11) claims it was the rule for an archdeacon to succeed to the episcopate at Rome in III. Whether or not this was the case, the passage testifies to the office at least at Rome in that century.

28. ἀρχιμύστης

At *New Docs 1977*, **2**, p.18, it was suggested that the ἀρχ- prefix was sometimes added to titles merely to make them sound more impressive: ἀρχιμύστης, 'chief initiate', was mentioned as one possible candidate. H. Waldmann, *Homm.Vermaseren* 3.1309–15 (pl.264; cf. *SEG* 1213) has published an inscription on a stone water vessel (Sagallasos in Pisidia, n.d.) which mentions that 'the *archimystes* N, son of Makedon, supplied the wash-basin at his own expense',]ων Μακέδονος | ἀρχιμύστης τὸν λου|τῆρα καὶ τὸ ὕ|δωρ ἐκ τῶν ἰδίων ἰσήγα|γεν. He lists most usefully other attestations of the word, nearly 80 examples, which occur only eastwards from Greece: Athens/Eleusis (7), the rest of Greece and the Islands (8), Macedonia/Thrace (10), Samothrace/Kyzikos/Nikomedeia (3, plus the variants μυστάρχης, μυστηριάρχης [= *TAM* 262], συμμύσται), Asia Minor (44; several of the cities mentioned in the NT, especially the Seven Churches of Rev., attest someone with this title). From Bithynion in Crete a Christian priest or bishop has the title μύστης (Waldmann, 1312 and n.8 for the reference). At *TAM* 42.4 (Nikomedeia, n.d.) a man whose name is lost is spoken of as ἀρχιμύστου διὰ βίου. An ἀρχιθιασίτης is the proposer of a motion to honour a man for his good will towards an association: Durrbach, *Choix* 85.3, 55 (Delos, c.153/2BC).

29. ἱερὰ βίβλος (cf. *New Docs 1977*, 46)

The wording quoted from *AE* (1977) 840 should be mentioned again since *ed.pr.* has now come to hand. G. Geraci publishes this inscription in S. Curto et al., *Dehmit* (Rome, 1973) 69-89. Loukios Lokeeios Kereairis, prefect of a cavalry cohort, has been instructed to mark out some territorial boundaries, and states that he did so κατὰ τὴν ἱερὰν βίβλον (*ll*.11-12). Another closely-related inscription (reprinted and discussed by Geraci, 71-73) found early this century near the site of this new text says that Lucius ὅριον ἔστησ[ε] ἐπὶ σκληροῦ | βαθμοῦ ἀκολούθως τῇ θείᾳ βίβλῳ γῆς Χονετμούεως (7-8), 'settled the boundary of the land of Chonetmouis at the hard rock in accordance with the divine book'.

Geraci's note (73) indicates that the two synonymous phrases are rare variants for the common ἱερὰ γράμματα and θεῖα γ., which refer to imperial ordinances or letters. Deissmann had long ago noted (*LAE* 375-76, followed by MM and BAGD, s.v. γράμμα) that this Graeco-Roman usage has applicability to 2 Tim. 3.15 no less than the occurrences in Hellenistic and Roman-Jewish writers where it refers to the OT. This neat — and conscious — conjunction of Graeco-Roman and Hellenized-Jewish usages at 2 Tim. 3.15 has a useful analogy in a word like κύριος. But it should not be forgotten that such Jewish usages in the Hellenistic period presuppose an awareness of the currency of such terms in the Graeco-Roman context.

For the hitherto-unattested form βυβλίς note *NIP* I.11 (Metropolis in Phrygia, 126/7; pl.6), the beginning of a letter from P. Ranius Castus, legate of P. Stertinius Quartus (proconsul of Asia in 126/7), in which he states his amazement (τεθαύμακα, 11) upon reading the petition (ἐντυχὼν βυβλίδι, 5) of Sosthenes, son of Pasikrates, that so many letters of (previous) governors [have been ignored (?) — text breaks off]. For discussion of the words in *l*.5 see Drew-Bear's commentary, pp.20-21, nn.81,82. Cf. *AE* 800; *SEG* 1169.

30. δεκάτη

Tithing was not a peculiarly Jewish institution in antiquity, although the NT allusions to it, such as Heb. 7.2–9 (where this noun occurs four times), may give that impression. Durrbach, *Choix* 5, is an inscription recording the dedication of a statue of Artemis (Delos, VBC): 'This is a statue of Artemis; Eupolis set me up to her, he himself, and his children, having vowed a tenth', [Ἀ]ρ[τ]έμιδος τόδ' ἄγαλ[μα]· ἀνέθεκε(ν) δέ με [Εὔ]πολις αὐτεῖ | αὐτὸς καὶ παῖδες εὐχσ[ά]μενος δεκάτεν. The early date of this inscription makes it well worth adding to a revised MM entry, to provide a wider perspective for the usage in the Hellenistic and Roman periods. Again from 1978 publications we may note *SEG* 1541 (Berenike in Cyrenaica, III/IIBC), a brief dedication: Εὐγένης [. . . . .]ντος δεκάταν | τῶι Ἀπόλλωνι.

A few examples of Christian vows have been noted previously, in *New Docs 1976*, **4**; *New Docs 1977*, **101**, pp.167–68; **116** p.207: to these a few more instances may be added here. C. Mango/I. Ševčenko, *DOP* 32 (1978) 19 no.22 (pl.22a, b; cf. *SEG* 1114) have published an inscription on a marble waterspout carved as a lion's head (Dorylaion (?) in Phrygia, c.VI): ὑπὲρ εὐχῆς Κοσταν|τίν[(ου)] πρήσμονος; Constantine gives his craft as 'sawyer of marble'. The phrase ὑπὲρ εὐχῆς occurs also on two silver plates, *IGLS* 2 (1939) 697, 698 (both from Stuma in Syria, dated 578–82 and VII init. respectively), as well as on an oil vial, *IGLS* 5 (1959) 2035 (Hama, VI). In all three cases the phrase is part of a longer formula 'for the vow and the salvation of X and for the repose of Y'. These three examples were noted by I. Ševčenko, *DOP* 17 (1963) 394–95, in the course of his publication of an inscription on two medallions, perhaps originally attached to a baptismal font in a basilica (Nikaia, VI):

– – – σοι	ὁ θεὸς
εὐξάμενος	ἐπέτυχον·
εὐχαριστῶν	ἀνέθηκα
τὰ σὰ ἐκ τῶν σῶ(ν)	σοι προσήγαγον.

. . . having made my vow to you, God, I succeeded and in appreciation I set up (this font ?). I offered to you your own things out of what is yours.

With the formula in *ll*.2–3 of this text Ševčenko compares an exact pagan equivalent, *SEG* 12 (1955) 503 (Cilicia, 307), in which Rufinus εὐξάμενος καὶ ἐπιτυχὼν ἀνέστησα τὸν βωμόν (3–4).

31. διατηρέω

This verb is common enough (NT: Lk. 2.52; Acts 15.29); but as an example not far removed from the time of the NT, note *SEG* 1540, an honorific decree for Apollodoros (Berenike in Cyrenaica, 62/1BC), in which he is said to have 'kept unity by introducing just judgement for all', ὁμόνοιαν | διετήρησε δικαίαν κρίσιν ἐς [ἅπ]αντας ἐσφερόμε|νος (17–19). For eight occurrences of the verb in a single inscription see **32**, ad fin.

The same decree employs the adverb παραχρῆμα (*l*.12), a word very popular in Lk./Acts but elsewhere in the NT found only at Mt. 21.19,20.

32. ἔγκλημα

OGIS 229, which records the establishment of *sympoliteia* between Smyrna and Magnesia on the Sipylos, was drawn upon by MM to illustrate several NT words (e.g., δακτύλιος, κατασκήνωσις, ὁρκωμοσία [the inscription has the neuter noun form]). This lengthy document (108*ll*.) has been reprinted and given an extensive commentary at *I.Magnesia Sip.* 1, pp.17–130 (pls.1–4), where 246/5BC is suggested as its date. The inscription also provides two attestations of the noun ἔγκλημα, though MM offered papyrus examples only under this lemma: συντελεσθέντων δὲ τῶν ὅρκων τὰ μὲν ἐγκλήματα αὐ|τοῖς τὰ γεγενημένα κατὰ τὸμ πόλεμον ἤρθω πάντα, κτλ (41–42), 'when the oaths have been completed the charges that have been made against them (i.e. the parties to the agreement) during the war are all to be put to an end'; and a little later, 'let every charge that is brought forward be invalid', πᾶν τὸ ἐπιφερόμενον ἔγκλημα ἄκυρον ἔστω (43). In the NT the noun occurs only in Acts, as a technical legal term (as here) at 23.29 and 25.16, though the more general sense, 'reproach', is the meaning required in the additional wording at Acts 23.24 preserved by 𝔓⁴⁸ = *PSI* 10 (1932) 1165, pl.2 (Oxyrhynchos, III; cf. Aland, NT48, p.278).

MM, s.v. διατηρέω, provide a couple of epigraphical attestations along with papyrus evidence; but the eight occurrences in this inscription could have been mentioned (NT: Lk. 2.51; Acts 15.29). Cf. **31** above.

33. μὴ εἴοιτο

MM, s.v. γίνομαι, provide no documentary attestations of μὴ γένοιτο to parallel the 15 NT occurrences (all but Lk. 20.16 are Pauline, with a heavy preponderance of those, 10, in Romans); for its function, expressing strong rejection in answer to a question, see BDF §384. MM do mention, however, that the exclamation is 'common' in Epiktetos: on this see A. Bonhöffer, *Epiktet und das Neue Testament* (*Religionsgeschichtliche Versuche und Vorarbeiten* 10; Giessen, 1911; repr. Berlin, 1964) 137–38.

While no non-literary example of this use of γίνομαι is known to me, Gignac (2.406) notes the clause ὃ μὴ εἴοιτο at *Stud.Pal.* 20 (1921) 35.7 (= *SB* 1 [1915] 5294; Herakleopolite nome, 235) where this unusual form for εἴη is being employed with the sense of γένοιτο. Another example which may now be noted is *P.Sakaon* 71, a lease of sheep and goats (Theadelphia, 6/3/306) in which the lessee accepts responsibility for the care, provisioning, 'and (may it not occur!) death' of the animals, καὶ, ὃ [μ]ὴ εἴοιτο, θανάτου (22; the clause had not been able to be read fully by Jouguet in his *ed.pr.*, *P.Thead.* 8).

34. ἐκκόπτω

MM provide some papyrus attestations of this verb, but no inscriptional evidence to illustrate its literal meaning, as found in the NT at Mt. 3.10 = 7.19 = Lk. 3.9; Lk. 13.7; cf. Rom. 11.24. *IGA* 2.44b is a fragment of a prohibition (Crocodilopolis (?), II/IBC) in which it is forbidden [--μή]τε ἐκκόπτειν | [--μήτ' ἐξ]άπτειν μηθὲν τῶν | [--πεφυτευ]μένων δένδρων, κτλ (2–4), 'neither to cut down nor to burn out any of the trees that are planted.'

35. ἐνορκίζω

This verb occurs at *IGCB* 23 (Corinth, V), a warning against adding further bodies to a tomb. With Bees' restorations the relevant lines (4–5) read [. . .] πρὸς τὸν θεὸν κα[ὶ κατὰ τῆς κρί]|[σεως τ]οῦ θεοῦ ἐνορκίζω. MM cite another couple of similar warnings where the verb is used: in the NT it is found only at 1 Thes. 5.27. For ἐξορκίζω/ὁρκίζω cf. the brief comment at *New Docs 1977*, **13**.

36. ἐνοχλέω

MM provide plenty of examples to illustrate this verb, although only two passives with the meaning 'be troubled'. To illustrate Lk. 6.18, οἱ ἐνοχλούμενοι ἀπὸ πνευμάτων ἀκαθάρτων ἐθεραπεύοντο, we might then add *P.Sakaon* 37 (Theadelphia, Jan./Feb.284), a document in which a woman complains that she is being required to pay dues owed by another woman: οὐ βούλεται διδόναι τὰ ἐπιπάλλοντα αὐτῇ δημόσια μετρήματ[α κ]ἀ[γὼ ἐνο]χλουμένη καὶ | [±17 ὑπὸ τῶν ἐν] μέρεσι δεκα[π]ρώτων ἀποδίδωμι τὰ ὑπὲρ αὐτῆς μετρήματα, κτλ (14–15), 'she is refusing to make the public payments impinging on her, and since I am under pressure and . . . by the regional *dekaprotoi* I provide the payments on her behalf'. At the end of their entry MM cite one papyrus example of the compound διενοχλέω (not found in the NT): for another, note *P.Sakaon* 30.6 (Theadelphia, 307–24) in a somewhat fragmentary context.

The rare example of ἐπιπάλλω in the passage quoted above deserves brief note: LSJ attest only one instance, from Aischylos. The resurfacing of the word eight centuries later provides a useful instance of the continuance of classical words through into the Roman and Byzantine periods, but often with a marked change in the stylistic level, as here. The fact that this IIIAD papyrus is a documentary text from an Egyptian village suggests a case for the word's continued existence throughout the intervening centuries — even though its presence is submerged from our view by the non-survival of texts — rather than its being a moribund word consciously revived in a later age. However, the shift in meaning from Aischylos ('brandish against') to this papyrus warns us against any *direct* line of descent from V BC (so J.A.L. Lee in a note to me). Cf. the comment at *New Docs 1977*, **39**; it may be more appropriate to think of the word under discussion there, διϊσχυρίζομαι, as also having had a continued existence, rather than being a 'revival'.

37. ἐπικουρία

Paul's speech to Agrippa is the only place in NT where this noun occurs: ἐπικουρίας οὖν τυχὼν τῆς ἀπὸ τοῦ θεοῦ (Acts 26.22). MM note one inscription, BAGD add a papyrus. To these may be added from the 1978 culling an occurrence in the much-discussed inscription from Kyrene — bibliography at *SEG* 1566 — comprising a dossier of letters and a decree from Hadrian and Antoninus Pius, now re-ed. by J.M. Reynolds, *JRS* 68 (1978) 111-21 (pls.

2–4). She dates the inscription to 154AD, and points out (111) that the Jewish Revolt of 115–17 can no longer be viewed as providing the background to the inscription. Rather, it was set up to publicize imperial backing for Kyrene when her position as *metropolis* of the province was under challenge. Though the context is somewhat fragmentary, the relevant line containing the word reads [... *35–45 letters* .. κα]θεστῶτας τὴν ἐπικουρίαν παρὰ τῶν Ἑλλή[νων? ...] (21–22), 'rallying help from the Greeks'.

38. εὐποιΐα

In the NT this noun occurs only at Heb. 13.16, τῆς δὲ εὐποιΐας καὶ κοινωνίας μὴ ἐπιλανθάνεσθε. MM provide one documentary attestation only, BAGD a couple more. From 1978 publications we may note the re-edition of an honorific decree for Stephanos (Balboura in Lykia, II²): C. Naour, *Anc.Soc.* 9 (1978) 170–76 no.2 (pl.4), repr. as *SEG* 1217. The honorand is said to be μαρτυρηθέντα δὲ καὶ ὑπ[ὸ] | [ἡ]γεμόνων πλεονάκις ἐπὶ ταῖς | *v* εἰς τὴν πατρίδ(α) εὐποιΐαις *v* (3–5), 'testified to also by governors frequently for his good deeds to his country'. The public testimonial for the man in this inscription is made not only by decree but also in letters, διά|τε ψηφίσματος καὶ ἐπιστολῶν (*ll.*19–20). For another, cf. *SEG* 1222 (Sidyma, II²).

39. τὸ θεῖον

MM's long entry on θεῖος includes several useful examples to illustrate the neuter noun at Acts 17.29 (cf. 17.27D, and the occurrence in the extensive variant reading at Tit. 1.9), among them three inscriptions. To these we may add *IG* IV².1.121 (Epidauros, IV²BC) where, in the first-listed divine healing — a woman, enabled to give birth after being pregnant for five years (T.G. Wright suggests to me that this should probably be understood as a case of Secondary Amenorrhoea), sets up her testimonial — it is said, 'It is not the size of her votive tablet that is to be wondered at, but the god', οὐ μέγε|[θο]ς πίνακος θαυμαστέον, ἀλλὰ τὸ θεῖον (*ll.*7–8). *CMRDM* 1.85 (Magnesia on the Sipylos, 184/5; not included in *I.Magnesia Sip.*) provides a further instructive text, on an altar dedicated to Men Axiottenos καὶ θείῳ which a certain Artemon set up as (divinely) instructed — κατ' ἐπ|(ιτα)γήν — on the footprints (ἐπὶ τὰ ἴχνη) made by the god in the place where the epiphany occurred. For divine footprints cf. the discussion at *CMRDM* 3, p.25, where two related dedications are mentioned.

In the NT divine ἴχνη provide a figure for an example to follow. Thus at 1 Pet. 2.21 readers are reminded that 'Christ suffered for you ...' ἵνα ἐπακολουθήσητε τοῖς ἴχνεσιν αὐτοῦ. Cf. 2 Cor. 12.18, οὐ τῷ αὐτῷ πνεύματι περιεπατήσαμεν; οὐ τοῖς αὐτοῖς ἴχνεσιν; Particularly imaginative is the phraseology at Rom. 4.12, alluding to those who walk in the tracks of the faith of Abraham. While the Men dedication above does not illustrate the NT metaphor, the link with the divine sphere renders it worth incorporating into a revised MM entry on ἴχνος. *P.Strasb.* 679.1-2 may be noted here, though it is much later in date (provenance unknown, VI fin.). This nearly complete letter to an archimandrite begins: ἐν προημίοις πολλὰ ἀσπάζομαι καὶ προσκυνῶ τὰ εὐλογιμένα ἴχνη τῆς ὑμετέ[ρ]ας ἁγιω[σ]ύνης (1-2), 'by way of preamble I offer many greetings and kiss the blessed footprints of your holiness'.

40. θυμιατήριον

CMRDM 1.28 (Smyrna, probably I; presumably to be included in G. Petzl, *Die Inschriften von Smyrna* 2 [*Inschriften gr. Städte aus Kleinasien* 23], vol. 1 of which appeared in 1982) is the longest single inscription in that corpus, though Men is hardly central to the text, for it is merely a statue of the god which is recorded among the cult objects housed at a shrine dedicated to Helios Apollo Kisauloddenos. Several of the words in this inscription (= *SIG²* 583 = *SIG³* 996) have been noted by MM (and thence BAGD) as relevant to NT vocabulary. At *l.*30 the phrase τὴν ἐνδώμησιν τοῦ τεμένους occurs ('the enclosing of the *temenos*'), which provides a useful parallel to Rev. 21.18, ἡ ἐ. τοῦ τείχους. But MM's lemma should be altered to ἐνδώμησις (currently ἐνδό(-ώ-)μησις) so that it is easy to find alphabetically.

One of the dedicated offerings is 'a square incense altar fashioned of Teian stone with an iron fireholder', θυμιατήριον τετράγωνον κα|τεσκευασμένον πέτρας Τηίας ἔχον περίπυρον σιδηροῦν (12-14). Dittenberger (n. in *SIG³*), followed by MM, thinks that θ. here means 'censer'; but one made of stone, and τετράγωνος in shape, seems considerably less likely to be in mind than 'altar' (so J.A.L. Lee, in a note to me). That being so, this inscription serves as a useful example to show that the meaning of the noun at Heb. 9.4 — 'incense altar' is more apposite here than 'censer' — is by no means exclusively Jewish. Rather, the word was taken over by the LXX translators from the *koine* and applied to the particular context for which they needed it, and thence it was employed by the writer of Heb.

Grenier, *Anubis* 59 (Iasos in Karia, Roman period) is a dedication to Anoubis, Isis Pelagia and Isis Boubastis by a Roman citizen and his wife of an 'altar with the adjacent censers', [τὸν] | βωμὸν μετὰ τῶν [περὶ] | αὐτὸν θυμιατη[ρίων] (4-6); the meaning here is not in doubt, in view of the contrast with βωμός. Grenier, *Anubis* 71 is a list of offerings deposited in the shrine of Anoubis on Delos (156/5BC), and includes two θυμιατήρια, one made of bronze, the other of stone; whether either or both is an altar is unclear.

CMRDM 1.28 mentions also the offering of a *trapeza;* for discussion of these in the cult of Men, and more generally, see B. Levick, *JHS* 91 (1971) 80-84; cf. *New Docs 1977,* **7**. For dedications of a *trapeza* in other contexts than Men note, from 1978 publications, *TAM* 87, 96 (at 84 the word is nearly totally restored). Durrbach, *Choix* 184 (Delos, Byzantine period) is an invocation to Christ to help the owner of a *trapeza*, and those who eat at it, τοῖς τρόγοτι (read τρώγουσι) εἰς | τούτην (*sic*) τὴν τράπεζαν (*ll.*3-4).

Only papyrological attestations are provided by MM for the noun χρῆσις; its occurrence in this inscription is worth noting, therefore: the context concerns a 'marble slab for the use of those who are sacrificing', ἀβάκηον μαρμάρινον πρὸς τὴν χρῆσιν τῶν | θυσιαζόντων (11-12).

Finally, this inscription provides another illustration of the need for consistent references and datings for epigraphical items in a work like MM (see **6** for further discussion of this problem). This Smyrna text is dated 'IAD?' for ἐνδώμησις; but doubt is removed s.v. θυμιατήριον (IAD), only to reappear s.v. σπαράσσω, where the noun σπ´

41. ἱματισμός

LXX use of τὰ ἱμάτια . . . τὸν ἱματισμόν at Ps. 21.19 (quoted at Jn. 19.24) indicates that these two nouns are scarcely to be differentiated. The latter occurs elsewhere in the NT at Lk. 7.25; 9.29; Acts 20.33; 1 Tim. 2.9. MM provide several documentary attestations ranging in date from IVBC-IIAD; many more are listed in *WB* and *Spoglio*. A nursing contract, *P.Oxy.* 1 (1898) 91.14 (187AD), includes the word, and though the papyrus was quoted s.v. ἔλαιον, it was not mentioned again s.v. ἱματισμός. For an example from the 1978 culling note *CPR* 18 (Pesla, undated, but from an early-IV archive) a fragmentary instruction to give (payment?) to N. the carpenter ὑπὲρ ἱματισμ[οῦ . . . (4).

42. καταρτισμός

CMRDM 1.121 (Burdur in Pisidia, n.d.; pls.55–57) records the offering to Men by one of his functionaries (πάρεδρος) of a number of items for the local shrine. Among these are κλεί|νας δύο σὺν καταρτισμῷ (2–4), 'two beds with their furnishing' (viz. cushions, etc.), and two tables. A banquet situation is presupposed, as L. Robert noted, *Hellenica* 9 (1950) 44, when first publishing this monument, pp.39–50. For adherents of Men banqueting in the god's presence see *CMRDM* 1.13, reprinted and discussed above at **6**.

The metaphorical use of καταρτισμός found at Eph. 4.12 is still not attested in the documentary sources, to my knowledge. But this inscription may at least be added to the two papyrus examples of the literal sense recorded by MM, s.v.

43. κεφάλαιον

Four examples of this noun with the meaning '(capital) sum of money' (cf. Acts 22.28) occur in *P.Sakaon*: nos.64–66 and 96 are documents recording loans of money, all from Theadelphia and ranging in date from 303–28. At 64.9–11 the borrower agrees to repay 'the sum mentioned above on the seventh day of the coming month Pachon, without procrastination', τὴν ἀπόδοσίν σ[ο]ι ποιήσομαι τοῦ [προ]κιμένου | κεφαλ[α]ί[ου τ]ῇ ἑβδόμῃ τοῦ εἰσιόντος μην[ὸς Παχ]ὼν | ἀνυπ[ε]ρθέτως. The other references are 65.8; 66.5; 96.8.

44. κῆνσος

This Latin loan word is not very common in non-literary sources. The earliest attested by far is R.M. Dawkins/F.W. Hasluck, *ABSA* 12 (1905/6) 177–78 no.2 (Bizye, Black Sea region, IBC), βασιλέα Κό[τυ](ν) βασιλέως Ῥησκουπορέως υἱ[ὸν] Ῥωμαῖοι οἱ πρώ(τ)ως κατακληθέντες εἰς κῆνσον ἑατῶν (*sic*) θεόν, clearly a reference to the Roman census and therefore relevant for the NT occurrences at Mt. 17.25; 22.17, 19; Mk. 12.14. Three attestations from II fin./III[1] are known. *SB* 1 (1915) 173.4 (Mendes, c.200; = *IGRR* 1[1911]1107) is a grave inscription for a man who, among other achievements, held the post of ἐπὶ κήνσων (= *a censibus*). By analogy with this phrase J.R. Rea, *CE* 43 (1968) 370-73, restores *P.Mich.* 6 (1944) 426.23 (Karanis, c.199/200) so that the man's title reads [--ἐπὶ κῆνσ]ον. *IGRR* 4 (1927) 1213 is an honorific decree (Thyatira, time of Caracalla) recorded by οἱ βαφεῖς for T. Antoninus Alphenos Arignotos in which his many offices are listed, among them ἐπὶ κῆν|σον τοῦ Σεβ(αστοῦ) (15-16). CPR 5.2 (1976) 4 (provenance unknown, c.237/8) appears to be a set of memoranda in which mention is made πε[ρὶ] κήνσου (13-14). Later again is *BGU* 3 (1903) 917.5-6 (Fayum, 348), which makes mention of τοῦ] | ἱερ[οῦ] κήνσου under the *censitor* Sabinus (here ἱερός means 'sacred', hence 'imperial'); while ἐν τῷ κήνσῳ occurs in *P.Amh.* 2 (1901) 83.2 (Fayum, late III/IV), a petition to a prefect mentioning the same Sabinus. Other texts from late III/early IV which use the word are *P.Beatty Panop.* (1964) 2.90, 132, 147 (Panopolite nome, 300); *SB* 1. 5356.6 (Fayum, 311(?)); and possibly also *P.Ryl.* 4 (1952) 653.3 (Theadelphia, 321), although the context is fragmentary. These papyri refer to the returns made by *censitores* who were responsible for land surveys. To this small tally we may now add *P.Oxy.* 3307 (IV), an assessment (κῆνσος, 1) of gold and silver contributed by certain individuals in the pagarchy of Teis. It should be noted that κῆνσος never occurs in census returns, where the standard word is the common ἀπογραφή. For a typical census return (II²) see *New Docs 1976*, 28; *P.Sakaon* 1 (Theadelphia, 27/2/310) illustrates a return rather later, with its more embellished wording.

To these Greek examples the following Latin papyri may be added. *P. Iand.* 4 (1914) 68 (= CPL (1958) 239) is the end of an imperial rescript from the Antonine period (provenance unknown, II) dealing with *chiristae* (administrators): there is a requirement that a *ch[i]rista* should have an assessment (*censum*) of not less than 30,000 sesterces (27-28; *cen[sum —* 10-12 lett. —] occurs at *l.*11). *WB* notes the phrase *censibus adscriptos* in a Latin papyrus, published in *Archiv für Urkundenforschungen* 5.227.12 (VI) — *non vidi*.

On the census in Egypt see M. Hombert/C. Préaux, *Recherches sur le recensement dans l'Egypte romaine* (*P.L. Bat. 5*; Leiden, 1952). More generally note G. Pieri, *L'histoire du cens jusqu' à la fin de la république romaine* (Paris, 1968).

45. κυκλεύω

This not very common verb — far more frequent is κυκλόω — is found once in the NT with the meaning 'surround', Rev. 20.9 κ. τὴν παρεμβολὴν τῶν ἁγίων; it is a *v.l.* at Jn. 10.24, of people surrounding someone. For the meaning 'turn the water-wheel', 'irrigate' MM provide two papyrus attestations. Other examples include *O.Strasb.* (1923) 753.7 (IIAD), ὑ]πολάλημα κυκλεύο[ντες . . ., but the context is too fragmentary to be helpful; and *O.Tait* 2 (1955) 1861, ἀρ]χιερεὺς κυκλεύει | [   ] ἐὰν δὲ μὴ κλυκλεύειν(sic; read κυκλεύῃ) |[   ] (1-3), and while this document is also very broken, it is more likely to allude to the priest's responsibility to see to some irrigation being performed. A new attestation is provided by *CPR* 31 (Pesla, before 300/1), in which Hyperechios instructs Apollonios: ἀποστείλητε ἐκεῖ βοὰς ἀπὸ τῆς ἐπαύλεως | τῆς παρ' ὑμῖν καὶ κυκλεύητ[ε τ]ὸν τοῦτον (10-11), 'please send there the oxen from the farm near you and irrigate this (place)'.

The noun ἔπαυλις occurs in this papyrus also at *l.*9; its single occurrence in the NT — Acts 1.20, quoting Ps. 68.26 — gives no indication of its true frequency: several examples in MM (from IIBC-VIAD), to which add the more than dozen in *Spoglio*.

46. λύτρον again (cf. *New Docs 1977*, 58)

Attention was drawn in the previous volume to two incriptions from Lydia which record ransom dedications relating to the god Men. *CMRDM* reprints and discusses both, and three other texts in that Corpus may also be noted here.

CMRDM 1.90 (pl.38), from Synaus, was reprinted in *New Docs 1977*, **58**, but Lane rejects Buckler's reinterpretation of the text, restoring the dative reading to the first word Γαλλικῷ. We are to understand Gallikos as an epithet of Men by analogy with Men Italikos (*CMRDM* 3, p.73). Asklepias is the name of the slave who dedicated the inscription as a ransom for her owner Diogenes, the implication being that the god requires recompense for the release of Diogenes from some affliction or punishment (cf. *CMRDM* 3, pp.21-22).

In the second text (= *CMRDM* 1.61, repr. in *TAM* 5.1 [1981] 255) reproduced in last year's entry, the phrase ἐξ ἰδότων καὶ μὴ ἰδότων is very difficult to understand. The same phrase occurs in *CMRDM* 1.66 (pl.27 is illegible; Kula in Lydia, 148/9; repr. in *TAM* 5.1 [1981] 254).

Μῆνα ἐγ Διοδότου
Ἀλέξανδρος Θαλού-
σης μετὰ Ἰουλίου καὶ
τῆς ἀδελφῆς ἐλυτρώ-
5 σαντο τὸν θεὸν ἐξ εἰδότων καὶ μὴ εἰδότων.
Ἔτους σλγ´.

Alexander son of Thalouse with Julius and his sister paid to the god Men of Diodotos
5 a ransom | for things known and not known. Year 233.

The name of the founder of the cult in this locality is given in the genitive (here with ἐκ), as quite frequently in Men inscriptions (*CMRDM* 3, p.67). The grammar of this inscription is very awkward: the god is referred to in the accusative (dative is expected), and the name of those ransomed is omitted, though the middle form of the verb implies that Alexander et al. are ransoming themselves. Although the middle verb occurs twice in the NT — Lk.1.68, αὐτός ἐστιν ὁ μέλλων λυτροῦσθαι τὸν Ἰσραήλ; Tit. 2.14, ἵνα λυτρώσηται ἡμᾶς ἀπὸ πάσης ἀνομίας (1 Pet. 1.18 is passive, but the same strong 'ransom' force is present) — the construction is different, since the notion of ransoming oneself is not in view there. This inscription could thus usefully be added to BAGD, s.v., 2, and to a revised MM entry for the verb, given its date and the particular appropriateness of its context for the NT usage. Most difficult grammatically is the wording at *ll*.5-6, which parallels *CMRDM* 1.61, and Lane is forced to the desperate strait of treating the participles as if they are passive: 'the only proper explanation, however difficult it may be even in the strange Greek of this area to take ἰδότων as passive, is that we here have people paying a λύτρον to secure their release from witting and unwitting sin' (*CMRDM* 3, p.22). So P. Herrmann, n. to *TAM* 5.1.255, p.87, where another text, unedited still, is quoted which contains the same wording.

With the simple verb in this text we may also compare the synonymous ἐγλυτρόομαι in *CMRDM* 1.57 (pl.23; Görnevit, n.d. [Roman period, presumably]; repr. in *TAM* 5.1 [1981] 576):

Ἀρτέμιδι Ἀνάειτι
καὶ Μηνὶ Τιάμου Ἀ-
λέξανδρος Τειμό-
θεος Γλύκων τῶν
5 Βολλάδος καὶ οἱ συν-
βο̣λαφόροι ἐγλυτρω-
[σάμεν]ο̣ι ἀνέστη-
[σαν . . . .]

To Artemis Anaeitis and Men of Tiamos, Alexander, Timothy (and) Glykon, sons of
5 | **Bollas, and the *symbolaphoroi*, having ransomed themselves, set up [this stele].**

Whether Τιάμου refers to the name of the founder of the cult located here is rather more problematical than in the case above of Diodotos at *CMRDM* 1.66 (cf. *CMRDM* 3, pp.68-69). The name Anaeitis is mentioned by Lane (ibid, 82-83) as a strong argument for seeing an Iranian link with Men. The *symbolaphoroi* appear to be a group within the association whose special function it was to carry certain cult objects in sacred processions. Lane speculates (ibid., 36) that a mishap during one such occasion involving these carriers and the three brothers offended the god, and caused them to seek release from some punishment by public confession of their fault. For other *symbolaphoroi* see Herrmann's n. to *TAM* 5.1.576, p.186.

All these texts are from Lydia; from Pisidian Antioch we have one other, semi-metrical, inscription (n.d., but presumably Roman period) involving an offering to Men in honour of a *tropheus* (*CMRDM* 4. new 127; pl.36):

Μ[ηνὶ] θεῷ Πατρίῳ θυμέλην [ταύτην]
ἀν[έθη]καν π[ά]ν̣τες ἴσω̣[ς καὶ πάντ]ες
ἐπὶ λιτα[ῖσιν ἴσαι]σιν. ἐκ [γὰρ ̣ ̣οἴ]κοιο
φίλου χρησ[τοῖο] τροφῆος εὐξάμενοι πάν-
5 τες ἀπεδώκαμεν ὡς ἔθος ἐστὶν καὶ λύτρον ἁγνείης τοὺς πλοκάμους [. . . . .]
Μᾶρκος   Ἴλαρος   Ἐπιτύνχ[ανος]
[Πε]ιθέρως   Λουκίλι[ος]

To Men the ancestral god they all set up this altar, equally and all of them after
adequate prayers. [For . . .] from the friendly home of our kind rearer we all made a
5 **vow | and gave our hair [. . .], as is the custom and holy ransom. Markos, Hilaros,**
Epitynchanos, Peitheros, Loukilios.

Here the meaning of *lytron* differs from that in the Lydian inscriptions, and with its dependent genitive is a poeticism to describe the offering of the hair. Lane notes that there is a long Greek tradition for this, extending back to Homer (*CMRDM* 4, p.59); and this may provide some further support for the suggestion offered briefly at *New Docs 1976*, **4**, p.24, that Paul's vow which involved the cutting of his hair (Acts 18.18) may not necessarily reflect a Jewish background.

A newly-published Christian inscription (Diocaesarea in Cilicia, end V/VI) reflects closely the usage in the Lydian Men texts: G. Dagron/J. Marcillet-Jaubert, *Belleten* 42 (1978) 417-18, no.45 (cf. *SEG* 1268). The text is a short verse dedication of two *pinakes* (here to be understood as painted wooden icons) with which, in demonstration of their piety, the clergy κοσμοῦσιν νηὸν τοῦ θεοῦ λύτρου χάριν (3), 'decorate the temple of God as a ransom' (i.e., for some sin committed). We may compare *SEG* 17(1960) 786(b), a mosaic from the Mount of Olives (VII) on which Symeon recorded that he built and decorated an oratory (εὐκτήριον) for 'our *despotes* Christ', ὑπὲρ λύτρου τῶν | αὐτοῦ ἁμαρτιῶν κ(αὶ) ἀναπαύσεως τῶν | αὐτοῦ ἀδελφ(ῶν) (3-5). This continuity of usage from pagan to Christian texts may be useful to bear in mind when the relevant NT passages are considered (Mt. 20.28 = Mk 10.45, λ. ἀντὶ πολλῶν; 1 Tim. 2.6, ἀντίλυτρον ὑπὲρ πάντων).

Other documentary attestations of λύτρον may be listed here more summarily. One further singular example is *SIG*³ 588. 68-69 (Miletos, 196BC), a peace treaty between Miletos and the Magnesians in which ὁ δῆμος ὁ Μαγνήτων ἔδωκεν (*sc.* τοὺς αἰχμαλώτους τοὺς Μιλησίων) [ἄ]|[ν]ευ λύτρου Ῥοδίοις. In a war context note also *SIG*² 863 (Delphi, IBC; not included in *SIG*³), which records that 'Ammia released Synphoros from obligation to remain in service after having achieved (her own) ransoming from the enemy', ἀπέλυσε Ἀμμία τᾶς παραμονᾶς Σύνφορον λαβοῦσα λύτρα ἐκ πολεμίων (4).

The largest single group of plural occurrences are manumission texts. *P.Oxy.* 1 (1898) 48 is a letter (86AD) requesting freedom for a slave who is being released under Zeus, Ge, and Helios upon payment of a ransom (ἐπὶ λύτροι(ς), 6) by her mistress. The same formula occurs in *P.Oxy.* 1.49.8 (100AD); while at *P.Oxy.* 4 (1904) 722 (91 or 107AD) allusion is made to 'the aforesaid ransom', τῶν προκει|[μ]ένων λύτρων (29-30), and the statement is made at the end (39-40) of the document, ἀπέχω | τὰ λύτρα, 'I have received the ransom' (viz., 200 silver dr.). The word is restored entirely at *l.*24. Close in time to these are *P.L.Bat.* 13 (1965) 23 (Oxyrhynchos, I fin.) where ἐπὶ λύτροις occurs (7) in another manumission document; and 13.24 (Oxyrhynchos, 98-117) where money is paid to the mistress as the ransom price (λύτρων, 6-7) for release of the slave woman. A century later is *Chrest.* II.2 (1912) 362 (Hermopolis, 211), a manumission document in Latin with Greek rendering following, in which the owner acknowledges his receipt of 2000 imperial drachmai for the ransom of his slave Helene, καὶ ἔσχον ὑπὲρ λύτρ[ω]ν αὐτῆς (19); the equivalent Latin text reads *et accepit pr*[*o*] *liber*[*t*]*ate eius*, etc. (7). J.A.L. Lee points out to me that λύτρα here seems to be equivalent to λύτρωσις.

To complete the tabulation of known non-literary occurrences of λ., the following may be noted. The earliest text is *SIG*³ 622B (Aetolia, c. 185-75BC) a letter in which mention is made of someone καταβαλὼν δὲ τὰ λύτρα, 'discharging the ransom' (8). The same idiom occurs in *P. Hamb.* 1 (1924) 91 (Herakleopolite nome, 2/7/167BC), a memorandum in which it is recorded that a woman offered 'to pay down her own ransom to me', ἑαυτῆς τε λύτρα μοι καταβαλεῖν (16-17), but that her relatives did not agree to give him [τὰ] λύτρα (21). *P.L.Bat.* 7a (= *P.Gen.* 1[1906] 20), 7b (= *P.Bad.* 2[1923] 3 = *SB* 1.5865) are two closely related documents (Pathyris, 18/2/109BC) in which a certain Harkonnesis acknowledges receiving from Nahomsesis, daughter of Spemminis, a certain amount 'as redemption money for a quarter-part of (the) wheat-bearing land above the inundation level in the south toparchy of the Latopolite nome', εἰς λύτρα τετάρτης μερίδος | γῆς ἠπείρου σιτοφόρου, κτλ (4-5, in both texts). On the problems of interpretation of these documents together with *P.L.Bat.* 6 see app. D, pp. 223-24 in that volume. A particularly useful parallel for the NT occurrences is *SIG*³ 708 (Istropolis, IBC), an honorific decree for a man, among whose virtues is the fact that τισὶν δὲ τῶν πολειτῶν ε[ἰς] | λύτρα προτιθείς (*sc.* χρήματα), 'he proffered (money) as a ransom for some of the citizens' (14-15). *P.Oxy* 4 (1904) 784 (IBC) is a fragmentary document which mentions [λ]ύτρα ἱερῶν ἐγ Μούχεω(ς) φ, 'a ransom for holy things from Moucheus, 500 (dr.)'.

Less weight should be placed upon the following items, which are included here for the record. Two are manumission documents: *SB* 1.5616 (Oxyrhynchos, late I; the full text of *P.Oxy.* 2 (1899) 349, given there only in resumé) has ἐπὶ λύτροις entirely restored (6), though the phrase would be expected there; while at *SB* 3(1926) 6293 (Ptolemais Euergetis, 195/6) ὑπὲρ λύτρων is entirely restored (10). The presence of the noun in *BGU* 6 (1922) 1260.12 (Pathyris, 102BC), τὴν λύτρα, is plausibly suggested by the ed. to be a confusion for ἐπίλυσιν. Nevertheless, its Ptolemaic date makes it of interest for its attestation of the word. Like *P.L.Bat.* 7a,b it emanates from a document concerned with land redemption; in this case λ. designates what is paid to free land sold under security.

From this survey there appears to be little difference between the use of the singular and plural of λύτρον; what is of great interest for NT work is, first, the incidence of occurrences involving dealings with the gods, whether confession texts or manumission documents; and second, the observation that the word is by no means confined to that sphere.

D. Hill's study (49-81) of the *lytron* word-group is one of several in his *Greek Words and Hebrew Meanings* (Cambridge, 1967), aimed to demonstrate that NT Greek vocabulary has a 'special Jewish-biblical character' (66; cf.18, 67, *et al.*). His case is not persuasive, even at the level of methodology, a matter to which his first chapter is devoted (1-22). We may note, for example, how 'classical Greek' comes to be equated with anything non-biblical: under the subheading 'Classical Greek Usage' (49-52) papyrus examples are adduced ranging in date from IIBC–VAD, while Lucian and Plutarch are discussed in the same sentences as Aischylos and Plato. Potential distinctions between prose and verse usage are ignored. With one exception, epigraphical evidence is not considered.

47. μέρος

At *New Docs 1977*, **2**, p.16, a new example of this noun with the meaning 'side' (NT: Jn. 21.6) was noted from *P.Oxy.* 44 (1976) 3195 (13-14/6/331) *col.* 2.40, 43). It occurs twice again in the introduction to a fragmentary mutual agreement to submit to arbitration, *CPR* 7 (Herakleopolite nome, VI): † τὸ παρὸν κομπρόμισσον ποιοῦν ται´ | πρὸς ἑαυτοὺς ἐκ μὲν τοῦ ἑνὸς | μέρος Αὐρήλιος Βίκτωρος | υἱὸς Ἰουλίου ἐκ δὲ τοῦ ἑτέρο῾υ´ | μέρος Αὐρηλίῳ (*sic*) Χῶνις υἱὸς | Πααραου, κτλ (1-6; read μέρους in both places), 'on the one side Aurelios Victor son of Julius and on the other side Aurelios Chonis son of Paaraos make the present agreement between themselves', etc. These κομπρόμισσον documents — the term is a Latinism — frequently lack a specific date: the earliest dated example is *P.Lond.* 3 (1907) 992 (Antinoopolis, 507). *CPR* 8 publishes the surviving first four lines of another, dated 509 (provenance unknown). Van Lith lists known examples in her commentary to *CPR* 7.

For another example of μέρος, 'side', note *P.Oxy.* 3314.8 (quoted below at **100**); a possible candidate is *IGA* 5.594, quoted above at **23**.

48. μετασχηματίζω

MM, s.v., refer to three documentary attestations of this verb; another six were already known by their time. Several of these are listed conveniently in *WB* 2.1 (1925), to which may be added *IGA* 5.587 = *SB* 5.3 (1950) 8701 (Philai, VI). This last records the transformation of a temple of Isis into a church: τ[ῇ] τοῦ δεσπότου ἡμῶν Χριστοῦ φιλαν|[θρω]πίᾳ μετασχημα-τισάμενος ὁ θεο|[φιλ]έστατος ἄπα Θεόδωρος ἐπίσκοπος [τὸ] ἱερῶν (*sic*) τοῦτο εἰς τόπον τοῦ ἁγίου Στε|φάνου ἐπ᾽ ἀγαθῷ ἐν δύναμει Χριστοῦ, κτλ, 'by the benevolence of our master Christ the most beloved-of-God abbot Theodoros, bishop, transformed this temple into the place of St. Stephen, for good, by the power of Christ' (1–5). The nearest NT parallel is Phil. 3.21, (Χριστὸς) μετασχηματίσει τὸ σῶμα τῆς ταπεινώσεως ἡμῶν.

The verb provides an illustration of the renewed popularity in early Byzantine times of classical words — this one occurs in Plato and Aristotle — testimony to whose continuing existence in the intervening period is comparatively sparse (in this case Josephus, NT, Diodorus).

49. μισθαποδοτέω

MM, s.v. μισθαποδότης, provide one papyrus attestation, τῷ μισ[θ]αποδότῃ θεῷ, *P.Gen.* 1 (1906) 14.27 (Fayum, Byzantine; corrected reading noted in Addenda section) to illustrate the sole NT occurrence at Heb. 11.6; but since it clearly draws upon that passage it offers no independent testimony to the word. No other documentary examples are known to me.

Their entry refers to a partly restored occurrence of the verb in a Christian epitaph, *CIG* 4.9124.5, repr. as *IGA* 5.608 = *SB* 5.3 (1950) 8731 (Coptic cemetery at Wadi Ghazal, n.d.): μισθαπο[δο]τήσας – – –. *IGA* 5.611 (same provenance) is an even more fragmentary epitaph where this verb is entirely restored, presumably by analogy with the other example. If *IGA* 5.608 does have the verb — which is not certain given the amount of restoration — then it continues to be the sole documentary attestation. LSJ lack an entry for the form.

The related noun μισθαποδοσία — confined in the NT to Heb. 2.2; 10.35; 11.26 — still awaits documentary attestation.

50. νεομηνία/νουμηνία

N/A[26] and UBS[3] continue to support the majority reading νεομηνίας at Col. 2.16, despite its anachronistic form. MM's useful entry differentiates persuasively Ionic νεομηνία from the contracted νουμηνία: the former is not found in documentary texts or in *koine* literature before IIAD, but prevails thereafter. *CPR* 5 (Theadelphia, 336-37) col.1 provides a new example to confirm this chronological distinction, mentioning 'our expenditure for a workman (ἐργάτου) for [four] months from Mecheir the first (νεωμηνίας) to Pachon (*ll.*5-6). Largely restored, but scarcely in doubt, is *P.Oxy.* 3293, a notification (26/5/262-65) to a man that he must 'put on the crown of office of *kosmetes* from the first to the *n*th day of the present month . . .', ἀναδήσα[σ]θ[αι] τὸν | τῆς κοσμ[ητείας στ]έφα|νον ἀπὸ νε[ομηνίας ἕως .] |

τοῦ ὄντος μ[ηνός, κτλ (11-14). *BE* (1946/7) 200 reports two identical graffiti (Dura Europos, 250-56) in which the dative νεομηνίᾳ occurs. Several examples of either form additional to those listed in MM may be gleaned from *Spoglio*.

The noun ἐργάτης occurs in *CPR* 5 at *ll.*2, 5 (restored at *l.*11), but is so common as scarcely to need mentioning in illustration of the numerous NT occurrences (Mt. 10.10; Lk. 10.7, etc.).

51. νουθετέω

Though very late (XI-XII), a small relief from Corinth may be noted for its attestation of this verb in the NT sense 'admonish': *IGCB* 12 reads † σῶζε | Πέτρον εὐθάρσει | καὶ νουθέ|τει, κύριε, 'Save Peter, Lord, give him good heart and admonish him'. But like the Byzantine Christian papyrus quoted by MM, this inscription provides no independent testimony to the NT usage.

52. κατ' ὄνομα

Some examples of this phrase in salutation sections at the end of papyrus letters (NT: 3 Jn. 15) were given at *New Docs 1976*, **15**, ad fin., and *New Docs 1977*, **20**, p.63. As well as in *P.Oxy.* 3312.15 (see **1** above), *P.Oxy.* 3314.21 (see **100** below), and *P.L.Bat.* 21 (Oxyrhynchos, VI) — a Christian letter, where it occurs at *ll.*16, 20, 24 — this phrase appears in another type of text among 1978 publications. *IGA* 3.481 is a *proskynema* inscription to the god Bes (Abydos, Ptolemaic period) made by a certain Aspidas, a victor at the Pythian games (πυθιονίκου, 3), and 'his brothers and their children, and Myron and his wife and their children and his friends, all those who love him from their soul, individually', . . . καὶ τῶν φίλων | αὐτοῦ τῶν πάντων ἐκ | ψυχῆς αὐτὸν φιλούν|των κατ' ὄνομα (9–12; an expanded version of this inscription occurs at *IGA* 3.580). That is, as he made his obeisance to the god he included the names of all his relatives and friends. Another such graffito (*IGA* 3.492) records a similar clause, where the dedicator makes his obeisance . . . (*lacuna*) . . . σὺν τοῖς ἀβασκάν|[τοις] τέκνοις κατ' ὄνομα καὶ τοῖς | ἡ[μ]ᾶς φιλοῦσ[ιν] (10–12). For the name Abaskantos in an ephebic catalogue (Athens, 146/7), note *SEG* 197. For the idea of 'those who love us with their soul' in 481 above, cf. *IGA* 3.617, . . . καὶ πάντων τῶν φιλούντων ἐν ψυχῆι . . .

Proskynema dedications are abundant in *IGA* 3. Elsewhere in 1978 publications note the two fragmentary examples in *Assuan*, pp.144–45: no.1 (Roman period) has Isis in view, while no.2 (Imperial period) has Anoubis. For discussion of these in both epigraphic and papyrus texts see *New Docs 1976*, **16**; *New Docs 1977*, **21**, p.68. In the former place reference was made to H.C. Youtie's publication of *P.Mich.* inv.346 (Arsinoe, IV): *ZPE* 28 (1978) 265–68, now repr. in his *Scriptiunculae Posteriores* 1 (Bonn, 1981) 451–54. In this indubitably Christian letter which 'must have been among the last to employ the formula, since the practice called προσκύνημα faded away under the attack of Christian doctrine' (Youtie, 265), the relevant wording is τὸ προσκύνημά σου | ποιῶ κατ' ἑκάστην ἡμέραν (2-3), 'I make obeisance for you daily'. Given that some Christian graffiti occur on the Memnonion at Abydos (e.g., *IGA* 3.491), is it possible that the fragmentary no.494 is another Christian *proskynema*? The text reads: τὸ προσκύνημα . . . . | τοῦ διακόνου καὶ τῶν παίδων | πάντων.

Whether the *proskynema* formula in letters can help us identify Alexandria as the place of writing because of its frequent association with Sarapis, is very doubtful. See Youtie, *ICS* 3 (1978) 90-99 (= *Scriptiunculae Posteriores* 1.36-45).

53. πάμπολυς

MM cite papyri only for this adjective, found in the NT only as a *v.l.*, at Mk. 8.1. It occurs twice in the lengthy Epidauros inscriptions recording divine cures (IV²BC). *IG* IV².1.121 attests the plight of a man from Mytilene (*ll.*122-25) who is embarrassed and teased by others because of his baldness despite having a bushy beard (οὗτος οὐκ εἶχε ἐν τᾶι κεφαλᾶι | τρίχας, ἐν δὲ τῶν γενείωι παμπόλλας, 122-23); the god effected the cure by anointing his head with a potion. At *IG* IV².1.122 (noted by BAGD, s.v., as '*Syll.*³ 1169') a Theban is cured from lice: οὗτος π[λῆ]|θός τι πάμπολυ φθε[ιρ]ῶν ἐν τῷ σώματι [ἔ]χων, κτλ (*ll.*45-46).

54. παραιτέομαι

An agonistic inscription from Pisidian Antioch set up after 293 (for the date see *CMRDM* 3, pp.63-64) records a certain Tiberius Claudius Marcianus as victor in the wrestling contest: his opponents declined, 'threw in the towel', when they saw him stripped for the match — ὃν | ἀποδυσάμε|νον παρητή||[σ]αντο οἱ ἀν|[ταγ]ωνισταί (*CMRDM* 1.164.14-18). For this use of the verb in the NT note Heb. 12.25; 1 Tim. 5.11 is not far removed in sense. MM include no epigraphical examples, so this may be useful for a revised entry.

55. παραλυτικός

Neither MM nor BAGD records documentary examples of this word, which occurs in the Synoptics nearly a dozen times, Mt. 4.24; 8.6; 9.2 (= Mk. 2.3); 9.2 (= Mk. 2.5); 9.6 (= Mk. 2.10 = Lk. 5.24); Mk. 2.4; Mk. 2.9.

P.Mon.Gr. inv. 123 (first ed. in 1951 — *non vidi*), re-edited by D. Fausti as *P.Carlini lett.* 32, pp.221-29 (pl.14), is a medical text written on one side of a roll (provenance unknown, I). The full height survives, with 39 lines of text, but the left hand side of the column is broken away. *Ll.*16-17 appear to refer to those suffering from epilepsy and paralysis: ... παθῶν οἷον ἐπιληπτικ[ῶν] | [---παρ]αλυτικῶν καὶ τῶν περὶ τὰ | [κτλ. For some literary attestations see Fausti's comment, p.227; this appears to be the first time it has occurred in the documentary material.

The Western variant at Mk. 2.9D, παράλυτος, remains unparalleled in papyrus and epigraphic texts.

For other items of vocabulary from *P.Carlini lett.* 32 see **26**, **57**.

56. παραμυθία

This noun is found in the NT only at 1 Cor. 14.3, and MM provide several papyrus attestations. *IGA* 2.318 is an epitaph (Alexandria, I/II) in which the deceased speaks of his tomb as a 'consolation of our life together (i.e., with his wife) which represents the piety of her three-year affection for me', παραμυθία συνζοίης | στοργῆς μοι τριετοῦς εὐσεβίην θεμένης (10–11). BAGD, s.v., notes this text as *SB* 4313.11, but the line numeration in *SB* is awry.

The neuter noun παραμύθιον occurs at *SEG* 953.30 in a long honorific inscription for Apollonis (Kyzikos, second quarter IAD), but the context is irrecoverable. For this text — *ed.pr.*: E. Schwertheim, *ZPE* 29 (1978) 213–28 (pls. 11–12) — see further the discussion in *BE* 393. This attestation should be added to the two in MM (both of later date) to illustrate the sole NT occurrence at Phil. 2.1, εἴ τι παραμύθιον ἀγάπης.

57. παραπλησίως

The first documentary example known to me occurs at *P.Carlini lett.* 32 (for details about this text see **55**) l.14, π]αραπλησίως αὔξειν δεῖ, κτλ (the particular context is irrecoverable). Given the dating of this papyrus to IAD, it offers a useful parallel to the NT *hapax* at Heb. 2.14, καὶ αὐτὸς παραπλησίως μέτεσχεν τῶν αὐτῶν.

As for the adjective παραπλήσιος, which occurs in the same papyrus at *ll.*23 (heavily restored) and 27, there have been several examples found since MM, some of which are in BAGD. One might add, e.g., *P.Beatty Panop.* (1964) 1.333 (Panopolis, 298-300), which speaks of bringing back into working order, for Diocletian's visit to Egypt, the bakery near the theatre, παραπλήσιον τοῦ θεάτρου. Further examples may be located via *WB* and *Spoglio*.

P.Tebt. 1 (1902) 5, *col*.3 *l*.71 (Tebtynis, 118BC) remains the sole documentary evidence to date for the adverbial use of this adjective, found in the NT only at Phil. 2.27 in the curious phrase ἠσθένησεν παραπλήσιον θανάτῳ. For this BAGD compares *P.Mich.* 3 (1936) 149.4, παραπλήσιον νεκρῷ.

58. παρασκευή

At *New Docs 1977*, **67**, a possible example was noted of an abbreviation for παρασκευή meaning 'Friday'. A more certain instance is afforded by *IGCB* 19 (Corinth, VI), a fragmentary Christian epitaph which concludes by providing the date when the deceased died (presumably): μη(νὶ) Σεπ[τεμβρίῳ] ἡμέρα | παρα[σκευή] (*ll.*8-9, Bees' reading). Though the final word is partly restored, it can hardly be in doubt in such a dating context. But it should be noted that ἡμέρα cannot be read in Bees' photo of the stone: should the text perhaps read [ἡμέρᾳ] | παρα[σκευῆς]? At *ll.*4-6 on the stone the wording λόγ(ον) δώ|ση τῷ κ(υρίο)υ (*sic*) alludes to Rom. 14.12.

Two instances of ἡμέρα κυριακή, 'Sunday', occur in 1978 publications: *SEG* 1395, 1396, both Christian epitaphs from Eboda in Palestine (577 and 581, respectively). Cf. *New Docs 1977*, **116**, p.207, where the earliest papyrus mention of Sunday was noted: *P.Oxy.* 48 (1981) 3407 (mid-IV).

59. πενιχρός

As so often, BAGD, s.v., has not gone beyond MM in collecting documentary attestations for words. From the 1978 culling we may now note *P.Oxy.* 3273 (I — '. . . more probably earlier . . . than later', *ed.pr.*), a fragmentary notification to an official concerning an inadvertent (κατὰ πλάνην, 4; on this phrase cf. *New Docs 1977*, **69**) confusion between two men of the same name and from the same village. One was mistakenly nominated for the office of *sitologos* although he was ἄθετος καὶ π[ε]νιχρός (8), i.e., lacking the financial means to bear the post. The phrase illustrates well the use of this adjective, which is not particularly common in documentary sources. As well as the two examples in MM and the new *P.Oxy.* text, the following further papyri — all Byzantine — may be listed; *P.Cairo Masp.* 1 (1911) 67002.I.12 (Antinoe(?), 522(?)); 67019.26 (Antinoe(?), 548-51); 67096.29 (Aphrodito, 11/573 - 5/574); 67097, *verso*, (c) 8 (Aphrodito, Byz.), superlative; 3 (1916) 67295.III.15 (Antinoe(?), VI²), εἰ καὶ πενιχραῖς ἐλπίσιν ηὐξάνοντο; *P.Lond.* 5 (1917, repr. 1973) 1708.221 (Antinoopolis, May – 13/11/567(?)). The epithet is used of people in all these passages except the one quoted (at *P.Cairo Masp.* 67019 the context is fragmentary).

MM offer no inscriptional attestations: three may be mentioned here, two Jewish and one Christian, all of which invest the epithet with a moral quality. *CIJ* 2.1123 (Beth-Shearim, n.d.), epitaph for Σαμουὲλ Ἰσαάκου πενηχροῦ Ἀναστα[σί]ου (for other Jewish examples of Anastasios see *New Docs 1976*, **73**); B. Lifshitz, *Rev.Bib.* 68 (1961) 410-11 (Besara, n.d.), epitaph for [Σα]μουήλο|[υ υἱοῦ] Γερμα|[νοῦ] πενι|[χρ]οῦ. Lifshitz's addition of υἱοῦ here is not necessary as the *CIJ* text illustrates, and is improbable given that the other line beginnings have lost only two or three letters each. W. M. Ramsay, *Cities and Bishoprics of Phrygia* I.2 (Oxford, 1897) 741, no.677 (Mikhail, c.370) is reprinted by Lifshitz (411): in this Christian inscription two brothers build a tomb and allow interment not only to their family but also to those who are 'heirs of the poor life', καὶ πάντων τῶ[ν ἄλλ]ων τῶν κληρονομούντων τὸν πενιχρὸν βίον. On Jewish attitudes to property and welfare for the poor cf. M. Hengel, *Property and Riches in the Early Church* (ET: Philadelphia, 1974) 12-22.

60. περιτέμνω

C.A. Behr, *Homm. Vermaseren* 1.13–24, discusses the problematic text of Ailios Aristeides 49.47, which reports a dream that he may have had c.148–49. Sarapis appeared with a lancet and seemed 'to make an incision around my face into what was somehow the root of the lips, close to the gum itself', περιτέμνειν μου τὰ κύκλῳ τοῦ προσώπου ⟨ἐν τῇ τῶν χειλῶν⟩ πως ῥίζῃ ὑπ' αὐτὸ τὸ οὖλον (the text given here is Behr's reconstruction, 19, although περιτέμνειν is not in doubt. One might compare *IG* IV².1, 123. 134–37 (Epidauros, IV²BC), which reports another divinely-performed mouth operation. The Aristeides passage provides a useful reminder of the more general meaning of the verb than the specific 'circumcise'. For the latter meaning, note among recent publications *BGU* 13 (1976) 2216 (Soknopaiu Nesos, 156; pl.4), a report of proceedings in which a man presents his three sons to the high priest for circumcision, proffering a letter from the *strategos* stating that the necessary conditions have been fulfilled: the verb occurs three times (3, 11, 28–29). *Spoglio* notes a few more examples not listed in MM. A further attestation of περιτομή to add to the sole example in MM, s.v., is *PSI* 9 (1929) 1039 (Oxyrhynchos, III), a report to the high priest at Oxyrhynchos which includes a list of boys who are candidates for circumcision: πρὸς τὲ (*read* δὲ) ⟨?⟩ τὴν μὲν τῶν παί|δων αὐτῶν περιτομήν (38–39; the list of names follows).

What Deissmann said about this word (*Bible Studies*, 151–53; echoed by MM, s.v.) is surely right. The currency of περιτέμνω and περιτομή in Egypt (at least) reflects the continuing practice of circumcision there, at least for candidates for Egyptian priesthoods in Roman times (whether it was more widely used before then is not certain — see E.M. Smallwood, *Latomus* 18 [1959] 334 n.2). The LXX translators thus had words ready to hand in the *koine* which could be applied to the Jewish ritual practice; cf. H.C. Youtie, *ZPE* 18 (1975) 152–53, repr. in his *Scriptiunculae Posteriores* 1 (Bonn, 1981) 220–21. As well as the literal meaning being found in the NT, these words undergo development there, reflecting the response to the pressures upon the first Gentile Christians to conform to the practices of Jewish Christians. Paul uses circumcision as a metaphor (though whether Youtie is right to see Paul alluding to 'baptism in Christ' is perhaps doubtful): περιτομὴ καρδίας ἐν πνεύματι οὐ γράμματι (Rom. 2.29); ἐν ᾧ (*sc*. Χριστῷ) καὶ περιετμήθητε περιτομῇ ἀχειροποιήτῳ . . . ἐν τῇ περιτομῇ τοῦ Χριστοῦ (Col. 2.11).

The problematic passage at Gal. 2.3, ἀλλ' οὐδὲ Τίτος ὁ σὺν ἐμοί, Ἕλλην ὤν, ἠναγκάσθη περιτμηθῆναι, should (I think) be taken to mean that Titos was *not* now obliged to be circumcised, since he was a Greek (cf. C.K. Barrett, *Essays on Paul* [London, 1982] 120–21). Certainly, the custom was repugnant to Greeks and Romans, as is reflected partly in the legislation against it under Hadrian and Antoninus Pius in II¹: on this see Smallwood, 334–47.

A group of seven circumcised phalli, originally strung on a necklace and functioning as an amulet, is reported from a funerary urn at Carthage (IVBC (?)) containing the charred remains of a child: see L.E. Stager, in J.G. Pedley (ed.), *New Light on Ancient Carthage* (Ann Arbor, 1980) 4 (pl.1.6 on p.133).

Since Aristeides has been mentioned in this entry it is apposite to note here C.P. Jones' re-edition of *IG* II².4531 (Mt. Pentelikon in Attika, 165–70 (?)), *Phoenix* 32 (1978) 231–34 (pl.; cf. *SEG* 229; *BE* [1979] 170): [Ἀσκληπιῷ καὶ] | [Ὑγ(ι)είᾳ] κα[ὶ] | [Τελε]σφόρ[ῳ] | [Ἀρι]στείδης | εὐ[ξ]άμενος, 'To Asklepios, Hygieia, and Telesphoros, Aristeides having vowed (this altar, set it up)'. This monument was erected by the orator on his second visit to Athens. Jones refers (232) to other inscriptional dedications from elsewhere (Mysia, Mytilene) in which he has been identified.

61. πιέζω

IGCB 5 (Corinth, IV²) provides the first few lines of a proconsular edict in which this verb occurs; the relevant portion (*ll*.6–7) is quoted (*qua SIG*³ 904) by MM, s.v., as their sole documentary attestation of the verb, found in the NT in this form only at Lk. 6.38. BAGD, s.v., notes that the word in this form (as opposed to πιάζω) is found in papyrus texts, but provides no references. In fact, it is quite rare: two examples only are known to me. *P.Cair.Zen.* 3 (1928, repr. 1971) 59378 (mid–IIIBC (?)) is a memorandum to Zenon from Alkimos, who points out: οὐ γὰρ οὕτως ὑπὸ τῶν ἔργων | πιεζομένου μου τηλικαύ|την ἐμοὶ βλαβὴν οἴσει | ἡλί κην οὐ καὶ σοί (10–13), 'For while I am being so pressed by my work you will not bring harm to me so much as to yourself' (i.e. if you refuse my requests). Also Ptolemaic is *P.Berl.Zilliacus* (1941) 1 (Abusir el-Melek, Herakleopolite nome, 156/5BC), although the context in which the verb appears here (*l*.41) is fragmentary: [διὰ τὸ πι]εσθῆναι | [±20]. On πιάζω/πιέζω see briefly G.P. Shipp, *Modern Greek Evidence for the Ancient Greek Vocabulary* (Sydney, 1979) 454–55.

The relatively common verb ἀποστερέω occurs in *IGCB* 5 (noted above) at *l*.5, τῆς τῶν νόμων (*sc.* μὴ) ἀποστερίσθω βοηθίας, 'let him not be deprived of the help of the laws'; and it is mentioned here because MM offer only one epigraphical attestation.

62. προχειρίζομαι

MM provide one epigraphical and several papyrus incidences of this word, ranging in date from Ptolemaic to II²AD, in illustration of the three examples in Acts, 3.20; 22.14; 26.16. To these BAGD adds another couple of documentary attestations. *P.Oxy.* 3275 (14-23/6/103-117) is an annual report to the district governor made on behalf of the priests of a village temple by two of their fellows, in which they tally the number of priests and certain amounts of grain and money. The men who report specify that they were 'selected by their fellow priests', προκεχειρισμένων ὑπὸ τῶν συνιερέων (7-8).

In making their report they use the verb προσφωνέω (17), poetical in classical Greek but a standard prose word in the *koine*. The NT use of this verb is different, however; at Mt. 11.16 = Lk. 7.32 and five other places in Lk./Acts it is employed of public (and formal ?) address to others, for which MM's entry provides a couple of parallels, most of their references illustrating the meaning 'report (officially)'.

63. πρωτότοκος

This word occurs at the beginning of a fragmentary epitaph, *IGA* 2.321 (Alexandria, III/IV). Given the accusative case ending, πρωτό το κον, this first-born son who died may have been the Herminos (also accus.) mentioned at *l*.5. The text provides a further example for MM, s.v.; Lk. 2.7 and Heb. 11.28 are the only NT instances to which no special theological connotation adheres.

64. Σατανᾶς

IGCB 15 (Corinth IV/V) is a Christian grave inscription consisting largely of a vivid curse upon any who open the tomb: let their family come entirely to ruin, let them be deprived of God's mercy, and 'may Satan enter their home and destroy them utterly,' Σα|τανᾶς αὐτῶν εἰς τὸν οἶκον εἰσ|έλθοιτο καὶ ἐξολεθρεύσαιτο αὐ|τούς (13–16). The attestation should be added to MM's entry, where two papyri are noted.

Other Christian epitaphs from Corinth — some very fragmentary — invoke curses on those who interfere with the grave: *IGCB* 16(?), 17 ('the curse of Annas and Kaiaphas', quoted at **100**), 18(?), 19, 20, 21(?), 22, 23 (see **35**) 24(?), 26, 27(?), 28, 29(?). In the course of his publication of a Christian inscription from Argos which reflects anti-Jewish sentiment (cf. *SEG* 26[1976/7] 437; repr. at *New Docs 1976*, **61**) D. Feissel, *BCH* 101 (1977) 224–28 discusses and re-edits several other Christian inscriptions which invoke a curse formulated with reference to Judas (cf. *SEG* 27 [1977] 29, 30, 528, 823). In the second of these, from the Laureion in Attika (IV), the warning reads that if anyone dares open the tomb 'he (will) have the portion of Judas, and may everything become darkness for him, and may God destroy him utterly on that day', ἔχι | τὴν μερίδαν τοῦ Ἰούδα κὲ γέ|νητε αὐτῷ πάντα σκ{τ}ότος | κὲ ἐξολεθρεύσῃ ὁ θ(εὸ)ς αὐτὸν | ἐν τῇ ἡμέρᾳ ἐκίνῃ (5–9). Note also the inscription published by C.Mango/I.Ševčenko, *DOP* 32 (1978) 10–11 no.13 (fig. 13), which warns that if any one of the deceased's heirs does anything contrary to his instructions ἔ]χι πρὸς τὼ | [ὄνο]μα τὸ φωβ|[ερ]ὸν κ(αὶ) τὶν μερί[δ]αν τοῦ εἰπό(ν)τ|[ος] Ἄρον, ἄρον, | [σταύρωσον αὐτόν], 'may he have to deal with the Aweful Name and have a portion with him who said, "Away with him, away with him, crucify him." ' On this text (provenance unknown, VI/VII; cf. *SEG* 1583), which concludes with a quotation from Jn. 19.15, cf. D.Feissel, *BCH* 104 (1980) 463–64 n.40, 466, 474.

In both the first two texts quoted in this entry the verb ἐξολεθρεύω occurs; MM, s.v., provide no documentary attestations to parallel the sole NT occurrence (Acts 3.23), and these two examples should therefore be noted. Their comments on the textual reading are now dated, as N/A[26] and UBS[3] both accept the form ἐξολε-; and the orthography of their lemma needs altering. BAGD, s.v., notes one papyrus example (VIAD).

65. σκώληξ

The first certain documentary attestation of this noun — *P. Erlangen* (1942) 148.2 may preserve the word in the form σκωλυκος, but Schubart was unsure since the remainder of this Byzantine text was written in tachygraphy — occurs as a curse inscription on a vase (provenance unknown, late imperial period): *ed.pr.* — L. Robert, *CRAI* (1978) 286–89 (fig. 3 on p.286); cf. *SEG* 1586. The text reads: Ἀγρυπνίου· τις ἂν ἄρι βοτηρίδιν | σκώληκας ποιεῖ, 'This belongs to Agrypnios. Anyone who takes this little vase gets worms.' The sole NT occurrence, Mk. 9.48 (quoting Is. 66.24; cf. Judith 16.21) uses the noun similarly: ὅπου ὁ σκώληξ αὐτῶν οὐ τελευτᾷ καὶ τὸ πῦρ οὐ σβέννυται. This application of the noun is not confined to Jewish sources: see Lucian, *Alex.* 59.2, quoted by Robert (also noted in BAGD, s.v.). Cf. the compound σκωληκόβρωτος, used similarly at Acts 12.33; *Spoglio* lists several documentary examples of the latter additional to MM's sole citation (though MM also note two closely related forms).

66. σπλάγχνον

Pace MM, s.v. (and cf. their comment on the verb σπλαγχνίζομαι), it is not necessary to perceive a 'distinctively "Hebraic" usage' in this noun when it has the meaning 'compassion'; references in BAGD, s.v., 1b, 2, confirm this. A recently published grave epigram for a child (Apollonia Mygdonia in the Chalkidike, late Hellenistic) serves to underscore the conclusion that *koine* texts containing the word in this sense do not involve Jewish influence in every instance, even indirectly. The epitaph, re-ed. by W. Peek, *ZPE* 31(1978) 265–69 (cf. *SEG* 541), devotes several lines to the child's grandfather, after whom he was named, who was honoured in various ways by his city, and of whom it is said, 'This tomb and dedication (worthy) of the heroes belongs to the same man as does his nobility compounded of compassion', τοῦ δ' αὐτοῦ τόδε σᾶμα καὶ ἡρώων ἀνάθημα | ἐστὶ καὶ ἁ σπλάγχνων σύνθετος εὐγένεια (13–14). In the NT, a Hebraic outlook does not have to be behind passages like Phil. 2.1 or Col. 3.12, though it may well be present at Lk. 1.78.

67. συναγωνίζομαι

This verb occurs in the NT only at Rom. 15.30, where Paul urges his readers to συναγωνίσασθαί μοι ἐν ταῖς προσευχαῖς ὑπὲρ ἐμοῦ πρὸς τὸν θεόν; MM cite three inscriptions of III/IIBC in illustration. A new attestation from that period may now be added, occurring in a lengthy honorific decree for Kallias of Sphettos (Athens, 270/69BC) — *ed.pr.*, Shear, *Kallias*; cf. *SEG* 60; M.J. Osborne, *ZPE* 35 (1979) 181–94, who argues, against Shear, for the revolt occurring in early summer 287; and *BE* (1981) 230–234 — in which he is said to have participated in embassies to King Ptolemy, and 'continued striving together in every way with the embassies despatched by the People, working for what was in the city's interests', ταῖς πρεσβείαις ταῖς ἀποστελλομέναις ὑπὸ τοῦ δήμου συναγωνιζόμενος | εἰς πάντα καὶ συνεργῶν εἰς τὰ συμφέροντα τεῖ πόλει (41–43).

A much more fragmentary decree from Athens (119/8BC) re-edited by J.S. Traill, *Hesperia* 47 (1978) 286–87 no. 15 (cf. *SEG* 89), mentions the meeting of the [ἐκκλησία κυρί]|α ἐν τῶι θεάτρωι. The same phrase is entirely preserved at Durrbach, *Choix* 73a.5 (Delos, 172/1BC). This common enough wording is perhaps worth passing mention to compare with the situation at Ephesos in Acts 19 where an irregular assembly (*v.*39) took place in the theatre (*v.*29).

68. συναντιλαμβάνομαι

I. Lampsakos 7 is a decree from Thasos recording the decision of Lampsakos in I¹BC to honour a Thasian, Dionysodoros, with *proxenia* and its attendant rights. At *ll.*15–16 it is said of him: συναντιλαμβάνετα⟨ι⟩ | δὲ καὶ τοῖς κατ' ἰδίαν ἑαυτοῦ ποιουμένο⟨ι⟩ς χρείαν, 'and he took an interest in those who made use of him privately'. In view of its date this example is well worth adding to MM, s.v. — cf. their comment, ad fin. — to illustrate the two NT occurrences, Lk. 10.40 and Rom. 8.26. *I.Lampsakos* 3 is another fragmentary example, dated c.200BC.

Proxeny decrees are common in the Classical Greek and Hellenistic periods. Among 1978 publications should be singled out Walbank, *Proxenies*, which collects and discusses the 94 examples from VBC Athens (68 are epigraphical); various elements in his volume are noted at *SEG* 11, 12, 48. Other proxeny decrees are picked up at *SEG* 438 (Megara), 453 (Haliartos), 465 and 466 (Thebes), 485 (Delphi), 714 (Samos). *IG* IV².1.48–58, 60, 63, 69, 96 are examples from Epidauros, ranging in date from IV/IIIBC–115/4BC. From Delos may be noted Durrbach, *Choix* 10–12, 15, 16, 20–22, 26–29, 34, 39, 42, 46–49, 54, 58, 63, 66, 112 (ranging in date from IV¹BC-end IIBC). Delphi is a rich source of these decrees: see *F.Delphes* III.4 (1976) nos.373–450. Apart from the εὐεργετ- word group, the constellation of honorific terms found in such decrees (ἀσυλία, ἀτέλεια, προδικαία, προεδρία, προμαντεία, προξενία, etc.) is — not surprisingly — entirely absent from both the NT and ECL. Walbank's discussion of these terms (5–7) is scarcely adequate. On proxenies note C. Marek, *Die Proxenie, eine historische Studie ihrer Bedeutung und Funktion* (Diss. Marburg, 1982) — *non vidi*.

69. συνείδησις

Two examples from the 1978 culling may be mentioned here. *CMRDM* 1.44 (Koresa (?) in Lydia, 156/7; = *TAM* 5.1 [1981] 318) records a case where a woman denied poisoning her son-in-law. In order to prove her innocence Tatia ἐπέστησεν | σκῆπτρον καὶ ἀρὰς ἔθηκεν | ἐν τῷ ναῷ ὡς ἱκανοποιοῦ|σα περὶ τοῦ πεφημίσθαι αὐ|τὴν ἐν συνειδήσι τοιαύτη (9–13), 'stood the sceptre (on the altar) and invoked curses (i.e., on herself) in the shrine to defend herself concerning her being slandered with such guilty knowledge'. In a quite different context the noun occurs in *IGA* 5.70 (Saqqara, IV), a Christian epitaph for Zenodora, originally from Antioch, remembered by her husband (?) for τ[ῶ]ν καλ[ῶ]ν | ἠθῶν καὶ τῆς συνειδήσεως κ|αὶ ἱστοργῆς (*sic*) τῆς πρὸς ἐμέ, κτλ (16–18), 'her good disposition and conscientiousness and affection for me'. Both these inscriptions would be useful additions to BAGD and MM, s.v.

70. συνέρχομαι

A new example of this verb in the common *koine* sense of 'marry' (NT: Mt. 1.18) may be noted here to provide attestation from a provenance rarely drawn on by MM. *SEG* 831 (environs of Brandon, in Suffolk, England, n.d.) is a silver finger ring on which is incised σύν|ηλθη (i.e., σύνελθε), 'marry me'. For a photo see *Britannia* 9 (1978) pl. 32a. From 1978 publications note also *P.Sakaon* 48.4, quoted at **101**.

71. συνοικέω

P.Sakaon 1 (a re-edition of *P.Strasb.* 1 [1912] 42) is a census declaration (Theadelphia, 27/2/310) in which Sakaon states, 'I live in my own house in the village, absolutely nobody living with me for a long while', οἰκῶ δ' ἐν ἰδίᾳ οἰκίᾳ τῆς κώμης, μηδενός μοι συνοικοῦντος ἐκ πολλοῦ χρόνου τὸ παράπαν (16). At Durrbach, *Choix* 73b (Delos, 172/IBC), news is reported that Queen Nysa, daughter of Antiochos, has married (συνωικηκέναι, 15) king

Pharnakes. The sole NT occurrence of the compound verb, 1 Pet. 3.7, has marriage as its specific context; but this papyrus example is rather more generalized. MM, s.v., provide two instances of the verb in this sense.

72. σωματικῶς

To illustrate the NT *hapax* at Col. 2.9, MM adduce as their sole documentary attestation *OGIS* 664.17 (Dimeh in the Fayum, 5/4/54AD; the date in LSJ, s.v., is wrong), an edict of L. Lusius Geta, prefect of Egypt. This inscription — = *SB* 5.3 (1950) 8900; most recently re-edited in E. Bernand, *Recueil des inscriptions grecques du Fayoum* 1 (Leiden, 1975) 75, pp.148-53 (pl.55) — concludes with a warning that anyone who ignores his edict κατὰ [π]ᾶν ἢ ἀργυρικῶς ἢ σωματικῶς κολασθήσεται, 'will be punished in every respect either financially or corporally' (for the question of the application of the different punishments see Bernand's note).

Several examples of this adverb are known from the papyri. *SB* 6.3 (1961) 9329 (Bakchias, 26/9/171; text also known as *P.Bacchias* 20, published by E.H. Gilliam, *YCS* 10 (1947) 254-58, pl.2) is a short document where the words of a legal counsel (*rhetor*) are quoted, that 'the officials are forcing the plaintiffs to labour in person', οἱ πραγματικοὶ βιά[[σ]]⟨ζ⟩ονται τοὺς συνηγορουμέ|νους σωματικῶς ἀπεργάζεσ[[τ]]⟨θ⟩αι τὰς ἐργασίας (4-5). The allusion is to priests of the village who are anxious to avoid dyke-work as a liturgy. Similar wording occurs in two other texts from the same decade and provenance: *SB* 6.3 (1961) 9339 (Bakchias, 178 or later; also known as *P.Bacchias* 21, published by Gilliam, op.cit., 259-60, pl.3; her text supersedes that in *SB* 5.3 [1950] 8748), a letter referring to a petition of the priests and *pa*[*stophoroi*] of the village, asking 'that they should not be forced to work in person on the dykes', μὴ ἄγεσθαι σωματικῶς | [ἐπὶ] τὴν τῶν χωμάτων ἀπεργασίαν (15-16). *P.Fouad* (1939) 13 (Bakchias, 178 (?)) is fragmentary but the final line of text — the papyrus is blank below it — reads σωματικῶς ἀπεργάζεσθαι ἱερε[ῖς (?).

Much later in date than these attestations are *P.Lond.* 4 (1910, repr. 1973) 1345.21, and 1367.19 (Aphrodito, both dated 710), which apparently employed an identical phrase μέλλομεν ἀποδοῦναι αὐτοῖς σωματικῶς καὶ ὑποστατικ[ῶ]/ (i.e., -ῶς, 1345; the text of 1367 here is largely restored), 'we intend to give them their due in person, and firmly'. (A possible addition to this list is *P.Warren* [1941] 3.19 (VI) — *non vidi*; *WB* Suppl.1, 2.Lief. [1969] lists both adjective and adverb attestations under the single lemma, σωματικός.)

From 1978 publications a further example can be added. *CPR* 6 (Hermopolis, 8/7/439; pl.5) is a settlement (διάλυσις) document in which it is said ἐνεμήθης σωματικῶς (text corrupt), 'you were assigned (the land) in person' (10). The notion 'in reality' is not far away in this phrase, which makes it of especial relevance for Col. 2.9 (cf. BAGD, s.v.; and s.v. σῶμα, 4).

This same papyrus includes several other words worth noting *en passant*. In the oath section the vendor states that he will not bring the purchaser to account in the future on any grounds, μήτε περὶ συντελείας ἢ προτελείας ... | ... μήτε περὶ οἱασδήποτε προφάσεως ... (15-16), 'neither concerning a contribution or advance payment ... nor on any kind of pretext'. The neat antithesis of the first two nouns here makes it well worth including in a revised MM entry, although this is not the NT usage (cf. MM, s.v.). For οἱοσδήποτε cf. *New Docs 1977*, 63. At MM, s.v. διαστολή, ad fin., it is noted that διαστολεύς (not found in the NT) is rare: *l*.26 of this document provides an attestation as one witness signs the document, 'Aurelios Pollon son of Hermes, cashier from Hermopolis'.

73. ὑπεράνω

For this word (NT: Eph. 1.21; 4.10; Heb. 9.5) MM supplied two IIIAD documentary attestations. Of far earlier date is *I.Lampsakos* 4 (= *SIG³* 591), an honorific decree (196/5BC) for Hegesias which contains at *ll*.1-2 (the text originally preceding this is lost) the wording ἐν] | [τοῖς ψηφίσμασι τοῖ]ς ὑπεράνω γεγραμμένο[ις, 'in the decrees recorded above'. This inscription was known to MM, for it is cited as '*Syll²* 276' for the attestation of ἀπόκρισις at *l*.28.

74. φιλάδελφος

C. Brixhe, *Le dialecte grec de Pamphylie. Documents et grammaire* (Paris, 1976), includes two IIBC inscriptions from Belkis-Camiliköy, near Aspendos, which use this adjective (nos. 146 and 154). Brixhe draws attention to the rarity of this word in Asia Minor — only one other documentary attestation is known to him — in contrast to its great frequency in Egypt. This point was noted at *New Docs 1977*, **80**, p.103; from 1978 publications note *SEG* 1511, a brief epitaph for Herakleides φιλά|δελφος (Terenouthis, III/IV; two further texts from this necropolis in Egypt, published earlier, are noted at **11**.

To supplement this sparse documentation from Asia Minor, we may note three inscriptions from *I.Bithynia*: III.2, pp.51-52 (Pelitcik, Roman period; pl.11; *SEG* 982), a man's children, who describe themselves as οἱ φιλάδελφοι (12), set up an epitaph for him; III.7, pp.56-57 (Göynük, Roman period; = *SEG* 1018), a funerary epigram which Attius Nikomedes had carved on a stele for his father, φι|λάδελφον ἔχων γνώμη⟨ν⟩ (13-14); and III.8, pp.57-58 (Göynük, Roman period; = *SEG* 1019), an epitaph for a man set up by his children who call themselves οἱ φιλάδελφοι (14). Further, the name [Φι]λάδελφος occurs on an epitaph from Bithynia, *TAM* 111 (n.d.), where the man appears to be a slave setting up the memorial for his master. 1 Pet. 3.8 is the only NT occurrence, and at the outset of this letter Bithynia is specified as one of the localities of the addressees.

75. φιλόκαισαρ

In the course of his discussion of the kingdom of Kommagene in relation to the Greek world, *Fest.Dörner* 1.359-74 (cf. *SEG* 1315), P.M. Fraser provides several examples and discussion of the word φιλόκαισαρ (369-71, with the notes). This is one of a cluster of epithets adopted, no doubt with official Roman approval, by individuals from the Greek East, particularly client kings although by no means them alone. The very common φιλορώμαιος begins to appear in early IBC, while φιλόκαισαρ and the rather less common φιλοσέβαστος are known from the early Principate. LSJ, s.v., provides two epigraphical examples of the latter; cf. *CIG* 2.3499, 3500, honorific decrees for M. Gnaeus Licinius Rufinus from Thyatira, which call him φίλον τοῦ Σεβαστοῦ (*ll*.4-5, and 5, respectively). MM, s.v. φίλος, misleadingly implies that these texts include the phrase φίλος τοῦ Καίσαρος. The most recent discussion of these terms in relation to client kings is to be found in D.C. Braund, *Rome and the Friendly King. The Character of Client Kingship* (London, 1984) 105–08.

That those who paraded the epithet φιλόκαισαρ were not only royalty is usefully indicated by *SEG* 17 (1960) 381 (Chios, c.150–60; discussed by Fraser, 363–71), where the word occurs eleven times — often partly restored, but hardly in doubt — after the names of both private individuals and monarchs. The word had a particular attraction for the kings of the Bosporos region: *Corpus Inscriptionum Regni Bosporani* (1965) lists 75 instances of φιλόκαισαρ in its index, s.v. A precursor to this terminology in the context of Rome's relations with other states may be seen in *I.Lampsakos* 4 (= *SIG*³ 591), an honorific decree for Hegesias (196/5BC), in which it is said of the city: σ[υγ]|[γενὴς ὢν κα]ὶ φίλος ὁ δῆμος τοῦ Ῥωμαίων δήμου (18–19), 'the people is of the same stock as, and a friend of, the Roman people' (see ed.n. on p.31 on the formal misuse of φίλος here). *OGIS* 379.16 (Iberia, 75) provides a less common attestation from the West. In the case of Judaea, both Agrippa I (who figures briefly in Acts 12.1–4) and Agrippa II (cf. Acts 25.13–26.32) are accorded the title in epigraphical texts: *OGIS* 419, 420, 424; while Agrippa I's nephew, Herod Eusebes, has it at *OGIS* 427.

The notion of *amicitia* is fundamental to Roman patronage, and among Roman citizens 'the *amici Caesaris* constituted an amorphous group including senators, *equites* and others who had access to the emperor' (R.P. Saller, *Personal Patronage under the Early Empire* [Cambridge, 1982] 59). While for some individuals the relationship with the Princeps was one of close friendship, for the majority it provided a much more formal tie involving the performance and reciprocal expectation of favours: Pliny's dealings with Trajan represent the situation well. Now it was not an empty title, especially for Romans acting abroad in an administrative capacity: for it indicates that they are 'representatives of the *auctoritas* of the emperor' (J.A. Crook, *Consilium Principis* [Cambridge 1955; repr. New York, 1975] 24). Accordingly, if a provincial governor were an *amicus Caesaris* this was likely to be known by any in the province who were close enough to him to be seeking his aid or important enough to be trying to manipulate him. F. Millar, *The Emperor in the Roman World* (London, 1977) 116, makes this point in his discussion of the emperor's friends and advisers (110–22; on *amici Caesaris* especially, 111–16); and he draws out the corollary, that such a person could be subjected to pressure by virtue of his relationship with the Princeps. Further, Millar speaks of the 'acute instability' of the *amicus* (113): for his patron to fall could well mean his own political demise.

This brings us to the words addressed to Pilate at Jesus' trial, ἐὰν τοῦτον ἀπολύσῃς οὐκ εἶ φίλος τοῦ Καίσαρος (Jn. 19.12). E. Bammel, *TLZ* 77 (1952) 205–10, has argued that the words here allude to Pilate's relationship with the Princeps, discussed above. C.K. Barrett (Comm. [1978²], ad loc.) is right to doubt the view that Pilate's fortunes were closely bound up with those of the recently fallen Sejanus (died October 31); for recent criticism of the opinion that Pilate was virtually Sejanus' appointee to Judaea see J.-P.Lémonon, *Pilate et le gouvernement de la Judée* (Paris, 1981), especially 275–76. However, Barrett rejects it because 'John would not have been aware of these political entanglements', and suggests that the phrase in 19.12 is to be understood more generally, that anyone who condones a monarchical pretender is no friend of the Emperor. This interpretation of the phrase is not altogether persuasive: the idea that the writer was unaware of the political 'loading' of the words does not mesh with such comments as that at Jn. 6.15. Even were Pilate not formally an *amicus Caesaris*, at least as a Roman of some standing the significance of the words cannot have been lost on him; hence he is portrayed as 'caving in' to their implied threat (19.13–16). Further, it is very reasonable to suppose that the words were deliberately chosen by the Jewish leadership. Although the term φιλόκαισαρ is not attested of the Jewish client kings as early as Jesus' trial, it is hardly likely that it was conferred upon these rulers but not on Herod the Great. And since the epithet is widely attested geographically, even had it not been accorded to a Judaean monarch before Agrippa I it is certain to be an epithet well-known to anyone in the early Empire as politicially attuned as the Jewish religious leadership clearly was. Moreover, every inhabitant of the Empire was personally committed by the terms of the oath to loyalty to the Caesarian family, including the obligation to report any disloyal intentions in others. On this subject see P. Herrmann, *Der römische Kaisereid* (*Hypomnemata* 20; Göttingen, 1968), whose App. 1 collects the surviving epigraphical texts (pp.122-26). Lémonon does not address the significance of Jn. 19.12 satisfactorily (187–89, 278).

While φίλος Καίσαρος is the most obvious rendering of the Latin *amicus Caesaris*, it is not the only Greek equivalent: H.J. Mason, *Greek Terms for Roman Institutions* (*American Studies in Papyrology* 13; Toronto, 1974) 176, notes also ἑταῖρος, οἰκιακός (cf. Mason, 14; and see 1 in the present Review), and σεβαστόγνωστος. See also J.M. Reynolds, *Aphrodisias and Rome* (*JRS Monograph* 1; London, 1982) 6, a II/IIIAD copy of a letter of Octavian to Plarasa/Aphrodisias (originally written in 38BC), praising their ambassador: among other things Octavian says, 'and I held him as one of my acquaintances', ἔσ|χον τε ἐν τοῖς ὑπ' ἐμοῦ | γεινωσκομένοις (*ll*.35-37); see Reynolds' n. on p.46, where she says that this is 'the earliest attested instance at present of the adoption of a specific individual as the *notus* of a great man'. In ibid., 10.2 we see the application of individual friendship by Octavian in foreign policy (letter of Octarian to Stephanos, II/IIIAD copy of an original to be dated late 39/early 38BC): 'you know my affection for my friend Zoilos', ὡς Ζοίλον τὸν ἐμὸν φιλῶ ἐπίστασαι.

76. Agape (cf. *New Docs 1976*, 49)

Lest the 1976 entry on this name allow the impression to remain that it is relatively uncommon, it should be noted that Solin, *GPR* 3.1191, lists 108 examples from Rome (one servile, all the rest *incertae*), with another possible candidate (a lacuna leaves it uncertain), 3.1340; and in a further two instances, both Christian, the name occurs as a cognomen (3.1355). Almost all of these are certainly Christian, the name becoming very popular in III and IV. From the 1978 culling we may add an instance of the name on a mummy label, *IGA* 4.14 (p.2*); from 1977 publications note *AE* (1977) 236 (Cannae). Several other names are attested with this stem, mainly diminutives (Agapetilla, Agapetion): see Solin, 3.1503. For the name Agapetos — for Rome see Solin, 2.880-81, where the 58 attestations include a couple of senators and one person of free birth — we may add from 1978 publications N.Asgari/N.Fıratlı, *Fest. Dörner* 1.74, no.SR5 (Kalchedon, III[1]), a tombstone set up by Aurelius Agapetos for himself, his wife, and their children. Solin's list for Rome attests Christian use of this name by II/III.

Ἀγα̣[πητήν (accus.) is the wife of a man commemorated in a Christian funerary epigram (Hadrianoi in Bithynia, IV): *SEG* 946, a text of *I.Bithynia* III.21, pp.68-69, improved by *BE* (1979) 363. The deceased Nikatorios was held in high esteem 'by all the people of the highest God', ἐν | [ὅλ]ῳ τε λαῷ θεοῦ ὑ[ψί]|[στ]ου (7-9). A possible allusion to Homer, *Od*.11.603 occurs at *ll*.9-11 (Şahin, n. ad loc. in *I. Bithynia*): for such quotations in Christian texts see *New Docs 1977*, 111, where it is noted that they may be a mason's clichés rather than conscious allusions to Homer by those who set up the stele. The word [πάν]|[τ]οτε may occur in this inscription at *ll.*13–14. In the NT and other *koine* πάντοτε was fast replacing ἀεί, as the condemnation of the Atticists indicates (cf. BDF §105; BAGD, s.v.).

77. Athanasios

This name is surprisingly less frequent than one might have expected. Solin, *GPR* 3.1193, lists three females, one male and an indeterminate Ἀθανασι---; on his dating this last may be the earliest attestation of the name from Rome (III[1]). Dates of the others (as late as VII) and other wording in these texts indicate that the name may be of exclusively Christian use. The theological outlook reflected by a name with such an etymology reinforces this presumption.

From the 1978 publications *P.Sakaon* registers in several texts an Aurelios Athanasios also called Philadelphos who acts as a *dekaprotos* at Theadelphia at the very end of III. The by-name is consistently introduced by καί, not ὁ καί; Jouguet's text at *P.Thead.* 27.7 restores [ὁ κ]αί, but Parássoglou's re-edition in *P.Sakaon* 12 reads καί. The relevant texts may be listed briefly.

1. *P.Sakaon* 11 (14/9/296 or 297), a wheat receipt in which he calls himself Aurelios Athanasios καί Philadelphos (3–4), and signs himself Aurelios Philadelphos (13);
2. *P.Sakaon* 82 (296 or 297), a wheat receipt in which he calls himself Aurelios [Ἀθα]|[νάσιος κ]αί Philadelphos (3–4), and signs himself Aurelios Philadelphos (13–14);
3. *P.Sakaon* 12 (26/10/298), a wheat receipt in which he calls himself Aurelios Philadelphos καί Athanasios (7), and signs himself Aurelios Philadelphos (18);
4. *P.Sakaon* 76 (Nov./Dec.298): it is very likely that the Aurelios Athanasis (*sic*) who signs (16) a land declaration for an illiterate man is the same individual (on -ιος > -ις see Gignac, 2.25);
5. *P.Sakaon* 86 (5/5/300), a receipt for money, in which he calls himself Aurelios Athanasios καί Philadelphos (8–10) and signs himself Aurelios Philadelphos (22). His colleague Aurelios Heroninos adds καὶ | Ἀθανάσιος after his own name (19–20), but this must be an error, since Heroninos nowhere else has this by-name.

No.3 above indicates how interchangeable name and by-name could be; while this man has a clear preference to sign himself Philadelphos, yet Athanasi(o)s occurs too, if we accept that the man in no.4 is to be identified with the Athanasios in the other documents. On such interchangeability G.W. Clarke draws to my attention the example of Cyprian: *Cyprianus qui et Thascius* (*Ep.* 66 *tit.*), whereas in *Act. Procons. Cyp.* 3.3 (Musurillo 172) we find *tu es Thascius qui et Cyprianus*? This letter of Cyprian is addressed to *Florentio cui et Puppiano*, the same individual whose name is to be extrapolated from *CIL* VIII.4 (1906) 26415 as Pullaienus Florentius Titinius Pupianus. On by-names more fully see *New Docs 1976*, **55**.

It is noteworthy that this person figures in this group of texts at the very end of III. Given his name, Athanasios may be presumed to have been a Christian. The majority of extant Decian *libelli* come from Theadelphia (34 out of 45; cf. *New Docs 1977*, **105**, pp.181, 182) and are a likely indicator — though not a certain one: cf. **101** — of an official perception that there was a Christian presence in that village in mid-III. Theadelphia is therefore likely not to have escaped the renewal of persecution under Diocletian at the beginning of IV. Is the disappearance of Aurelios Athanasios also called Philadelphos from Theadelphian papyrus records at the very end of III to be associated with the Great Persecution?

78. Crescens

This Latin name is common enough, but its Greek transliterations seem scarcely attested: MM have no entry to illustrate the sole NT occurrence at 2 Tim. 4.10, Κρήσκης. At *BCH* 102 (1978) 621 G. Daux mentions two attestations of Κρήσκηνς (*sic*), one being from Rome, though he does not provide the references: cf. *SEG* 1630. The item from Rome is *CIL* VI. 4.2 (1902) 30780, a dedication to the Mother of the gods by Κρήσκηνς and others.

Some other attestations of the name may be noted. The Jory/Moore index to *CIL* VI lists over 200 examples (including fragmentary occurrences (pt. 7, fasc. 5, pp. 6350–53); cf. Vidman's *Index cognominum* to *CIL* VI. Elsewhere the name is not particularly common. *IGRR* registers the name at 1.432 (Naples, n.d.; cognomen), 496 (Syracuse, n.d., cognomen); 3.501 (Oinoanda, n.d.); 4.749 (Stektorion in Phrygia, 161–69 or 176–80; cognomen — imperial freedman), 1296 (Iulia Gordos, n.d.; re-ed. as *TAM* 5.1 [1981] 745 [pl.25]). Two papyrus attestations are known to me: *PSI* 9 (1929) 1063.10 (provenance unknown, 117), and once in the long tax list *P. Mich.* 4.1 (1936) 224 (Karanis, 172/3; cognomen). The incorrect reference to *O. Tait.* P275 should be deleted from Foraboschi, vol.4, s.v. Τιβέριος Κλαύδιος Κρήσκης.

79. Philemon

MM provide four documentary examples of this name (NT: only at Philem. 1), two papyri and two inscriptions from Asia Minor. From Rome alone Solin, *GPR* 2.738-40, provides over 60 attestations ranging in date from IBC-IV/VI, with the clear predominance occurring in IAD. Of these only one is certainly of free status. *CMRDM* 1.149 (Ikonion in Lykaonia, n.d.) provides another Roman citizen (the *tria nomina* are given) in a tombstone set up for the man's son, in which Men is referred to. At *CMRDM* 4. new 6 (pl.14) Μάρκιοι Φιλήμων | καὶ Μάρκ[ος ... set up a brief dedication to Men Askaenos (Pisidian Antioch, n.d.). *I.Bithynia* II.10, p.42 (= *SEG* 1054) is an epitaph for Dorema (Strobilos, Roman imperial period) consisting of a relief of a funerary banquet and the words Δώρημα Φιλήμονος. As illustrations of the NT occurrences at Rom. 5.16 and Jas. 1.17 this text is worth adding to a revised MM entry for δώρημα, where two papyri and one inscription are the documentary texts given. (A further example from the 1978 culling to be noted in passing is *IG* IV².1.128 — mentioned in BAGD, s.v. — the so-called 'hymn' of Isyllos [Epidauros, c.280BC], which praises Apollo and Asklepios' ability to cure disease and bestow health, describing this as a μέγα δώρημα βροτοῖς [*l.*53]). From Egypt a Christian epitaph for a certain Philemon may be noted (*IGA* 5.309; Akhmim, n.d.). Another Philemon, son of Laios, appears at *TAM* 8.15, in a fragmentary list of names (Nikomedeia, n.d.). The name is possibly to be restored at *TAM* 151.7 (Nikomedeia, n.d.). A Philemon is mentioned in *IG* IV².1.401 (Epidauros, somewhat after 400).

80. Trophimos

In Acts this companion of Paul is called both Ἀσιανός (20.4) and 'The Ephesian' (21.29); 21.28-29 makes clear that Jews hostile to Paul perceived Trophimos to be a gentile. The (same?) Trophimos is mentioned at 2 Tim. 4.20 as being left behind by the writer at Miletos because he was sick.

Solin, *GPR* 2.990-95, illustrates how extremely common (with almost 300 examples it is the 12th most frequently attested name in Solin: *GPR* 3.1439) is this name at Rome, particularly for slaves and freedmen, although a very small number with free status possess it too. While the name is attested from IBC-IV/V, its popularity peaks markedly in I, remaining frequent in II. MM provided two documentary examples; a considerable number of epigraphical attestations have come to notice in the 1978 culling. From Asia Minor some examples from *CMRDM* may be mentioned: 1.35, 45, 46, 49, 54, 122, 210; 4.26 (on p.8; a combination of 1.272 + 276 + 285); 4. new 8 (on p.15). All these people — or their descendants, since some occurrences are patronymics — have an involvement in the cult of Men, ranging geographically from Lydia to Pisidia. Also from Lydia is an epitaph for a certain Trophimos (Saittai, 98/9) published by G. Petzl, *ZPE* 30 (1978) 258-61 no.4 (pl.10), repr. as *SEG* 917 (cf. *BE* [1979] 436) and *TAM* 5.1 (1981) 167a. From the same locality Petzl has published an epitaph (254/5) for Aurelia Iulia set up by her husband Aurelios Trophimos (ibid., 262-3, no.9; cf. *SEG* 924; *TAM* 5.1.168c). In *Fest. Dörner* 2.746-52, no.1 (pl.177), Petzl has also published an inscription (Lydia, n.d.; cf. *SEG* 899) for a certain Glykon, whom a number of people and groups have collaborated in honouring with crowns: the members of an association (ὁ ἱερὸς δοῦμος, 5), members of his family (7-15), a priestly colleague (15-17), a friend (17-19), two brothers who share with Glykon membership of an association (τὸν συνβ[ι]|ωτήν, 21-22), a relative called Trophimos (22-24), and two *threptoi*, Grapte and Trophimos (24-26). In passing, note the participle συνπαθῶν (or gen. pl. συνπαθῶν, from συμπαθής?) in the fragmentary *l.*2 of this inscription. It is unclear whether it indicates an expression of sympathy for the relatives, or whether the dedicatee is being praised for his attitude to his city. If the form is to be understood as being from συμπαθής, it is a further example to add to a revised MM entry; cf. *New Docs 1977*, **18,** p.60. For other epigraphical examples of the συμπαθ- word-group see L. Robert, *AC* 37 (1968) 411-12. Another Trophimos, ὁ θρέψας, is involved in setting up an epitaph (N.E. Lydia, 182/3) for a certain Aphrodisia in conjunction with her husband, Ammianos (E.P. Gibson, *ZPE* 31 [1978] 238-39, no.1 [pl.12]; cf. *SEG* 934). *New Docs 1977*, **103,** p.176 mentioned an epitaph (*SEG* 27 [1977] 1238) for a certain Trophimos (Bithynia or Pontus) which *may* be crypto-Christian. From Bithynia note *TAM* 16.14 (Aurelios Trophimos; text dated to 124/5), 307 (Trophimos; n.d.). We may add the following papyri: *P.Oxy.* 14 (1920) 1648.16 (late II); *P.Gen.* 1 (1906, repr. 1967) 41.1 (Fayum, 222/3); *SB* 1 (1915, repr. 1974) 2232 (Alexandria, n.d.).

Are any Jewish occurrences of the name known? *CPJ* records none, while it is found twice at Rome in *CIJ*: 1.169, regarded as Jewish solely on the basis of the formula ἐν εἰρήνῃ ἡ κοίμησις αὐτῆς (*ll.*7-9); while 1.10* is regarded as Jewish no longer, because of the presence of *D(is) M(anibus)* — yet see *New Docs 1976*, **76** for some Jewish and Christian texts where this abbreviation occurs — and 'l'allure toute classique des noms' (*CIJ*, ad loc.; the name here is M. Junius Trophimus; Solin, 1.993, dates this text to II).

Even if we admit both these texts as Jewish — possibly neither is if the formula in 1.169 is not as exclusively Jewish as is sometimes thought (see below) — it remains clear that the name Trophimos was used almost solely by non-Jews of (past or present) servile status. Granted the few occurrences from Egypt in contrast to the ready attestation from Asia Minor, a good proportion of the numerous Trophimi mentioned at Rome may originally have been slaves from Asia. With this the sparse information in Acts about Paul's companion accords very comfortably.

Returning to the formula found in *CIJ* 1.169 (mentioned above), we may compare *IGA* 5.189 (necropolis of Antinoopolis, n.d.), an epitaph for Maria daughter of Phamsothis: ἐν εἰρήνῃ | ἡ κοίμη|σίς σου (5-7). *IGA* 5 comprises Christian texts only, and though nothing indicates this text to be Christian *per se*, it would be natural to take it as such since the great majority of other inscriptions in this necropolis (*IGA* 5.167-212) are demonstrably Christian by virtue of phraseology or symbols, such as crosses. Therefore, either there is no compelling reason to view *CIJ* 1.169 as necessarily Jewish, or *IGA* 5.189 may be a Jewish epitaph included in the necropolis. More distinctively Christian is the related formula μνήθητι κ(ύρι)ε τῆς | κοιμήσεως τῆς δού|λης σου, κτλ (*IGA* 5.16); for other examples of this or very similar phraseology note 5.15, 22, 28, 48, 51, 609, 610 — these last two have ἡ ἡμέρα τῆς κ|οιμήσεως τοῦ μακαρίου ἀδελφοῦ ἡμῶν, κτλ. The overlapping usage of κοίμησις, of sleep and the sleep of death, is clearly illustrated by the NT *hapax* at Jn. 11.13. The temptation to see this as a distinctive Jewish usage which passed across into Christian terminology should be resisted: not only does LSJ, s.v., include an example from a curse tablet, but their examples of the verb, s.v. II.3, show how thoroughly Greek is the idea.

One way in which the 'sleep of death' phraseology was given a distinctively Christian stamp was in the formula κοιμάομαι ἐν κυρίῳ/ἐν Χριστῷ: the starting point is provided by Paul at 1 Cor. 15.18, οἱ κοιμηθέντες ἐν Χριστῷ; cf. 1 Thes. 4.14, ὁ θεὸς τοὺς κοιμηθέντας διὰ τοῦ Ἰησοῦ ἄξει σὺν αὐτῷ. Examples of this formula on epitaphs from Egypt (the earliest date V/VI) include: *IGA* 5.2-12, 14, 121, 123, 124, 528, 541. An interesting variation is provided by *IGA* 5.577 (Assuan, n.d.), an epitaph for ἡ ἅγι|α Σούσαννα παρ|θένος (2-4) who ἐκοιμήθη | ἐν ὀνόματι κ(υρίο)υ | καὶ τὸ θέλομα | αὐτõ (i.e., κατὰ τὸ θέλημα αὐτοῦ, 8-10). The verb alone occurs in epitaphs, without the rest of the formula, and is a sufficient indicator of a Christian milieu for such tombstones. Examples abound in *IGA* 5, but it is by no means confined to Egypt: note from this year's culling *NIP* IV.49 (vicinity of Eumeneia in Phrygia, 350; cf. *SEG* 1129), in which a certain Tryphon ἐκοιμήθη (2). In passing, we may record Drew-Bear's observation that the stele on which this inscription was written is carved in the shape of a door (cf. pl.36), 'type de monument funéraire dont l'origine était liée à des croyances paiennes: sans doute s'agit-il, d'un remploi, à cette époque tardive, avec martelage de l'inscription précédente' (*NIP*, p.110; cf. his discussion of the term θύρα, pp.59-62).

81. Tryphaina

MM provide several papyrus attestations for this name, found in the NT only at Rom. 16.12. Solin, *GPR* 2.783-84, provides over 60 examples from Rome alone, not one of whom is indubitably of free status. While these occurrences range in date from Augustus-IV[1], the bulk is concentrated in IAD. To these we may add from elsewhere *CMRDM* 1.71 (Tarsi(?) in Lydia, 93/4), which mentions Tryphaina ἡ θρεπτή. From Egypt, and of earlier date, we may note from the year's culling *IGA* 3.177, τὸ προσκύνημα Τρυφαίνης· τὸ προσκύνημα; and 3.538, consisting of the name alone. Both these graffiti were written on the Memnonion at Abydos, and may be Ptolemaic in date. *IGA* 2.40b (probably Naukratis, 58BC) is a brief honorific decree for Tryphaina τὴν τρόφον of Ptolemy XIII. W. Peek, *Fest. Dörner* 2.697-99, no.6 (cf. *SEG* 954), has republished a metrical inscription (Kyzikos, 37/8) in which a certain Tryphaina dedicates a statue to Poseidon.

C. BIBLICAL AND RELATED CITATIONS

82. The Greek OT — new fragments

Following on from *New Docs 1977*, **87**, which reported K. Treu's publications of several OT Greek fragments, some further items published by others are reviewed here briefly. Editorial criteria and abbreviations applying to last year's catalogue (see the first paragraph) are followed here.

1. Ps. 5.12; 6.9-10 (provenance unknown, mid-VI); fragment of a papyrus codex leaf (11.5B × 6.5H cm.), with text written in stichic form as is usual for OT metrical books (cf. *New Docs 1977*, **87**, p.116 no.11). Edd. calculate that the full page originally was c.21B × 35H cm., with room for c.34 lines. No variants of particular interest; *nomina sacra* are unexceptional (κ̅ς̅ at *verso ll.*1, 3, and to be restored at *l.*4).
   P.*Vindob.* G.36022; *ed.pr.* — T. Luzzatto/A. Roselli, *Athenaeum* 52 (1974) 13-15 (pl.4c), repr. *P.Carlini lett.* 19, pp.145-48 (pl.8); van Haelst 98; Aland AT46; Rahlfs 2152; cf. K. Treu, *APF* 26 (1978) 152; id., *APF* 27 (1980) 251.

2. Ode 4 (Hab. 3).8-10 (provenance unknown, VII); papyrus fragment (13B × 6.7H cm.) written on *recto* only, therefore not from a codex. Probably a private copy for personal use — an amulet? The text is to be thought of as belonging to the Ode, not to Hab. (so Treu, *contra ed. pr.*). From the text surviving on this fragment the original breadth must have been about twice what now exists, as is clear from a comparison between the papyrus and Rahlfs' text:

```
   πο.[            ].....[           3.8
    ἦ ἐν θαλάσης τὸ ὅρμημά σ.[
   ὅτι ἔπιβήσῃ ἐπὶ τοὺς ἵππ[
   ἐντύνων ἐντενῆς τὸ δο.[            9
 5 ποταμῶν ῥακήσεται κῆ ο[           10
   σκορπίσον[...]δα πορ...[
       ].. [
```

Note the gen./dat. confusion in *l.*2, and confusion of δ/τ (*ll.*4,6), κ/γ (*l.*5), σ/ζ (*l.*6). P.*Vindob.* G.36114; *ed.pr.* — A. Carlini, *P.Carlini lett.* 20, pp.149-53 (pl.9); a virtually identical discussion was published contemporaneously by id. in *Studi in onore di A. Ardizzoni*, edd. E. Livrea/G.A. Privitera (*Filologia e Critica* 25; Rome, 1978) I. 157-64 (pl.); cf. K. Treu, *APF* 27 (1980) 252.

3. Job 9.2, 12-13 (Aphroditopolis, III); a tiny fragment with three complete words of 9.2 on *verso*, two complete words of 9.12-13 on *recto*.
Included with *P.Chester Beatty V* (Pap. 962), though not part of that codex; ed. pr. — A. Pietersma, *P.Chester Beatty IV/V*, p.175 (pls. 4.3 and 3.2, respectively).

4. Is. 48.6-8; 48.11-14, 17-18 (provenance unknown, late III/early IV); two fragments (the larger, B, is 8B × 23H cm., and preserves parts of two columns) of a papyrus roll, blank on *verso*. *Ed.pr.* suggests that the use of a roll rather than a codex in this period may suggest an origin 'in ambiente giudaico'. Yet, as K. Treu has pointed out, *Kairos* 15 (1973) 138-44 (esp. 140-41), over-simplistic distinctions have led to some misleading conclusions about Jewish use of the Greek Bible in the early Christian centuries: it is simply not the case that all LXX mss of the Christian era must be Christian. Nor is it true that Jews used only rolls, and that any codex of the Greek OT must therefore be Christian. Finally, while there is no doubt that Christians used *nomina sacra* pervasively, it was not their monopoly; and there are undoubted Jewish uses attested for *kyrios* and *theos*. (The Is. fragment under discussion here has κϲ̅ at frag. B., col. 2, *l.*15, while *ed.pr.* restores θϲ̅ for reasons of space in the next line, both of which form part of Is. 48.17.) In this excursus to a longer article on the importance of Greek for Jews under the Empire, Treu proceeds to list Greek OT mss (both rolls and codices) which contain Jewish elements. *P.Alex.* inv. 203; *ed.pr.* — A. Carlini, *ASNP* 2 (1972) 489-94 (pl.33), repr. *P.Carlini lett.* 14, pp.119-24 (pl.6); van Haelst 300; Aland AT135; Turner OT198A; Rahlfs 850; cf. K. Treu, *APF* 24/25 (1976) 253-54, who follows C.H. Roberts' dating (*per litt.* to Carlini) of early IV, excluding late III; id., *APF* 27 (1980) 252.

5. Jer. 5.29-6.4; 6.5-10 (provenance unknown, IV); five fragments (largest is B, 7.5B × 5.2H cm.) of a papyrus codex leaf with pagination surviving (23/24), which suggests that the codex may have begun with Jer. The last surviving line of the *recto* (*l.*24) breaks off with the first word of 6.4, παρασκευ|[άσ]ασ[θε, while the first surviving word on *verso l.*1, θε]μέλια (6.5) occurs in mid-line. On this basis it can be calculated that c.7 lines have been lost from the bottom of the page which would have carried the rest of the wording of 6.4-5; i.e., originally c.31 lines for the complete page. See *New Docs 1977*, **91**, pp.130-31, no.5 for discussion of NT codices with so many lines to the page. Some lines end short: thus, *recto l.*10 for Jer. 6.1 begins the next line; *verso l.*19, with 6.10 beginning the new line. *Nomina sacra* consistently suspended. Textually problematic is *recto ll.*19-20 (Jer. 6.3), for the lacuna from ἥ|ξ[ο]υσιν[to ἐπ' αὐτὴν (*l.*21) only has λη surviving (in *l.*20); if these letters (at the bottom of frag. D) have been read correctly they appear to reflect a text different from LXX ἥξουσιν ποιμένες καὶ τὰ ποίμνια αὐτῶν καὶ πήξουσιν ἐπ' αὐτήν . . . Furthermore, comparison between the relative space needed for other verses in this papyrus and in Rahlfs' text suggests that the largely lacunose *ll.*19-20 could have accommodated a little more than the words just quoted.
P.Gen inv. 252; *ed.pr.* — A. Carlini, *Athenaeum* 52 (1974) 6-12 (pl.1), repr. *P.Carlini lett.* 4, pp.57-64 (pl.3); van Haelst 305; Aland AT140; Rahlfs 851; cf. K. Treu, *APF* 26 (1978) 153; id., *APF* 27 (1980) 252.

6. Dan. 3.51-52 (provenance unknown, V-VI (*ed.pr.*); III-IV (E.G. Turner, *per litt.* to Carlini)); small parchment fragment (4.2B × 3.8H cm.) of parts of 7 lines written on one side only; possibly from a roll. The 'Song of the three children' occurs also in the OT as Ode 8, but given the presence in this fragment of the words introductory to the verse section this extract is to be thought of as from Dan. rather than the Ode.

]. [καὶ εὐλό-   3.51
γουν τὸ[ν θ̅ν̅ ἐν τῆι καμίνωι λέγον-
τες εὐλογη[τὸς εἶ, κ̅ε̅ ὁ θ̅ς̅ τῶν πατέρων   52
ἡμῶν, καὶ ὑπε[. . . . . . . καὶ ὑπερ-
5 υψώμενος εἰς [τοὺς αἰῶνας, καὶ εὐλο-
γημένον τὸ ὄν[ομα τῆς δόξης σου τὸ
ἅγιον καὶ ὑπεραι[νετὸν καὶ ὑπερυψου-
μ]ένον εἰς πάντ[ας τοὺς αἰῶνας
].. . [

Ed. pr. and Carlini (who re-edits the fragment) link it textually with the version of Theodotion (?), due to the presence in *ll.*1-2 of [---εὐλό]|γουν τὸ[ν θ̅ν̅, which allows no room for LXX ἐξύψουν. But this falls a little short of certainty, especially as the LXX version is very similar at this point. The *gamma* at the beginning of *l.*2 is subject to some doubt (Carlini's pl. is not very clear), and the next three letters would equally form part of ἐξύψουν as εὐλόγουν. Even apart from this, word-order varies occasionally in textual witnesses, and given the number of similar letters in these two verbs that possibility cannot be ruled out. That his piece reflects the Theodotionic text is, perhaps, 'not proven'. On the Köln pap. 967 portion of LXX ch.3-4 see W. Hamm's edition (Bonn, 1977), discussed briefly at *New Docs 1977*, **89**. Note the presence in *l.*8 of πάντ[ας, which accords with a few other witnesses; while Carlini suggests that the gap in *l.*4 is to be restored as ὑπε[ρύμνητος or ὑπε[ραίνετος.

Cod.Mon.Gr. 610.7; *ed.pr.* — W. Baars, *Textus* 6 (1968) 132-33 (pl.); re-ed. — A. Carlini, *SCO* 22 (1973) 24-26 (pl.2), repr. *P.Carlini lett.* 38, pp.283-87, pl.14; van Haelst 321; cf. K. Treu, *APF* 22/23 (1970) 370; id., *APF* 26 (1978) 154.

83. MSS of Psalms and Genesis in the Greek OT

P. Chester Beatty XIII/XIV comprises not newly discovered texts, but ones which have lain unedited in the Chester Beatty collection for some years and are edited by A. Pietersma for the first time. They are: (a) *P. Chester Beatty* XIII (numbered 2149 by the Septuaginta-Unternehmen), four bifolios of a papyrus codex, comprising Ps. 72.6-76.1, 77.1-88.2, with some short lacunae and one larger one (Ps. 76.2-77.1); (b) *P. Chester Beatty* XIV (= 2150), a single folio, unrelated to the preceding and much briefer and more fragmentary, containing Ps. 31.8-11; 26.1-6, 8-14; 2.1-8 (in that order), possibly part of an amulet. Both are of unknown provenance, and both are dated (by E.G. Turner) to IVAD.

Pap. 2150 is too short and fragmentary for much to be done in the way of textual analysis, and 'cannot be assigned to any textual family' (Pietersma, 38). Pap. 2149 is of much greater significance, being 'the fourth largest Psalter papyrus discovered to date' (5-6). It presents a large number of variant readings (107 unique), many of which are discussed in detail by Pietersma. Careful attention is given to the question of Hebraizing corrections (i.e., alterations bringing the Greek text into closer conformity with MT), but Pietersma finds only one clear-cut instance of this. The textual affinities of the MS are set out in full, the conclusion being reached that '2149 does not align itself with any particular text group' (66). Taking into account the new evidence of 2149, Pietersma argues for revisions to the text of Rahlfs' *Psalmi cum Odis* in some 13 instances.

With one exception *nomina sacra* are abbreviated throughout Pap. 2149, including a rare instance of the complete abbreviation of θεῶν as θ̄ν̄ (cf. **102**). Stichometric divisions are indicated throughout by the use of spaces, and there are numerous deviations from Rahlfs. The orthography of the MS provides an interesting glimpse of the practice of some scribes in the fourth century: deviations from 'correct' spelling, reflecting phonetic developments in the language, are abundant, just as in uneducated documents of the period. In short the orthography is, as Pietersma says, 'poor'. Not only this; it exhibits the same bilingual interference phenomena as are found in many Egyptian documents (see Pietersma, 3; cf. especially Gignac, I, *passim*). This indicates not so much that the scribe was a non-native speaker of Greek (Pietersma, 3 n.1) as that he reflects the pronunciation of Greek in Egypt as it had come to be as a result of influence from Egyptian (cf. Gignac, I.47).

In *P. Chester Beatty IV/V* Pietersma re-edits two important papyri of Genesis, a task made necessary by the discovery of errors in Kenyon's *ed.pr.* of 1934. They are: (a) Pap. 961, dated IVAD, containing Gen. 9-44, with numerous lacunae; (b) Pap. 962, dated IIIAD, containing Gen. 8.13-17, 21-9.2; 24.13-25.21; 30.20-35.16 with lacunae; 39.3-46.33 with lacunae.

Pietersma provides a full analysis of the readings of the MSS, comparing them with the text established by Rahlfs. In a substantial number of cases Pietersma finds grounds for revision of Rahlfs' text. The question of correction in the direction of the Hebrew text is also examined, and such influence is found to be minimal.

The contribution of these two papyri to the restoration of the Old Greek is described by Pietersma as 'invaluable' (174). 'Even though (virtually) uniquely preserved original readings are rare in Pap. 961 and 962, there are many instances in which the papyri furnish support for otherwise poorly supported readings of G' (ibid.). As to their textual affinities Pietersma finds that they contain a 'mixed' text, and neither can be regarded as a member of one or other medieval textual family. They are more closely related to each other than to any other MS among our most ancient textual witnesses. Of the two, Pap. 961 'contains, *generally* speaking, the better text' (173-74).

Pietersma brings to light (149ff.) an interesting feature of the translation technique of LXX Gen. In the use of plural or singular verb with a neuter plural subject, it seems that the choice was determined by the number of the verb in the Hebrew: if the Hebrew verb is singular the translator uses a singular verb in the Greek (e.g., 47.24 τὰ μέρη ἔσται MT *yhyh*), but if it is plural he uses a plural (e.g., 29.20 ἔτη ἑπτὰ ... καὶ ἦσαν MT *wyhyw*).

(J.A.L. LEE)

84. Miscellaneous OT quotations

As may be expected most items noted here are from Psalms, and from Christian funerary contexts. *IGA* 5.283 (Akhmim, n.d.) is a stele in the shape of a mummy label which includes a cross and a quotation of part of Ps. 24.5-7 (half *v.*6 is omitted). Ps. 50.3 is quoted in a long epitaph for Theodike, *IGA* 5.663.7-13 (Nubia, n.d.). *IGA* 5.33c is one of the texts in a Christian funerary chapel found at Karmouz (III or IV) which quotes Ps. 90.13 above a picture of Jesus treading upon serpents. It is possible that *IGA* 5.660 includes an innovative allusion to Ps. 83.11 (ἐξελεξάμην παραρριπτεῖσθαι ἐν τῷ οἴκῳ τοῦ θεοῦ μᾶλλον ἢ οἰκεῖν ἐν σκηνώμασιν ἁμαρτωλῶν); for in this epitaph for Elizabeth (Nubia, n.d.) God is requested to grant her repose in the bosom of Abraham, Isaac, and Jacob, ἐν σκηναῖς τῶν δικαίων. Finally, we may note *IGA* 5.783 (provenance unknown, n.d.), B (= ?) μόνος θη|ὸς ἐν οὐρ|ανῷ, but the allusion to 2 Paralip. 20.6 suggested by Lefebvre seems tenuous.

85. The 'prodigal son' parable, spiritualized

Provenance unknown

VI fin.

ed.pr. — R. Cingottini, *SCO* 22 (1973) 27-29 (pl.2)

> μου ἐσκορπισμένα, (καὶ) λιμῷ
> ἀπόλυμε τὸν θίον καρισ-
> μάτον· τί [. . .] ποιῆσαι ἵνα
> 4 σωθῶ ὁ ἁμαρτολός; πορεύο-
> με{ν} πρὸς τὸν πατέρα τὸν
> οἰκτηρμὸν (καὶ) βόα πρὸς αὐτὸν,
> δέξε με σωτὴρ μετανοοῦν-
> 8 τα (καὶ) ἐλέησόν με (καὶ) σῶσομε.

Bottom section of a papyrus leaf, written on *recto* only (9.7B × 11H cm.); the number of lines missing above is indeterminable. Vertical folds still visible. *P.Vindob.* G. 25683.

Bib. — A. Carlini (reporting views of K. Treu), *Athenaeum* 52 (1974) 5; van Haelst 1019; K. Treu, *APF* 26 (1978) 156; *ed.pr.* repr. with some alterations in **P.Carlini lett.* 18, pp.141-43 (pl.8).

. . . The things squandered (by) me, and I am dying with hunger for (your) divine
5 favours . . . What [ought] I the sinner do to be saved? I | go to the father of mercies
and cry to him, 'Receive me, saviour, for I repent, and have pity on me and save me'.

The folds in this papyrus suggest that this prayer of repentance — originally from a liturgical context, perhaps? — has been copied or transferred into private use an an amulet. The wide spacing between the lines of text, and even between the letters may lend weight to the suggestion that it may have been used for public recitation in church, and subsequently passed into the keeping of an individual who kept it about his person for reasons of piety, its apotropaic potency, as a reminder of some past sin forgiven, or a mixture of all three.

The passage is a mélange of NT phraseology, though the main source is the 'prodigal son' story in Lk. 15. For σκορπίζω in the first line cf. Lk. 15.13. The literal wording of the NT parable has been spiritualized in some places: thus at *ll.*1-2 λιμῷ . . . ἀπόλλυμαι of Lk. 15.17 is made metaphorical in its connection with τῶν θείων χαρισμάτων. Treu, reported by Carlini, makes this point and draws attention to similarly figurative usages of λιμώσσω noted in Lampe, s.v., e.g., Eus., *Comm. in Is.* 5.13; 65.11-12 (Migne, *PG* 24.120a, 512b). *Ll.*4-6 also spiritualize Lk.15.18, πορεύσομαι πρὸς τὸν πατέρα μου, but in addition conflates the Lukan

wording with the Pauline phrase at 2 Cor. 1.3, ὁ πατὴρ τῶν οἰκτιρμῶν. The active form
πορεύω is perhaps unexpected (only middle in NT), and *ed.pr.* suggests that it may be an error
for πορεύομε{ν} = πορεύομαι. The next verb, βόα, can only be imperative, and even though
the grammar does not follow easily the thrust of the passage is quite clear. The use of βόα
here as an equivalent of ἐρῶ in the Lukan parable (15.18) reflects a conscious use of language
with a biblical flavour, since βοάω was already obsolescent in NT times, being replaced by
κράζω. For the 'weak' meaning of βοάω one might compare the use of ἐβόησεν λέγων at Lk.
9.38 and 18.38. MM, s.v., needs complete rewriting to take account of a wider range of usage
than they briefly cite. In view of the jerky grammar in *ll.*4-6 K.L. McKay suggests to me an
alternative text: πορεύο|μεν⟨ος⟩ πρὸς τὸν πατέρα τὸν | οἰκτιρμῶν βόα, κτλ. The καί inserted
editorially in *l.*6 is rendered unnecessary if a participle had preceded.

The cry of the Philippian jailer (Acts 16.30) is clearly in view at *ll.*3-4. How are we to
understand σοσομε at the end of the text, as σώσομαι or σῶσό(ν) με? The latter seems
preferable, following the two previous imperatives; but Treu (reported by Carlini) notes that
the former would express 'the confidence of the sinner' (the passive σωθήσομαι would, but
how could the middle σώσομαι do this? — J.A.L. Lee).

86. Scribal carelessness in 𝔓³⁶ (Jn. 3.14-18, 31-35)?

Oxyrhynchos   after 400
ed.pr. — E. Pistelli, *PSI* 1 (1912) 3, pp.5-6

A *recto*

λε

καὶ καθὼς [Μωυσῆς ὕψωσεν   3.14
τὸν ὄφιν [ἐν τῆι ἐρήμωι, οὕτως
ὑψωθῆναι [δεῖ τὸν υἱὸν τοῦ ανου,
ἵνα πᾶς ὁ [πιστεύων ἐν αὐτῶι   15
5 ἔχῃ ζωὴν [αἰώνιον. οὕτως γὰρ   16
ἠγάπησ[εν ὁ θς τὸν κόσμον, ὥστε τὸν υἱὸν [τὸν μονογενῆ
ἔδωκεν, [ἵνα πᾶς ὁ πιστεύων ἐν
αὐτῷ μὴ [ἀπόληται ἀλλ' ἔχῃ
10 ζωὴν α[ἰώνιον. οὐ γὰρ   17

A *verso*

ἀπέστειλε]ν ὁ θς τὸν   3.17
υἱὸν εἰς τὸν κόσ]μον ἵνα
κρίνηι τὸν κόσμον ἀλ]λ' ἵνα
σωθῆι ὁ κόσμος δι' αὐτο]ῦ. ὁ πιστεύ- 18
5 ων εἰς αὐτὸν οὐ κρί]νηται· ὁ δὲ
μὴ πιστεύων εἰς] {τὸ / ὄνομα}
ἤδη κέκριται, ὅτι μὴ πεπ]ίστευκε(ν)
8 εἰς τὸ ὄνομα τοῦ μο]νογενοῦς

B *verso*

..[ἐπάνω   3.31
πάν[των ἐστίν· ὁ ὢν ἐκ τῆς γῆς
ἐκ τῆ[ς γῆς λαλεῖ. ὁ ἐκ τοῦ ουνου
ἐρχόμ[ενος ἐπάνω πάντων
5 ἐστίν. [ὁ ἑώρακεν καὶ ἤκουσεν   32
τοῦτο μ[αρτυρεῖ
.[

B *recto*

].
τὰ ῥήματα τοῦ] θυ   3.34
λαλεῖ· οὐ γὰρ ἐκ μέτρου] δίδω-
σιν τὸ πνα. ὁ πηρ ἀγαπᾷ τὸ(ν)   35
5 υἱὸν καὶ πάντα δέδ]ωκεν
]..

Two papyrus fragments (8.5B × 6.8H; 5B × 5H cm.) from separate, non-consecutive leaves of the same single-column codex containing parts of ten and eight lines respectively.

Bib. — *re-ed.*, A. Carlini, *APF* 22/23 (1974) 219-22 (fig.13); id., **P.Carlini lett.* 28, pp.193-99 (pl.12); K. Treu, *APF* 26 (1978) 154; Aland NT36, van Haelst 437 (both contain further bibliography); Turner NT36

The preservation of the page number 34 at the top of frag. A *recto* allows several conclusions to be drawn about this codex. Since the bottom margin of that *recto* is preserved, working with an average of ten lines per page, the previous 34 pages would be room enough for Jn 1.1-3.13. On this basis the entire gospel in this codex would have needed c.360pp. (180 leaves, 90 sheets). The verses preserved on frag. B show that two leaves have been lost between A and B, and that therefore the two sides of B would have been paginated 41/42. Yet the format of this codex, broader than high, is unparalleled for the dimensions suggested by *ed.pr.* and Carlini (c.14B × 9/10H cm.): see Turner, 147 n.134.

The date originally suggested by *ed.pr.* (VI (?)) has generally been thought too late: Carlini suggests V (?), while post 400 is the view of C.H. Roberts/T.C. Skeat, (noted by Carlini, 195-96 n.4). Aland (p.258) reports opinions about the date ranging from V-VII.

Carlini's re-edition of this piece has resulted not only in the reading of several letters from Jn. 3.34-35, on frag. B *recto;* he has been able to read an extra line on B *verso* and so has suggested some significant differences to the word arrangement posited by Pistelli for that page. There is little to be gained by providing a comparative table here. The cancellation of the words at the end of A *verso l.*6 calls for brief comment, however. Pistelli read εἰς τὸ] ὄνομα, but Carlini has noticed that τό is written in small superior letters above ὄνομα; these two words (and presumably εἰς) were crossed out with two horizontal strokes. Carlini suggests that the same scribe who wrote the text did this, and that the error is easily accounted for by the presence, later in the verse, of the same phrase following a form of the verb πιστεύω. This reconstruction appears to leave out one step: the addition of the article τό in a superior position implies a realization by the copyist that he had made an error of omission. After including this word he then realized that in fact the whole phrase was wrongly included, and it was then scored out. Double errors of this kind in the mechanical copying out of texts ought not to occasion surprise; but it does confront us with the question whether Christian scriptoria were as meticulous as Jewish scribes in their attitude to copying sacred text.

Now, C.H. Roberts has pointed out (*Manuscript, Society and Belief in Early Christian Egypt* [London, 1979] 21-22) that the addition of marginal notes, reading aids (accents, breathings, punctuation), and corrections in some Christian texts indicates a 'scrupulous reproduction of the text [which] may be a legacy from Judaism'. This may well hold good in general, but examples like that in 𝔓[36] should alert us to the fact that the standard of care devoted to copying texts will not be consistently high between all scriptoria and all copyists. And further, it is at least conceivable that by V Christian scribes may be thinking of 'Jewish meticulousness' merely as a catchword to embody a standard of excellence to be aimed for in theory, though disregarded or held unattainable in practice. Nevertheless, the very recognition and rectification of the mistake provides minor testimony to the gradual trend from IV onwards to establish a uniform and controlled text, in contrast to the period c.150-300 when most NT textual variants arose (cf. J. R. Royse, *Scribal Habits in Early Greek New Testament Papyri* [Diss., Graduate Theological Union, 1981] 21-24).

87. Miscellaneous NT quotations

A small number of items not incorporated elsewhere in this volume is listed summarily here. *IGA* 5.773 (provenance unknown, IV (?)) records μὴ μοιχεύσῃς engraved on an iron spoon, though why this citation of Mt. 19.18 (= Mk. 10.19) should have been put on such an object is hard to imagine. Need it be a certain allusion to the gospel saying? There is no external reason to consider a link with Christianity otherwise.

Mt. 25.34 is quoted in an epitaph for Thekla, *IGA* 5.107.8–13 (Fayum (?), n.d.), though there are some orthographical eccentricities (e.g., ἐδυμασμέ|νην at *ll.*10–11 for ἡτοιμασμένην).

C. Mango/I. Ševčenko, *DOP* 32 (1978) 15–17 no.20 (pl.; cf. *SEG* 574) have published a fragmentary Christian magical inscription (Byzantium, VI), which contains references to angels (Michael — largely restored — Gabriel, Ouriel), to James Ζαβαι[--- (son of Zebedee?), as well as an allusion to the logion at Mt. 26.39 :]οὐ μὴ παρελε[ύ]σ[ε]τ[αι] τὸ ποτήριον το[ῦτο---].

A Christian funerary chapel from Alexandria (III or IV) has several inscriptions in different locations: 1 Cor. 1.30 appears to be alluded to in one of them, *IGA* 5.33b, the second line of which reads σοφία ῑ̅ς̅ χ̅ς̅. Elsewhere in the same complex (no.33g) John the Baptist is depicted carrying an opened roll on which the wording of Mt. 3.3 (= Mk. 1.3) can be made out.

A brief Latin epitaph for three women buried in a common grave, *AE* 868 (Belalis Maior in Africa proconsularis, n.d.), concludes with the words *pax fidis* (sic) *karitas*, which is taken to be a reminiscence of Eph. 6.23. *AE* notes (*ed.pr. — non vidi*) that these virtues appear to be related to the three deceased. While it is not impossible that Eph. 6.23 is in mind, the triad may be more simply a list of virtues. For a certain instance of the latter note *IGA* 5.613 (Taphis in Egypt, n.d.): πίστις, | ἐλπίς, | ἀγάπη, | δικαιοσύνη, | ἐνήνη (i.e., εἰρήνη), | ἀλήθεα, | μακροθυμείλ (i.e., -εία), | [ἐγκρά]τεια | [--]κραα[--] (= πραότης?). The first three in the list will make us think of 1 Cor. 13.13; several of the group occur in the NT virtues list at Gal. 5.22–23; cf. Col. 3.12; 2 Tim. 3.10.

At *New Docs 1976*, **59** several examples of the light/life formula were given from the 1976 culling. The claim made there in the second sentence that it occurs only on epitaphs and is unattested before VI is wrong on both counts. W. Brashear has drawn to my attention (*per litt.*) *IGA* 5.762 (Luxor, V/VI), 770 (Fayum, n.d.), both bronze crosses with the monogram, and one at least possibly pre-VI. A variant of the φῶς/ζωή monogram is possibly to be detected at *IGA* 5.772 (Medinet el-Fayum, VI/VII):

ɑ̅
F † C
ω

This inscription on a buckle should be taken as φῶς, A/ω, and a central cross, all formed into the shape of a cross. In this connection mention may also be made here of N. Asgari/N. Fıratlı, *Fest.Dörner* 1.80–81, no.SR19 (pl.23), a sarcophagus with the following inscription between the arms of a very ornate cross (Kalchedon, VI; cf. *SEG* 1014):

	φ(ῶς)	Χ(ριστοῦ)
	φ(αίνει)	π(ᾶσιν).
†	ἐνθάδε	ὧ μοναχὼ[ς]
	κεῖτε	Ἀντώνιος
	ὧ ἁμαρ	τωλῶς.

For Christ as Light cf. Jn. 8.12; for the active use of φαίνω + dative in the NT cf. Rev. 21.23 (of the sun and moon not being needed to 'shine upon' the heavenly city). This text has now been reprinted as R. Merkelbach, *Die Inschriften von Kalchedon* (*Inschr. gr. Städte von Kleinasien* 20; Bonn, 1980) 80.

88. The Lord's Prayer in a necropolis

el-Bagawat
ed. — G. Lefebvre, *IGA* 5.357

n.d.

```
      ✝ εἷς θεὸς λόγος
      [ἐ]ν ὀνόματι τῆς [ἁ-]
      [γί]ας μ[ ]να δριάς  πρω
          ]ἁγίου πνεύματος θεοῦ ἀλήθια
    5 μὴ εἰσνγγας ἡμᾶς εἰς π.ασμον
      β̄ δαμ[      ]ς κακοῦ κυφυλαι
              ] μου
```

One of several inscriptions on the wall of a funerary chapel. Read τριάς (3); πρός (3) for πρω, perhaps; εἰσενέγκῃς (5); πειρασμόν (5); *l.*6 could perhaps be restored as ἀλλὰ [ῥῦσαι ἡμᾶ]ς (so Lefebvre).

> **(cross) (There is) one God, the Logos. In the name of the holy, (one and) only (?)**
> **5 Trinity, Father (?) . . . Holy Spirit of God, truth. | Do not bring us into testing . . . evil**
> **. . .**

Explicit mention of the Trinity here rules out the possibility that the reminiscence from the Lord's Prayer (Mt. 6.13) reflects direct acquaintance with the Bible; we are to infer a liturgical background. Quite what is the significance of the quotation within a context also mentioning the Trinity is unclear, unless πειρασμός is intended here as an allusion to post-mortem judgement. Whether any doctrinal polemic is implied in this necropolis inscription is uncertain: one might feel more confident about this if μ[ ]να were not in doubt. This text is by no means unique in posing us the question whether the Bible or the liturgy is the source of its phraseology. The 'bosom of Abraham' formula discussed at **89** is relevant to this issue, as also is *IGA* 5.749, a lamp (provenance unknown, n.d.) with the following wording on it: υ̅ς̅ θ̅υ̅ ἐλέ[η]σον ἡμᾶς. Lefebvre sees this as a reminiscence of Mt. 9.27 (= Mk. 10.48 = Lk. 18.38), but the NT passages have 'son of David' and the change to 'son of God' reflects a doctrinal development consonant with a liturgical context.

The Lord's Prayer written on papyrus and related materials is found most frequently in a magical context, such as an amulet. A list of these is provided below, with the two most recent items reproduced.

1. *P.Ant.* 2 (1960) 54 (Antinoopolis, III), Mt. 6.10-11 (*recto*), 11-12 (*verso*); fragment of a miniature codex, probably used as an amulet. Aland, Var.29 (p.353); Turner, p.150 (no number); van Haelst 347.

2. *P.Oxy.* 3 (1903) 407 (III/IV), including Mt. 6.13 in a prayer; amulet, possibly. Van Haelst, 952.

3. *PGM* 2 (1931/1941, repr. 1974) 04 (= *O. Athens* inv. 12227; Megara, IV), Mt. 6.11-13 on an ostrakon; van Haelst 348.

4. *P.Princ.* 2 (1936) 107 (provenance unknown, IV/V), nearly incoherent resume of the Lord's Prayer at *ll.*13-15 in a gnostic amulet against fever; van Haelst 967. Text also quotes Ps. 90.1-2 (*ll.*10-13), and alludes to Is. 6.3 (*ll.*15-16). *Ll.*13-15 read: πατὴρ ὑμῶν ἐν τῆς | οὐρανῆς, ἁγίασθήτω τὼ θέλημά σου, τὼ|ν ἄρτον ὑμῶν τὼν ἐπιούσιων.

5. *P.Oslo* inv.1644 (*ed.pr.* — L. Amundsen, *SO* 24 [1945] 141-47; Oxyrhynchos, IV fin.), Mt. 6.9-13, 2 Cor. 13.13, and Ps. 90.1-4 on *recto* (*verso* blank) of what is probably an amulet; Aland, Var.27 (p.351); van Haelst 345.

6. *PSI* 6 (1920) 719 (Oxyrhynchos (?), IV/V; = *PGM* 2.P19), includes the beginning of the Prayer (Mt. 6.9), along with a cento of other incipits: Jn. 1.1, Mt. 1.1, Jn. 1.23 (the 'odd one out'), Mk. 1.1, Lk. 1.1, Ps. 90.1, doxology; van Haelst 423.

7. *P.Köln* 4 (1982) 171 (provenance unknown, V), Mt. 6.12-13 plus doxology plus magical repetition of sacred words; amulet, one side only written on (*recto*):

[τὰ ὀφ-]
1   [ειλή]μ[ατα ἡμῶν ὡ]ς καὶ ἡ-
    [μ]εῖς ἀφή[καμεν το]ῖς ὀφει-
    [λ]έταις ἡ[μῶν· κα]ὶ μὴ εἰσ-
    [εν]έγκῃς ἡμᾶς εἰς πει-
5   ρασμὸν, ἀλλὰ ῥῦσαι ἡμᾶς
    ἀπὸ τοῦ πονηροῦ· διὰ τοῦ μο-
    νογενοῦς ⟨σ⟩ου Ἰη(σο)ῦ Χρ(ιστο)ῦ ἀμήν.
    ἀμήν ≡ ἀμήν ≡ ἀμήν ≡
    ἅγιος ≡ ἅγιος ≡ ἅγιος

8. *P.Iand.* 1 (1912) 6 (Hermopolis Magna, V-VI; = *PGM* 2.P17), Mt. 6.9-13, with doxology; 8.1; Lk. 11.1-2; Ps. 90.13 — all on *recto* (*verso* blank), amulet; Aland, Var.30 (p.354); van Haelst 917.

9. *P.Vindob.* L.91 (Fayum, V/VI; *ed.pr.* — R. Seider, *Paläographie der lateinischen Papyri* 2.2 [Stuttgart, 1981] no.47, pl.22), parts of Mt. 6.10-12 (*vetus Latina*) with interlinear Greek transliteration (improved text of A. Martin, *Latomus* 42 [1983] 412-18, given here):

1a [---   νοστ]ρουμ
2   [ε]d [in terra. pan]em
2a κωτ[ ]θιδιανουμ ‖ δα νοβις
3   nostrum coth `θ´ -i-dianum
3a οδιε   ε δεμεττε νοβις
4   da nobis hediẹ ‖ e demette
4a   δεβιττα νοστρα
5   nobis ‖ debitta no[stra]
5a σικ . . . ε[δ---]
6   s[icu]d [---]

This text has been most usefully discussed by Martin, who places it in the context of Latin speakers in Christian Egypt who did not know Greek or Coptic. Probably an amulet rather than a school exercise (the comment at *New Docs 1977*, **91**, p.138 no.4 thus needs correction, and this item removed from that list).

10. *BGU* 3 (1903) 954 (Herakleopolis Magna, VI; = *PGM* 2.P9), Mt. 6.9-13 with doxology, plus allusions to Mt. 1.1 (?); 4.23; Jn. 1.1 (?); used as an amulet; Aland, Var.28 (p.352); van Haelst 720.

11. Paris Louvre *MND* 552B (Antinoopolis, VII; *ed.pr.* — A.Passoni dell'Acqua, *Aeg.* 60 (1980) 107-09, pls.4-5); beginning of the Lord's Prayer (Mt. 6.9) on the *recto* of a wood tablet — a school exercise (cf. *New Docs 1977*, **91**, p.138 no.3) or an amulet; van Haelst 349.

12. *P.Baden* 4 (1924) 60 (Qarara, VII/VIII), Mt. 6.9-13 with doxology; wood tablet (*verso* blank), found in a tomb (cf. the inscription with which this entry began), together with nos.61-65 (also wooden tablets), which appear to have had a magical purpose; Greek text apparently written in Coptic lettering. van Haelst 346.

13. Chicago MS 125 ined. (Egypt (?), XII-XIII), Mt. 6.9-13 together with Mk. 1.1-8; Lk. 1.1-7; Jn. 1.1-17; Nicene Creed and Ps. 68, on a parchment roll which appears to have been used for magical purposes; van Haelst 386.

89. The bosom of Abraham

Alexandria

409

ed. — G. Lefebvre, *IGA* 5.48

✠ ✠ ✠

ὁ θεὸς ὁ παντοκράτωρ
ὁ ὢν προὼν καὶ μέλλων,
Ἰησοῦς ὁ Χριστὸς ὁ υἱὸς τοῦ
θεοῦ τοῦ ζῶντος, μνήσθητι
5 τῆς κοιμήσεως καὶ ἀναπαύσεως
τῆς δούλης σου Ζωνεήνης
τῆς εὐσεβεστάτης καὶ (*leaf*)
φιλεντόλου· καὶ αὐτὴν
καταξίωσον κατασκηνῶσε
10 διὰ τοῦ ἁγίου σου καὶ φωταγωγοῦ
ἀρχανγέλου Μιχαηλ
εἰς κόλπους τῶν ἁγίων πατέρων
Ἀβρααμ Ἰσακ καὶ Ἰακωβ· ὅτι σοῦ ἐστιν
ἡ δόξα καὶ τὸ κράτος εἰς τοὺς αἰῶνας
15 τῶν αἰώνων ἀμην. ἔζησε δὲ
μακαρίως ἔτη ο̅ζ̅. ἐστιν δὲ
ἡ μνήμη αὐτῆς Φαμενωθ κ̅γ̅
μετὰ τὴν ὑπατίαν Βάσσου καὶ Φιλίππου.

God almighty, the one who is, who was and who is to come, Jesus Christ, son of the
5 **living God, remember | the sleeping and repose of your slave Zoneene, who was most**

10 **pious and loved the Law. And deem her worthy to dwell, |through the agency of your holy and light-bringing archangel Michael, in the bosoms of the holy fathers Abraham,**
15 **Isaac and Jacob. Because yours is the glory and the power to the ages |of ages, amen. She lived in blessedness 77 years and this is her tomb. Phamenoth 23rd, after the consulship of Bassos and Philip.**

The pervasive influence of liturgical forms and, behind them, of NT phraseology, in a text dated to within a century of official state acceptance of Christianity provides some indication of how quickly it became normative by late IV. Rather than comment on every relevant phrase here, a few are selected for brief notes.

Zoneene is described as a 'lover of the Law': for the word φιλέντολος see discussion at *New Docs 1976*, **74**, where a brief list of Jewish examples (and one Christian) is provided. Another possible addition would be *IGA* 5.89 (Fayum, n.d.) a Christian epitaph for Zoe τῇ | ιλεντολει (*sic*) — was the *phi* accidentally omitted by the mason? While for a Jewish user φιλέντολος and its rarer synonym φιλόνομος may be taken to refer to the Torah, quite what is alluded to in a Christian context is less clear: more generally the scriptures as a whole, perhaps? The single citation in Lampe (Palladius) is rendered 'lover of God's commandments'.

The verb κατασκηνόω is found four times in the NT, though only once of people (Acts 2.26, quoting Ps. 15.9). BAGD, s.v., note this text as *SB* 1540. To include this occurrence in a revised MM entry may not be particularly useful, since the text's pervasive use of biblical phraseology means that we are not provided with an attestation of the NT meaning which is clearly independent of the NT.

The allusion to repose with the patriarchs stems from liturgical use, a wording expanded from that in the parable of Dives and Lazarus at Lk. 16.19–31. That it derives from liturgy rather than directly from the NT is clear from a text like *IGA* 5.647, a Byzantine epitaph (Nubia, 913) in Coptic with portions of the liturgy inserted in Greek (as expected): among the latter occurs the 'bosom of Abraham' formula (*ll*.15–16). Nevertheless, the form of the borrowing is not so firmly established that variations are excluded. Leaving aside orthographical and syntactical eccentricities (e.g., εἰς κόλπων at *IGA* 5.654) the following items noted from *IGA* 5 (cf. *New Docs 1976*, **58** for a couple of other examples) occur which deviate from the most common type (listed first in the table below).

1. εἰς κόλπους (ἐν κόλποις) Ἀβρααμ καὶ Ἰσακ καὶ Ἰακωβ 107, 484, 541, 623–25, 626 (probably to be included here, though the text breaks off after Ἀβρααμ — see n. ad loc.), 629, 636, 641 (part restored), 642, 647, 649, 652, 654, 655, 658, 659, 664–66, 667 (some words accidentally omitted by the mason), 668;
2. ἐν κ. τῶν π(ατέ)ρ(ω)ν Ἀ. καὶ Ἰ. καὶ Ἰ. — 635;
3. ἐν κ. τῶν π. ἡμῶν Ἀ. καὶ Ἰ. καὶ Ἰ. — 645, 646 (ἡμῶν restored, and text broken off after Ἀβραα[μ);
4. εἰς κ. τῶν ἁγιῶν π. Ἀ. καὶ Ἰ. καὶ Ἰ. — 48 (printed above), 608;
5. εἰς κ. τῶν ἁ. π. ἡμῶν Ἀ. καὶ Ἰ. καὶ Ἰ. — 661;
6. ἐν κ. τῶν ἁ. σ[ου] Ἀ. καὶ Ἰ. καὶ Ἰ. — 657;
7. εἰς κόλπ(ον) Ἀ. καὶ Ἰ. καὶ Ἰ. — 484 (plural might equally be understood here);
8. εἰς κόλιπον (*sic*) Ἀ. — 622 (the only certain singular example, and the only certain one containing Abraham alone of the triad of patriarchs, though cf. 626 noted above under group 1).

Few of these epitaphs are dated internally, but as a general caveat we should be cautious about according to these variants a relative chronological sequence from simplest to most complicated form. There are too few instances noted here to test this possibility, but the fact that only one example occurs for each of several categories makes it reasonably likely that they are mere idiosyncrasies.

The Latin equivalent of this phrase, *in gremio Abraham* . . . , is among those considered by I. Kajanto, *Arctos* 12 (1978) 27–53 (cf. *AE* 7), in his examination of eschatological ideas in Christian epitaphs (another is *pax, in pace*, etc.). He finds that Christian poetry (Paulinus of Nola and Prudentius are taken as representative) provides a closer analogy with epigraphical formulae than anything in the Fathers. Whereas in the first couple of centuries the distinction remained between the pre-resurrection state of the Christian dead and the immediate bliss of martyrs (cf. Rev. 6.9–11), gradually the situation enjoyed by the latter was widened in popular thinking to include the souls of all the faithful dead, whose bodies had to await the Apocalypse. Kajanto suggests (33) that the increasingly popular acceptance of this notion is reflected on Christian gravestones and *consolatio* poems, where the desire to offer comfort was paramount. He argues (41–42) that occasionally the 'bosom of Abraham' formula appears to indicate an intermediate state where the soul remained between death and resurrection; although of the three examples adduced one clearly refers to Heaven, one gives no indication whether Heaven or Hades is meant, and the third is only a possible candidate for this interpretation in view of restorations in the text (as Kajanto acknowledges). Since in the Greek epitaphs where this wording occurs (noted above) it is never an issue whether celestial rest or some intermediate abode is implied, the former may be the preferable and consistent way to understand it. For an instance where this appears certain note *IGA* 660 (Nubia, n.d.) where God is requested to grant repose in the bosom, etc. . . . ἐν σκηναῖς τῶν δικαίων.

An illustration of the beatific state enjoyed by the soul from the moment of death is provided by *IGA* 5.423 (Herment, n.d.):

> πρίν σε λέγειν, ὦ τύμβε, τίς ἢ τίνος ἐνθάδε κεῖται
> ἡ στήλη βοάα πᾶσι παρερχομένοις·
> σῶμα μὲν ἐνθάδε κεῖται ἀειμνήστου Μακαρίης·
> ὡς ἔθος εὐσεβέων γευσάμενον θανάτου,
> 5 αὐτὴ δ' οὐρανίην ἁγίων πόλιν ἀμφιπολεύει,
> ☧ μισθὸν ἔχουσα πόνων οὐρανίους στεφάνους.

> ☥   ✝   ☧

Before you say, grave, who or whose child lies here, this tombstone proclaims to all passers-by: here lies the body of ever-remembered Makaria; as is customary for the 5 pious it (i.e., her body) tasted death, | but she serves the heavenly city of the saints having as a reward for her labours heavenly crowns.

Biblical phrases might be thought to pervade the second half of this metrical text. In fact, only γεύομαι θανάτου occurs in the NT. (Mt. 16.28 = Mk. 9.1 = Lk. 9.27; Jn. 8.52; Heb. 2.9, of Christ). Neither the wording 'heavenly city' nor 'heavenly crown' is found in the NT — Heb. 11.10,16 and especially 12.22 are close for the former, however, as K.L. McKay points out to me — though in this epigram both appear to allude to the vision of the new Jerusalem in Rev. and to the crowns given there. Similarly 'reward for labours' may appear to have an appropriate Christian resonance, but does not recall any NT phrase. The separation of body and soul at death is presupposed in the Pauline comment, ἐκδημῆσαι ἐκ τοῦ σώματος καὶ ἐνδημῆσαι πρὸς τὸν κύριον (2 Cor. 5.8). It appears also to be implied in an epitaph for Alexander (Tomis, V) which begins: εἴλεος | σὺν ἀσωμ[άτοις] — I. Barnea, *Les monuments paléochrétiens de Roumanie* (Rome, 1977) 6 (pl.4).

Kajanto makes the point (53) that though the resurrection is rarely mentioned explicitly, it is tacitly assumed in many epitaphs. The very fragmentary *IGCB* 26 (Corinth, VI) provides an instance of explicit reference, where the grave is said to be . . . πληρω[θὲν σώματι] | ἕως ἀ[ναστάσεως] | [ἐ]ωνί[ας], κτλ. For further examples and discussion see Bees' n., ad loc. Another explicit example is published in *I.Bithynia* III.5 (pp.53–54; fig.), which begins οὐ χρυσὸς οὐκ ἀργύ|[ρ]ιν ἀλ⟨λ⟩' ὀστέ[α] κατακί|μενα, περιμένοντα φωνὴν σάλπινγος (cf. *SEG* 986; *BE* [1979] 567). The NT allusion in this text (Kandamiş in Bithynia, early Christian — *ed.pr.*) is more appropriate to 1 Thes. 4.16 than to Rev. 1.10 and 4.1 as suggested by ed.pr. For another text implying bodily resurrection see *New Docs 1977*, **113**.

The tacit implication of the future resurrection is instanced by Christian use of the cliché θάρσει, οὐδεὶς ἀθάνατος, usefully discussed by M. Simon, *RHR* 113 (1936) 188–206, repr. in his *Le Christianisme antique et son contexte religieux. Scripta Varia* (*Wiss. Untersuchungen zum Neuen Testament* 23; Tübingen, 1981) 63–81. He shows that we may detect its rise in Egypt, and that it is used alike by pagans, Jews and Christians. A number of Christian examples from Tyre were listed at *New Docs 1977*, **116**, p.208; cf. ibid., **112**. The reprinting of *IGA* 5 allows the opportunity to tabulate a few examples from Egypt from this year's culling. The most common form which the statement takes is represented by no.462, μὴ λυπηθῆς καὶ γ|ὰρ οὐδεὶς ἀθάνατ|ος ἐν τῷ κόσμῳ τούτ|ῳ; again, cf. 465, 476, 479, 482, 494, 507, 515, 782 (not all include the final demonstrative adjective). At nos.526, 556 and 620 ἐν τῷ βίῳ occurs as a variant. A few shorter alternatives are found occasionally: μὴ λυποῦ . . . οὐδεὶς ἀθάνατος (485, 525, 619); omission of the introductory prohibition (486, and possibly 490 where it is unclear whether the stone is broken away after οὐδεὶς ἀθάν|ατος, or whether this is all of the formula which was included; note also *IGA* 2.338); at 557 the broken stone reads]μν (read μὴ) λυπ|ῇ Μαρία. From Nikomedeia note *TAM* 357 (n.d.), Κυδία, ἣν (sic) ἡ|ρήνη ἡ ψυ|χή σου· οὐ|δὶς ἀθάνατος. The hint of a future expectation of resurrection comes in the phrase 'in this world'. The latest pagan examples known to me are an inscription from Raphia in Palestine, dated 410 (D. Barag, *IEJ* 24 [1974] 128–31 [pl.19c]), and another from Elusa in the Negev, dated 426 (referred to by Barag, 130).

A metrical variation of the mortality formula is provided by an inscription from near Karacabey in Mysia (III): S. Şahin, *Homm. Vermaseren*, 3.1000–02 no.3 (pl.218; = *SEG* 948; E. Pfuhl/H. Möbius, *Die ostgriechischen Grabreliefs* 2 [Mainz am Rhein, 1979] 1930 [pl.]), which concludes: 'I lie in Hades having completed my allotted portion; do not weep father, nor you, mother. Mortality is common (to all), for no one can escape the lot of men', κεῖ|μαι πρὸς Ἅιδαν μοῖρα|ν ἐμὴν τελέσας· μηκέτι κλαῖε, π|άτερ, μήδε σύ, μῆτερ· κοινὰ τὰ θ|νητῶν· οὐδεὶς γὰρ προφυγεῖν | μοῖρα⟨ν⟩ βροτῶν δύναται (10–15). A much rarer variation is provided by *NIP* IV.36, pp.99–100 (Uğurlu near Eumeneia, n.d.; cf. *SEG* 1158) which reprints an epitaph for several people; it concludes with the words καὶ σύ (16), i.e., 'you, too (must die)'. See Drew-Bear's commentary for discussion and references to other examples.

The first known example of this idea in West Semitic burial inscriptions is published by J. Naveh, *'Atiqot* (ES) 14 (1980) 54–59 (pl.9.4), a short Aramaic graffito on an ossuary lid found in a burial cave on Mt. Scopus (early Herodian period). Naveh reads and translates the text thus:

לא סכל אנש למעלה
ולא אלעזר ושפירה

Nobody has abolished his entering (into the grave/Sheol), not even Eleazar and Shappira.

Naveh suggests that this may reflect an attempt to paraphrase a Greek οὐδεὶς ἀθάνατος text. Given that the handwriting indicates a person of some education (Naveh, 59), 'we may assume that the writer knew Greek at least to a degree of reading epitaphs' (ibid.).

J. Fink discusses ideas and practices in Greek, Roman and Christian burials, *Fest.Dörner* 1.295–323 (on Christianity see especially 316–22).

90. A Christian invocation from Arabic Egypt

IGA 5.69 is a four-line Greek inscription followed by a Coptic dating formula, carved together with two scenes from the life of Christ (the entry into Jerusalem, the Ascension) on a wooden lintel of the Coptic church of el-Moallaqa in Old Cairo. This text has been restudied by L.S.B. MacCoull, who has kindly allowed me to refer to her discussion in advance of publication in ZPE (1984). Her article includes bibliography for the text and sculpture.

The most significant aspect of her re-examination concerns the dating clause. Whereas VI(?) is given in *IGA*, MacCoull shows that the date in fact corresponds to 734/5. This accords perfectly with the mention of Abba Theodore (*l.*4), patriarch of Alexandria from 731–743. The language and the art scenes confirm the appropriateness of an eighth-century date. The Greek text is full of biblical phraseology and allusions. Among them attention may be drawn particularly to *l.*1, κατῳκεῖ πᾶν τὸ πλήρωμα τῆς θεότητος (drawn straight from Col. 2.9, though note the change of tense of the verb) followed immediately by mention of 'the heavenly Sinai above' ἐπουρανίου Σιναὶ ἄνω[θεν(?)].

With this we may compare the allusion to the heavenly Jerusalem (Rev. 12.22), as well as the allegorical treatment of Mt. Sinai at Gal. 4.24–25. Together with emphasis on the Incarnation (*l.*4), the insistence on Christ's full divinity and the looking towards a better place beyond is all consistent with a context of Christians living under Arab domination 'in an atmosphere of defensive argument' (MacCoull). The art scenes of the triumphal entry juxtaposed with the Ascension are also to be viewed in this light, as 'an expression of hope for the future triumph of a persecuted Church' (ead.).

The survival as late as VIII of good quality Greek in the Coptic church is not really a matter for surprise, given such related factors as the conservatism of the liturgy (cf., briefly, *New Docs 1977*, **95**, p.153); see O.H.E. Burmester, *OCP* 2 (1936) 363–94, and (relating to music), I. Borsai, *Akten des XVI. Intern. Byzantinistenkongresses October 1981*, II.7 — = *JÖB* 32.7 — (Vienna, 1982) 109–18.

91. Miscellaneous liturgical quotations

Early Christian remains from the necropolis at el-Bagawat together with other locations in the el-Khargeh oasis are discussed at **106**. Several texts from that burial area were included in *IGA* 5, among them no.354 (n.d.) an early version of the Trisagion: ἅγιος | ἅγιος | ἅγιος | κύριος | σαβαωθ· | πληρε̄⟨ς⟩ ὁ οὐρανὸς | κα[ὶ] ἡ [γ]ῆ τῆς [δόξης σου]. For discussion of the

Trisagion see *New Docs 1977*, **95**. The Monophysite example included there rounds off with the formula Ι̅Σ̅ Χ̅Σ̅: on this statement see F.J. Dölger, *Ant. und Christ.* 1 (1929) 22–26. Among further examples from the 1978 culling is *IGA* 5.513 (Herment(?), n.d.), an epitaph for Theodoros which concludes with the monogram:

ι̅ς̅	χ̅ς̅
νι	κᾷ

A graffito from el-Kharga (n.d.) begins, Ἰ(ησοῦς) Χ(ριστὸς) νικᾷ (*IGA* 5.358). *TAM* 371 (Nikomedeia, n.d.) reads: ἡ ἁγί|α Τρίας ἡ ὁμο|ούσιος. | Χρ(ιστὸς) νι|κᾷ. *IGA* 5.590 (Philai, c.537) verbalizes the cross motif in an inscription on the temple of Isis: ✝ ὁ σταυρὸς | ἐνίκησεν, | ἀεὶ νικᾷ ✝✝✝. Together with a closely adjacent inscription this text refers to the transformation of the temple of Isis into a Christian Church: see M. Guarducci, *Epigrafia greca* IV (Rome, 1978) 466–69. Such slogans as these last four quoted illustrate the response — not necessarily contemporaneous — to pagan acclamations like *IGA* 2.89a, for Diocletian (provenance unknown in Egypt, end III), *Iovi Aucuste vincas* (*sic*). Another example of a *nike* inscription has been published by G. Dagron/J. Marcillet-Jaubert, *Belleten* 42(1978)292–93 no.24 (Çemkale in Cilicia, n.d., cf. *SEG* 1264):

[ἐν τού]	τῳ νικᾷ
[α]	ω
[Ι Χ(?)]	CH

Ed.pr. suggests that the unparalleled last line could be expanded as Ἰ(ησοῦς) Χ(ριστὸς) σ(ωτὴρ) ἡ(μῶν). *TAM* 369 gives us a related example from Nikomedeia (n.d.):

Ἰ(ησοῦ)ς   Χ(ριστό)ς
Ἐ
μ
μ
μεθ' ἡμ   α   ὧν ὁ θ(εό)ς
ν
[νι]   ο   κᾷ
[υ]
[ή]
[λ]

For Ἐμμανουήλ here cf. *TAM* 366 (Nikomedeia, n.d.), and the very late Coptic amulet recently published by A. Alcock, quoted in translation at **93**. As for other references to the cross we may note *IGA* 5.560, a graffito in a tomb (Gebel el-Silsila, n.d.): σταυρὸς δῶν (*sic*) χριστιανῶν; and 5.746 (provenance unknown, n.d.), a lamp decorated with a frog and carrying the inscription: τωχημα (i.e., τὸ ὄχημα) ✝ σταυρός ✝, 'the cross is (my) support (?)'. A pavement laid down in May 559 by bishop Abraamios — who was present at the Second Council of Constantinople in 553 — in a basilica at Resafa-Sergiopolis (Syria) mentions that he built it 'for the honour of the holy cross, in order that he might merit God's mercy', πρὸς τιμὴν τοῦ ἁγίου σταυροῦ ἵνα ἀξιώθη | ἐλέους θεοῦ (2-3): *ed.pr.* — T. Ulbert, *Arch.Anz.* (1977) 563–69 (figs. 2–4); cf. *BE* 521.

It was at el-Kharga oasis that Athanasios spent some of his exile, and passing mention may therefore be given here to the near-contemporary Greek copy of his encyclical letter — a Latin version also exists — to the monks of his see, preserved by one of the recipients: ['Aθ]αν΄ ασιος τοῖς ἀπ[ανταχοῦ ὀ]|[ρθ]οδόξοις μοναχο[ῖς τοῖς τὸν μ]|[ον]ήρη βίον ἀσκοῦσ[ι, κτλ (*IGA* 5.380.4-6; Qurna, near Luxor, IV). The adjective ὀρθόδοξος here, as elsewhere (cf. *New Docs 1977*, **95**, pp.151-52), reflects current polemic. Two other examples of the word which crops up in this year's culling are *IGCB* 9 (Corinth, 7/12/574-4/10/578), a fragmentary inscription which makes mention of the emperors Justinus (name restored) and Tiberius, [δεσπο]τῶν ὀρθοδόξων; and *SEG* 868, a bibliographical reference to E.K. Chrysos, *DOP* 32 (1978) 74-75, who dates the edict concerning orthodox churches (. . . ταῖς ἐκκλ]ησίαις τῆς ὀρθοδόξου πίστεως, H. Grégoire, *Recueil des inscriptions grecques-chrétiennes d'Asie-Mineure* [Paris, 1927; repr. 1968] 107.5) to the time of Heraclius or later (Grégoire suggested 535/6 for this inscription from Ephesos, now repr. with some other readings in H. Engelmann et al., *Die Inschriften von Ephesos* IV [*Inschriften gr. Städte aus Kleinasien* 14.4; Bonn, 1980] 1353). Implied polemic is probably to be detected in an epitaph for John, 'presbyter of the holy, true church', ἁγίας ἐκκλησίας ἀληθινῆς (*IGA* 5.481; Herment, n.d.).

One of the longest well-preserved inscriptions in *IGA* 5 is a painted text (237) from the monastery of Shenute at Sohag. This includes (1-7) the *Gloria in excelsis* in its Greek form (prior to the Latin version), but containing variants some of which appear to reflect knowledge of the Latin version; while *ll.*8-18 draws upon several doxologies, notably the *Te Deum*.

The trichotomy 'body, soul and spirit' was discussed at *New Docs 1976*, **64**, where papyrus allusions to the NT phrase at 1 Thes. 5.23 were listed. Worth noting in this connection, though not of direct relevance, is *IGA* 5.656 = *SB* 5.3 (1950) 8740, an epitaph for Maria (Nubia(?), 707), which begins: ὁ] θεὸς τῶν πνευμά|[τ]ων καὶ πάσας (*sic*) σαρ/κός, ἀνάπαυσον τῆς ψυχῆς τῆς | μακαρίας Μαρίας (1-5), 'God of the spirits and of all flesh, give repose to the soul of blessed Maria'. This formula does not involve a trichotomy: the first two nouns suggest a comprehensive dichotomy, while ψυχή is a particular application of the first of them. This wording is a liturgical formula (derived from Num. 16.22; 27.16), occurring also at, e.g., *IGA* 5.608 = *SB* 5.3.8731 (Coptic cemetery at Wadi Ghazal, n.d.). It is not confined to Christian texts, however, appearing in the two identical Jewish inscriptions (originally from Delos, II/IBC) which beseech God for vengeance against the killer of two girls (noted briefly at *New Docs 1976*, **5**, ad fin.). On these Jewish texts see Deissmann, *LAE* 416-17, where the phrase is discussed; see also now Guarducci, *Epigrafia greca*, 4.236-38.

92. Papyrus testimony to Christological controversies

A.C. Mancini republishes as *P.Carlini lett.* 25 (provenance unknown, V init.; pl.10) a patristic text, *P.Pis.* inv. 4, first dealt with by A. Carlini et al., *Nuovi papiri letterari fiorentini* (Pisa, 1971) 16-24, 33, no.4 (pl.3) — *non vidi* (cf. van Haelst 1091). There survive two fragments from separate sheets of a papyrus codex — parchment, according to van Haelst — but they are too mutilated to merit reprinting here since, lacking complete lines, no connected sense can be derived from what remains. However, several words in the surviving portions give a clear enough general indication of the subject. Christ's name is not preserved at all, but words like μονόειδ[ες (or -δ[ης; frag.A *verso*, *l.*5) and ἄρχων ἢ βασιλε΄ υς (frag.B *verso*, *l.*15; cf. Rev. 1.5 where Christ is spoken of as ὁ ἄρχων τῶν βασιλέων τῆς γῆς, and note Mancini's references, p.179, to Lampe) fairly certainly allude to him. The most constantly recurring terms are ἀπάθεια, πάσχω, and related forms; and it is a reasonable inference that — at least until the *paragraphos* at frag.B *recto*, *l*.25 — the subject concerns the suffering of Christ, contrasting his real suffering as a man with the *apatheia* of his divine nature. An allusion to the 'death of God', ἐν θανάτῳ θ(εο)ῦ, occurs at frag.B *verso*, *l*.13 (with the abbreviated *nomen sacrum* here contrast frag.A *recto*, *l*.5, θεῷ; for such inconsistency cf. comments at *New Docs 1977*, **91**, pp.126-27, 132, 136, 138; **115**, p.205).

Mancini suggests that the text reports the different views of the nature of Christ epitomized by Nestorius and Cyril, a debate which culminated in the council of Ephesos in 431; for the background see briefly H. Chadwick, *The Early Church* (Harmondsworth, 1967, repr.) 194-200, or in more detail in id., *JTS* 2 (1951) 145-64, repr. in Chadwick's *History and Thought of the Early Church* (London, 1982) ch.16. If so, then given the date of the papyrus we have a contemporary witness to this controversy. Furthermore, the occurrence of προαιρέσεω[ς at frag.A *verso*, *l*.10 could allude to the Arian debate over the free will of Christ (Mancini, 176, reporting the suggestion of K. Treu [not made in his comments on this papyrus at *APF* 22/23 (1974) 379]).

Direct NT quotations — or even allusions — are sparse. With the augmented form of ἀποκαραδοκέω at frag.A *recto*, *l*.7 cf. ἀποκαραδοκία at Rom. 8.19; Phil. 1.20. This papyrus attestation could well be included in MM, s.v. Note also the use of ἐνεργί[ας---] | μὴ καταγωνιζομένης (frag.B *recto*, *ll*.14-15; the noun probably occurs also at B *verso l*.4, ἐν]εργίας), whose affinity with Col. 1.29 may be coincidental (ἀγωνιζόμενος κατὰ τὴν ἐνέργειαν αὐτοῦ . . .). *Energeia* is used only in Pauline epistles in the NT, mostly of God, but once of Satan (2 Thes. 2.9).

The ordering of the sides is open to doubt. Mancini prints frag.A *verso* then *recto*, followed by B *recto*, *verso*. Now, it is not common for writing on the *verso* of a codex leaf to precede that on the *recto* (although an example is noted above at **82**, a tiny fragment of Job); the main situation where this occurs is with codices with gatherings of 'ones' (*uniones*). For discussion with examples see Turner, 60-61, 66-67; and it may be that in the two fragments of *P.Pis.* inv.4 we are seeing an example of a *unio*. While such an arrangement is not unparalleled, therefore, it still remains hard to see why this order for frag.A is a necessary reconstruction. True, frag.B *recto* gives particular attention to πασχ- words, and A *recto* contains ἀπάθεια twice; this appears to be Mancini's ground, p.172, for B *recto* following on from A *recto*. Yet A *verso* contains ἀπάθους at *l*.2, so that even if they are consecutive leaves (which is not certain, though perhaps likely given the concentration on πασχ- words), a *recto* then *verso* order for frag.A is no less conceivable.

The interest afforded by this papyrus is increased considerably by the possibility that it may be connected with two other papyri which reflect christological disagreements. The more important one — because it is a largely complete codex leaf — is *P.Palau Rib.* 68 (provenance unknown, IV fin./V init.; this date is K. Treu's [in the *APF* reference given above], who rejects *ed.pr*'s dating to second quarter IV as too early). This text (*ed.pr.* — F. de P. Solá, *Stud.Pap.* 9 [1970] 21-33, pl.; van Haelst 1159) includes a polemical report concerning Arian and Sabellian views (*verso, ll*.15-19):

15   τὸν γὰρ υ̅ν̅ τοῦ [αὐτοῦ θ̅υ̅
    υ̅ν̅ τυγχάνιν κ(αὶ) τὸν π̅ρ̅α̅ τοῦ υἱοῦ εἶ[ναι θ̅ν̅
    ὁμολογοῦμεν, ἀναθεματίζοντε[ς αἵρεσιν
    ἀθεότηταν τῶν χριστομάχων ἀριο[μανιτῶν
    καὶ τὴν ἀσέβιαν Σαβελλίου τοῦ φά[σκοντος . . .

For we confess that the Son is Son of the same God and the Father of the Son is God, placing an anathema upon the heresy (and(?)) godlessness of the Ariomaniacs who fight against Christ, and upon the impiety of Sabellios who claims that, etc. . . .

(The text above alters *ed.pr.* θ̅ν̅ at end of *l.*15 to genitive, and fills out a restoration for end of *l.*16. J.A.L. Lee wonders whether the restoration at the end of *l.*17 is satisfactory, given that ἀθεότηταν is a noun; add καί after αἵρεσιν, perhaps.)

On the basis of its content R.M. Grant, *Stud.Pap.* 11 (1972) 47-50, suggests that this papyrus should be associated with the synod of Alexandria in 362. On the *recto* the text insists on the equality (ἰσότητα, 4) of the Son to the Father; he is τὸν ἐν τῇ σαρκὶ θ̅ν̅ (10), even while being ἐν μο]ρφῇ . . . δούλου (12); and there is mention of 'God the *Logos* who lives in the body', τοῦ κατοικοῦ|[ντος ἐν σώ]ματι θ̅υ̅ λόγου (16-17). This theme continues over to the *verso*, where Christ is spoken of as ἐνσαρκωθέντα and born of Mary (2); while *ll.*6-7 speak of the *ousia* of the Son and his *isotes* with the Father. Several NT quotations and allusions may be noted: *recto ll.*7-8 (Jn. 14.18), *l.*12 (Phil. 2.7), *ll.*20-24, cf. 15-17 (Eph. 4.13), *ll.*24-26 (Col. 2.9); *verso ll.*10-11 (Col. 1.16).

The same date (IV fin./V init.) is to be accorded *P.Palau Rib.* 72 (provenance unknown), *ed.pr.* — F. de P. Solá, *Stud.Pap.* 7 (1968) 49-64 (pl.); van Haelst 1160. This papyrus preserves the left-hand side of a codex leaf. Like *P.Palau Rib.* 68 this one also concerns the anti-Arian controversy, emphasizing the identical substance of the Son and the Father. At *verso l.*1 [πατέρες ἐν τῇ] Νικαίᾳ may well allow the inference of an allusion to the Council of Nicaea in 325. The following NT quotations and reminiscences may be noted: *recto l.*3 (Phil. 2.6), *ll.*10-11 (Heb. 1.3.; cf. ἐκείνου τὸν χαρακτῆρα at *l.*2); *verso l.*3 (Jn. 1.1-2), *l.*12 (Jn. 1.6-7).

Because it is most complete *P.Palau Rib.* 68 is the most informative of these three papyri; but the intriguing question raised by their similar content and date is whether they all emanated from the same scriptorium (as Treu suggests), or even from the same codex (so Solá for the two *P.Palau Rib.* texts; cf. van Haelst, 1091). If the latter view is to be entertained as a possibility then these three fragments, alluding to three separate Church councils, may have formed part of a collection of reports and refutations of various near-current theological stances on the nature of Christ. To be within the ambit of a Christian scriptorium in early V is no surprise; but is there any evidence for such in Egypt prior to Constantine? G. Zuntz has argued that there was a Christian scriptorium at work in Alexandria by II² (*The Text of the Epistles* [London, 1953] 271-75; cf. his synopsis of this book's conclusions in *Rev. Bib.* 59 [1952] 5-22, repr. in English in his *Opuscula Selecta* [Manchester, 1972] 252-68). C.H. Roberts suggests that the presence of another at Oxyrhynchos by late II or III is 'not unlikely' (*Manuscript, Society, and Belief in Early Christian Egypt* [London, 1979] 24). To these hypotheses may now be added a further intriguing possibility. C. Gallazzi has published *P.Mil. Vogl.* inv. 1224, containing Acts 2.30-37; 2.46-3.2, in *BASP* 19 (1982) 39-45 (pls), which he dates mid-III (provenance unknown). S.R. Pickering tells me that 'this fragment contains, on both front and back, the same verses as *P.Macquarie* inv. 360 (𝔓⁹¹) and is written in a similar hand and format, possibly even by the same scribe despite some differences in the script. There is a minor amount of overlapping in the portions of the text represented by the two fragments. The textual characteristics of the two are essentially the same'. The Macquarie fragment was described briefly in *New Docs 1977*, **91**, *ad fin*. Since there is overlap of text and difference of script, and the two fragments therefore cannot be from the same codex, the possibility of such a connection between these two Acts papyri of such early date is tantalizing for our thinking about the mass production of Bible texts in Egypt's early Christian milieu.

93. Credal formula in a Christian amulet against fever

Provenance unknown   VI(?)

ed.pr. — P.W.A.T. van der Laan, *P.L.Bat.* 20, pp.96–102 (pl.14)

```
         † † † †
     ⳁ    Χ̄Σ̄ . . . . φ[
     ⳁ    Χ̄Σ̄ ἐφάνη
     ⳁ    Χ̄Σ̄ ἔπαθε[ν]
     ⳁ    Χ̄Σ̄ ἀπέθα[ν]εν
  5  ⳁ    Χ̄Σ̄ ἀνηγέρθη
     ⳁ    Χ̄Σ̄ ἀνελήμφθη
     ⳁ    Χ̄Σ̄ βασιλεύει
          Χ̄Σ̄ σῴζει . . . κον (?)
        ὃν ἔτεκεν Γενναία,
 10   ἀπὸ παντὸς πυρετοῦ
      καὶ παντὸς ῥίγους,
      ἀμφημερινοῦ,
      καθημερινοῦ,
      ἤδη ἤδη, ταχὺ ταχύ.
         † † † † † † †
```

A complete papyrus, *verso* blank.

5 (*crosses*) Christ . . . ; Christ appeared; Christ suffered; Christ died; |Christ was raised;
10 Christ was taken up; Christ reigns; Christ saves . . . kos(?), whom Gennaia bore, |from
   every fever and every shivering fit, one-day, recurrent(?) — now, now! quickly, quickly!
   (*crosses*)

This amulet is arresting chiefly because of the credal statement which comprises the first
seven lines. The nearest NT analogy to such a spare formulation is 1 Cor. 15.3–4, Χριστὸς
ἀπέθανεν . . . ἐτάφη . . . ἐγήγερται, a passage fleshed out only slightly with the theological
implications of those events. But the new amulet is not harking back to that or any other
NT passage: its reference point appears to be the Niceno-Constantinopolitan creed of 381.
Ed.pr. draws attention to the links with this creed — the verbs used are not in every case
identical — and also to those with Justin Martyr, *Apol.* 1.37.7, on the basis of which it is
suggested that the verb in *l.*1 may possibly have been προεφητεύθη. Like the Justin passage
(quoted by *ed.pr.*) the amulet employs φαίνομαι of the Incarnation (2), and ἀνεγείρομαι of
the Resurrection (5): neither is an NT usage. Yet given the long gap in time between Justin
and the amulet, the possibility that the latter owes any debt to the former is very remote.

This is not the only recently published apotropaic sickness amulet which begins with a
credal statement. *P. Turner* (1981) 49 (provenance unknown, V/VI) is a nearly complete text
written on a very long, narrow papyrus strip. The text in *P. Turner* supersedes W. Brashear's
ed.pr. in *ZPE* 17 (1975) 31–32 (pl.2b) in view of his subsequent discovery of a new fragment,
although the original notes are still relevant.

παρθ]ένου Μαρία⟨ς⟩ καὶ ἐστ(αυ)ρ(ώ)θη ὑπὸ Ποντίου Πιλάτου καὶ ἐτάφη εἰς μνημῖον καὶ

ἀνέστη ἐν τῇ τρίτῃ ἡμέρᾳ καὶ ἀνελήμφθη ἐπὶ τοὺ⟨ς⟩ οὐρανοὺς καὶ ε . . . . [

] ̣εν Ἰ(ησο)ῦ ὅτι ἐθεράπευες τότε πᾶσαν μαλακίαν τοῦ λαοῦ καὶ πᾶσαν νόσον συ̣ῖ πρ Ἰ(ησο)ῦ

πιστευ ̣ μου ὅτι ἀπῆλθες τό[τ]ε εἰς τὴν [ο]ἰκίαν τῆ[ς] πενθερᾶς Πέτρου πυρεσ[σούσης]

[καὶ ἀφῆ]κεν αὐτὴν ὁ πυρετός· καὶ νῦν παρακαλοῦμέν σε, Ἰ(ησο)ῦ, θεράπευσον καὶ νῦν τὴν

δούλην σου τὴν φοροῦντα (sic) τὸ ἅγ[ιον] ὄνομά σου ἀπὸ πάσης νόσο̣υ καὶ [ἀπὸ παν-

]

[τὸς π]υρετοῦ καὶ ἀπὸ ῥιγοπυρέτου καὶ ἀπὸ κροτάφου καὶ ἀπὸ πάσης βασκοσύνης καὶ ἀπὸ

παντὸς πν(εύμ)α̣(τος) πονηροῦ ἐν ὀνόματι π(ατ)ρὸς καὶ υ(ἱο)ῦ καὶ ἁγίου πν̣(εύματ)ος.

[He was born of the] Virgin Mary, was crucified by Pontius Pilate, and was buried in
2 **a tomb; on the third day he rose, was taken up to heaven, and . . . | Jesus, because you**
healed at that time every sickness and every disease of the people . . . Jesus (we?) trust
(you?) because you went at that time into the house of Peter's mother-in-law, who was
3 **suffering from fever, | and the fever left her. So now we ask you, Jesus, heal also now**
4 **your slave, who wears your holy name, from every disease, every | fever, every shivering**
fit and every headache (?), as well as from all bewitching and every evil spirit; in the
name of Father, Son and Holy Spirit.

This document provides a fascinating Christian use of the common literary *topos*, δύνασαι
γάρ, by which a person seeking to enlist the god's aid reminds him that he has the power
to do the thing asked. In this example the credal section — more reminiscent of the Apostle's
Creed — leads to a plea that since Jesus healed Peter's mother-in-law of fever (Mk. 1.31 =
Mt. 8.14–16 = Lk. 4.38–41) he will heal the wearer of this amulet. In *P. Turner* 49 healing
is requested in both the physical and the spiritual realm. Now, in the gospel accounts to
which this papyrus alludes the narrative continues by pointing to Christ's healing of those
physically and spiritually ill: ἐθεράπευσεν πολλοὺς κακῶς ἔχοντας ποικίλαις νόσοις, καὶ
δαιμόνια πολλὰ ἐξέβαλεν (Mk. 1.34, cf.32; Mt. 8.16 has ἐξέβαλεν τὰ πνεύματα — cf. *l*.4 of
the papyrus).

Several analogies may be drawn between *P. Turner* 49 and the much more fragmentary
Christian amulet, *P.Coll.Youtie* (1976) 91 (provenance unknown, V/VI; pl.33a), reprinted
at *New Docs 1976*, **64**.

(i) The δύνασαι γάρ *topos* appears to occur also in *P.Coll.Youtie* 91.3–4.
(ii) The name of the wearer (*P.Coll.Youtie* 91.4 — τὸν φοροῦντα{ν}) is unspecified; *ed.pr.* (O.
Montevecchi) regarded the *P.Coll.Youtie* amulet as providing a model of the formula rather than
one for actual use, in view of the large size of the papyrus, 13 x 8 cm. She restored [ἡ] δ[εῖ]να at
l.7, which the owner of an amulet following this model would replace in her own version with her
own name. Yet anonymity occurs elsewhere in similar texts, e.g., *P.Princ.* 2 (1936) 107.6–7
(provenance unknown, IV/V), which emanates from a Gnostic milieu.
(iii) *P.Coll.Youtie* 91.5 has π̄ν̄(εῦμ)[α, although the *nomen sacrum* does not apply to the Holy Spirit
there. *P. Turner* 49.4 has πν(εύμ)α̣(τος) πονηροῦ . . . ἁγίου πν(εύματ)ος, which illustrates strikingly
both the expanded use of this *nomen sacrum* and also the inconsistent abbreviation of the word.
While on the subject of *nomina sacra* we may note that in *P. Turner* 49.1 ἐσταυρώθη is abbreviated
as εϲ✝θη: 'the figure between sigma and theta is not so much a tau-rho monogram as a cross with
a circle on it — almost a pictorial representation of the crucifixion' (ed. n., ad loc.).
(iv) First-person plural request: *P. Turner* 49.3; in *l*.2 is the speculative restoration πιστεύομ⟨εν⟩ worth
consideration? At *P.Coll.Youtie* 91.2 the reading [π]οιησαμ̣εν is difficult (see pl.33a): aorist
participle, or is an augment also lost at the beginning of the word, [ἐπ]οιήσαμ̣[εν]?

Returning to the credal statements in *P.L.Bat.* 20 and *P.Turner* 49, both begin with this and then proceed to request recovery from illness. What is the nexus between these two elements? In my judgement the function of the prior credal section is to establish the wearer's *bona fides* as Christ's follower, and on this basis the request for help can then be made. The fact that these credal formulae reflect knowledge of the great orthodox statements of faith indicates that the owners of these talismans participated in the mainstream Church, and were conversant with its liturgical forms. Now, in IV² especially there was much ecclesiastical opposition to the use of amulets, both from bishops like Chrysostom and Augustine and from certain Church synods, most notably the Council of Laodicea (held some time between 341–381). Canon 36 of the latter reads (Migne, *PG* 137, col.1388): ὅτι οὐ δεῖ ἱερατικοὺς ἢ κληρικοὺς μάγους ἢ ἐπαοιδοὺς εἶναι, ἢ μαθηματικούς, ἢ ἀστρολόγους, ἢ ποιεῖν τὰ λεγόμενα φυλακτήρια, ἅτινά ἐστι δεσμωτήρια τῶν ψυχῶν αὐτῶν· τοὺς δὲ φοροῦντας ῥίπτεσθαι ἐκ τῆς ἐκκλησίας ἐκελεύσαμεν, 'that priests or clergy ought not to be wizards or enchanters, or numerologists(?) or astrologers, or to make so-called amulets which are prisons of their souls. Those who wear them we commanded to be cast out of the Church'. For discussion of this passage and further references see B.M. Metzger's expanded commentary on *P.Princ.* 3 (1942) 159 in his *Historical and Literary Studies: Pagan, Jewish and Christian* (*NT Tools and Studies* 8; Leiden 1968) 106–07. The continued prevalence of Christian amulets witnesses to the Church's powerlessness to stamp out the practice: it was too deeply engrained. The Laodicea canon informs us that those in orders made amulets, though not for themselves alone, we are to presume (otherwise we should perhaps expect φορεῖν rather than ποιεῖν). Was this because they had readier access to biblical/liturgical texts to copy extracts, or because they were more likely to be literate? (For people in orders who are illiterate at least in Greek see *New Docs 1976*, **80**, p.124; for intending deacons who cannot even write Coptic see Deissmann, *LAE* 221–24.) This synodical canon may help to illuminate for us the occurrence of first person plural forms in a text like *P. Turner* 49 (παρακαλοῦμέν σε, Ἰ(ησο)ῦ, 3) and the possible one in *P.Coll.Youtie* 91 ([ἐπ]οιήσαμ[εν, 2; see comment above). Behind these personal documents of V/VI are we able to perceive the laity's acceptance that those in orders had special access to Christ? This is not the place to test this hypothesis, for which a thorough chronological study of the extant Christian amulets is needed. Even if only approximately correct, it means that these brief texts provide a hitherto unappreciated resource for our understanding of the relationship between laity and clergy as it developed in the period c.IV–VIII.

P.Lit.Lond. (1927) 239 (VI/VII) comprises nine vellum sheets containing the Niceno-Constantinopolitan creed, and has been claimed by *ed.pr.* to be an amulet. For brief discussion of this and other passages from creeds preserved on papyrus see *New Docs 1976*, **66**. To these should be added O. Montevecchi, *Aeg.* 55 (1977) 58–69 (pl.), a wooden tablet (*tab.lignea Med.* inv. 71.00A) which preserves a nearly complete version of the Niceno-Constantinopolitan creed (Oxyrhynchos(?), VI). She suggests that the text on this tablet may have been used in a liturgical context: the different line lengths, following sense breaks, support this, as perhaps, too, does the very limited use (only side 1, *l.*4) of *nomina sacra* — elsewhere such words are written out in full. Textually there are few deviations, but we may note side 1, *l.*12, [καὶ] σαρκοθέντα ἐκ πνεύματος ἁγίου ἐκ Μαρία⟨ς⟩ τῆς ἀειπαρθένου, in place of the usual ἐκ π. ἁ. καὶ Μαρίας τῆς παρθένου. On the word ἀειπαρθένος see Montevecchi, 66–69; and, more recently, A.M. Emmett, *JÖB* 32.2 (1981) 507–10, who argues that none of the three papyri in which the word is used other than of Mary — *P.Lips.*1 (1906) 43 and 60; H.C. Youtie *ZPE* 37 (1980) 216–17, no.6 (pl.7a): all dated IV — need be referring to nuns (although patristic texts of this period use it in this way), but rather to 'still unmarried' women/daughters.

The following further references to the Niceno-Constantinopolitan creed culled from 1978 publications may be noted here. Knowledge of this creed is exhibited on two lamps, *IGA* 5.752, 753, both of unknown provenance, the former dated by Lefebvre to end IV/early V, shortly after the Council of Constantinople in 381. Both have the words φῶς ἐκ φωτός. An additional phrase from this creed occurs in *IGCB* 1 (Corinth Isthmos, 551–65), a prayer to God for protection for Justinian and 'his slave' Victorinus, which begins: † φῶς ἐκ φωτός, θεὸς | ἀληθινὸς ἐκ θεοῦ ἀληθινοῦ, | φυλάξῃ τὸν αὐτοκράτορα, κτλ. This inscription has been reprinted in numerous places (e.g., Deissmann, *LAE* 459 n.4), most recently in W. Wischmeyer, *Griechische und lateinische Inschriften zur Sozialgeschichte der Alten Kirche* (*Texte zur Kirchen- und Theologiegeschichte* 28; Gütersloh, 1982) 49, no.23. A linguistic commentary on the creed is provided by R.J.H. Matthews, *Prudentia* 14 (1982) 23–37; for recent general discussion of the Council see J. Taylor, *Prudentia* 13 (1981) 47–54, 91–97.

Reverting to *P.L.Bat.* 20, it remains to consider the second half of the text. *Ed.pr.* notes that the indicative is used in *l.*8 instead of the expected imperative, and thereby suggests that an apotropaic function is not to the fore in this amulet. But there may merely be a confusion of the forms σῴζει/σῷζε; and certainly, given the frequent use of nominatives for vocatives, the presence of X̄Σ̄ rather than X̄Ē does not confirm that an indicative was intended. At *ll.*9 and 14 we are given an indication of the tenacity of magical formulae, surviving here in a Christian text from VIAD. It is a standard feature to define the person in view by adding the mother's name: for an example of this in a love charm see *New Docs 1976*, **8** (Antinoopolis, III/IV; the Antinous invoked there is probably to be interpreted as Hadrian's favourite — see R. Lambert, *Beloved and God. The story of Hadrian and Antinous* [London, 1984] 192 and n.39 on p.271). Note also *New Docs 1977*, **11**, another love charm (provenance unknown, n.d.) in which as well as the maternal defining there occurs the common formula ἤδη ταχύ. For the latter van der Laan's n. to *P.L.Bat.* 20, p.102, provides numerous parallels.

Also fairly standard in amulets against sickness is the specifying of a range of fevers and cold sweats, in order to cover all the possibilities. How much we should distinguish ἀμφημερινός/καθημερινός (12–13) is uncertain (see translation at beginning of this entry), though this pair of adjectives occurs elsewhere in similar contexts: see, e.g., *P.Berl.* inv. 21165, published by W. Brashear, *ZPE* 17 (1975) 27–30 no.2 (pl.2a; Fayum (?), III/IV), a text which includes as well *nomina barbara*, a list of angel-names, and various magical signs including an *ouroboros*. The *ouroboros* makes it apposite to mention here another magical charm, on a silver plate (Homs (?) in Syria, n.d.): *ed.pr.* — P.J. Sijpesteijn, *OMRL* 59/60 (1978/9) 189–92 (pl.37); cf. *SEG* 1334. The 15 lines of text, encircled by the snake, mostly comprise *nomina barbara*; but in addition seven angel-names are listed (*ll.*9–11), followed by the words 'the picture of the god' (11–12). Concerning this phrase *ed.pr.* says (n. ad loc.), 'the words τὸ ζωγράφημα τοῦ θεοῦ probably meant that on this plate the picture of a certain god had to be engraved but that these words were simply taken over [from his exemplum by the engraver] without any real understanding'. After more *nomina barbara* and vowel combinations the text concludes εἴλεως ἔσται τῷ φορο[ῦν]|[τ]ι [καὶ] τῇ φορούσῃ (14–15), 'it will be propitious for the wearer, whether male or female'. It is uncertain what εἴλεως goes with grammatically — indeclinable in *koine*: some examples in *ed.pr.*'s n. ad loc. — though Sijpesteijn doubts that it is to be taken with τὸ ζωγράφημα; is ὁ θεός to be understood, perhaps? The identity of the god is unknown.

The most recently published amulet against fever known to me is *P.Mich* inv.6660: R.W. Daniel, *ZPE* 50 (1983) 147–54 (pl. 7c; provenance unknown, III). This article is particularly useful for its commentary on the interpretation of *nomina barbara*, the use of vowels set out in various carefully devised schemas (palindromes, etc.), and other regular features in magical texts. Do many amulets seeking to allay illness survive? In the course of his publication of a rare Coptic example, P.J. Sijpesteijn, *CE* 57 (1982) 377–81 (2 pls.), lists (377 n.1) 19 in Greek, including Christian items such as *P.L.Bat.*20, *P. Turner* 49 — both discussed above — and *P. Princ.* 2 (1936) 107, a gnostic piece (provenance unknown, IV/V). To these we may add *P.Princ* 3 (1942) 159 (provenance unknown, III/IV); the fragmentary Christian *P.Coll.Youtie* 91 discussed above; and F. Maltomini's re-edition of *P.Erlangen* (1942) 15 (provenance unknown, *c*.IV), now identified as a fever amulet: *SCO* 32 (1982) 235–40 — *non vidi*. Its legibility is difficult, and R.W.Daniel/P.J.Sijpesteijn, *ZPE* 54 (1984) 83–84, offer several different readings. The name Ἰωάννης (3; partly restored at 8) suggests that the owner of this text was Christian; and at *l*.7 Daniel/Sijpesteijn discern mention of a 'guardian angel', τὸν ἡμῶν ἀθάρατον (= ἀθάνατον) ἄγγελον. (Another such occurs in *P.Yale* inv. 1773 (late VI/early VII), re-ed. by H.C.Youtie, *ZPE* 16 [1975] 259–64 — repr. in his *Scriptiunculae Posteriores* 1 [Bonn, 1981] 163–68 — 'I was expecting to come and do obeisance to your guardian angel', ἐπροσδόκων ἐλθῖν καὶ προσκίνησα τὸν ὑμῶν ἄγγελον, 3.) However, in *l*.2 Daniel/Sijpesteijn read κύριοι θεοί, which could count against a Christian milieu, and therefore the ἄγγελος might be 'a specific god who acts as the agent' of the *kyrioi theoi* (ibid.).

A very late Coptic amulet on paper (Oxyrhynchos, XI), has been recently published by A. Alcock, *BASP* 19 (1982) 97–103 (pl.). This last item comprises *c*.50 short lines in three sections, which includes use of the *Sator-Arepo* word-play (sect. 1.3–5) as a formula against fever. Part of the text requests the owner's pain to be removed ' . . . in the name and by the nails which were driven (?) into the body of Emanouel, our Nouel, our God on the cross, by the Jews' (sect.1.16–20, trans. *ed.pr.*). For the anti-Jewish comment see **100**. On the *Rotas-Sator* acrostic W. Moeller has more to say (cf. *New Docs 1976*, **99**), at *Homm. Vermaseren* 2.801–20. Two other acrostics from the year's culling appear as graffiti at Abydos, *IGA* 3. 456, 456 *bis* (neither is dated). The latter is not a true acrostic, reading 'God, lead me. Lead me, God.'

θεὸς

ἡγοῦ

ἡγοῦ

θεός

Whether this inscription is Christian is uncertain. The ed. n., ad loc., suggests that the layout is indicative that the text was felt to have a magical potency.

Finally, since Brashear's article in *ZPE* 17 (1975) has been drawn upon above for two of its amulets, its two other texts — both of interest — may be mentioned here briefly: *P.Berl.* inv. 21227 (Brashear, 25–27 no.1, pl.1b; provenance unknown, III/IV) is an invocation to Sarapis, calling upon him as κύριε πα[ντοκράτωρ] (4); ed. notes several more examples of παντοκράτωρ in magical papyri which should be added to the paucity of non-Jewish/non-Christian examples included in MM, s.v. From 1978 publications we may note the adjective used of God in a Christian letter, *P.L.Bat.* 21.4 (Oxyrhynchos, VI). D. Feissel, *BCH* 104 (1980) 463–65, lists several Christian epitaphs in which the adjective occurs. *P.Berl.* inv. 21230 (Brashear, 30–31 no.3, pl.2c; provenance unknown, V) is a Christian prayer to Mary requesting a cure from an eye ailment.

✝ λαβοῦσα χάριν ἐκ τοῦ
μονογενοῦς σου υἱοῦ
στῆσον τὸ ῥεῦμα, τοὺς
πόνους τῶν ὀφθαλμῶν
5   Φοιβάμμωνος υἱοῦ Ἀθα-
νασίου· ὁ κατοικῶν ἐπὶ βο-
[η]θίᾳ τοῦ ὑψί[στο]υ ἐν σκέπῃ
[τοῦ θεοῦ τοῦ οὐ]ρανοῦ αὐλισ-
[θήσεται·

(*cross*) Receiving grace from your only-born son, check the discharge, the pains in the
5 **eyes | of Phoibammon, son of Athanasios. 'He who dwells with the help of the Highest**
will lodge in the shelter of the God of Heaven'.

The reading ἐπί (6) for ἐν may be noted in this quotation from Ps. 90.1. On this psalm
and its great popularity among Christians see most recently R.W. Daniel, *VC* 37 (1983)
400–04, who publishes a Christian amulet (*P. Vindob*. G. 348; provenance unknown, VI/VII)
which begins with incipits from the four gospels, in canonical order (*ll.*1–4) followed by most
of Ps. 90 (*ll.*5–29); parts of *vv.*7 and 8 are omitted at *l.*15.

D. JUDAICA

94. The earliest mention of a synagogue
Schedia (Egypt)   246–221BC
ed. — E. Breccia, *IGA* 2.11, p.6

ὑπὲρ βασιλέως
Πτολεμαίου καὶ
βασιλίσσης
Βερενίκης ἀδελ-
5   φῆς καὶ γυναικὸς καὶ
τῶν τέκνων
τὴν προσευχὴν
οἱ Ἰουδαῖοι.

Bib. — *CIJ* 2.1440 (pl.); *CPJ 3, App.1, p.141.

5   **For King Ptolemy and Queen Berenike, his sister | and wife, and for their children, the Jews built the synagogue.**

This inscription which mentions Ptolemy III Euergetes is one of the two earliest references to a synagogue 'in Egypt or indeed anywhere' (D.M. Lewis, n. ad loc. in *CPJ*). The other text, to be dated to the same reign, is *CPJ* 3, App.1, no.1532a (not in *CIJ* 2), from Arsinoe-Crocodilopolis, which follows a similar format and concludes before breaking off: οἱ ἐν Κροκ[ο]δίλων πόλει Ἰου[δαῖ]οι τὴν προ[σ]ε[υχήν] | --- (*ll.*9–11).

A synagogue built at Alexandria during IIBC was dedicated to Theos Hypsistos, as the fragmentary *IGA* 2.116 (= *CIJ* 2.1433 = *CPJ* 3, App.1, pp.139–40) shows (*CPJ* text printed here): ---θε]ῶι ὑψίστωι | [---τ]ὸν ἱερὸν | [περίβολον καὶ] τὴν προσ|[ευχὴν καὶ τὰ συγ]κύροντα, 'To the Highest God [the Jews of Alexandria (?)] (dedicated) the sacred precinct and the synagogue and the things belonging to it'.

An individual benefactor provided another synagogue at Alexandria in 37BC (*IGA* 2.41 = *CIJ* 2.1432 = *CPJ* 3, App.1, p.139): [ὑπὲρ βασιλίσ]|[ση]ς καὶ β[ασι]|[λ]έως θεῶι [με]|γάλωι ἐ[πηκό]|ωι, Ἄλυπ[ος τὴν] | προσε[υχὴν] | ἐπόει. [?*vacat*] | (ἔτους) ιε΄ Με[χείρ .], 'For the queen and the king, to the great God who hears (prayers) Alypos made the synagogue. Year 15, Mecheir . . .' The royalty referred to are Cleopatra VII and Ptolemy XVI Caesarion.

In all these examples 'synagogue' is the appropriate meaning for προσευχή; whether it is also the case at Acts 16.13, 16 is not certain. For the word συναγωγή from this year's texts note *IGCB* 6, a building inscription (Corinth, c.100BC–200AD): [συν]αγωγὴ Ἑβρ[αίων]. This text has already been picked up by MM, s.v. Ἑβραῖος; but Bees' commentary in *IGCB* is full of useful references. *TAM* 376 and 377 (= *CIJ* 2.799) are the concluding lines of epitaphs (both Nikomedeia, Roman period) which provide that those who disturb the tomb must pay one fine to the synagogue (τῇ συναγωγῇ, 376.9; τῇ συναγωγῇ τῶν | ᾿Ιουδέων, 377.4–5), and another to the town treasury. It is likely that *TAM* 319 should be restored somewhat similarly, δώσει τῇ ἁγειωτ[άτῃ συναγωγῇ---] (cf. *BE* [1976] 684, p.558; [1979] 557). For a non-Jewish use of συναγωγή cf. **11**, ad fin.

Other evidence of Judaism at Nikomedeia in *TAM* may be mentioned here briefly. *TAM* 374 (= *CIJ* 2.798), and 375 are epitaphs (III?) which conclude with the words εὐλογία πᾶσιν. Another possible candidate is *TAM* 364, a very fragmentary epitaph in which ᾿Ιο[υδαίῳ] is a suggested restoration at *l*.4 (see ed. n.), and which contains the wording --ἐν] | εἰρήνῃ ψ[υχή σου (5–6). The name ᾿Ιοῦστος at *TAM* 197 may well indicate that the deceased was a Jew: cf. **17**.

With the words above, εὐλογία πᾶσιν, note for comparison the mosaic from what appears to have been a Samaritan synagogue (Ramat-Aviv in Israel, end VI/VII init.) which includes two Greek and one Aramaic inscription, the latter written in Samaritan script. One of the Greek texts reads: εὐλογία καὶ ἡρήνη τῷ ᾿Ισρα[ὴ]λ καὶ τῷ τόπῳ, ἁ[μ]ήν, 'Blessing and peace to Israel and to this place, Amen.' See J.Kaplan, *Rev.Bib.* 84 (1978) 284–85 (pl.14); cf. *BE* 532.

95. A governor of Judaea under Vespasian

Jerusalem, near the temple   78-79
ed.pr. — M. Gichon/B. H. Isaac, *IEJ* (1974) 117–23 (pl.19)

> *Imp(erator) Caesar*
> *Vespasian[us]*
> *Aug(ustus), imp(erator) T(itus) [Cae-]*
> *sar Vesp(asianus) Aug(usti) [f(ilius)]*
> 5 *L(ucio) [Ant(onio) Sat(urnino) leg(ato)]*
> *Aug(usti) pr(o) pr(aetore)*
> *leg(io) X Fr(etensis).*

A round pillar in the shape and size of a milestone.
Bib. — *R. Syme, *JRS* 68 (1978) 12-21; *AE* 825.

Imperator Caesar Vespasian Augustus, Imperator Titus Caesar Vespasian son of the Augustus; legion 10 Fretensis (set this up) when Lucius Antonius Saturninus was legate of Augustus as pro-praetor.

Despite its shape and dimensions suggesting an affinity with *miliaria*, the inscription carved on this stone speaks for its most likely being to mark the dedication of a building in or near the camp of the legion which provided the Jerusalem garrison. From Vespasian to Hadrian the commander of legio X Fretensis also served as governor of Judaea. This legion served at the siege of Jerusalem in 70: *IGA* 2.61a, tablet A, face 4, mentions veterans *qui militaverunt Hierosolym{n}is* | *in leg(ione) X Fretense* (*ll.* 3-4), who were granted their honourable discharge on 29/12/93 after beginning service in 68 and 69. On this text see further the n. in *IGA* 2, pp.269-71. *Ed.pr.* suggested that *l.*5, where all but the initial *L* had been deliberately erased in antiquity, the name L. Flavius Silva should be restored. While governor of Judaea (from 73, but probably not until 78) Silva had been responsible for the capture of Masada, probably in 73 (possibly 74). Syme shows that this name is not a tenable restoration, and proposes instead L. Antonius Saturninus, governor of Judaea from 78-81. He may not have been Silva's immediate successor: a (still unknown) governor should perhaps be postulated between them (Syme, 15). After his service in Judaea, Saturninus became suffect consul in 82; but he is best remembered for his short-lived attempt at rebellion while legate of Germania Superior in 89 (cf. R. Syme, *Chiron* 13 [1983] 121-22). The failure of this endeavour accounts for the erasure of his name from the Jerusalem inscription. For a survey of the contribution of documentary texts to the literary evidence on Saturninus' revolt see B.W. Jones/R.D. Milns, *The use of Documentary Evidence in the Study of Roman Imperial History* (*Sources in Ancient History* 5; Sydney, 1984) 171-76.

In this context it is appropriate to mention the unique epigraphical reference to Pontius Pilate. First published in 1961, the most recent re-edition and discussion is in J.-P. Lémonon, *Pilate et le gouvernement de la Judée. Textes et Monuments* (Paris, 1981) 23-32 (pl.). His textual restorations make the stone read:

> [---]*s Tiberiéum*
> [? *Po*]*ntius Pilatus*
> [*praef*]*ectus Iuda*[*ea*]*e*
> [*fécit* ?]

The stone is not large, and it is certain it had only four lines of text, though much of it (including all the fourth line) has been erased. It was found at Caesarea, and possibly marks the dedication of a building to Tiberius, or identifies such a building as the 'Tiberieum' (a word not previously attested). Lémonon suggests (276) that the inscription is to be dated after 31, and its intention was to manifest Pilate's loyalty to Tiberius. Apart from its great interest for NT studies because of the attestation of Pilate's name, *l.*3 settles the dispute about the title used for the early governors of Judaea: they were *praefecti* not *procuratores*.

96. A judaizer from the Second Sophistic

During the course of an enlightening study of curses on Greek epitaphs L. Robert, *CRAI* (1978) 241-89 (cf. *SEG* 311, 358, 1609; the new inscription at his pp. 286-89 [= *SEG* 1586] is repr. at **65**), pays attention (245-52) to *IG* XII.9 (1915) 1179 (Chalkis in Euboia, II; repr. with one small change at *SIG*³ 1240; cf. *SEG* 721), a copy of which — minus the preceding six-verse epigram — appears also as *IG* XII.9.955. This epitaph for his son was set up by T. Flavius Amphikles, a pupil of Herodes Attikos. On his family see C.P. Jones, *HSCP* 74 (1970) 223-55, together with his remarks at *GRBS* 21(1980)377-80 which update the information about Amphikles.

The prose section of the inscription consists of 'cursing and blessing', the latter portion (35–41) much briefer than the former (13–34). There is an undoubted quotation of Deut. 28.22,28 at *ll.*22–27: τοῦ|τόν (i.e., the person who interferes with the site and with the herm of the dead son) τε θεὸς (LXX has κύριος) πατάξαι ἀπορίᾳ καὶ | πυρετῷ καὶ ῥίγει καὶ ἐρεθισμῷ (καὶ φόνῳ follows here in LXX except in Vaticanus) | καὶ ἀνεμοφθορίᾳ καὶ παραπλη|ξίᾳ καὶ ἀορασίᾳ καὶ ἐκστάσει δια|νοίας, 'God will strike this person with poverty, with fever and cold shivers, irritation, blight, derangement, blindness, and distraction of mind'. Once this debt to Deut. 28 is perceived (as was done by A. Wilhelm in his *ed.pr.* of 1892) it follows that certain other common features are also to be attributed to that origin (so Robert, 249–50), namely the use of ἐπικατάρατος (14) and εὐλόγοιτο (37), terms which appear with some frequency in that section of Deut. (27.15–28.68). Yet a caution should be sounded: is *direct* knowledge of the LXX ruled out by the fact that portions of two verses are quoted as though they were a continuum even though some of the intervening wording would also have been quite appropriate? The inference would be that the LXX material has therefore been mediated indirectly, perhaps via a collection of suitable formulae; one may compare the way in which Jewish influence in magical texts does not necessarily require direct acquaintance with Judaism.

In propounding a view somewhat like this, that 'the composer had simply adopted a syncretic formula of cursing which had been influenced by the Septuagint' (*LAE*, 23 n.4), Deissmann went a step further, claiming that there was nothing in the inscription to suggest that the author was anything but a pagan. Against this, Robert shows that the wording of the inscription reflects the impression made on Amphikles by Jewish monotheism. The mention of the Erinyes (34), Charis and Hygeia (41) does not necessarily testify to a pagan milieu: 'they are moral personifications not tainted with paganism' (Robert, 247–48, at 248). Further, the use of θεός and the omission of certain expected phrases (such as πρὸς θεῶν καὶ ἡρώων; cf. Robert, 247), together with these other elements, indicate cumulatively that the author of the inscription was either a Jew or a judaizer. Since the first option is ruled out by what we know of the man's identity, it is to be concluded that Amphikles 'had leanings to Judaism' (Jones, 378).

This is a matter of considerable surprise, for it has been customary to think of Greek intellectuals of this period as looking back over their shoulders to their own heritage. Yet here is a participant in the Second Sophistic consciously looking elsewhere, and the inscription thus gives us a hitherto unrecognized witness to the penetration of Jewish monotheism among the intelligentsia of Old Greece under the early Empire (cf. Robert, 250). If this interpretation by Robert of the inscription and its author is sustained, it underscores the considerable advance in NT work that may be expected from the re-evaluation of the importance of rhetoric for men like Paul and Apollos. Cross-fertilization between the Graeco-Roman and Jewish intellectual traditions is exemplified in Philo; but whether such intercourse occurred during I and IIAD in specific areas like rhetoric is now beginning to be investigated. As one example, C.B. Forbes discusses the rhetorical convention of 'comparison' (σύγκρισις) in Paul, in an article forthcoming in *NTS*.

Though the amount of quotation is brief, this inscription deserves not to be neglected for the comparatively early witness it provides — and the sole one outside Egypt — to the Greek text of Deut. It receives no mention in, e.g., J.W. Wevers, *Text History of the Greek Deuteronomy (Abh. der Ak. der Wiss. in Göttingen, Mitteil. des Septuaginta-Unternehmens* 13; Göttingen, 1978). On the lexicographical front it may be noted that LSJ cites both the two *IG* inscriptions and the Deut. passage under several lemmata; the unwary user might think several independent testimonies to the same word were being provided. Their entry on παραπληξία needs correction: the reference to the inscription (s.v., I) should join the Deut. reference (s.v., II).

On the question of 'Godfearers' see **17**, containing brief discussion of articles by M. Wilcox and A.T. Kraabel. A synagogue inscription from Aphrodisias in Karia soon to be published by J. Reynolds — cf. the report in *AJA* 81 (1977) 306 — lists separately several individuals as *theosebeis*. The text 'seems to confirm that θεοσεβεῖς could be a formal designation for a group distinct from both proselytes and native Jews, but still enrolled in the membership of a synagogue' (W.A. Meeks, *The First Urban Christians* [New Haven 1983] 208 n.175). The evidence of this inscription may well prove to undermine the force of Kraabel's argument.

For another curse-warning on a tombstone from 1978 publications see *I.Magnesia Sip.* 28.6–13 (n.d.).

E. ECCLESIASTICA

97. A Christian woodcarver

Nikomedeia   not later than III

ed.pr. — L. Robert, *BCH* 102 (1978) 413–19 (pl.3b on p.412)

Εὐμοίρι͜ος
(*mallet*)   Πάπο͜ς *(chisel)*
Ἀράδιος ξυλο-
γλύφος κῖμε
5 λείψανον ἐν-
θάδε, πρόμοι-
ρος κακῶν, ἐτῶν
† μα΄. Χαίρετε
παροδῖτε.

Stele from the west necropolis
Bib. — *SEG* 1037

5 **Papos the Fortunate from Arados, woodcarver, I — my remains — lie |here, forestalling troubles, aged 41. Greetings, wayfarer!**

Papos' home town is in Phoenicia, but his presence at Nikomedeia is no cause for surprise, given his trade. The cultivation of large forests for timber export was important to the economy of cities and towns in this part of Asia Minor (see Robert, 415–19). The tools depicted on the gravestone draw attention to his occupation.

It cannot be doubted that Papos was a Christian: Robert (414) regards the cross carved at the beginning of *l.*8 as an integral part of the epitaph, not added later. He refers to two other pre-Constantinian epitaphs from Bithynia, one with a cross, the other referring to the deceased parents as τοῖς ἀγνοτάτοις καὶ τῷ θεῷ πιστεύσασιν, 'to the most holy ones who also trusted God'. The epigraphical evidence thus provides testimony to continuing Christian activity in Bithynia in the century and more after Pliny served there (cf. *Ep.* 10.96). Furthermore, in this new epitaph Papos has adopted the surname Eumoirios, placing it first as another indication of his own religious outlook; Robert points out (414–15) that the epitaph formula εὐμοίρει is universally Christian, occurring in the Greek East as well as in the West. Whether there is intended a play on words with πρόμοιρος κακῶν (6–7) is uncertain, though likely enough. The latter phrase should probably not be pressed to mean more than that he forestalled the troubles of old age by dying at 41 (so Robert). Yet though we have no more specific a date than before the end of III, the possibility of a passing allusion to persecution in these words makes this inscription most tantalizing.

98. Christian inscriptions from Phrygia

1. Χριστιανοὶ Χριστιανοῖς Inscriptions

Eymir (Upper Tembris Valley, N.Phrygia)   IV(?)

ed.pr. — E. Gibson, *'Christians for Christians'* 19, pp.50–51(pl.19)

Χρηστιανοὶ
Χρηστιανοῖς.
(*wreath*)
Αὐρ. Πατρίκις κὲ Μακεδόν-
ις κὲ Ζωτικὸς κὲ Ἀμμιὰς κὲ Ἐ-
5   πικτῆς γνησίῳ πατρὶ Κυρίλλῳ κὲ μητρὶ Ἀμμίᾳ κὲ υἱοῖς
Ὀνησίμῳ κὲ Κυρίλλῳ κὲ Πα-
τρικίῳ κὲ ἀδελφῇ Δόμνῃ
μνήμης χάριν.
10   A

White marble grave stele with projecting top and base. The large *alpha*, near the bottom of the stone, probably denotes the order in which this stele stood next to others in a graveyard. It is not part of the main inscription.

Bib. — *SEG* 1100; A. Strobel, *Das heilige Land der Montanisten* (Berlin, 1980) 110

> **Christians for Christians. Aurelios Patrikis and Makedonis and Zotikos and Ammias**
> 5 **and | Epiktes, for their dear father, Kyrillos, and their mother, Ammia, and their sons**
> **Onesimos and Kyrillos and Patrikios and for their sister Domna, in remembrance.**

This is one of seven new χριστιανοὶ χριστιανοῖς epitaphs published by Gibson in her corpus of these inscriptions (Gibson 3 = *SEG* 1096; 5 = 1107; 7 = 1108; 8 = 1104; 9 = 1097; 10 = 1098; 19 = 1100). Gibson considers her no.11 (= *SEG* 1099) to be an eighth new χρ.-χρ. epitaph, perhaps incorrectly as it only contains the single word χρηστιανοῖς. Gibson 4 (not in *SEG*) is a ninth new tombstone which may have contained a χρ.-χρ. inscription, but the text is missing. Previously published χρ.-χρ. epitaphs (Gibson 1–2, 12–14, 17–18, 20–24, 27–29) and one (no.6), better classified as a 'χριστιανοί inscription' (see below), complete the corpus (cf. *BE* [1979] 522). Some new (Gibson 16, 25–26, 31–34, 42) and a number of previously published (15, 30, 35–41, 43–45) Phrygian inscriptions are given for comparison (see *SEG* 1078 for tabulation of all inscriptions republished by Gibson and for a summary of additional relevant information provided by her).

The formula χριστιανοὶ χριστιανοῖς, entirely confined to inscriptions from the Upper Tembris Valley (N. Phrygia), indicates that the Christians named on the tombstones constructed the tomb for, or 'to the memory of', their Christian relatives. As in this instance, the formula often stands apart at the beginning (cf. 2, 18, 22, 24) or as the last phrase (cf. 1, 3, 5, 7–9, 12, 21). Nevertheless, at least during the early stages of its development, it could be adapted grammatically to suit the sense of the main inscription (see below) or be split up (e.g., no.10).

Orthography

The orthography of the word 'Christian' varies on the χρ.-χρ. epitaphs: χριστιανός (Gibson 18, 23), χρειστιανός (1–2, 22), χρηστιανός (3, 8, 10–11, 14, 20–21, 24, 27–29). The last of these forms occurs on a large number of Christian inscriptions from Phrygia (e.g., Gibson 6, 32, 44) and elsewhere (e.g., A. Ferrua, *Riv. Arch. Chr.* 31 [1955] 97–100 [Rome]; *IGLR* [1976] 10 [Tomis]). *Codex Sinaiticus* uses χρηστιανός consistently: Acts 11.26; 26.8; 1 Pet. 4.16. W.M. Ramsay (*Expositor* 8 [1888] 251–55), followed by J.G.C. Anderson (in W.M. Ramsay [ed.], *Studies in the History and Art of the Eastern Provinces of the Roman Empire* [Aberdeen, 1906] 198, 214–16), used these variations as a basis for dating the χρ.-χρ. monuments, arguing that those which used χρειστιανός were the earliest, χρηστιανός next (both pre-IV), and χριστιανός last. This is pure speculation. Although the spelling χρειστιανός occurs on some epitaphs (not of the χρ.-χρ. type) with an indisputable third-century date (e.g., Gibson 42 = *SEG* 1202) the spelling is attested as late as VIII (cf. *New Docs 1977*, **102**) and was popular on post-Constantinian Phrygian monuments (e.g., Gibson 35, 38, 40, 43). Moreover, it is evident from Gibson's pl.4 of one of the only three χρ.-χρ. monuments employing χρειστιανός (her no.2) that χρ.-χρ. was carved in that instance by a later hand, suggesting that, even if the monument itself dates from III, its formula may not. Besides, the attempt to distinguish these spellings chronologically founders upon the linguistic fact that there is a nearly complete overlapping of the sounds represented by ι, ει, η in *koine*. Confusion between ι/ει occurs in classical dialects (see C.D. Buck, *The Greek Dialects* [Chicago, 1955] §28–29), and occurs in Attic inscriptions from 300BC (Gignac, 1.191 n.2). By the Roman period ει is commonly written for short ι: forms like δειά, εἶνα, ἐστείν, and τει are all attested in IAD papyri (further examples in Gignac, 1.190–91; *NIP* IV.48 [mid-III], quoted below, has τεις at *l*.6). By this same century η is also occurring frequently for ι, with such forms as ἠδιοτικῶν, βασιληκή (numerous other examples listed in Gignac 1.237–39). In inscriptions from Attika and Asia Minor the interchangeability of η/ι is attested from II (Gignac, 1.242 n.1); and Gignac provides plenty of evidence (1.239–42) from Roman and Byzantine papyri for the interchange of η/ει, with forms like εἰμῖν for ἡμῖν, ἠ for εἰ, and ἠμί for εἰμί. 'This interchange of η with ι and ει reflects the phonological development of the Greek Koine, in which the sound originally represented by η generally merged with /i/ by the second century A.D. In the later papyri, however, there is a noticeable increase in the frequency of these interchanges' (ibid., 241–42).

Yet, this said, the similarity between Χριστός/χρηστός (cf. Suet., *Claud.* 25.4) seems to have led to the widespread ancient assumption that χριστιανός/χρη-/χρει- derived from χρηστός (see Tert., *Apol.* 3.5; Lact., *Div. Inst.* 4.7.5; F. Blass, *Hermes* 30 [1895] 468–70). Some of the Fathers, although themselves consistently employing the spelling χριστιανός, occasionally connected the term with χρηστός by a play on words (e.g., Just., *1 Apol.* 4.1; Thphl. Ant., *Autol.* 1.12). A similar play on words, but using the spelling χρηστιανός, is evident in an inscription from Syracuse: [Χ]ρυσὶς χρηστὴ χρησσιανὴ (*sic*: see below) Χρ(ιστὸν) πιστεύσασα (S. Agnello, *Silloge di iscrizioni paleocristiane della Sicilia* [Rome, 1953] 34). Gibson ingeniously suggests (p.16) that there may even be some intended word play in the two clear examples of the use of χρηστός in the NT: Lk. 6.35; Eph. 4.32. Attestations of χρηστιανός/-ή on papyri dating from III[2] are given in *New Docs 1977*, **102**, showing that the term was used by civil servants to describe people whom they knew to be Christians.

Turning now to the consonant cluster -στ- in χριστιανός, some papyri attest the omission of the τ: *PSI* 14 (1957) 1412 (with Rea's correction noted at *P.Oxy.* 36 [1970] 2785, n. to *l*.2); *P.Oxy.* 42 (1974) 3035 (for the quotations from these texts, dated II/III, and 256, respectively, see *New Docs 1977*, **102**). A similar omission of the τ is evident in some Phrygian inscriptions (e.g., Gibson 27, 30). One of Gibson's newly published χρ.-χρ.

inscriptions (9) substitutes an extra σ for the τ: χρησσιανοὶ χρησσιανῷ. The·use of the -σσ- is also attested in Sicily (Agnello, no.34) and, in its Latin form, in Rome (Ferrua, *Riv.Arch.Chr.* 17 [1940] 71) and Salona (O. Montevecchi, in *Paradoxos Politeia* [Festschrift G. Lazzati] 490 [cited in *New Docs 1976*, **76**]). These variations are not unexpected, for the voiceless stops π, κ and τ are occasionally omitted when they occur with other consonants (Gignac, 1.64). Where σ is found for στ, either τ has been omitted or it has been assimilated without any orthographic replacement by σ. For the assimilation of τ after σ note for example ἐσσί for ἐστί, and πισσικίου for πιστικίου (further examples at Gignac, 1.66). This occurs most commonly before ι — as in the case of χρησσιανός — though not exclusively so (e.g., ἐπισόλιον for ἐπιστόλιον, σαδίου for σταδίου; see further, Gignac, 1.67). Alteration from χρηστιανός to χρησιανός/χρησσιανός is probably to be connected with the following /i/ rather than with the vowel preceding the -στ- cluster. The papyri also provide evidence of false correction of this phenomenon: προφεστίονα for προφεσσίωνα; εὖ πράστιν for εὖ πράσσειν: cf. Gignac, 1.66 for the former; the latter occurs at *P.Oxy.* 31 (1966) 2600.2 (III/IV). The papyrus evidence from Egypt, together with the epigraphical evidence from such regions as Phrygia and Italy, confirms it as a general feature of *koine* that -στ- was being assimilated in speech to -σσ- before ι, and perhaps before other vowels.

These two phonological developments in *koine*, the overlapping of ι/η/ει, and the assimilation of the consonant cluster -στ- to -σσ- (especially before ι), result in the fluid orthography of χριστιανός. Apart from the linguistic phenomenon, however, masons' errors in inscriptions are a factor not to be overlooked, as is illustrated by the χρ.-χρ. formula in Gibson 5 = *SEG* 1107 (Karaağaç, IV(?)); the first three lines are entirely lost:

> [- -] Ἑρμόδωρος Τροφίμ[ῳ]
> 5   πατρὶ κὲ μητρί· κὲ Λου-
>   κειανῆς νύνφη
>   κὲ τὰ ἔγγονα αὐτῶν Χα-
>   ρίτων κὲ Εὐγενία.
>   Χριστιανοὶ Χρηστιανοῖς.

5 . . . and Hermodoros for Trophimos | his father and for his mother; and Loukeianes, their daughter-in-law (for her parents-in-law) and their grandchildren Chariton and Eugenia (for their grandparents). Christians for Christians.

The juxtaposition of the different ways of spelling 'Christians' in this inscription not only indicates genuine confusion on the part of the engraver, but puts paid to the theory that the various forms, by themselves, can be used to date the χρ.-χρ. epitaphs. (This section on orthography owes a great deal to the comments of A.L. Connolly.)

A Montanist connection? The problem of dating

Ever since the discovery of the first of these epitaphs, over a century ago, the question of the date and religious origin of the χρ.-χρ. monuments has remained controversial, and unresolved. After surveying the major theories, Gibson suggests (125–44) that they are possibly Montanist, but that the evidence is inconclusive. Similarly, in his recent discussion of the χρ.-χρ. formula, Strobel (104–12) is undecided, although he suspects that they are not, or at least not exclusively, Montanist.

It was W.M. Ramsay who first suggested the possible Montanist nature of the χρ.-χρ. epitaphs, noting the similarity between the attitude of the dedicators of these tombstones and some alleged aspects of Montanist theology and practice: *JHS* 4 (1883) 370-436; id., *Cities and Bishoprics of Phrygia* (2 parts, cited below as *CB* 1 and *CB* 2; Oxford, 1895-97) 2.510 n.1; id., *Byzantion* 6 (1931) 1-35. This suggestion was popularized by W.M. Calder, who argued that the dedicators' 'provocative' attitude to the State was consistent with Montanist views encouraging voluntary martyrdom and refusing to allow flight during persecution: *BJRL* 7 (1923) 309-54; id., in *Anatolian Studies presented to Sir William Mitchell Ramsay* (Manchester, 1923) 15-26; id., *BJRL* 13 (1929) 254-71; id., *Byzantion* 6 (1931) 421-25; id., *AS* 5 (1955) 25-38. This view has found its way into many modern text-books on Church History. But can the major premise on which it rests, i.e., that the tombstones are third-century monuments, be sustained? The case for a third-century date, accepted by all editors from Ramsay to Strobel, is based almost entirely on the following inscription from Altıntaş republished by Gibson (no.22 = W.H. Buckler et al., *JRS* 18 [1928] 21-22 no.231, fig.1; text given here is Gibson's but amended to conform with Buckler et al.; stone not seen by Gibson [p.56]):

[τ]λγ´.
Χρειστιανοὶ
Χρειστιανο[ῖς].
Αὐρ. Ἀμμεία
5 σὺν τῷ γαμβρ[ῷ]
αὐτῶν Ζωτι-
κῷ κὲ σὺν τοῖ[ς]

ἐγόνοις αὐτῶ[ν]
Ἀλλεξανδρείᾳ
10 κὲ Τελεσφόρῳ
κὲ Ἀλλεξάνδρῳ
συνβίῳ ἐποίη-
σαν.

5 **(In the year) [3(?)]33. Christians for Christians. Aurelia Ammeia, | with their (*sic*) son-**
10 **in-law Zotikos and with their (*sic*) grand-children Allexandreia | and Telesphoros and**
Allexandros, constructed (this tomb) for her husband.

This is the only dated example of a χρ.-χρ. inscription (for dated χριστιανοί inscriptions, see below). Although the word ἔτους is not visible, there is little doubt that λγ´ in *l*.1 represents part of a date. However, the restoration [τ]λγ´, 333 (Sullan era) = 248/9AD is by no means unchallengable. Perrot, the earliest publisher of this inscription (in G. Perrot et al., *Exploration archéologique de la Galatie et de la Bithynie, d'une partie de la Mysie, de la Phrygie, de la Cappadoce et du Pont* [2 vols., Paris, 1862-1872; reprinted N.Y., 1972] 1, no.90), did not notice the date. Ramsay, who also saw the stone and published the inscription in translation only (*Expositor* 8 [1888] 251-52, no.2) wrote, 'Part of the first line is illegible, and there remain only the two symbols indicating thirty and three' (251). Ramsay based his restoration on two pre-suppositions, neither of which has been challenged to date. Firstly, he compared this inscription with another from Akmonia(?) which contains both the single word χρειστιανοί and a clearly visible date: Ἔτους τξγ´, 363 (id., no.1 = Gibson no.36; pl.31). Ramsay classified this as one of the χρ.-χρ. inscriptions. But it is important to emphasize the difference between inscriptions which are only prepared to reveal the Christianity of the deceased by the use of the single word χριστιανοί and inscriptions which openly declare the adherence of the dedicators as well as that of the deceased by the use of the χρ.-χρ. formula. The χρ.-χρ. texts are likely to be later in date than the χριστιανοί type of inscription.

Consequently, restoring a date on a χρ.-χρ. inscription so as to precede a date found on a χριστιανοί one is open to serious doubt, at best; at worst, it is illegitimate. Ramsay supported his restoration by pointing to the use of the *nomen* Aurelia in this inscription, but this is not a foolproof criterion by which to establish a third-century date. It provides a likely *terminus post quem* but not necessarily a *terminus ante quem*, as many people who took the name Aurelios or Aurelia after 212 in honour of the emperor who granted them Roman citizenship handed their *nomina* on to their children. Many post-Constantinian inscriptions still bear the letters Αὐρ.

Anderson, influenced by Ramsay's arguments and in possession of Ramsay's notebook, made a new copy of the stone on a visit to Asia Minor in 1897, noting his restoration as ΤΛΓ (Anderson, op. cit., p.214). It is certain that he saw the lower portion of the λ, and the γ. Whether he actually saw a faint τ, even though he thought he did, is not as certain. The rough texture of the projection on which the letters were carved makes it extremely difficult to distinguish a faint capital Τ from alternatives such as a faint Υ. A number of *upsilons* carved on the shaft of the stone have quite small left and right diagonal bars at the top. Anderson, influenced by Ramsay, may have mistaken the remnants of Υ for the remnants of Τ. If so, the date should be restored to read [Ἔτους υ]λγ΄, 'in the year 433' (Sullan era) = 348/9AD. Buckler et al. (p.21) were adamant that only the lower part and the right-hand tip of the Γ and part of the right bar of the Λ were visible when they saw the stone. They made another observation which would tend to support a later date. Anderson, following Ramsay, read an ω as the last letter in *l*.3. The resulting formula: χρειστιανοὶ χρειστιανῷ is grammatically consistent with the content of the text, in that a number of Christians buried *one* Christian. A squeeze taken by Buckler et al., however, supported their reading of an *omikron*. Unless the *omikron* was simply a mistake for ω (common in papyri) the grammar of the resultant reading, χρειστιανοὶ χρειστιανο[ῖς], no longer coheres with the content of the inscription. On most other tombstones the grammar of the formula specifies that a *number* of Christians were burying *one* Christian (Gibson 12, 18, 20–21). A plausible reason for the inconsistency between the use of the plural form of the formula and the text of some of the tombstones may be found in Gibson's discovery that the formula χρειστιανοὶ χρειστιανοῖς in a previously published inscription (2 [pl.4]) was added by a later hand (see above, under 'Orthography'). The text declares that only *one* Christian, Aurelios Zotikos Markianos, prepared the tomb for a *number* of his relatives, yet the (later) engraver chose to use the plural formula: 'Christians for Christians'. Could it be that by the time he added the formula the, by then familiar, plural form had become a cliché which overrode the particular content of any text? If so, inscriptions which link the formula grammatically to the text are likely to be earlier than ones which use the plural form despite its grammatical inconsistency with what is revealed by the text — suggesting that the dated inscription under discussion is not one of the earliest of the χρ.-χρ. type, but one of the later ones. The date 348/9AD would be consistent with this. Gibson (p.64) dates nos. 27–29 to IV[1], arguing that they are the latest occurrences of the χρ.-χρ. formula; but this is based on the assumption that χρ.-χρ. is a third-century phenomenon. If the dated χρ.-χρ. inscription under discussion really does belong to mid-IV, as argued here, all other χρ.-χρ. inscriptions, including Gibson 27–29, can be placed well into IV, where they become part of a consistent pattern. Open profession of Christianity, including references to χρηστιανοὶ πρεσβύτεροι (no.29), is not provocative in the post-Constantinian era.

Postulating a post-Constantinian date for the χρ.-χρ. monuments also removes any obvious link with Montanism other than the coincidental one of geography; and even that link is very tenuous. Whilst it is true that Montanism commenced in *southern* Phrygia, the χρ.-χρ. inscriptions are all from the Upper Tembris Valley in the *north* of Phrygia and there is no independent evidence of Montanism having spread to that region. Moreover, positive epigraphical evidences for the spread of Montanism to other places outside of southern Phrygia do not contain the χρ.-χρ. formula. In any case, irrespective of their date, explanations of the religious origin of the χρ.-χρ. monuments based on 'Montanist zeal' are not convincing. There is no suggestion on any of the tombstones that the dedicators flaunted their Christianity in the face of persecutors, or that they intentionally provoked martyrdom. There is certainly no hint that any Christians named on the tombstones had been martyred. Nor can the contention that voluntary martyrs were invariably Montanists be substantiated. Although some Montanist oracles may appear to have encouraged the desire for martyrdom — see, most recently, D.E. Aune, *Prophecy in Early Christianity and the Ancient Medieval World* (Grand Rapids, 1983) 313–16 — there is no evidence to suggest that, whilst Montanists might pray to be deemed worthy to receive the martyr's crown, they answered their own prayers. Montanist and Catholic theology, in fact, differed little on the issue; both condemned voluntary martyrdom as irresponsible (W. Tabbernee, *Opposition to Montanism from Church and State* [Diss. Melbourne, 1978] 189–287). Finally, neither the formula itself (see H. Grégoire, *Byzantion* 1 [1924] 708; S. Mitchell, *JTS* 31 [1980] 203) nor the artwork (see H.W. Pleket, *VC* 34 [1980] 197) gives any of the signs we would expect to see if they were Montanist epitaphs.

Chi carved as a cross

Viewing the χρ.-χρ. inscriptions as remnants of post-Constantinian Christian orthodoxy rather than as remnants of pre-Constantinian Montanism enables us to ultilise them to discover a great deal more about what it was like to be a Christian in a remote part of the Empire during IV. A good example of this is Gibson, no.3 = *SEG* 1096 (Yalnizsaray, IV):

Αὐρ. Εὔτυ†ος Μενάνδ[ρου]
κὲ Πρόκλα τέκνῳ Κυρίλλῳ κὲ [νύ-]
μφῃ Δόμνῃ κὲ ἐγγόνῳ Κυριακῷ
καταλιπόντες τέκνα ὀρφανὰ
5 Ἀλέξανδρον κὲ Πρόκλαν· κὲ Αὐ[ρ.]
Εὔτυχος ἀδελφῷ Κυρίλλῳ κὲ ἐνατρὶ Δόμνῃ· κὲ Εὐτυ†ιανὴς δαέρι
[Κ]υρίλλῳ κὲ ἐνατρὶ Δόμνῃ.
†ρησ-
10 τιανοὶ †ρησ-
τιανοῖς.

Aurelios Eutychos, son of Menandros, and Prokla (made this tomb) for their child Kyrillos, his wife Domna, and their son Kyriakos, who leave orphaned their children
5 **|Alexandros and Prokla; and Aurelios Eutychos for his brother Kyrillos and his sister-in-law Domna; and Eutychianes for her brother-in-law Kyrillos and her sister-in-law**
10 **Domna. Christians |for Christians.**

The tombstone containing this inscription — *ll.*9–11 are encircled with a wreath — is typical of the χρ.-χρ. funerary altars of the Upper Tembris Valley (cf. Gibson, 4–5, and probably 6-7). They, like the more elaborate χρ.-χρ. *stelai* (8-15), were probably products of the same workshop (Gibson, pp.41-45). The main shaft of these altars is separated visually from their trapezoidal top and their base by means of horizontal garlands and the shaft itself is normally divided into registers. The lowest register invariably contains teams of oxen (with or without ploughs) suggesting the agricultural life-style of the people, and the top register contains a large wreath encircling a cross. Both oxen and wreaths are carved in relief and are usually of better artistic quality than other symbols contained on the shaft, indicating that the altars (with garlands, wreath, cross, and oxen) were prepared beforehand. The inscription was added at the time of purchase as were any other symbols particularly relevant to the deceased. To facilitate this, the shaft could be subdivided into further registers by simple double horizontal lines.

Because the inscription of this particular epitaph was lengthy, the engraver decided to use the space beneath the wreath to create a middle register in which he carved open tablets with stylus (denoting literacy), spindle, distaff and carding comb. Insufficient room on the shaft necessitated the engraver using the trapezoidal top for the main inscription and the blank space within the wreath for †ρηστιανοὶ †ρηστιανοῖς. Apart from in the name Εὔτυχος in *l*.6, the engraver consistently carved *chi* in the shape of a Greek cross. Even in *l*.6 the *chi* is tilted slightly, although not as much as the *chi* in the same name in *l*.1. Although these 'crosses' could be intentional indications of Christianity, this is extremely doubtful. On this, and other Phrygian Christian tombstones, intentional symbolic representations of a cross are normally in the shape of a Latin cross (cf. Gibson 4-5, 8-10, 12, 15) or, if in the shape of a Greek cross, are drawn with parallel double lines (see 25-27; cf. *New Docs 1976*, **86**). In a number of Gibson's inscriptions the *chi* is tilted at various angles (5, 8, 10, 12-13, 16, 31; cf. *BE*(1979) 527), often inconsistently within particular inscriptions, as in the χρ.-χρ. formulae of nos.8 and 13. In the light of the irregular formation of these, and the other letters of the inscriptions, and the fact that *chi*s are carved like 'Greek crosses' on obviously non-Christian Phrygian inscriptions (no.16 and discussion, p.39) it seems best to conclude that no suggestion of 'Greek crosses' was intended by the dedicators of the χρ.-χρ. inscriptions. What is clear, however, is that the dedicators and the deceased belonged to extended families (cf. nos.27-29).

Hence, a fairly comprehensive picture emerges about the people whose lives and deaths are recorded on the χρ.-χρ. inscriptions of the Upper Tembris Valley. They were orthodox Christians, literate agriculturalists who belonged to extended families which included people involved in civil and ecclesiastical affairs. For a most illuminating study of what may be learned from the decoration on votive inscriptions and gravestones about social and economic life in Roman Phrygia see M. Waelkens, *Anc.Soc.* 8 (1977) 277-315 (cf. *BE* 466).

2. Χριστιανοί **Inscriptions**

Akmonia (Central Phrygia)   III/IV(?)
ed.pr. — E. Gibson, *'Christians for Christians'* 32, pp.103-04 (pls.26-27)

(*leaf*) ἔτ[ους] ταπ´.   τῷ γλυκυτάτῳ
Αὐρ. Ἰουλία τῷ   μου τέκνῳ Σεβή-
πατ[ρὶ - - - -] Α   ρῳ καὶ Μουνδάνῃ
ΤΟ [καὶ τῇ μητρὶ] Βε-   νύμφῃ μνήμης χά-
5 ρονεικιαν[ῇ] καὶ   10 ριν. Χρειστιανοί.

White marble funerary altar with projecting moulding. On the left side an unrolled scroll above a stylus case; on the back, a highly stylized wreath above a corbel.
Bib. — *SEG* 1082; *BE*(1979) 534; Strobel, 112–13

5 **In the year 381. Aurelia Julia for her father . . . and her mother |Beroneikiane, and for my sweetest child Severus and my daughter-in-law Moundane, in remembrance.**
10 **|Christians.**

This is a good example of inscriptions which, unlike the χρ.-χρ. ones, use the single word χριστιανοί to declare that the *deceased* were Christians without explicitly designating the religion of the dedicators (cf. 33–36, 42); in most cases the inflexion of the word is decisive for this view. Its date, ἔτ[ους] ταπ΄, 'in the year 381', is clearly visible, as is the date on a similar inscription from the same region: ἔτους τξγ΄, i.e. 'in the year 363' (Gibson 36: the inscription used by Ramsay as a precedent for restoring the date 333 on one of the χρ.-χρ. inscriptions [see above]). These dates suggest that the tombstones were set up in III². If the Akmonian inscriptions employed the Sullan era, reckoned from the reconquest of Asia by Sulla in 85/84BC, their dates refer to 296/7AD and 278/9AD respectively. However, it is not inconceivable that they used the Actian era, reckoned from Augustus' victory over Antony and Cleopatra in 31BC, in which case the intended dates are 349/50AD and 331/2AD. Despite Ramsay's claim (*The Historical Geography of Asia Minor* [London, 1890] 441–42) that it was not used in pro-consular Asia, a number of dated inscriptions from Phrygia make sense only if they employed the 'Actian era'; e.g., W.H. Buckler, *JHS* 37 (1917) 8. One of the most interesting examples (*IGRR*, 4 [1927] 626) is from Uşak (Trajanopolis(?)) in the region of Akmonia. It is dated ἔτους σπβ΄, 'in the year 282', and contains the name of the emperor Trebonianus Gallus (251–53), revealing that the Actian and not the Sullan era was used (Tabbernee, op. cit., 317–31). Whilst some second-century inscriptions discovered at Uşak (e.g., Ramsay, *JHS* 8 [1887] pp.517–18; P. Le Bas and W.H. Waddington, *Voyage archéologique en Grèce et en Asie Mineure* 3.5 [Paris, 1870; repr. Hildesheim, 1972] no.1676) definitely used the 'Sullan era', the ancient city on whose site Uşak stands, or even the whole Akmonian region, may have decided to adopt the Actian era during III.

This is not to argue that all Phrygian inscriptions which openly profess the Christian allegiance of the deceased must be post-Constantinian in date. A newly discovered dated inscription of this type from Uckuyu, further south in Phrygia (Gibson, no.42 = *SEG* 1202; cf. Strobel, 117–20), is indisputably III. Its clearly visible date: [ἔ]τους τκζ΄, 'in the year 327' must refer to III irrespective of whether it employed the Sullan era (= 242/3) or, as is unlikely in this case, the Actian era (= 295/6). Hence, even if the Akmonian χριστιανοί inscriptions are pre-Constantinian, they, like the Uckuyu inscription, still fit into the pattern emerging about Phrygian inscriptions in which Christianity is openly professed. During III², if not earlier, Christians and pagans co-existed relatively peacefully in Phrygia (Strobel, 117). Consequently, Christians from mid-III on appear to have felt sufficiently secure to acknowledge publicly the religion of the *deceased* — something which most of their neighbours would have known anyway. They, however, were not yet ready to declare on public monuments that the (still living) dedicators were also Christians. Whilst this latter declaration may not have supplied new information, it would have supplied indisputable evidence which could have been used against them if the prevailing tolerant attitude ever changed for the worse. In the pre-Constantinian period there was a vast difference between being known as, or suspected of being, a Christian and openly declaring this on a public monument during one's life-time. Inscriptions (such as Gibson 37–39, 44–45) which use the single word χριστιανοί inclusively to refer to the dedicator(s) as well as to the deceased are, like the χρ.-χρ. inscriptions, surely post-Constantinian.

3. The formula ἔσται αὐτῷ πρὸς τὸν θεόν

Eumeneia (S. Phrygia)   III
ed.pr. — T. Drew-Bear, *NIP* IV.44, p.106 (pl.34)

Ἀγαθεῖνος κα[τ]εσ-   ἴ τι⟨ς⟩ δὲ ἕτερος ἐπιχ-
κεύασεν τὸ ἡρῷ-   ειρήσει θεῖνέ τινα,
ον ἑαυτῷ καὶ τῇ (γ)-   ἔστε αὐτῷ πρὸς τ-
υνεκὶ αὐτοῦ καὶ το-   ὸν θεόν.
5 ῖς τέκνοις αὐτοῦ· ε-

White marble block, decorated at top by two akroteria in relief framing a diadem.
Bib. — *SEG* 1161; *BE*(1979) 520

5 **Agatheinos constructed the tomb for himself and for his wife and for | his children; but**
if any one attempts to intrude another, he shall be answerable to God.

This is the first of five new (*NIP* IV.44 = *SEG* 1161; 46 = 1155; 47 = 1148; 48 = 1144; 49 = 1129) and one republished (45 = *CB* 2.358 = *SEG* 1156) Phrygian inscriptions classified by Drew-Bear as Christian. The text of this inscription, and of four of the others, contains variants of the so-called Eumeneian formula: ἔσται αὐτῷ πρὸς τὸν θεόν (see *New Docs 1976*, **86**).

It was extremely common for people in Asia Minor to try to protect their tombs by means of sepulchral threats. In Lydia and Lykaonia-Kilikia, for example, the god Men — particularly Μὴν καταχθόνιος — was often invoked as protector of graves: *CMRDM* 1.145–47, 149–51 (Ikonion); 154 (Lystra); 2.AD6, p.179 (Perta). After stating who is buried, these inscriptions adjure Men to protect the tomb against damage and unauthorised burials. Transgressors are threatened with Men's anger. In no.147 a fine is prescribed.

Christians, as well as others, felt the need to protect their graves. One of the earliest known Christian tombstones, that of Aberkios Markellos from Hieropolis (Phrygia), prescribed a fine for people who attempted to place another in the tomb (*CB* 2.657; discussed most recently by M. Guarducci, *Epigrafia Greca* 4 [Rome, 1978] 377–86, where dated c.170–200). Some of the χρ.-χρ. inscriptions, whilst not levying (impossible to enforce) fines, threaten impending doom (e.g., Gibson 27). Another contains the phrase τὸν θεόν σοι ἀναγνοὺς μὴ ἀδικήσῃς: 'By God, having read (this inscription), do not abuse (the tomb)' (Gibson 29, cf. 28). Variants of this formula (on which see Gibson pp.62–63) were popular amongst Christians in N.W. Phrygia, whereas δώσει λόγον τῷ θεῷ ('he shall render account to God') and ἕξει (ἔχει) πρὸς τὸν θεόν ('he shall have to deal with God') were common in E. Phrygia (Calder, *AS* 5 [1955] 25–28). For a recently published example of the latter see C. Mango/ I. Ševčenko *DOP* 32 (1978) 12–13 no.15 (provenance unknown, VI; = *SEG* 1582), where a useful note on the phrase is provided. This text concludes with the warning καὶ λάβῃ | τὴν θλῖψι|ν τῆς μητ|ρός μου (7–10), 'and may he have upon himself my mother's grief' (trans., *ed.pr.*); for θλῖψις here cf. *New Docs 1976*, **38**.

By far the most common Phrygian sepulchral threat was the 'Eumeneian formula' which is also to be found in the Plain of Kırbasan, the likely headquarters of Montanism (Strobel, 65–86) and the Upper Tembris Valley (cf. *New Docs 1976*, **86**). The ambiguity of πρὸς τὸν θεόν means that it is not clear from the formula alone whether a pagan god, YHWH, or the Christian God is intended. G. Kaibel, *Epigrammata Graeca ex lapidibus conlecta* (Berlin, 1878) 426, n. on p.169, first suggested that the formula may be Christian. L. Duchesne, *RQH* 34 (1883) 5–33, and Ramsay, *JHS* 4 (1883) 370–436, proved that it was definitely used by Christians, Ramsay, later, commenting (*CB* 2.496–98) that the formula contained the smallest possible modification of the pagan form used in the region. F. Cumont, *MEFR* 15 (1895) 245–99, argued that it was exclusively Christian, providing a safe clue to the identification of Christian tombstones. This view was popularized by Calder who suggested, however, that the formula was occasionally imitated by Jews (*BJRL* 7 [1923] 309–54, especially 309–17; id., in *Anatolian Studies Presented to W.H. Buckler* [Manchester, 1939] 15–26; id., *AS* 5 [1955] 25–38, especially 25–27; id., *MAMA* 7 [1956] xxxvii). A.R.R. Sheppard, *AS* 29 (1979) 169–80, has recently proposed the (opposite) view, that the Christians of Eumeneia in fact imitated the Jews in their use of the formula (cf. Ramsay's similar comment at *CB* 2, p.653). On the Jewish use of the formula in Phrygia see also L. Robert, *Hellenica*, 11–12 (1960) 399–406, 412–13; D. Feissel, *BCH* 104 (1980) 463; *New Docs 1976*, **61**; and especially W. Schepelern, *Der Montanismus und die phrygischen Kulte* (Tübingen, 1929) 86–87, who argues that at least some variants (e.g., τὸν θεὸν τὸν ὕψιστον [*CB* 2.563]) may have been employed by pagans influenced by Judaism. M. Waelkens (*Actes du VIIe Congrès international d'Épigraphie grecque et latine, Constantza 9–15 Sept. 1977* [Bucharest, 1979] 105–28), who redates one of the earliest examples of the Eumeneian formula (*MAMA* 4 [1933], 31) to the first quarter of III (see also *SEG* 29 [1979] 1376; cf. 1778), is also convinced of the pagan nature of some of the inscriptions.

Whilst Jewish use of the formula is assured and pagan usage is not to be ruled out, it remains likely that the majority of the tombstones displaying the Eumeneian formula are Christian — pagans, after all, had no reason to be ambiguous about the name of their gods. Hence, Drew-Bear is almost certainly correct in classifying the inscription under discussion as Christian. The dedicator's name, Agatheinos, tends to support this. D. Feissel, *BCH* 104 (1980) 459–70, discusses in detail the features of a recently published Christian epitaph for a woman from Attika (VAD) which includes as part of its lengthy curse formula an instance of the Eumeneian formula, though it is considerably embellished: ἔχῃ | πρὸς [τὸ]ν | [θ]εὸν τὸν | [π]αντοκρά|τορα κὲ πρὸ(ς) | τὰς ἐν οὐρανῷ | δυνάμις [κὲ] | πρὸς τὰς ἐ|ν ἀέρι κὲ ἐν | [γῇ] κὲ κατα|[χθ]ονίας | δυ(νά)μις καὶ | τὴν μερί|δα μ(ε)τ(ὰ) τῶν | ἰρηκότων | ῏Αρον, σταύ|ρωσον αὐ|τόν, κτλ (*ll*.20–37), 'He will have to deal with Almighty God, and with the powers in heaven, those in the air, those on earth and the subterranean powers, and have the portion with those who have said, "Away (with him), crucify him!"'

The context, or expansion, of the formula, often provides a clue to the likely Christian character of a particular inscription. For example, the imprecation on a tombstone from Eumeneia (Calder, *AS* 5 [1955] p.38) reads: εἰ δέ τις ἕτερον ἐπε|νένκῃ πτῶμα ἔστα[ι] | [α]ὐτῷ πρὸς τὸν θε|ὸν καὶ νῦν καὶ τῷ π|[α]ντὶ αἰῶνι καὶ μὴ τύ|[χ]υτο (*sic*) τῆς τοῦ θεοῦ [ἐ]|πανγελίας (*ll*.13–19), 'and if anyone intrudes another in the tomb he shall be answerable to God both now and in all eternity, and may he have no part in God's promise' — an allusion to the general resurrection? Similarly, the restored imprecation on *NIP* IV.47: ἐπάρατο[ς ἔσ]|[τε ἰς] τὸν αἰ[ῶνα παρὰ] | [θεῷ], 'he shall be accursed for eternity by God' (cf. *MAMA* 4.354, 356), may indicate Christianity, although it may also be Jewish. The addition of adjectives describing the nature or action of the god whose wrath is invoked may provide better clues to the origin of the inscriptions, especially the following: ἔσται αὐτῷ πρὸς τὸ | μέγα ὄνομα τοῦ θεοῦ; [ἔσ]|ται αὐτῷ πρὸς τὸν ἀθάνα[τον θεόν]; ἔσται αὐτῷ π[ρ]ὸς τὴν χεῖρα τοῦ θεοῦ; ἔστε αὐτῷ πρὸς τὸν κριτὴν θεόν; [ἔσ]ται αὐτοῖς πρὸ[ς] | [τὴ]ν δικαιοσύ[ν]|[ην] τοῦ θεοῦ (respectively, *CB* 2.369, 388, 392, 394, 457). Each of these points in the direction of Christians or Jews (see also Sheppard, 171–80).

A popular form was ἔσται αὐτῷ πρὸς τὸν ζῶντα θεόν (e.g., *CB* 2.378, cf. 353, 356, 362, 364 and variants 355, 374). This version of the Eumeneian formula, though with the characteristically Phrygian Greek πός for πρός (cf. *New Docs 1976*, **86**), is found also on *NIP* IV.48 = *SEG* 1144, dated 257/8:

ἔτους τμβ΄, μ[η(νὸς) - - ὁ δεῖνα]	5 καὶ τοῖς πεδίοις μου· εἴ
πρευσβύτερος κατεσ-	τεις δὲ ἕτερον ἐπενβά-
[κ]εύασεν τὸ κοιμητήριον	λει, ἔστε αὐτῷ πὸς τὸν
ἑαυτῷ καὶ τῇ γυνεκί μου	ζῶντα θεόν.

In the year 342, the month - - - presbyter, constructed the grave for himself and for
5 **my (*sic*) wife | and for my (*sic*) children; but if anyone intrudes another, he shall have to answer to the living God.**

This inscription is probably Christian because the dedicator, whose name is missing, calls himself a πρευσβύτερος and because of the invocation of 'the living God'. The word κοιμητήριον, 'sleeping-place', used here instead of the more normal ἡρῷον ('tomb'), may also indicate Christianity as it is used in the sense of 'family grave' on a number of indisputably Christian Phrygian inscriptions (e.g., *MAMA* 4.353–55). Whilst cumulatively they suggest that this inscription is Christian, taken individually not one of these is a conclusive indicator of Christianity. First, πρεσβύτερος also appears in Jewish epigraphy. *CIJ* 1 has several instances: nos.595, 663; cf. [πρεσβ]ύτερος at 378 and the feminine πρεσβυτέρα which appears in nos.581, 590, 597, 692. Πρεσβύτ(η)ς occurs at 400. (See also the discussion in *CIJ* 1, pp.lxxvi–vii, and L. Robert, *RPh* 32 [1958] 41–42.) Second, the phrase τὸν ζῶντα θεόν is as likely to be Jewish (or Jewish-influenced pagan) as Christian (Schepelern, 87); and third, κοιμητήριον is also used on Jewish as well as on Christian tombstones (see *NIP*, pp.109–10). H.W. Pleket (n.ad *SEG* 1144) appears to question the Christian origin of this inscription. Support for the Christian use of κοιμητήριον here, however, may come from *NIP* IV.49 which, although later in date, uses ἐκυμήθη (*sic*), a term popular amongst Christians describing the faithful who had 'fallen asleep in Christ awaiting the resurrection' (1 Cor. 15.18, 20; see Lampe, s.v. κοιμάομαι).

If *NIP* IV.48 is indeed Christian, it is the earliest known dated example of an inscription containing both the Eumeneian formula and the title πρεσβύτερος. In this instance there is no reason to question the era, as the 'Sullan era' was still in use in Eumeneia in VI (cf. Drew-Bear's n. to IV.50, p.111). A non-dated inscription from Eumeneia concluding with ἔστε αὐτῷ πρὸς τὸν ζῶντα θεόν which also contains the word ἐπισκόπῳ (*CB* 2.362), therefore, may also be III and Christian (as argued by Calder in W.H. Buckler, et al., *JRS* 16 [1926] 58), although as with πρεσβύτερος, the title is not exclusively Christian (cf. BAGD, s.v. ἐπίσκοπος).

That the people who set up these third-century tombstones, if Christian (as is likely), were only prepared to reveal their Christianity through ambiguous terms and phrases is a conclusion consistent with the pattern of Christian profession outlined above. As the formula spread to other parts of Phrygia, it was combined with (and later replaced by) more overt expressions of Christianity, e.g., ἔσται αὐτῷ | πρὸς τὸν ✳ (*CB* 2, p.527). Ramsay argued that the monogram ✳ predated ☧ and published the reading ἔσται αὐτῷ | πρὸς τὸν Ἰ(ησοῦν) Χ(ριστόν) (*CB* 2.371, cf. *MAMA* 7.96: ἔσται αὐτῷ πρὸς τὸν | θ(εὸν) καὶ Ἰη(σο)ῦ(ν) Χ(ριστό)ν). Three inscriptions from the Upper Tembris Valley, in particular, illustrate this: the inscription given in *New Docs 1976*, **86** combines the variant ἔ[[σ]]τη αὐ|τοῦ πὸ[[ς]] τῶν παντωκράτ|ωρα θεόν with a conspicuous cross; *MAMA* 6(1939) 235 combines the normal Eumeneian formula with the heading χριστιανοί; and *MAMA* 6.234 (= Gibson, no.40) not only concludes with the normal formula but contains in its text the variant ἔσται αὐτῷ | πὸς τὸν ἐξουσειάζοτα (*sic*) πά|σης ψυχῆς ('he shall be answerable to him who has authority over every soul'). The first line of this inscription reads ΖΩΕΠΔ ☧ ΧΧΡΕΙ. Apart from the *chi rho* (cf. *New Docs 1977*, **101**, pp.171-72), the meaning of these abbreviations is not certain. Buckler and Calder suggested ζῶ(σιν) ἐπ(οίησεν) δ(οῦλος) Χρ(ιστοῦ) χ(ρειστιανὸς) χρει(στιανοῖς). The restoration, if accurate, would make this the only known 'Christians for Christians' inscription also to contain the Eumeneian formula. Neither Buckler et al., nor Gibson (who prefers ζῶν to ζῶσιν, p.111), is convinced about this conjecture, however, as alternative reconstructions viz.: ζῶ(ντες) ἐπ(ιφωνεῖτε)· δ(όξα) Χρ(ιστῷ), χ(αρὰ) χρει(στιανοῖς) make perfect sense. The Christian nature of the inscription, however, is beyond doubt.

4. Conclusion

The Christian inscriptions from Phrygia show a clear progression in the degree of their open profession of Christianity but in the reverse order to which they are discussed in this entry. The earliest inscriptions employing the Eumeneian formula are ambiguously Christian, although use of certain words and phrases gives clues to their Christian nature; these clues become more obvious as time progresses. From the middle of III onwards, isolated examples of a preparedness in some regions to acknowledge the religion of the deceased by the single word 'Christian' are to be found, although some of these may, in fact, belong to IV. Open declaration that the dedicators as well as the deceased are Christians, culminating in the χρ.-χρ. inscriptions, is most likely a post-Constantinian phenomenon.

(**W. TABBERNEE**)

99. A model epitaph for Mercurinus

Lyon
26/3/618 or 619

ed.pr. — F. Descombes/J.-F. Reynaud, *Riv.Ant.Crist.* 54 (1978) 291-96 no.4 (fig.13)

Humata sub <hoc> tetolo Mercurini sibi Cict-
ato bembra quiscunt; bonetate benign(u)s,
caretate perfecta, pietate iargu[[u]]s, cum
magnebeletate magnus, dulcissemus, fede
5 *praecepus, semplecetate magnus, amatus,*
familiae uriunius, pauperebus semper pius; qua-
ter denus decim aetate annus lxxv portauit in
pace; obiit subdii vii kalendas aprilis,
lxxviiii pos(t) con(sulatum) <Jus>tini uiri cla(rissimi) con(sulis). indic(tione) sexta. (cross, star)

Epitaph on a flagstone covering a sarcophagus in the porch of the church of St. Laurent de Choulans. Numerous orthographical idiosyncrasies and mistakes: confusion of *i/e*, *u/o*; contractions (*quiscunt* for *quiescunt*; *praecepus* for *praecipuus*); read *sive* (1), *membra* (2), *largus* (3), *oriundus* (6); *magnebeletate* (4) appears to be a confused blending of *magnanimitas* and *affabilitas*.
Bib. — *AE* 491

> **Buried under this epitaph the body of Mercurinus or Cictatus lies at peace: obliging in goodness, his love was perfect, abounding in piety, great in magnanimous-**
> 5 **courteousness, a very charming man, distinguished in faith, |great in candour, loved, descended from a (good) family, always pious to the poor. (Having) four times ten years in age (*sic*) he lived 75 years in peace. He died on the 7th day of the April Kalends, the 79th (year) after the consulship of Justin, *vir clarissimus*, consul. In the sixth (year of the) indiction. (*cross, star*)**

The most arresting blunder in this text is the reference to Mercurinus' age (6–7): he can hardly have been both 40 and 75 when he died. *Ed.pr.* demonstrates effectively, however, that this epitaph is modelled closely upon one for a certain Felemoda (discovered over a generation earlier in the same necropolis), now to be redated to 599, within a generation of this new text. Felemoda died at 40, and a considerable number of the other expressions found in Mercurinus' epitaph occur also in hers. There is nothing surprising in this: stonemasons will have had stock phrases to offer their clients. But because perfunctory repetition and clichés are expected to occur in very short texts there is a danger in not allowing their presence equally in fuller and apparently more individual documents. In this particular example we have two epitaphs based on the same model; were only one of these to have survived there might be a temptation to allow that the epitaph helped us 'flesh out' something of the deceased's personality; but in fact the inscription is of no help to us in that regard. What we have here is a late example of a list of virtues, with emphasis on Christian graces (love, faith, a proper attitude to the poor), though by no means to the exclusion of some classical elements (magnanimity/courteousness, charm, of [good] family). The same editors also publish several other Latin Christian epitaphs, among which are two (same necropolis, VII) which include mention of *caritas* and *fides* as attributes of the deceased: Descombes/Reynaud, 285–87 no.1 (fig.11), 288–89 no.2 (fig.12); = *AE* 488, 489 respectively. For another list of virtues (in an epitaph?) see *IGA* 5.613, quoted at **87**.

Christian use of the Roman theophoric name Mercurinus is to be noted at this late date: see brief discussion of this question at *New Docs 1976*, **80**; and in the present volume see **100** for discussion of the adoption of OT names by Christians of non-Jewish background. One other name worth mention here among the new Lyon epitaphs is [A]manda, [r]apt{i}ata in ☧ (2) who died at age six and is described as *ennox [e]t sinceres* (3–4; i.e., *innox*): Descombes/Reynaud, 279–81 no.6 (fig.7) = *AE* 487 (necropolis of Saint-Just, V[1]). The editors mention that the name Amanda is well attested in the Christian onomasticon at Rome, Spain and Africa, though it is rare in Gaul. The phrase *raptata in Christum* is unique, but perhaps is developed from the notion of *mors* as a *raptor* (*ed.pr.*); more likely, it alludes to the 'rapture' of the saints (as E.A. Judge points out to me) — cf. 1 Thes. 4.16 (Vulg.), *rapiemur cum illis in nubibus obviam Christo in aera*. The Christogram ☧ used here to represent *Christum* serves as a further epigraphical example to those noted in my article (written jointly with E.R. Waterhouse) forthcoming in *Scriptorium*, dealing mainly with the *nomen sacrum* XP in Latin and Old English MSS.

100. Divine Providence in a letter of Judas

Oxyrhynchos   IV

ed.pr. — J. R. Rea, *P.Oxy.* 3314, pp.103-05 (pl.7)

κυρίῳ μου πατρὶ Ἰωσῆ καὶ τῇ συμβίῳ μου
    Μαρίᾳ   Ἰούδας.
προηγουμένως εὔχομαι τῇ θίᾳ προνοίᾳ
περὶ τῆς ὑμῶν ὁλοκληρίας ἵνα καὶ ὑγιαίνοντας
5 ὑμᾶς ἀπολάβω. πᾶν οὖν ποίησον, κυρία μου
ἀδελφή, πέμψον μοι τὸν ἀδελφόν σου, ἐπιδὴ εἰς
νόσον περιέπεσα ἀπὸ πτώματος ἵππου.
μέλλοντός μου γὰρ στραφῆναι εἰς ἄλλο μέρος,
οὐ δύναμαι ἀφ' ἐμαυτοῦ, εἰ μὴ ἄλλοι δύο ἄνθρωποι
10 ἀντιστρέψωσίν με. καὶ μέχρις ποτηρίου
ὕδατ[ο]ς οὐκ ἔχω τὸν ἐπιδιδοῦντά μοι.
βοήθησον οὖν, κυρία μου ἀδελφή. σπουδαῖόν σοι
γενέσθω ὅπως τὸ τάχος πέμψῃς μοι, ὡς
προεῖπον, τὸν ἀδελφόν σου. εἰς τὰς τοιαύτας
15 γὰρ ἀνάγκας εὑρίσκονται οἱ ἴδιοι τοῦ ἀνθρώπου.
ἵνα οὖν καὶ σοὶ παραβοηθήσῃς μοι τῷ ὄντι
ἐπὶ ξένης καὶ ἐν νόσῳ ὄντι. καὶ πλοῖον
ἐπεζήτησα ἐνβῆναι καὶ οὐχ εὗρον τὸν
ἐπιζητοῦντά μοι. ἐν τῇ γὰρ Βαβυλῶνεί εἰμει.
20 προσαγορεύω τὴν θυγατέρα μου καὶ πάντας τοὺς φιλοῦντας ἡμᾶς κατ' ὄνομα.
       (*vac.*)
καὶ ἐὰν χρίαν ἔχῃς κέρματος, λάβε παρὰ
Ἰσὰκ τὸν κολοβόν, τὸν ἔνγιστά σοι μένον[τ]α.
       (*vac.*)
    (*m. 2*) ἐρρῶσθαι ὑμᾶς εὔχομαι
25   πολλοῖς χρόνοις.
verso ἀπόδος συμ . . . . ±*50 letters*

A complete papyrus sheet (14B × 21.5H cm.). The text above follows *ed.pr.* with the addition of a full stop in *l.*10. Read σύ (16); genitives for accusatives at *l.*23.

Bib. — G. Tibiletti, in *Scritti in onore di O. Montevecchi*, edd. E. Bresciani et al. (Bologna, 1981) 407-11; E. A. Judge, *Rank and Status in the World of the Caesars and St. Paul* (*Broadhead Lecture* 4; Christchurch, 1982) 28-31.

To my lord father Joses and my wife Maria, Judas. In the first place I pray to divine providence concerning your all-round health so that I may hear that you are also in
5 **good health. |Make every effort, my lady sister, send me your brother, since I've fallen ill after a fall from a horse. For when I want to turn over to my other side I cannot**
10 **do it on my own without two other fellows |turning me. And I don't have anyone to give me as much as a cup of water. So send help, my lady sister. Make it your serious**

concern to send your brother without delay to me, as I said above. For in straits like
15 these | a man finds out who his own folk (really) are. You too, therefore, please send
help to me since I am at a strange (town) and in sickness. I searched for a ship to
20 embark on, and found no-one to search for me; for I am in Babylon. | I greet my
daughter and all who love us individually. And if you need some money, get it from
Isaac the cripple who lives very near you. (*m.2*) I pray you may be well for many years.
(*verso*) (*m.1*) Give . . .

A man of some means — he has a horse — has an accident which incapacitates him while
far from his own family and friends; from Babylon (Old Cairo, in the Delta) he writes to
his wife and father at Oxyrhynchos, urging them to send him help. An ordinary enough
calamity, no doubt; yet this papyrus has quickly aroused interest since it was first published
because it raises in acute form the question, how are Christians and Jews distinguishable in
a period like the fourth century? *Ed.pr.* inclines to the view that the family mentioned here
was Christian, while both Tibiletti and Judge concluded independently that the letter
concerns Jews. (These are the only options, for the biblical names of the four people
mentioned rule out the possibility of a pagan context.) Even if an unassailable conclusion
is not attainable this papyrus affords a useful example with which to consider the problem.
Apart from the explicit content of the letter there are several criteria to be weighed,
distinctive phraseology, nomenclature, and less tangible hints about the social context.

First, a more general point. In form, the document is a typical letter of the fourth century.
It is a matter for considerable surprise to discover in *CPJ* almost no private letters written
by Jews: *CPJ* 1 (1957) 4 and 5 are both written by the same man on the same day (12/5/257
BC) in Transjordan; 2 (1960) 424 (Ptolemais Hermeiou, 15/12/87 AD) is written by a Jewess,
Joanne. *CPJ* 3 has none. To these we may add *CPJ* 1.132, a letter written to a Jew. There
are, of course, other more public letters, of a business or official nature; but the number of
surviving Jewish personal letters is very tiny. This scarcity is thrown into sharp relief by the
relatively plentiful number of Christian personal letters in III and IV. The major reason for
the dearth of Jewish-originated documentary texts in Egypt is the suppression of the Jewish
revolt in 115-17 under Trajan, and the decimation of their numbers. (The most recent
discussion of the factors which gave rise to the revolt is by M. Hengel, in *Apocalypticism
in the Mediterranean World and the Near East*, ed. D. Hellholm [Tübingen, 1983] 655-86,
in which the fifth Sibylline Oracle is particularly examined as testifying to Jewish Messianic
hopes and political 'radicalism'.) Jews very largely had to 'go underground' and though there
remained numerically significant communities in a number of larger towns in Egypt (see *CPJ*
3, app.3, pp.197-209, their invisibility in very many others — so far as the evidence indicates
— suggests that those who survived Trajan had to live near others for solidarity and security.
A low profile was all the more necessary with the official acceptance of Christianity in early
IV. If this personal letter from Judas is Jewish, it would be our first such example from this
period. That is no argument against its being Jewish, of course, for Jews will have written
letters no less than anyone else. But at least in view of the dearth of contemporaneous Jewish
personal letters the onus at this stage rests more heavily upon those who think this new text
is Jewish.

Phraseology

Three passages in this letter claim our attention for their phraseology. It is readily admitted
that the opening and closing formulae (1-2, 24-25) have parallels in undisputed Christian
letters of III-V; for some examples see *New Docs 1976*, **83-85**; *New Docs 1977*, **103**, as well

as such collections as Naldini's. But the formulae are not distinctively Christian, as examples in G. Tibiletti, *Le lettere private nei papiri greci del III e IV secolo d.C. Tra paganesimo e cristanesimo* (Milan, 1979) show. Two business letters from III-IV in *CPJ* 3, nos.469 and 479 (provenance unknown for both), share the same formulae (479 lacks any closing phrase); and as the editor of no.469 concedes, it 'might have been written by a gentile as well as by a Jew or a Christian'. These formulae reflect a stylistic trend of the period, and without the presence of distinctive elements such as *nomina sacra*, they are rarely a reliable guide to religious affiliation. Even where this may occur, in a letter like *P.Oxy.* 3314 (almost all of which is written by a scribe — so *ed.pr.*, n. to *ll.*24-25), we may well be learning more about the adherence of the scribe than of the sender (on this question see *New Docs 1977*, **22**).

In need of closer scrutiny is the clause in *l.*3. (Divine) Providence was a fundamental aspect of Stoic thought: see, for example, Cicero's discussion in *de nat. deor.*, where he says that 'providence' is an elliptical expression for divine providence (2.74), by which the world is governed (*deorum providentia mundum administrari*, 2.73); as for the Greek term θεία πρόνοια its occurrence in Philo, *in Flacc.* 125 (noted by Rea) suggests it had currency in educated Jewish circles by I. In papyrus texts from mid III-end IV this wording (or its near approximation) occurs nearly two dozen times, as tabulated below. (There are examples from V and later, some listed conveniently in a note to *P.Strasb.* 676.)

(a) In official proclamations, petitions, etc., where it is clearly a conventional public formula:
   — *P.Oxy.* 33 (1968) 2664.3 (c.245-48), ἡ θ]εία πρόνοια τῶν κυρίων ἡμῶν Σεβαστῶν. With this use of πρόνοια of people cf. Acts 24.2, διὰ τῆς σῆς προνοίας ... κράτιστε Φῆλιξ ...
   — *P.Cair.Isidor.* (1960) 63.14 (20/11/296–6/6/324), δαὶ (= δὲ) θεοῦ προνοίας·

(b) In opening prayer for health of addressee(s) in private letters:
   — *P.Vindob.* G. 39838 = *SB* 6.5 (1963) 9605 = Naldini 53 (provenance unknown, IV init.), [εὔχο]μ[αι τ]ῷ [ὑ]π[ίσ]τῳ (*sic*) θ[εῷ] | καὶ τῇ θείᾳ προνοίᾳ τοῦ κυρίου | ἡμῶν Ἰησοῦ Χρηστοῦ 'night and day for your health' (*ll.*3-8, following text in *SB*);
   — *P.Abinn.* (1962) 10.5-6, εὐχόμενος τῇ θείᾳ | προνοίᾳ 'for your health'; texts in this archive range in date from March 340–Feb. 351;
   — _____ 11.3-4, προηγουμένος εὔχομε τῇ θίᾳ προ|νοίᾳ, κτλ;
   — _____ 25.3, προηγουμένως εὔχομαι τῇ θίᾳ προνοίᾳ, κτλ;
   — *P.Oxy.* 48 (1981) 3396.3 (IV), προηγουμένους εὔχομαι τῇ θίᾳ προνοίᾳ, κτλ;
   — *P. Ant.* 1 (1950) 44.19 (late IV/V; = Naldini 92), I pray for your health τῇ θείᾳ προνοίᾳ;
   — cf. *P.Oxy.* 14 (1920) 1682.6 (IV; = Naldini 52) ἡ μὲν τοῦ θεοῦ πρόνοια παρέξει 'your return home in health';
   — *P.Oxy.* 3314.3, the letter printed above.
Of these texts *P.Vindob.* G. 39838 is definitely Christian, the editor of *P.Oxy.* 3396 specifies this (p.76) as one of several in an archive which is Christian, and *P.Oxy.* 1682 is regarded by its first ed. as 'perhaps' a Christian letter. *P.Ant.* 44 has no clear indication of Christianity (*pace* Naldini). From these examples it is apparent both how conventional is the clause in the letter of Judas, and that it occurs in Christian and non-Christian letters alike.

(c) In a prayer that the recipient may be kept safe, usually near the end of the letter:
   — *P.Abinn.* 12.23, ἐρρωμέ[ν]ως | σε εἴχετε | ἡ θία πρόνοια, | κύριε ἄδελφε;
   — _____ 28.27-28, ἐρρωμένον σε ἡ θία πρό|νοια [δι]αφυλάξειεν πανοικί;
   — *P.Lond.* 6 [= *P. Jews*] (1924, repr. 1972) 1929.19 (Heracleopolite nome, mid-IV), ἐρ]ρωμέν[ο]ν σε ἡ θεία διαφυλάξει〈ε〉 πρόνοια;
   — *P.Oxy.* 17 (1927) 2156.5-7 (late IV/V; = Naldini 89) ὁμοῦ τῇ | θείᾳ τοῦ θεοῦ προνοίᾳ εὐχόμενος ἀεὶ | διαφυλάξαι σε ἡμῖν. The wording here conflates the phraseology of (b) and (c).
   — *P.Strasb.* 676 (provenance unknown, V), a concluding portion of a Christian letter, θεία πρόνοια πολλοῖς διαφυλάξει χρόνοις.
The last three of this group are definitely Christian.

(d) Miscellaneous:

— *P.Oxy.* 12 (1916) 1492.7-8 (late III/early IV; = Naldini 30), ταῦτα (viz., salvation, etc.) γάρ ἐστιν τὰ ἐ[ν τῇ] | θείᾳ προνοίᾳ, 'these things are the objects of divine providence' (trans., *ed.pr.*); Christian letter.

— *P.Oxy.* 48 (1981) 3417.16-17 (IV), μὰ τὴν γὰρ θίαν πρό|νοια⟨ν⟩. Part of the same archive as *P.Oxy.* 3396, and like it specified as Christian by *ed.pr.;* with the phrase in this letter cf. *P.Lips.* (1906, repr. 1970) 40 (Hermopolis, IV fin./V init.), col.3, *l.*3, μὰ τὴν πρόνοιαν (the context is a judicial hearing).

— *P.Lond.* 3 (1907, repr. 1973) 982.10 (provenance unknown, IV; = Naldini 54), εὐ[χ]αριστῶ | [τῇ θείᾳ] προνοίᾳ (for recovery from illness). Private letter, containing no clear-cut indication of Christianity (*pace* Naldini).

— *P.Laur.* 2 (1977) 41.3 (Memphis, III), a clearly pagan private letter, which speaks of τῆς τῶν π[ατ]ρῴων ἡμῶν θεῶν προνοίας.

— A.H. El-Mosallamy, *Actes du XVᵉ Congrès international de Papyrologie, deuxième partie* (*Pap.Brux.* 17; Brussels, 1979), no.20 (Oxyrhynchos (?), late III/early IV); *ll.*3-4 read πρὸ μὲν πάντων εὔχομαι τῇ θείᾳ προ|νοίᾳ 'that you receive my letter'. The letter is clearly Christian, in view of the occurrence of the *nomen sacrum* at *l.*2.

While several of these texts are definitely Christian only one is definitely not, judging by the plural θεῶν in *P.Laur.* 41.

Given its Stoic pedigree, the most we can say at present about the phrase ἡ θεία πρόνοια is that by late III Christians were comfortable in their use of it in private correspondence. Yet, as a criterion to assess the problem whether *P.Oxy.* 3314 is Christian or Jewish, on its own it is inconclusive.

The third phrase for consideration, Judas' claim that he has no one to provide him μέχρις ποτηρίου | ὕδατ[ο]ς (10-11), appears at first to offer more scope for a decision. Rea notes that this phrase is reminiscent of Mk. 9.41, ὃς γὰρ ἂν ποτίσῃ ὑμᾶς ποτήριον ὕδατος ἐν ὀνόματι, κτλ (cf. Mt. 10.42, ποτήριον ψυχροῦ), but concedes that it is not an indubitable allusion to the NT. On quotations and allusions to the NT in papyrus letters see *New Docs 1977*, **97**, esp. pp.156-58. In this instance the wording is not distinctive enough as a parallel to the NT phrase to allow us to determine that Judas' letter comes from a Christian circle. If it is an allusion to the Marcan passage, then given the context Judas may be saying loosely, but very covertly, 'There are no other Christians here to help me'. Yet a further point may be noted about the phrase. When Judas writes this he is using hyperbolic, metaphorical language for 'I have no one to attend to me'. It is not impossible that he means rather more, viz., 'I am isolated from my family and will have no one to look after my burial if I die'. What suggests this, admittedly, outside possibility is an Egyptian phrase found from Old Kingdom sepulchral inscriptions onward, as N. Kanawati tells me. In Greek texts this sentence reads, 'May Osiris give you cold water', or the like. The adjective ψυχρός appears to be an addition to the Egyptian notion to bring the formula into conformity with Greek funerary traditions: see R. A. Wild, *Water in the Cultic Worship of Isis and Osiris* (*EPRO* 97; Leiden, 1981) 124-25. This appears to be borne out by the presence of the wording ψυχρὸν ὕδωρ twice (*ll.*7, 12) in the intriguing gold tablet found in 1969 in a grave at Hipponion in Italy. It provides the latest addition to a small corpus of 16 such texts from Italy and Greece, all but one dated IV or IIIBC; and it is the earliest in date (c.400BC). The proliferation of articles proposing different readings serves to indicate that no consensus has yet been reached in interpreting this 16-hexameter text (*SEG* 775 *bis*, with considerable bibliography; add M. Guarducci, *Epigrafia greca* IV [Rome, 1978] 258-65, fig.72). Whether it is Orphic, Pythagorean, or Dionysiac — for the last see S.G. Cole, *GRBS* 21 (1980) 223-38 — remains to be settled, but in essence the *lamella* provides advice for the deceased what to do upon arrival in the underworld. For the most recent discussion of the text see E. Feyerabend, *RhM* 127 (1984) 1-22.

Returning to the 'Osiris cool water' formula, Wild lists (248-49 nn. 154,155) the known examples (twelve, plus four closely-related variants) which come from Egypt (6 + 2), Italy (5 + 2) and Carthage (1); the latter is to be linked with the Italian attestations on the ground that Carthage was a Roman *colonia*. Where they are able to be dated these texts — all emanating from funerary contexts — range from I to III fin. From 1978 publications we may note the following republished examples: *IGA* 2.332 (Alexandria, n.d.), Ἀμμ[ώνιε(?)] | (ἐτῶν) λε ἡ(μερῶ)ν ζ | εὐψύχι | δο[ίη] σο[ι Ὀ]|σιρις | [τὸ] ψυχρὸν ὕδωρ; 341 (Alexandria, II/III), εὐψύχι | Γαλατιανέ | (ἐτῶν) κε | δοί σοι | ὁ Ὄσειρος | τὸ ψυχρὸν | ὕδωρ; 375 (provenance unknown, undated). εὐψύχι Ταῆσι | μητρῶον μόρον | ἐκτανύσασα σω|φροσύνη καὶ φιλάν|δρια ἐβίωσεν ἔτη κε | καὶ κατὰ γῆς δῶκε ψυχρ|ὸν Ὄσιρις ὕδωρ. Dr. Kanawati informs me that this notion still survives among Copts in Egypt today via the custom of pouring or sprinkling water at the tombs of dead relatives. This idea thus has a long ancestry and has been adopted by people of different religion in that time. On the link between Osiris' cool water and the Christian notion of *regrigerium* cf. M. Simon, *Le Christianisme antique et son contexte religieux. Scripta Varia* (*Wiss. Untersuchungen zum Neuen Testament* 23; Tübingen, 1981) 1.78-79.

Now, whether or not Judas is alluding to this sepulchral terminology as a hyperbolical way of conveying to his family the impression that he is on his death-bed — and I do not think the point should be pressed; it would be the only example from a non-funerary context — we may at least ask whether it is a mere coincidence that the alternative reading of D and some other witnesses at Mt. 10.42 is ποτήριον ὕδατος ψυχροῦ instead of ποτήριον ψυχροῦ. Could it be reflecting the phraseology of the longstanding Egyptian custom, while altering the context in which it is applied? (J.A.L. Lee suggests to me that the addition of ὕδατος is readily explicable by the desire to make ψυχροῦ clear, and harmonization with Mk.) At Acts 18.25 D appears to reflect some awareness of Egyptian Christianity in the comment it adds about Apollos. While that does not constitute an argument in favour of the correctness of Mt. 10.42D, the reading is comprehensible against the background of wording in an Egyptian custom of great antiquity which has been able to cross the boundaries of more than one religious outlook. Furthermore, Wild notes that the water alluded to in the 'cold water' inscriptions 'offered life and immortality to those dead who shared in it'; it was viewed as a 'source of life after death . . . a means by which [Isis worshippers] might conquer death' (125-26). 'Such water in Egyptian religious thought has too close an association with Osiris and his son Horus to allow it here [ie., in the 'cold water' formula] to have a separate identity apart from the god. Instead, in giving this water Osiris gives himself' (127). If Wild's interpretation of the symbolic significance of the water in such contexts is correct (see also his comments at 102-03), we are provided with a very interesting analogy to some of Jesus' statements in his encounter with the woman at the well (Jn. 4.1-26, especially vv.10, ὕδωρ ζῶν, and 14, ἀλλὰ τὸ ὕδωρ ὃ δώσω αὐτῷ γενήσεται ἐν αὐτῷ πηγὴ ὕδατος ἁλλομένου εἰς ζωὴν αἰώνιον). We are not speaking of influence here, but of independent development of a similar idea along slightly divergent lines. The Jewish background should not be lost from view, as Jn. 7.37-38 shows (where Is. 58.11 is quoted), in addition to the passages in Rev., 7.17; 21.6; 22.1, 17.

The conclusion to be drawn from consideration of this phrase in *ll.*10-11 is that there is no reason to associate it with Judaism, while that it points to a Christian background is at best a fairly remote possibility. The three passages considered so far — opening/closing formulas, 'divine providence', and the 'cup of water' — are all inconclusive for determining whether the letter is Christian or Jewish, although the cumulative effect of the last two cases perhaps favours a Christian milieu slightly.

Nomenclature

All four individuals mentioned here have distinctively Jewish names; yet by IV it was much more common for Christians who did not convert from a Jewish background to be giving Bible names to their children. There is no exact date which can be pinpointed for this trend becoming apparent, and it is perhaps too easy to see the reign of Constantine as the *terminus post quem* for all such developments. In fact, Harnack suggested that the change came a little before mid-III (*The Mission and Expansion of Christianity in the first three Centuries*, I [ET: 1908; repr. Gloucester, Mass. 1972] 424). Rea himself draws attention to a 'virtually certain' third-century Christian called Judas, mentioned by Eusebius (*HE* 6.7). A gnostic 'Gospel of Judas' is known from Irenaeus and other patristic sources: see C. Hennecke/ W. Schneemelcher, *New Testament Apocrypha* (ET: London, 1963) 1.313-14, where the references are given and c.130-70 is suggested as its date. Of the four names in our letter Judas ought to be the one least likely to be adopted by Christians because its association in the NT with the betrayer so heavily overshadowed — though did not obliterate — the link with one of the apostles (Lk. 6.16; Acts 1.13). That Christians used the name Judas in anti-Semitic contexts is one indication of this; cf. the sepulchral inscription, invoking 'the curse of Judas' upon any who exhume the corpse, discussed at *New Docs 1976*, **61**. From 1978 publications compare *IGCB* 17.7-8 (Corinth, VII; already repr. at the same 1976 entry, p.100), ἔστω αὐτῷ τὸ ἀνάθεμα Ἄν|να κ(αὶ) Καιάφα †. This text has now been reprinted in W. Wischmeyer, *Griechische und lateinische Inschriften zur Sozialgeschichte der Alten Kirche* (*Texte zur Kirchen- und Theologiegeschichte* 28; Gütersloh, 1982) no.32, p.53. *DACL* 8.1 (1928) 277 reprints a warning in a MS (dated VIII) that if anyone removes the book from the monastry *cum Iouda proditore, Anna et Caiapha | atque Pilato damnationem | accipiat* (*ll*.7-9). Cf.**64**. For further comment on this motif see D. Feissel, *BCH* 104(1980) 466,474.

CPJ discusses the presence of Jewish names in papyri as a major criterion for the assessment of whether the text is Jewish or Christian: 1 (1957) xvii-xix (where it is pointed out that it is better to risk omission of some Jewish texts than include ones which are only potentially so), 27-30, 83-85. The less than half-dozen Judases to appear in that corpus range in date from Ptolemaic to IV. Yet the editors' discussion of *CPJ* 3 (1964) 501 (= *P.Aberd.* 68; provenance unknown, IV) provides an analogy for our text which illustrates the danger of getting caught in a circular argument. That text is a list of people who pay a certain tax. Because so many of the names are Jewish they are claimed to be Jews. 'Besides, we would hardly expect to meet a Judas among Christians' (*CPJ*, comm. ad loc.). The presence of the name Judas in a fourth-century text is here regarded as a sufficiently strong indication to warrant its inclusion in the corpus. This kind of argument leaves out of account the further possibility of a Jew converting to the new faith, such as may have been the case with the man mentioned in Eusebius (noted above). From 1978 publications note *IGA* 5.342 (the name is partly restored), 563 and 742 (J. the apostle) (all Byzantine in date). As well as these *NB* and Foraboschi alert us to a few other Judases, at least one of whom is Christian: *P.Iand.* 6 (1934) 132.11 (provenance unknown, VI-VII). G. Petzl, *Die Inschriften von Smyrna* 1 (*Inschr. gr. Städte aus Kleinasien* 23; Bonn, 1982) 297 is a fragmentary funerary inscription (n.d.) which mentions a certain Anna and her child Judas.

The problem of identifying Christians via their names has been taken up recently by R. Bagnall, *BASP* 19 (1982) 105-24. In this very stimulating 'preliminary exploration' he seeks to discover the 'pace of conversion' to Christianity in Egypt by examining shifts in the pattern of naming (108). The reason why so few of those with OT names are to be regarded as Jews by IV is the long-lasting effect of Trajan's drastic suppression of the Revolt in 115-17, a revolt documented in the papyri, for which see *CPJ* 2. Those Jews who were still left in Egypt tend to be clustered in several big towns, not the rural areas (105, 110). The giving of Bible names to children is an indication of the religion of the parents at the time of the child's birth (109). Bagnall argues from the evidence he collects that in the period 310-320 there was 'an enormous leap' in the rate of conversion, which he attributes to a combination of factors: the church was now free to proselytize, many now converted who had held back till then in fear of repercussions, and official sanction allowed people to be open about their adherence (117). Perhaps two-thirds of the Christian population possess Christian names by late IV (117-20). The rise in the number of Christians increases sharply in the period 310-60 (it was *c*.50% of the population by the mid 320s), then continues to increase but more slowly. This fits in very well with evidence elsewhere in the papyri that the 330s/340s witnessed the large growth of church institutions (121). It is also consistent with the beginning of major ecclesiastical controversies, when the Christian population no longer needs to be a covert minority. Bagnall's main conclusion is that the pace of conversion was rapid and that the process began earlier than is sometimes believed (121). For the evidence of *P.Landl.* — land registers of the 340s — on this question see **104**.

The implications for our interpretation of great numbers of papyri of IV and V are very great. If Bagnall is correct then, in view of the need by Jews to be much more circumspect and to keep a low profile after 117, it is to be expected that a number of the texts in *CPJ* of IV and later which have been included on the ground of Jewish nomenclature could be Christian. *CPJ* 469 and 501 (both discussed above) may be cases in point. One may ask why, if we accept Bagnall's thesis, personal Christian letters of IV are not more explicit; this is a question which will require further consideration. Whether his conclusions can be applied to other parts of the Empire is another issue which will need to be weighed.

To return to the letter of Judas, the general thrust of Bagnall's argument appears to give some further ballast to the claim that the papyrus may be Christian, given its date and the names which are used. Given Christian hostility to the name Judas (though there are exceptions to this) our Judas may have to be considered a Jewish convert. Yet it should not be forgotten that Jews will have kept on employing their traditional names, even allowing for the inroads of Hellenism; just because Christians were adopting them in rapidly increasing numbers from IV does not mean that Jews abrogated their use themselves. If the letter is Jewish names like these are what we should expect to meet.

Reading between the lines

Judge points out (30) that Judas is unlikely to be a Christian because he speaks of being isolated at Babylon; this suggests that he is unaware of the links Christians established to provide hospitality and protection for other believers. The argument from silence here cannot be given much weight, although Babylon is not a locality for which Jews are attested. But this comment by Judas at *l*.19 may merit further consideration. It is surprising that he expects his brother-in-law to come and help him, but provides no more directions of his whereabouts than the town he was in. Owning a horse suggests he is a man of means who may therefore have had slaves with him who might convey the letter to his family. But this is unlikely since, as *ed.pr.* points out, the address on the back must have been fairly long and perhaps contained detailed instructions. Is it conceivable that 'Babylon' is a 'secret' name, used for its figurative significance? This is very speculative, but we may compare the use of 'Babylon' for Rome in late Jewish writings (see BAGD, s.v., for some references), as well as in the NT at 1 Pet. 5.13, and 'Great B.' at Rev. 16.9; 17.5; 18.10, 21. Note also Rev. 11.8 where Jerusalem is called πνευματικῶς Σόδομα καὶ Αἴγυπτος. G.J. Cowling points out to me that while such allegorical use of names may be not unexpected in a literary work, it would be rather more surprising in a private letter. Yet even if this suggestion can be entertained we are helped no further, for this use of Babylon occurs in the NT no less than in Jewish texts; and for Judas to employ it here would not clarify his own background.

Consideration of these factors has in each case been fairly inconclusive. Yet in the light of Bagnall's study on nomenclature, and the fact that Christians were quite at home in their use of the phrase 'divine providence', together with the 'cup of water' not being entirely ruled out as a Christian allusion, there is some cumulative force which perhaps leads us to think that the letter of Judas may after all emanate from a Christian milieu, as *ed.pr.* had tentatively suggested.

Finally, a few items of a philological nature may be noted briefly. With the adjective θεῖος at *l.*3 cf. 2 Pet. 1.3, 4, θ. δύναμις . . . θ. φύσις. For πρόνοια Acts 24.2 has already been noted above; but I am unaware of any instructive documentary parallel to Rom.13.14, τὴν σαρκὸς πρόνοιαν. Although ἵνα . . . ἀπολάβω (4-5) is not a biblical reminiscence cf. Lk. 15.27, ὅτι ὑγιαίνοντα αὐτὸν ἀπέλαβεν. With περιπίπτω εἰς νόσον (6-7) cf. Acts 27.41, περιπεσόντες δὲ εἰς τόπον διθάλασσον; though the force is different no parallel to the construction is provided by MM, BDF or BAGD. The causal use of ἀπό (7) may be added to BAGD, s.v., V, 1, where only one other papyrus example is provided. The use of μέλλω + aor.infin. is not a cause for surprise from *koine* onwards: for NT examples note Acts 12.6; Rom. 8.18; Gal. 3.23; Rev. 3.2, 16; 12.4. But in addition this verb is a weakened periphrasis for the future, almost = βούλομαι/θέλω (for NT examples see BAGD, s.v. I, c. β); but I have not noticed any places in the NT where the two functions are combined. For μέρος, 'side', cf. **47**; ἀφ' ἐμαυτοῦ, cf. BAGD, s.v. ἀπό, 5. The use of simple verb followed by a compound form occurs twice here (*ll.*8 and 10-11; *ll.*12 and 16), although neither compound, ἀντιστρέφω and παραβοηθέω, is found in the NT. For ἐπιδίδωμι treated as a thematic verb see Gignac 2.382-83; cf. B.G. Mandilaras, *The Verb in the Greek Non-Literary Papyri* (Athens, 1973) §92. Rea takes οἱ ἴδιοι (15) to refer to 'true friends'; in the NT it is used of relatives at Jn. 1.11b and 1 Tim. 5.8; fellow-believers at Acts 4.23 and 24.23; and perhaps of disciples at Jn. 13.1.

As for the instance of imperatival ἵνα (16), it should be noted that N. Turner's claim, in J.H. Moulton's *A Grammar of NT Greek III, Syntax* (Edinburgh, 1963) 94-95, is false: 'In view of this wealth [of LXX and NT examples] and the secular poverty of examples we may claim the imperatival ἵνα as virtually a Semitism, illustrating the homogeneity of Biblical Greek and its distinction from the Koine.' This comment reflects Turner's long-held commitment to the notion that 'Biblical' Greek is *sui generis*. (My review article which includes discussion of his latest book, *Christian Words*, is forthcoming in *Biblica*.) The construction without an introductory word like κελεύω, γράφω, θέλω is rare in classical Greek; but Mandilaras §585-589 provides examples from both Ptolemaic and especially post-Ptolemaic papyri. In the NT note Mk. 5.23; Eph. 5.33.

Ed.pr. reports the suggestion of P.J. Parsons that γάρ (19) looks back two lines to ἐπὶ ξένης. For classical precedents see J.D. Denniston, *The Greek Particles* (Oxford, 1954², repr.), s.v. γάρ, III.4, p.63. With Judas' greeting to 'all who love us, by name' (20-21) we have an exact parallel to *SB* 3.2 (1927) 7253.18-20 (296 AD), noted at BAGD, s.v. φιλέω, 1a; cf. Tit. 3.15. See further, **52**. The noun κέρμα (22) occurs in the NT only at Jn. 2.15; MM already has several other references; κολοβός provides another example to add to those collected in *WB* I and *Spoglio*; while this adjective does not occur in the NT, see BAGD, s.v., for some ECL uses. The related verb κολοβόω is used in the Synoptics of shortening time, Mt. 24.22 = Mk. 13.20. For μένω, 'live (in a house)', cf. NT examples in BAGD, s.v., 1α,a.

101. A family feud

Theadelphia 6/4/343

ed.pr. — J.W.B. Barns, *Studia Patristica* 1. *Papers Presented to the Second International Conference on Patristic Studies held at Christ Church, Oxford, 1955.* Part 1, edd. K. Aland/F.L. Cross (*Texte und Untersuchungen* 63; Berlin, 1957) 3-9

Αὐρηλίῳ Ἰσίωνι πολ(ιτευομένῳ) πραιποσίτῳ [η] // πά[γο]υ νομοῦ Ἀρσι(νοΐτου)

παρὰ [Αὐ]ρηλίου Ζωΐλου Μέλαν[ο]ς δ[ι]άκονος τῆς καθολικῆς ἐκκλη[σ]ία[ς] ἀπὸ κώμης Θεαδ[ε]λφίας τοῦ αὐτοῦ νομοῦ.

οἱ τὸν ἀν[αιδ]ῆ [κ]αὶ ληστρικὸν [τρό]πον ἠρημ[έ]ν[ο]ι, καθαρώτατε τῶν [ἀ]νδρῶν, δίκα[ιοί εἰ]σι ⟨τῆς⟩ τῶν νόμων

ἐπεξελ[ε]ύσεως τυχεῖν. ἔτι [περ]ιόντος τοῦ [μα]καρί[ου μου] υἱοῦ Γεροντίου τοὔνομα [συ]νῆλθεν, ὡς εἴθε

5 μήποτε, πρὸς γάμου κοινωνίαν [γυ]ναικὶ Νόννᾳ θυγ(ατρὶ) Ἀννοῦτος ἀπὸ τῆς αὐτῆς κώμης. νομίζων εὔνοιαν κα[ὶ] στ[ο]ργὴν αὐτὴν [δ]ι[ασ]ῴζ[ε]ιν πρὸς τὴν συμβίω[σί]ν μου, τοὐναντία διεπράξατο· τοῦ γὰρ αὐτ[οῦ]

προ[κι]μένου μου υἱοῦ νόσου κατακ[λι]θέν[τ]ος καὶ μέλλοντος τ[ὸ] χρέον τοῦ βίου ἀποδοῦναι, οὐκ οἶδα ὅπως

Σακα[ῶ]ν τις τουνομου (*sic*) ἀπὸ τῆς αὐτῆς κώμης ἴδι[ό]ν μ[ου] οἶκον ἀναλαβόμενος ἐπιστὰς διήρπαξεν τὴν γυναῖκα τοῦ αὐτοῦ μου υἱοῦ καὶ προκιμένην Νόνναν [καὶ] αὐτὴν ἀπήγαγεν εἰς τὴν ἑαυτοῦ οἰκίαν

10 οὐ δεόντως καὶ παρὰ πάντας [τ]οὺς νόμους, συνεργοὺς ἐσχηκὼς τῆς τηλικαύτης παρανομίας τοὺς ἑαυτοῦ

ἀδελφοὺς καὶ τὴν μητέρα τῆς [γυναικὸς] καὶ προκιμένην Ἀννοῦ. ἀλλὰ πάραυτα τοῦ αὐτοῦ μου υἱοῦ τελευ-

τήσαντος ἐβουλόμην τότ[ε τῇ] τῶν ν[ό]μων ἀκολουθίᾳ χρήσασθαι περὶ οὗ [ἐτ]όλμησαν ῥιψοκινδύνου πράγματος· καὶ δὴ εἶξα τὸν [ἀπ]ράγμον[α βίο]ν ἀσκῶν. ἀλλ' οὐκ οἶδα τίνι λόγ[ῳ ο]ὖν, τοῦ ἑτέρου υἱοῦ Πάσει τοὔνομα θεωρήσαντος τὸν ἑαυτοῦ πάππον ὑβριζόμενον ὑπὸ τῶν πανκακίστων ἀνδρῶν

15 κ[α]ὶ προκιμένων ἐσθῆ[τα] αὐτοῦ καταπελεκίσαι καὶ δικαιολογουμένου πρὸ[ς] αὐτοὺς περὶ τούτου, οἱ δὲ πάλιν, ἐκ τῶν ἐναντίω[ν] ἤθ[ο]ς πανκάκιστον καὶ ἀπονοίας μεστὸν ἀναλαβόμενοι, ἐπελθόντες κ[α]ὶ αὐτῷ μετὰ πελέκων καὶ ῥοπάλων ἐβούλοντο αὐτῷ καὶ τοῦ ζῆν ἀνελῖν — εἰ μὴ γὰρ τύχης ἔργον γεγένη-

ται, τοῦ φυγῇ αὐτὸν τὴν ζωοποίαν ποιήσασθαι, πάλε ἂν καὶ τοῦ ζῆν αὐτὸν ἀνῖλον — καταφρονήσαντες

τ[ῆς] τῶν καιρῶν εὐνομίας καὶ τῆς ἡμετέρας ἀπραγμοσύνης. ἐπὶ τοίνυν καὶ ἅπερ εἶχαν ἐν μισθώσει

20 οἱ αὐτοί μου υἱοὶ πρόβατα πε[ν]τ[.]ια καὶ βόας ὀκτὼ καὶ ὀνικὰ τετράποδα πέντε ἀφήρπαξαν καὶ διεσπάθησαν, κἀγὼ αὐτὸς ὁ ἄθ(λ)ιο[ς] ἀ[ν]αγκίζομαι ὑπὸ τῶν δεσποτῶν ταῦτα ἀποδοῦναι, διά τοι τοῦτο τάδε τὰ βιβλία ἐπιδίδω[μι], ἐν [ἀσφ]αλ[ί]ᾳ ἀξιῶ[ν] ἀχθῆναι αὐτοὺς ἐπὶ σοί, [κα]ὶ πρῶτον μὲν οὗ ἐτόλμησαν παρανόμου καὶ ῥι[ψοκινδύνου] πράγματος [ἐκ]δικίας τυχεῖν, ἔπιτα ἐπαναγκασθῆναι αὐτοὺς τὴ[ν] τῶν προειρημένων [τετρ]απόδων ⟨ἀπόδοσιν⟩ ποιήσασ[θ]αι· εἰ δὲ μή, ἐκπέπεσθαι αὐτοὺς [εἰ]ς τὸ μέγα δικασ-

25 τήριον τοῦ κυρίου μου διαση[μοτά]τ[ο]υ ἡγεμόνος τῆς Αὐγουστοποταμίας Φλαουίου Ὀλυμπίου, ὅπως ἡ δέουσα ἐπιστρέφια προ[σταχθήσηται] κατ' αὐτῶ[ν]. διευτύχει.

ὑπατείας Φουρίου Πλακίδ[ου] καὶ Φλα]ουίου Ῥωμύλ[ου] τῶν λαμπροτάτων, [Φ]αρμοῦθι ια.

(*m.* 2) Αὐρήλιος Ζωΐλος ἐπιδέδ[ωκα· . . . .] . . . . ου ἔγραψα ὑπὲρ α[ὐ]τοῦ ἀγρ(αμμάτου).

A virtually complete papyrus sheet, 32B x 26H cm. At *l.*7 νόσου is genitive for dative; read χρέων (7), τοὔνομα (8); τοῦ ζῆν, gen. for acc.(17,18); ἐκπέμπεσθαι (24).
Bib. — P.J. Sijpesteijn, *Mnem.* 12(1959)134; *SB* 6.5 (1963) 9622; E.A. Judge/S.R. Pickering, *JbAC* 20(1977) 63; **P. Sakaon* 48, pp.119–23.

To Aurelius Ision *curialis, praepositus* **of the 8th pagos in the Arsinoite nome, from Aurelius Zoilos son of Melas, deacon of the catholic church, from the village of Theadelphia in the same nome. Those who have chosen a way of life that is shameless and piratical, o purest of men, deserve to encounter the vengeance of the laws. When**
5 **my late son, called Gerontios, was still alive, he entered — if only he |hadn't! — into a marriage partnership with a woman, Nonna, daughter of Anous, from the same village. Although I thought that she was maintaining good will and affection towards living with me, she effected the reverse. For when my son, mentioned above, was lying ill and about to pay back life's debt, unaccountably a certain man, Sakaon by name, from the same village, setting upon my own house and laying hands upon the wife (Nonna, mentioned above) of the said son of mine, he abducted her and removed her**
10 **to his own house, |though it was quite improper and quite illegal, having obtained as accomplices in this blatant transgression of decency his own brothers and the woman's mother, Anous (mentioned above). But since the said son of mine died immediately I wanted at that time to conform to the laws concerning the reckless act which they had the effrontery (to commit); and what is more I gave way to them (i.e., the abductors) since I practise the quietist life. Well then, unaccountably, when my other son called**
15 **Pasis saw his grandfather being assaulted by the villainous men |(mentioned above), who had chopped up (?) his clothing with an axe, and took issue with them about this, they in turn adopted on their side an attitude that was most villainous and full of rebelliousness; and setting upon him with axes and clubs, wanted to deprive him even of life — for had not a stroke of fortune occurred, the making safe of his life by flight, they would long ago have deprived him even of life — since they scorned the good order of the times and our quietism. Since, therefore, they have also snatched away and**
20 **plundered five sheep, eight [   ] and oxen and five asses which |these same sons of mine held on lease, I myself, poor wretch, am required by the owners to return them. For this reason, then, I present this petition, asking that they be brought before you in custody, and that, first, they may meet with the penalty of law for the illegal and reckless act which they had the effrontery to commit; next that they may be compelled to make restitution for the aforesaid livestock. And if they do not, that they may be**
25 **taken away to the great court |of my lord the most eminent** *praeses* **of Augustopotamia, Flavius Olympios, so that the appropriate severity will be prescribed against them. Fare well. In the consulship of the most illustrious Furius Placidus and Flavius Romulus, Pharmouthi 11. (***m.2***) I, Aurelius Zoilos, have presented the petition. I . . . wrote for him since he is illiterate.**

This is the sole text among the one hundred collected together in *P. Sakaon* which provides explicit testimony to the presence of Christianity in the small, dying village of Theadelphia. Parássoglou's volume assembles and provides a re-edition of 76 texts — ranging in date from c.280 (no.36) to 352 (no.10) — belonging to the 'archive of Sakaon', an influential member of the village who appears to have been related by marriage to a large proportion of the others who lived there. Sakaon himself figures in 46 of these texts. The remaining 24 documents — the most recently published item, an ostrakon, is included in an appendix, p.263 — are contemporary to this period, and although there is no direct link with Sakaon, we hear more about individuals who do figure in 'his' archive. Over half the texts gathered in *P. Sakaon* had been published previously by P. Jouguet in *P. Thead.* (1911, repr. 1974); his notes and commentaries thereto are still important in the absence of any by Parássoglou to date (cf. R. Bagnall, *BASP* 17 [1980] 97–104).

In early IV the village was on the way to becoming a 'ghost' town, gradually being abandoned to the desert because the irrigation system could not be made to work properly, despite pleas to the government. *P. Sakaon* 42 (c.323), 44 (331/2) and 35 (c.332), in which Sakaon and others request tax alleviation, testify to the depopulation of Theadelphia: 'we are living in a deserted village', ἡμᾶς ... | ... ἔρημον κώμην οἰκοῦν|τας (32.11–13). Barns suggests (9) a link could be made between the decay of the town and the presence there of Christianity; but did he overstate his case? For him, Theadelphia was 'a village which the authorities must have regarded as a hotbed of Christianity and disaffection', and this 'made the government less inclined to keep it alive' (9). Barns notes that the finding at Theadelphia of a considerable number of *libelli* from the time of Decius — 34 of the 45 known at latest count; cf. *New Docs 1977* **105**, p.182; none are included in *P. Sakaon*, being outside the relevant time zone — implies that a Christian presence was suspected there. Yet that such a large number of these texts came from one site merely reflects the haphazard nature of such finds, one which in this case may distort our picture of mid-III Theadelphia; and this is all the more something to be cautious about if G.W. Clarke is correct, *Antichthon* 3 (1969) 68–73, that citizens throughout the Empire, and perhaps even the entire populace, were obliged to sacrifice. There are at least indisputable instances of non-Christians being required to sacrifice (cf. *New Docs 1977*, ibid.). That said, the *libelli* ought not to be discounted entirely as a witness to localities where Christianity was believed to have taken root; for as we may infer from the text printed above, 90 years after Decius there was a church and all the usual hierarchy. Such developments would be expected to require more than the three decades since 312.

Further, Barns claims (9) that not only Zoilos and his family, but his adversary Sakaon and his family were Christians. In this he depends on a doubtful argument from silence, that Zoilos identifies himself as a church official, rather than as a Christian complaining about the behaviour of a non-Christian when 'it would have been natural, and by this time safe and even advantageous, for him to have said so'. But the earliest attestations of the word χρηστιανός in papyrus texts (from mid-III) are consistent: it is applied by outsiders to Christians as a way to define them, not used by Christians for self-identification (cf. *New Docs 1977*, **102**). For discussion of the 'Christians for Christians' inscriptions from Phrygia see **98**. But Barns' view may be supported more generally by the thrust of R. Bagnall's argument about the rapid pace of conversion during IV, *BASP* 19 (1982) 105–24, discussed at **100**; and it gains strength particularly from the presence of the names Gerontios and Nonna in the respective families. The latter appears to be a Christian usage (cf. Barns' n. to *l.*5 on p.6); while the former appears to be almost entirely confined among Christians (for the evidence from Rome see *Solin, GPR* 2.947, where of 29 attestations ranging in date from III–VI² only one is certainly Jewish and a small number of others may be non-Christian, although given the period of attestation this possibility becomes increasingly remote with successive centuries). One may wonder, too, whether Nonna would have been acceptable to Zoilos and his family if she were not a member of the Church. A study of the influence of Paul's dictum at 2 Cor. 6.14, μὴ γίνεσθε ἑτεροζυγοῦντες ἀπίστοις, is beyond the scope of the present discussion; but the extent to which it was taken seriously by the Church — for patristic references see *Bib.Pat.* 1.478, and 2.397–98, among which Tertullian and Cyprian both figure prominently — may have some relevance for Bagnall's view about the speed with which Egypt was Christianized in this century.

Barns notes that the high-sounding phraseology in *ll*.3–4 contrasts with the errors (especially καί for the definite article) and misspellings of the scribe. The latter was not the author of the petition for the illiterate Zoilos (for another deacon illiterate at least in Greek see *New Docs 1976*, **80**; some intending deacons did not even know how to write Coptic — see Deissmann, *LAE* 221–24). To this *P. Sakaon* 38 (*ed.pr.* — *P. Flor.* 1 [1906,repr.1960] 36, dated 17/8/312) provides more than a passing parallel; and Barns suggests that the same person composed the wording of these two documents. This petition a generation earlier reflects a previous stage of the family feud going on at Theadelphia. In that document Aurelios Melas, father of Zoilos, complains that his son's wife Taeus was abducted by Sakaon on the ground that he had not received sufficient marriage gifts (ἕ[δν]ων, 11). Nonna, the wife abducted in *P. Sakaon* 48 — was she the daughter of Anous by Sarmates, Sakaon's nephew by marriage (*P. Sakaon* 38.24–25)? — may have been removed for a similar reason: she and Gerontios appear to have had no children (see Parássoglou's family tree in *P.Sakaon*, p.xx), a *possible* indicator that they had not been long married. Now it is very curious that in the petition printed above Zoilos has made no reference to Sakaon's action in kidnapping his wife Taeus thirty years earlier. Furthermore, the relationship between the two protagonists has been suppressed — given the bureaucratization of Egypt it will not do to say that it was too well-known to require specification that Zoilos was son-in-law to Sakaon, Taeus being the latter's daughter by his first marriage.

It must not be forgotten that in the two petitions *P. Sakaon* 38 and 48 we are hearing only one side of the family feud. Whether or not the Pauline injunction noted above about marriage to unbelievers was taken to heart, the gospel advice on how believers should resolve their disputes (Mt. 18.15–17) appears to have had little impact. Only two early patristic discussions of the three-verse passage occur (cf. *Bib.Pat.* 1.269; 2.274). In contrast, *Bib.Pat.* 1.452 and 2.381 assemble over 50 patristic discussions of 1 Cor. 6.1–11 (or parts thereof), and it is clear that this passage provided the basis for what became the institution of the episcopal court (*audientia episcopalis*) set up under Constantine. His edict of 318 concerning this — R.P. Coleman-Norton, *Roman State and Christian Church* (3 vols; London, 1966) 1.28, pp. 74–76 — 'raises the Christian episcopate to the status of judges in such cases involving private law as litigants agree to plead before bishops. The law allows litigants to transfer suits from civil judges to bishops, whose verdicts are recognized as final' (Coleman-Norton, n. ad loc.). His allusion to a papyrus which illustrates the working of the court refers to *P. Lips.* (1906) 43 (Hermopolis(?), IV), the earliest surviving documentary attestation to the existence of ecclesiastical courts, in which Bishop Plousianos adjudicates a dispute between Thaesis, a nun (ἀειπαρθ[ένο]υ, 4; for the possibility that the word here may mean 'still unmarried' woman see A.M. Emmett, *JÖB* 32 (1981) 507-10), and the heirs of a certain Besarion. The heirs produced witnesses who accused Thaesis 'concerning the removal of Christian books', περὶ ἀφαιρέσε[ω]ς | βιβλίων χρε[ιστ]ια῾νι῾κῶν (12–13). Because the fourth-century date of *P.Lips.*43 cannot be defined more specifically, it is impossible to decide whether Zoilos' recourse to the civil authority in *P.Sakaon* 48 only a generation after Constantine's legislation reflects more about the personalities involved or about the slowness of such changes to take effect in small, and dying, rural villages. On the subject of ecclesiastical jurisdiction see A. Steinwenter, '*Audientia episcopalis*', *RAC* 1(1950) 915-17; and more recent and fully G. Thür/P.E. Pieler, 'Gerichtsbarkeit', *RAC* 10 (1976–1978) 466-492 (papyrus references at col.486); note earlier in that article cols. 384–91 (Roman legal treatment of Jews and Christians), and 465-66 (Jewish legal jurisdiction). E.A. Judge has drawn my attention to a specific recent study, K.M. Girardet, *Kaisergericht und*

Bischofsgericht. Studien zu den Anfängen des Donatistenstreites (313-315) und zum Prozess des Athanasius von Alexandrien (328-346) (*Antiquitas* 21; Bonn, 1975).

Zoilos speaks of practising a life of quietism (13; cf.19). On the verb ἀσκέω in general see H. Dressler, *The Usage of* ἀσκέω *and its Cognates in Greek Documents to 100 A.D.* (Washington, 1947); it occurs in the NT only at Acts 24.16, ἀσκῶ ἀπρόσκοπον συνείδησιν ἔχειν πρὸς τὸν θεὸν καὶ τοὺς ἀνθρώπους. At *New Docs 1977*, **18** a posthumous inscription for Theophilos of Iulia Gordos (75/6) praises him as one of those ἀσ|κήσαντες βίον ὑπὲρ τῆς πατρίδος (23-24); quoted in the discussion there is a closer parallel to the present situation, *SB* 1 (1915) 5100, an epitaph for David τὸν μοναδικὸν ἀσκήσας βίον (4). Cf. the related noun ἀσκήτρια, 'nun', in a brief epitaph for Irene (provenance unknown, V/VI): *ed.pr.* — C. Mango/I Ševčenko, *DOP* 32 (1978) 23 no.27 (fig.27); cf. *SEG* 1576. For ἀπραγμοσύνη as reprehensible non-involvement in VBC Athenian politics see Perikles' funeral speech (Thuc.2.40), which provides the *locus classicus*; for other contemporaneous examples of both noun and adjective see LSJ, s.vv. Yet Zoilos has taken on his share of civic responsibilities: he was *sitologos* in 312 (*P. Sakaon* 38.12) and 320 (*P. Sakaon* 7.4-5); later he was *komarch* of the village (*P. Sakaon* 52.4,27), in 326. If the word is to reflect some such colouring here — unless Zoilos has taken orders late and opted out of such involvement — may ἀπραγμοσύνη here refer to a vow(?) to non-violence, presumably related to his being in orders? In *P. Coll.Youtie* (1976) 77 (cf. *P.Col.* 7 [1979] 171; *New Docs 1976*, **81**) a man claims in a petition (Karanis, 6/6/324) that he would have been killed by his assailants but for the help of Antoninos the *diakon* and Isak the *monachos* who happened to be passing by; but quite what βοηθεία means there in *l.*13 is hard to specify. In *P. Sakaon* 41 (*ed.pr.* — *P.Ryl.* 4[1952] 659, dated 14/7/322) a certain Arion, who figures quite often (over a dozen times, mostly in financial documents) in *P. Sakaon*, petitions against the threatened violence of the local tax-collectors because of a presumed partnership (μετουσίαν, 10) with his father-in-law. He complains that these men are 'despising my modest circumstances and my quietism', καταφρονοῦντες τῆς μετριότητός μου καὶ | ἀπραγμοσύνης (7-8), along with his widowhood and childlessness; his wife and his children have all predeceased him. It is by no means certain, but are we to detect another Christian family here? This suggestion deserves consideration in view of the word ἀπραγμοσύνη (which by its coupling with μετριότης may suggest here the more general moral quality of 'inoffensiveness'), and more particularly as the wife's name, Eirene, is predominantly — though not exclusively — Christian in usage, its frequency in Rome, at least, being most marked in III and IV (Solin, *GPR* 1.422-26, cites a few Jewish examples, and others that are certainly pagan, but indubitably Christian attestation preponderates). *If* Arion is a Christian then *P. Sakaon* 41 taken together with *P. Sakaon* 48 may be taken to reflect the shift from allusiveness to overt self-identification. Even allowing for factors like personal idiosyncrasy, personality, etc., the dramatic shift apparent in 20 years would be quite consonant with Bagnall's hypothesis about the rapid rate of conversion.

Some items of vocabulary relevant to the NT and ECL may be noted briefly; for τρόπος (3) with the sense 'way of life' cf. Heb. 13.5, ἀφιλάργυρος ὁ τρόπος. Although μακάριος (4) used of the dead is especially common as an epithet in Christian contexts (see Lampe, s.v., E.1), in fact the usage goes back to Plato at least (see LSJ, s.v., I.3; cf. the similar use of μάκαρ, going back to Hesiod, LSJ, s.v. III). The example of εἴθε in the parenthetical comment at *ll.*4-5 (with this exclamation συνῆλθε is to be understood) may be worth noting at BDF §359(1). With the phrase πρὸς γάμου κοινωνίαν (5) we may compare *P. Sakaon* 38 (= *P.Flor.* 36), discussed above, where the same wording occurs in *ll.*5, 25. It too goes back at least to Plato (*Laws* 721a) as a classical usage. For discussion of κοινωνία/κοινωνός in another context cf. **4**. The noun συμβίωσις (6) might be expected to mean 'marriage' here (for the meaning 'private association' see **17**, where several attestations are noted); cf. *P. Sakaon* 38.32–33, where the note is appended to the petition, 'If the girl is satisfied with her marriage to her husband, let this very matter be made clear to the *logistes* in accordance with the laws' εἰ ἀρέσκεται τῇ πρὸς τὸν ἄνδρα συμβιώσει ἡ παῖς, αὐτὸ τοῦτο φανερὸν γενέσθω παρὰ τῷ λο|[γιστῇ ἀκολούθ]ως τοῖς νόμοις. But μου following συμβίω[σι]ν in Zoilos' petition makes that meaning considerably less certain; the translation given above, '(their) living with me', attempts to reflect the pronoun and provides consistency with the fact that the assault occurs in Zoilos' own house (8). It appears that Gerontios and Nonna were living with him, as were his son Pasis and his father (14). Alternatively, given the frequency of μου in this papyrus (8 occurrences, one of which is partly restored, *l*.8; in addition, Barns restored μου at *l*.4), is it an unnecessary scribal 'filler' in the text, at least in a passage like *l*.6? For the euphemism τ[ὸ] χρέον τοῦ βίου ἀποδοῦναι (7), Barns (n. ad loc.) provides a near contemporary parallel, *SB* 1(1915) 4426.8–9, διὰ τὴν νόσον ἀποδοῦναι τὸ χρέως (late III). The participle ἐπιστάς (8; J.A.L. Lee suggests to me that this ought to go loosely with οἶκον, ἀναλαβόμενος governing γυναῖκα) provides a parallel to Acts 17.5, where the Jews are ἐπιστάντες τῇ οἰκίᾳ Ἰάσονος. The verb διαρπάζω (8) occurs in the NT only at Mk. 3.27, τὰ σκεύη . . . δ.; with a personal object it is found in ECL at Ign. *Rom*.7.1. At *P. Sakaon* 38.10 the simple verb is used of abducting Zoilos' wife, ἁρπάξας τὴν κόρην. Another compound, ἀφαρπάζω, occurs in *P. Sakaon* 48.20, of the subsequent cattle-duffing; at *P. Sakaon* 36.15 the verb is used of sheep-stealing in a petition by a widow (c.280) concerning the behaviour of a certain Syrion when her husband died (cf. **5** above); it is found with an identical force at *P. Sakaon* 46.8–9 (29/3/342). The pejorative sense of συνεργός here, found elsewhere in the papyri but going back to classical writers (see LSJ, s.v.,I), is quite distinct from the semi-specialized meaning attached to the word in the NT epistles: note especially 1 Cor. 3.9, θεοῦ γάρ ἐσμεν συνεργοί; 1 Thes. 3.2, Timothy συνεργὸν τοῦ θεοῦ; and above all 3 Jn. 8, ἵνα συνεργοὶ γινώμεθα τῇ ἀληθείᾳ. Christian specialization of another kind is to be understood in a Christian necropolis inscription, *IGA* 5.191 (Antinoopolis, n.d.), where St Kollouthos is asked to 'be a fellow-worker (σύνεργοε — *sic*) with the one who writes with a chisel (i.e., the mason), and the builder, and Paul your humble slave'. The noun συνεργασία (not NT) occurs in *SEG* 741, a funerary epigram (Gortyn, II/III). The noun παρανομία (10) appears only as a *v.l.* in the NT, at 2 Pet. 2.16, and could usefully be added to the few examples in MM, if a revision of that work is to include documentary attestations of NT variants.

The example of πάραυτα (11) may be added to BAGD, s.v., to illustrate Ign., *Trall*. 11.1, as may ῥιψοκίνδυνος (12; largely restored at *l*.23) to illustrate the related adverb in *1 Clem*. 14.2, a largely restored example of which occurs at *P. Sakaon* 38.2–3. So too with ἀπόνοια (16), found in ECL at *1 Clem*. 1.1; 46.7. In the NT μεστός is used of people and the qualities they are filled with: Mt. 23.28; Rom. 1.29; 15.14; Jas. 3.17. At 2 Pet. 2.14, however, the personal reference is made slightly more remote for the adjective qualifies 'eyes', ὀφθαλμοὺς ἔχοντες μεστοὺς μοιχαλίδος; and *l*.16 in our papyrus offers a helpful analogy, where μ. is a predicative epithet of ἦθος. With ζωοποία (18) cf. the verb ζωοποιέω found several times in the NT; MM's entry offers only one documentary example of the adjective, a sixth-century Christian text. With adjectival ὀνικός (20) cf. Mt. 18.6 = Mk. 9.42 = Lk. 9.2. The verb διασπάω here (20–21) lacks the meaning occurring at Mk. 5.4 and Acts 23.10. For the phrase ἐν ἀσφαλείᾳ (22) cf. Acts 5.23, τὸ δεσμωτήριον εὕρομεν κεκλεισμένον ἐν πάσῃ ἀσφαλείᾳ.

Finally, since this text deals with marital matters it may be appropriate to refer to the few related texts noted in the 1978 culling. *P. Strasb.* 668 (provenance unknown, II) is the fragmentary conclusion of a marriage contract. *P. Sakaon* 38 (= *P.Flor.* 36) has already been referred to several times above and requires no general comment here; but we may note the verb κοινωνέω of marriage at *l*.6; in *l*.9 the statement τοὺς παῖδας [συ]νέ[ζ]ευξα is noted by MM, s.v. συνζεύγνυμι; the 'children' being married here are Zoilos whose petition has been the focus of this entry, and his betrothed relative Taues, later abducted by Sakaon. This text is the only example illustrating μνηστεύω noted in MM, s.v.

102. An uncommon *nomen sacrum*

CPR 11 (Fayum, VI/VII; pl.8) is an order for payment which provides an addition to a small archive (van Lith details the other texts in her commentary). It begins: † Στέφανος δοῦλ(ος) τῆς θεοτόκ(ου) | Ἰωάννῃ ἀπαιτ(ητῇ) Πτολεμαίδ(ος)· | παράσχ(ου) Ἀλεξάνδρῳ | τέκτ(ονι) ἐργαζομ᾽έ᾽(νῳ) εἰς τὸν σὺν ᾽θ᾽(εῷ) | κτιζόμ᾽ε᾽(νον) οἶκ(όν) μου, κτλ (1-5), 'Stephen, slave of the Mother of God, to John, tax collector of Ptolemais: provide for Alexander the carpenter working on my house being built with God's help (20 artabas of corn)', etc.

The noun θεότοκος is not at all rare in this period, but the formula δοῦλος τῆς θ. is not common, clearly derived as it is from δοῦλος τοῦ θεοῦ/Χριστοῦ. This same Stephen uses it in two other documents with exactly the same abbreviations: *Stud.Pal.* 8 (1908, repr. 1965), 1134, 1135 (both Fayum, VI). Among 1978 publications where θεότοκος occurs we may note *IGCB* 2 (Corinth Isthmos, 551-65), an invocation to Mary. On this inscription and *IGCB* 1 (same provenance and date; referred to at **93**) see D. Feissel, *BCH* 101 (1977) 220-24.

Of rather more interest, perhaps, is the abbreviation of the common phrase σὺν θεῷ — a typical example from 1978 texts, σὺν θ̅ω̅, occurs in the address on the *verso* of a letter, *P.Strasb.* 680 (provenance unknown, VII init.) — as ${}_{σὺν}^{θ̶}$: the long bar through the *theta* is probably to be put down to style (cf. in the same line the superior *epsilon* above εργαζομ; the plate is excellent), though it ought not to be ruled out that it *may* act as the superior bar would over a more normal *nomen sacrum*. At *Stud.Pal.* 3 (1904, repr. 1965) 183.4 (provenance unknown, VI) the arrangement is similar (no long bar) except that the *theta* follows the end of the word [σ]ὺν θ. More interesting is *Stud.Pal.* 3.191 (Arsinoite nome, VII) where *m*.1 wrote σὺν θεῷ (3), while *m*.2 has σὺν θ (5). Only one approximately comparable example is provided in A. H. R. E. Paap, *Nomina Sacra in the Greek Papyri of the First Five Centuries AD* (*P.L.Bat.* 8; Leiden, 1959) 76-78, namely *PSI* 7 (1925) 757. In this portion of *Ep.Barn.* 9.1-6 (provenance unknown, IV (?)), we have ὁ θ· at *verso*, *l*.10 and *recto*, *l*.31. But the interchangeability of this form of abbreviation is apparent by analogy with the different ways of writing κύριος in this text: in full, *verso ll*.4, 11; κ̅·, *verso l*.8; κ·, *verso ll*.16, 18 (restored at *ll*.3,10). Note the phrase πρὸς τὸν θ(εόν) in *MAMA* 7.96, quoted above at **98**. No examples of θ(εός) are cited in K. McNamee, *Abbreviations in Greek Literary Papyri and Ostraca* (*BASP Supp.* 3; Chico, 1981). A variant of the 'fish' acrostic, painted in a funerary chapel, includes the abbreviation θ(εοῦ): see *IGA* 5.20, printed above at **7**.

For the uncommon suspension θε in the phrase παρὰ τῷ θε(ῷ) see *P.Mich.* inv. 337, published by H.C. Youtie, *ZPE* 22 (1976) 63-68 with his n. to *l*.4 on p.66 (repr. in his *Scriptiunculae Posteriores* 1 (Bonn, 1981) 345-50).

A rare example of the complete abbreviation of θεοί (θ̅ν̅ for θεῶν) occurs in *P.Chester Beatty* XIII (Pap.2149), folio 7, *l*.5; for further comments on this text see **83**.

103. The earliest trace of Christianity at Lampsakos

Included in *I.Lampsakos* along with its inscriptions are the testimonia for that city. In T.134 = *Acta Martyrum* [Ruinart] 205, a certain Peter is ordered by the proconsul: *sacrifica magnae deae Veneri*. Since the text mentions Decius this instruction is to be related to the persecution of 249-51; and, in view of the name of the man under pressure to show his religious (and thereby political) orthodoxy, it provides our earliest evidence — if genuine historical material is preserved in these *Acta* — for a Christian presence at that city. For discussion of the Decian *libelli* cf. *New Docs 1977*, **105**, where it is pointed out that, whatever Christians at the time (and Eusebius, later on) may have felt, the measure may well not have been specifically and solely anti-Christian in its focus.

104. Christians in mid-IV land registers

P. Landl. collects and (re)edits four land registers from the Hermopolite nome written up for taxation purposes. By far the most important in view of their length and the correspondences between them are nos. 1 (*P.Giss.* 1.117; 593*ll.*) and 2 (*P.Flor.* 1.71; 824*ll.*); no. 3 (*P.Flor.* 1.87) contains extra material from the same codex as no. 2. No. 4 is a re-edition of *Stud.Pal.* 5.120 with a new fragment, a similar register from Hermopolis. It is possible to show that no.1 precedes no.2 probably by less than a decade, since a very high proportion — some 75% — of the names in no.1 occur also in no.2, although in some cases the amount of land owned has altered in the interim.

The editors of *P. Landl.* suggest (18) that these documents are to be placed within the timespan c. 313-25. In a very useful review article R. Bagnall, *BASP* 16 (1979) 159-68, holds that this is too early and that a date after c.340 but before the 370s is more appropriate. Bagnall's examination of onomastic evidence for the pace of conversion to Christianity, *BASP* 19 (1982) 105-24 — discussed above, **100** — draws upon the *P. Landl.* evidence (114-15), and his onomastic argument provides some confirmation for a date in the 340s.

These land registers deserve mention here for they document just a generation after the end of persecution the *volte face* of state recognition of the Church. In these lists we see the 'use by official recordkeepers of church titles as an official means of designating a taxpayer, of distinguishing him in the tax rolls. The state in effect recognizes the occupation of the person as it would that of a weaver or of a military veteran' (Bagnall [1979]: 164). Those with such titles may be listed here:

— Makarios ἀποτακτικός: 1.505 = 2.722; for other *apotaktikoi* who own property see *New Docs 1976*, **82**, p.128. In a petition, *P.Oxy.* 3311 (c.373/4) two sisters — to be regarded as Christians in view of the name of one, Martha; cf. Bagnall's onomastic argument, noted above — attempt to gain control of an estate of a cousin. When he was about to die (ὃς μέλλων τελευτᾶν, 4) he left his property under the authority (ὑπὸ τὴν ἐξουσίαν, 4-5) of his maternal uncle Ammonios, an *apotaktikos* (5, 7; at *l.*10 he is said to have remained in this vocation till death, ἀποτακτικὸς δὲ ὢν ἐτελεύτα τὸν βίον). What the phrase in *ll.*4-5 means is not certain, but may hint at the theoretical situation — as opposed to actual practice — by which *apotaktikoi* could not *own* property. See *ed.pr.*'s n. ad loc.; cf. E. A. Judge, *Proc. XVIth International Congress of Papyrology, New York, July 1980* (*American Studies in Papyrology* 23; Chico, 1981) 618-19.

— Pkulis διάκων: 1.200
— Amonianos ἐπίσκοπος: 1.298 = 2.510
— Arion ἐπίσκοπος: 1.305 = 2.519
— Dios ἐπίσκοπος: 2.147
— Makarios ἐπίσκοπος: 1.512 = 2.731 = 3.50
— Pankrates πρεσβύτερος: 1.522 = 2.771 = 2.809 = 2.818.

Over this list one might pause to wonder whether the number of bishops in the area is surprisingly large for the date. Yet note the comment of W. H. C. Frend, (*Carthage* 3.32) that in early V there were more than 700 bishops in N. Africa: even some villages and landed estates could boast having one. On bishops see H. Chadwick et al., *The Role of the Christian Bishop in Ancient Society* (*Center for Hermeneutical Studies, Colloquy* 35; Berkeley, 1980), especially 2, 30, on the number of bishops in a city. To this group of land-owning ecclesiastics we should add the reference to church property at 1.534, οὐσίας ἐκκλησίας (on the problem of the reading see edd. n. on p.60).

If Bagnall's argument about the pace of conversion in IV is correct, then quite a proportion of those listed in these registers may have been Christians. On the basis of names alone the following minimal list can be devised:

— Athanasios son of Eudoxios: 1.100 = 2.304
— 12 Makarioi: 5 are sons of fathers with pagan names, two are fathers of children with pagan names. One has a double name, M. ὁ καὶ Κλώμιος 1.159 = 2.375. Of the remaining four, three have a title instead of a patronymic: *apotaktikos*, *episkopos* (both listed above), λιβλάριος 1.506 = 2.723 = 3.41. The significance of περαξ after the name M. at 1.508 = 2.725 = 3.52 is unclear. Makarios is not exclusively a Christian name, but is uncommon until III, when it begins to occur more frequently: for evidence from Rome see Solin, *GPR* 2.814-15 (28 examples, only two certainly before III according to his dating). Its increasing attestation from then seems to reflect its popularity among Christians.
— Nonna daughter of Olympios: 1.522 = 2.742; for this name see, briefly, **101**
— Paul: 1.30 = 2.171 = 2.700 = 3.44
— Paul father of Papnouthis: 2.419
— Paul father of Timotheos: 2.449
— Paul son of Moros: 2.762
— Peter: 2.273
— Timotheos father of Silvanos: 2.441
— Timotheos son of Mouses: 2.446
— Timotheos son of Paul: 2.449.

Two other occupations may be noted here in passing: at 2.641 Diokoros is a πορφυροπώλης, an addition to the list collected at *New Docs 1977*, 3, p.27. L. Casarico, *Stud. Pap.* 22(1983) 23-37, has collected papyrus examples of nouns ending in -πωλης/-πρατης. She lists eight examples of πορφυροπώλης, dated between 399 and the Byzantine period. Two individuals, Mouses and Petbes, are each defined as θυρουρός: 1.161 = 2.380, and 1.201 respectively; cf. *New Docs 1977*, **53**.

105. Christianity at Carthage

The collaboration of archaeological teams from several countries in rescue digs at Carthage since the early 1970s has achieved results whose full significance remains to be assessed, but which are already providing indications that some views about the ancient city in the Late Roman and Byzantine periods will need to be revised. The most recent bibliography seen by me related to the 'Save Carthage' excavations is by J.H. Humphrey in *New Light on Ancient Carthage*, ed. J.G. Pedley (Ann Arbor, 1980) 123–27.

The Michigan team has been working on a VIIAD ecclesiastical complex — see S. Ellis, *Carthage* 3.41–67 (with an appendix of locus lists by Humphrey and Ellis, 69–94); id., *Carthage* 5.7–124 (locus lists, 135–83) — adjacent to an early Christian basilica, and also on the so-called 'House of the Greek Charioteers' (named after a mosaic found there: see K.M.D. Dunbabin, *Carthage* 1. 30–31, with pls. 12–13, colour pls. 1–2, and end figure 1) which had occupancy during late Roman and Byzantine periods. Humphrey's survey within this time zone of new finds being made by the various teams (in Pedley, op. cit., 85–120) helps to put the contributions in different areas into a larger perspective of the overall project.

Apart from the speed of publication achieved by the Michigan team, a feature of their preliminary reports (*Carthage* 1–5; further volumes have appeared: vol. 6 [1981], not yet seen by me, concentrates on the cisterns, and a statue group of Ganymede and the Eagle, dated to the time of Augustine) very useful to non-specialist archaeologists is the inclusion of 'chapters which attempt in the light of current research to update the historical and economic picture of the periods the levels of which we are now excavating' (*Carthage* 4, preface p. v). A notably successful example is W.H.C. Frend's 'The Early Church at Carthage' (*Carthage* 3.21–40), which surveys the half-millennium of Christian presence in the city from II²–VIII, paying particular attention to what can be inferred about the state of the Church from building remains. The Byzantine basilicas with mosaic floors and marble fittings 'reflect a wealthy, influential and self-reliant Church' (31; cf. 28). The earliest focus for Christian worship was provided by cemeteries outside the city walls; martyrs' graves acquired especial sanctity. Frend mentions (25–26) probable epigraphical references to Vibia Perpetua, martyred with other Christians in 203. In his discussion (26–27) of the Damous el Karita, a major cemetery basilica located outside the city walls, he notes that the way this site was developed over several centuries encapsulates 'the whole history of Christianity in Carthage from *area* church [i.e. those located in the cemeteries] to great ecclesiastical complex and then in Byzantine times to a small, rather neglected suburban church' (27). In contrast to the Nubians and Copts, Carthaginian Christianity put up no resistance to Islam in VII/VIII, for the Church there can be perceived from the archaeological record to have been already in decline before the Arabs arrived (34). In addition to 22 churches at Carthage known from the literary sources, archaeological work has located a further six (see Frend's appendix, 36–40). Other matters discussed include the development of the ecclesiastical hierarchy from IV onwards (29), and the powerful role exercised by the 'lay elders', *seniores laici*, in relation to church property (30).

A very readable evocation of Carthage in Augustine's day is provided by F.M. Clover (*Carthage* 4.1–14); this survey concentrates upon the importance of public entertainment (exemplified in the chariot races) together with the Church's increasing denunciation of it, and the role of senatorial aristocrats who owned estates at Carthage. The many new buildings — ecclesiastical, public, and private — erected in late IV/early V indicate a time of great prosperity; local mosaic and pottery manufacture flourished, as did pagan religion (cf. Humphrey, in Pedley, op.cit., 116). Evidence of the latter may be derived in part from the surviving mosaics; new finds are discussed by Dunbabin in *Carthage* 1.21–46, and together with material discovered earlier in the century in Pedley, op.cit., 73–83. In the latter she argues (74) that several of the mosaics dated late IV/early V, including the 'Offering of the Crane' (pl.6.2) and the 'Mosaic of the months and seasons' (pl.6.3), were commissioned by a pagan patron in view of the classical religious motifs present in these works. Furthermore, another mosaic depicting Venus, while not to be regarded as pagan *per se* in view of the motif's use by Christians in other contexts, is to be understood as pagan in view of its location: it was used to cover over a walled-up access to a below-ground room in which had been cached statues and statuettes of various gods, votive offerings and an inscription to Jupiter Hammon Barbarus Silvanus. These items had probably been hidden away to avoid damage at the hands of the Christians (77). Dunbabin suggests that these mosaics may all reflect the work of one factory, but that their 'strong pagan tone' presumably reflects the interests of the patrons rather than that of the mosaic craftsmen; 'and one may ask whether the Christians patronized the workshop for the decoration of the basilicas constructed at this period' (80). Given the strong feelings held by the Carthaginian Church both *inter se* (Catholics vs. Donatists) and with regard to non-Christian practices, it may be wondered whether Christians in a mosaic factory would have taken on a commission with an avowedly pagan motif. Conversely, it may well be likely that Christians would approach such a factory with a commission regardless of the fact that the craftsmen were pagans, simply because the latter were skilled at their trade. It would be tantalizing if we could discern any hint of Christians giving such work to other Christians in conscious preference to pagans, even if it entailed work of inferior quality.

The Michigan volumes published so far include various lamps with Christian decorations, such as the ⚹ monogram (e.g., Carthage 2.234 no. 58). Few inscriptions have been presented so far (*Carthage* 3.167–73): all seven are very fragmentary, probably IV/V, and nearly all are probably Christian (only one is certainly so). Along with these Frend and Humphrey have also published (3.167–68) a bronze cross (of North African provenance(?), VI(?)) with elaborate decoration, for which two apparent parallels are known. While it must have had an ecclesiastical function, it is not clear whether it may have been used as a bishop's pectoral cross, or perhaps in connection with a reliquary (these two suggestions had been put forward previously for the piece most akin to the new example).

106. Early Christianity in the Egyptian Sahara — new finds

In 1978 the Toronto-based Dakhleh Oasis Project began its first detailed field season of archaeological survey in the Egyptian Sahara at the Dakhleh Oasis. Since then five seasons of survey work have been successfully completed and the entire area of the oasis examined. Evidence of man's activity can be documented from the Palaeolithic in an almost unbroken sequence to the present day: A. J. Mills/M. M. A. McDonald, *JSSEA* 9-13 (1979-1983); C. A. Hope in C. A. Hope/J. R. Zimmer (edd.), *Ancient Middle-Eastern Ceramics and Australian Archaeology in the Middle East* (Melbourne, 1982) 59-66. Amongst the sites which have been discovered are many which can be dated to the late antique period in Egypt when Christianity was developing and expanding throughout that country. The information from these sites pertinent to our understanding of Christianity in the region is still being analysed and its significance assessed; the following comments are of a preliminary nature.

The Dakhleh Oasis lies some 800 km SSW of Cairo roughly on the same latitude as modern Luxor and covers an area of between 2-3,000km². It is now connected with the Nile Valley by a road from Assiut which runs through the neighbouring oasis of el-Khargeh. In antiquity it was reached by one of two caravan routes: one via Khargeh Oasis following more or less the route of the modern road, and the other leaving the Nile Valley further to the south of Assiut at Abydos, which by-passed Khargeh Oasis. Although Christianity was known to have reached Khargeh Oasis by late III, as is indicated by the references to Christians, some holding church offices, amongst papyri discovered at Qasr Dush in that oasis in 1893 (A. Fakhry, *The Necropolis of El-Bagawat in Kharga Oasis* [Cairo 1951] 11-12 with references), in the Dakhleh Oasis nothing was previously known of Christian origin other than the remains of one church, Deir Abu Metta, of a later date (H. E. Winlock, *Ed Dakhleh Oasis* [New York 1936] 24; A. J. Mills, *JSSEA* 11 [1981] 185). Christianity apparently flourished in Khargeh Oasis, which was the seat of a bishop from IV onwards (Fakhry, op. cit. 12). As a result of the discoveries made by the Dakhleh Oasis Project it can now be shown that Christianity reached Dakhleh probably no later than late III and certainly flourished there also from IV to VII. Thereafter the archaeological record is silent, though bishops of Khargeh were appointed until XIV (ibid.). Famous church figures who can be associated with Christianity in the area are Athanasios and Nestorios, both of whom spent some of their time in exile there, during IV and V respectively.

On the basis of various criteria, e.g., architectural types, inscribed material and coins, details of interments, artefacts (especially ceramics), it has been possible to identify Christian activity in the oasis and to obtain approximate dating for it. The types of sites identified from this activity range from settlements to cemeteries, the former including several churches of importance at large urban centres, isolated churches and also caves possibly used by Christian hermits. Many temples in the oasis were re-used by Christians, though the exact date of this re-use has yet to be determined. Only the most important finds are mentioned here; short descriptions of all Christian sites discovered will be found in the works cited above by Mills, and illustrations and discussions of the ceramics, vital for their dating, appear in Hope, *JSSEA* 9-11 (1979-1981) and 13 (1983).

Undoubtedly one of the most important sites with remains of Christian origin is the large city of Ismant el-Kharab at the eastern end of the oasis (Mills, *JSSEA* 12 [1982] 99-100, and 13 [1983]; Winlock, op.cit.). This important urban and administrative centre, which has two temples, one dating to the Ptolemaic period, contains three churches. One of these is badly preserved while the other two are extant to the capitals of the columns which once supported the roofs (Mills, *JSSEA* 12 [1982] pl. XIIIa, c-d; Hope, in Hope/Zimmer [op. cit.] pl. 10A-B). These two churches form one complex. Excavation in the larger of the two, carried out in 1982 in one of the diaconicons, produced at floor level a large quantity of ceramics associated in part with a hoard of bronze coins. While the cleaning of the coins of this hoard is as yet only in its initial stages, it would appear to belong to the time of Constantine the Great and his immediate successors (Mills, *JSSEA* 13 [1983]). Amongst the ceramics were several fragments of imported North African red-slipped ware of a type known from mid-IV. It would seem, therefore, that the building can be ascribed to mid-IV. This would make it one of the earliest well-dated, large Christian monuments yet to be unearthed in Egypt, pre-dating the basilica of St Menas begun by Arcadius and apparently completed in 412 in the desert west of Alexandria (R. Krautheimer, *Early Christian and Byzantine Architecture* [London, 1981³] 117-19 and n.29).

Other sites of IV date have been found in different parts of the oasis. Located in the central part of the oasis is the church and small settlement of Deir Abu Metta (Mills, *JSSEA* 11 [1981] 185; Hope, *JSSEA* 11 [1981] 235). Coins of Constantine the Great and Theodosius I were found here in levels below the surviving church building. Ceramics from the site can be dated from late IV to VII. The church of tri-apsidal form (Mills, ibid., pl. XI) is of a type known from V onwards (Krautheimer, 119-24; see also C. C. Walters, *Monastic Archaeology in Egypt* [Warminster, 1974] 19-78, for a discussion of monastic church architecture). A settlement with possibly non-ecclesiastical, monumental architecture in the western part of the oasis has yielded large quantities of ceramics including imported North African red-slipped wares datable to late IV-early V (Mills, *JSSEA* 9 [1979] 182; Hope, *JSSEA* 10 [1980] 299-303). One final church of a later date is located near Ismant el-Kharab, namely the church of Deir el-Molouk (Mills, *JSSEA* 11 [1981] 184-85). Of a square plan with nine rooms it is the only example of its type yet found in the Dakhleh oasis.

Despite the large number of Christian sites found to date the amount of inscribed material which they have yielded is small. Of the pottery ostraca all are unimportant, fragmentary or poorly preserved, though one refers to Apa Shenoute. Demotic ostraca from sites of the Roman Period, some of which may be contemporary with the early Christian sites, are more plentiful, but are yet to be studied. Of the fragments of papyrus and parchment all are extremely small save one.

recto			ⲣ ⲡ		*verso*	ⲚⲀ	
1	ϥ	ⲠⲈⲤⲦⲢⲀⲦⲈⲨⲘⲀ · Ⲛ	23.27		1	ⲈⲄⲤⲀⲄ ⲚⲈⲘⲘⲞϤ	31
	ⲘⲀ	ⲦⲈⲢ ⲓ Ⲉ ⲓⲘⲈ · ⲬⲈⲞⲨⲄ ⲢⲰ				ⲚⲀⲨ · ⲀⲨⲦⲀⲖⲈⲠⲀⲨ	
	ⲂⲰⲔ	ⲘⲀ ⲓ ⲞⲤⲠⲈ · ⲀⲈ ⲓ ⲦⲞⲨ				ⲖⲞⲤⲚⲦⲈⲨ[ⲱ]Ⲏ · ⲀⲨ	ⲣ
	Ⲁ · ⲀⲨ	ⲬⲞϤ · ⲈⲈ ⲓ ⲞⲨⲰϢⲀⲈ	28			Ⲭ ⲓ Ⲧϥ ⲈⲀⲚⲦ ⲓ ⲠⲀⲦⲢ ⲓⲤ ·	ⲄⲎ ⲓ
5		ⲈⲤⲞⲨⲚⲦⲀⲞ ⲓ ⲄⲈ · Ⲉ			5	ⲘⲚⲈϥ ⲢⲀⲤⲦⲈⲀ[Ⲉ]ⲀⲨ	ⲹⲚ-
		ⲦⲞⲨⲈⲄ ⲔⲀ ⲖⲈ ⲓ ⲚⲀϥ				ⲦⲢ ⲈⲚ ⲄⲄ ⲓ ⲠⲠⲈⲨⲤ ·	32
		ⲈⲦⲂⲎⲎⲦⲤ · ⲀⲈ ⲓ Ⲭ ⲓ				ⲂⲰⲔⲚⲘⲘⲀϥ · ⲀⲨ	
		Ⲧϥ ⲈⲄ ⲢⲀ ⲓ ⲈⲠⲈⲨⲤⲨ–				ⲔⲞⲦⲞⲨⲈⲦⲠⲀⲢ ⲈⲘ	
		ⲄⲈⲀⲢ ⲓ ⲞⲚ · ⲀⲈ ⲓ ⲄⲚ	29			ⲂⲞⲖⲎ · ⲚⲦⲞⲞⲨⲀⲈ	33
10		ⲦⲤⲈⲨⲈⲄ ⲔⲀ ⲖⲈ ⲓ			10	ⲚⲦⲈⲢⲞⲨⲂⲰⲔⲈ ⲄⲞⲨ	
		ⲚⲀϥ ⲈⲦⲂⲈ Ⲅ ⲈⲚ				ⲈⲦⲔⲀ ⲓ ⲤⲀⲢ ⲓ Ⲁ · ⲀⲨ†	
		ⲦⲎⲘⲀⲚⲦⲈⲠⲈⲨ				ⲦⲈⲠ ⲓ ⲤⲦⲞⲖⲎⲘ ⲫ Ⲏ	
		ⲚⲞⲘⲞⲤ · ⲈⲘⲚⲀⲀ				Ⲅ ⲈⲘⲰⲚ · ⲀⲨⲠⲀⲢ	
		ⲀⲨⲚ Ⲅ Ⲁ ⲠⲈⲢⲞϥ Ⲉϥ				Ⲅ ⲓ ⲤⲦⲀⲚⲀϥⲘⲠⲀⲨ	
15		ⲘⲠ Ϣ ⲀⲘⲠⲘⲞⲨ			15	ⲖⲞⲤ · ⲚⲦⲈⲢⲞϥⲞϢ	34
		ⲎⲘⲢⲢ Ⲉ · ⲚⲦⲈⲢⲞ[Ⲩ]	30			ⲀⲈⲚϬ ⲓ Ⲡ ⲄⲎ Ⲅ Ⲉ	
		ⲦⲀⲘⲞⲈ ⲓ ⲀⲈⲈⲨ				ⲘⲰⲚ · Ⲁϥ	
		ⲔⲢⲞϥ · ⲈϥⲚⲀ				Ϣ ⲓ ⲚⲈⲬⲈⲞⲨⲈ	
		ⲰⲰⲠⲈⲈⲄⲞⲨ				ⲂⲞⲖⲚⲈ Ⲅ [ⲚⲀ]ϢⲚⲈ	Ⲉ
20	ⲚⲘ	ⲈⲠⲈ[ⲓ]ⲢⲰⲘⲈⲈⲂⲞⲖ			20	ⲠⲀⲢⲬ ⲓ ⲀⲚ[ⲧ]ⲈⲢ Ⲉϥ	Ⲟϥ>
	ⲀⲦ ⲓ	Ⲅ ⲓ ⲦⲚ ⲓ ⲞⲨⲀⲀ ⲓ · Ⲛ				Ⲉ ⲓ ⲘⲈⲀⲈ[ⲬⲈⲞ]ⲨⲈ[ⲂⲞⲖ]	Ⲉ
		[ⲧ]ⲈⲨ[Ⲟ]ⲨⲀⲈ ⲓ ⲦⲀⲨⲞϥ				ⲠⲈⲄⲚ	Ⲕ ⲓ Ⲁ
		[Ϣ]ⲀⲈⲢⲞⲔ]Ⲉ ⲓ ⲠⲀⲢⲀⲄ				ⲠⲈⲬⲀ[ϥ][ⲬⲈ]ⲈⲈ ⲓ [ⲈⲤⲰ]	35
		Ⲅ[Ⲉ] ⲓ ⲖⲈ[ⲚⲚ]Ⲉϥ ⲔⲀ				ⲦⲘⲈ[ⲢⲞⲔⲄ]ⲞⲦ[Ⲁ]Ⲛ	
25		ⲦⲎ[ⲄⲞⲢⲞⲤ]Ⲭ ⲓ Ⲅ ⲀⲠ			25	ⲈⲨ[ϢⲀ]ⲚⲈ ⲓ	
		Ⲅ[ⲓ ⲱⲱ]Ⲕ[Ⲛ]ⲘⲘⲀϥ ·				[Ⲁ]ϥⲞⲨ[Ⲉ]Ⲅ Ⲅ ⲤⲀ[ⲚⲈ]	
		ⲘⲘⲀⲦⲞ ⲓ [Ⲕ]Ⲁ					
		ⲦⲀⲠ[Ⲉ]Ⲛ					

(emendations : *recto, l.*10-Ⲉ ⲓ ⲔⲀ ⲖⲈ ⲓ (?); *l.*20-ⲠⲈⲢⲰⲘⲈ)

This is half a page from a parchment codex written in Sahidic (10.6B × 18.0H cm.), preserving two columns of text, one on each side, with a few letters extant from the other column originally on each side. The text of Acts 23.27-35 is preserved, written in a clear and well-formed hand; it may be ascribed tentatively to IV-V. The text may be compared usefully with that published by E. A. Wallis Budge in *Coptic Biblical Texts in the Dialect of Upper Egypt* (London, 1912) 254-55. The piece was found in grave 1 at the important cemetery numbered 31/435-D5-2 by the Project, and it carries the registration number 31/435-D5-5/1/1 (see Mills, *JSSEA* 13 (1983) 128-29). The text of this fragment is given here without commentary. It will be published in full with the other Coptic texts found by the Project in one of the volumes of the publication of the survey of the Dakhleh Oasis under the auspices of the Society for the Study of Egyptian Antiquities, Toronto, Canada.

Co-existent with the Christian churches and communities of IV were numerous pagan communities. A discovery of major importance for the study of art in late antique Egypt was made in Dakhleh in 1979 at the site of Amheida in the western part of the oasis. This comprised a series of frescoes decorating a room in a large complex of buildings, illustrating themes taken from classical sources (see below). Despite the large number of Christian sites and monuments found in Dakhleh, no paintings on a comparable scale of Christian origin have been discovered. However, in the nearby oasis of el-Khargeh, important Christian frescoes of V decorate two of the tomb chapels in the large cemetery of el-Bagawat (see below).

(C.A. Hope)

Frescoes in Dakhleh and Khargeh Oases

The revelation of a series of wall paintings illustrating mythological themes in a room at the site of Amheida must be regarded as one of the most important art-historical discoveries in recent archaeology in Egypt. The following remarks on the Amheida paintings are greatly indebted to the report published by L. M. Leahy in *JSSEA* 10 (1980) 331-78. They are briefly discussed and illustrated in colour in A. J. Mills, *Rotunda* 13 (1980) 19-25.

While there is ample evidence in the minor arts of late antique Egypt for a lively continuation of pagan art into the Christian period, these paintings provide unique testimony on a monumental scale. Their cultural significance is sharpened by their geographical proximity to programmes of Christian paintings executed perhaps a century later in two mausolea in the nearby Khargeh oasis. The Amheida paintings decorate two walls of the ground floor room in a building on the edge of the town site. Several of the five or six separate events from the repertoire of Graeco-Roman mythological themes illustrated can be identified with certainty and the remarkably good state of preservation of many sections reveals the work of trained and competent craftsmen.

The manner in which the paintings are executed and their arrangement on the walls in clearly delineated registers above an ornamental painted dado set them firmly within the Roman tradition of wall painting, but their sometimes exaggerated proportions and tendency toward frontality and occasional linearity reveal traits of the late antique period and suggest that they may be dated to IV.

On the north wall of the room two single scenes are separated by a doorway. One of these is only partly preserved but the lower half of the painting is sufficient to allow positive identification of a popular and much-illustrated event in antiquity: the rescue of Andromeda by Perseus; cf. J. M. Woodward, *Perseus* (Cambridge, 1937), *passim*. The scene on the other side of the door is less common, but can be confidently assumed to illustrate Odysseus' return to Penelope in disguise and his identification by his old nurse, Eurykleia, as she bathes the 'stranger's' feet (Homer, *Od.* 19).

On the east wall the principal scene in the lower register is a portrayal of the adultery of Aphrodite with Ares witnessed by the cuckolded Hephaistos and a group of the Olympian gods. While the romance between Aphrodite and Ares — Love and War — was an extremely popular subject in Roman painting (cf., A. Maiuri, *Roman Painting* [Geneva, 1953] 78), antique illustrations of Homer's description of the discovery of their adultery (*Od.* 8), do not seem to have survived. The portrayal closely follows Homer's narrative in many details, although it includes Herakles and omits Hermes from the assembled witnesses. The physiognomy and attributes of the gods comply with those commonly found in Roman painting.

The enthroned figure of Polis to the left of this scene also conforms in many ways to antique norms, but the precise meaning of her appearance in this context is not immediately apparent; for other examples and discussion of iconography see K. Weitzmann, *Age of Spirituality* (New York, 1979) 173-82. Only the lower half of the paintings on the upper register of the east wall has survived and the sketchy remains have so far defied identification.

The predominance of Homeric themes among the identifiable sections of the Amheida decoration suggests a romantic and heroic emphasis, but it is possible to interpret the appearance of events from the lives of Odysseus and Perseus together with the adultery of Aphrodite and Ares as a conscious juxtaposition of contrasting moral attitudes. The portrayal of Polis also tends to lend an element of secular moral formality to the programme. However, pending the identification of other components no conclusions can be drawn on the possible meaning of the programme as a whole, if indeed there was a dominant theme or unity of purpose.

Dominant theme and unity of purpose are, on the other hand, very clear in the decoration of the two Christian mausolea at Bagawat in the Khargeh oasis to the east. These sketchy but intriguing paintings have been the subject of some study in the past — see bibliography below — but further work, together with fresh archaeological investigation, is needed to attempt a more positive dating and to compare their iconography with other early Christian sepulchral art. In common with their Roman counterparts the programmes emphasise the dominant message of early Christian sepulchral art — salvation through faith — and many of the characters depicted can be related to the ancient prayers for the dying. In the Chapel of Peace these messages of hope and faith are encapsulated in abbreviated images of OT and NT events. These include the Sacrifice of Isaac, Noah in the Ark, the Fall of Adam and Eve, Daniel in the Lion's Den and St Paul and St Thekla, together with single figures, including personifications. Many of these themes are found in Roman catacombs and on sarcophagi of IV in similar formats: A. Grabar, *The Beginnings of Christian Art* (London, 1967), *passim*. But there are some interesting variations on the common Roman iconography, such as the prominence of St Thekla and the inclusion of personifications of Prayer, Justice and Peace.

The Chapel of the Exodus takes its name from the conspicuous portrayal of this event on its cupola. The stylistic and iconographic character of these paintings is different from those of the Chapel of Peace: the paintings are not organized into an orderly radiating pattern around the cupola, but are arrayed across the surface, often employing a sequence of scenes rather than a single image to illustrate the biblical events. In addition to the Exodus, the Parable of the Ten Virgins(?) and events from the life of St Thekla are illustrated. Other OT themes include Jonah and the Whale, Noah's Ark, the Sacrifice of Isaac and the Three Hebrews in the Fiery Furnace, while the higher sections of the dome are decorated with an enormous grape-vine inhabited by birds which peck at the abundant fruit. The iconography in this chapel seems more highly developed in that it offers a sequential narration of some events, but the predominant theme is again the highly appropriate one of salvation through faith.

The paintings in the Amheida building and those in the Christian mausolea at Bagawat furnish important material which extends our knowledge of late antique art in a remote frontier of the Empire. They also provide fascinating fresh insights into the continued diversity of cultural and religious life into the Christian era. Further research and archaeological investigation in the area will undoubtedly be fruitful in adding to our understanding of developments in art in Roman Egypt.

Select Bibliography of 'Chapel of Peace' and 'Chapel of the Exodus' at Bagawat: P. du Bourguet, *L'Art copte* (Paris, 1962) 88-89; A. Fakhry, *The Necropolis of el-Bagawat in Kharga Oasis* (Cairo, 1951); A. Grabar, *CArch* 7 (1956) 9-26; M. Guarducci, *Epigrafia Greca* IV (Rome, 1978) 461-64; W. Hauser, *BMMA* 27 (1932) 38-50; A. M. Lythgoe, *BMMA* 3 (1908) 203-08; G. Millet, *CArch* 7 (1956) 1-8; J. Schwartz, *CArch* 13 (1962) 1-11; H. Stern, *CArch* 11 (1960) 93-119; K.Wessel, *Koptische Kunst* (Recklinghausen, 1963) 175 and 182; H. Zaloscher, *Die Kunst im christlichen Ägypten* (Vienna and Munich, 1974) 89 and 148-50.

(M. Riddle)

107. Edessa again (cf. *New Docs 1977*, 115)

H.J.W. Drijvers discusses the gods of Edessa in *Fest. Dörner* 1.263-83, drawing attention to the need for a systematic treatment of the city's religious history; the notes provide useful bibliography for the subject.

The Syriac text and translation of the *Doctrine of Addai* has recently become available in G. Howard, *The Teaching of Addai* (*SBL Texts and Translations* 16; *ECL Series* 4; Chico, 1981).

General reference ought to have been made to the recent treatment of the city as a whole: J.B. Segal, *Edessa 'The Blessed City'* (Oxford, 1970). In addition to Youtie's article, *HTR* 23 (1930) 299-302, on Jesus' letter to Abgar, mention should have been made of his article the following year, *HTR* 24 (1931) 61-65 which related the Coptic version of the letter to *P.Got.* (1929) 21.

F. VARIA

108. In brief

Where possible reference is made below only to conspectus volumes (like *SEG*), where fuller details of *ed.pr.* etc., are given.

(a) **Divine healings** at Epidauros in epigraphical records ranging in date from IV¹BC–224AD: *IG* IV².1.121–127. None reprinted in this Review, a representative section of no.123 having been included at *New Docs 1977*, **2**, pp.21–23. Allusions to portions of these texts occur in the present Review at **39, 53, 60**. Note also no.123.22–33, the case of a man who disbelieves the miraculous cures testified to by the votive tablets; in a dream the god shows that he can cure him, and accords him the nickname Ἄπιστος. Cf. the NT anecdote about Thomas, Jn. 20.24–29 (esp.v.27).

(b) **Foreign teachers** and pupils who reside there provided by Lampsakos with tax-immunity: *I. Lampsakos* 8 (IVBC?).

(c) **Black marketeers** (so L. Koenen, *ZPE* 27 [1977] 212) in regulations (III²BC) concerning the activity of κάπηλοι in the *temenos* of the Temple of Hera on Samos: *BE* 369. The text uses the hitherto unattested verb παρακαπηλεύω (*ll*.8, 11). In the NT καπηλεύω only once, and pejoratively, at 2 Cor. 2.17.

(d) Senators and equestrians whose **behaviour is likely to disgrace their** *ordo* in the 21*ll.* surviving of a new *senatus consultum* of Tiberius (Larinum, 19AD): *AE* 145. Clearly the decision to which Tac., *Ann.* 2.85.1 and Suet., *Tib*.35.3 refer.

(e) **107 slaves** possessed by an estate owner (Kibyra in Lykia, IAD): *SEG* 1219. For an individual in Egypt owning so many slaves cf. *New Docs 1976*, **24**, p.70.

(f) List of θεραπευταί added in I/II to a IIBC dedication to Sarapis and Isis: *I Magnesia Sip.* 15.

(g) The philosopher **Epiktetos** mentioned in a brief inscription on a herm at Epidauros: *IG* IV².1.683.

(h) A **bakers' strike** at Ephesos, c.200: *SEG* 863.

(i) **Stoic hymn** on the creation of the world, 12 fragmentary lines (vicinity of Monte Fortino in Italy, II/III): *SEG* 793, *BE* 573. *Ed.pr.* places the text within the milieu of the Second Sophistic. It is orthodox Stoicism, with no trace of Jewish/Christian syncretism.

(j) The **'Christian' (?) missionary** from Syria at Lyon (cf. *New Docs 1976*, **23**): further bibliography at *SEG* 826.

(k) Funerary epigram for a tailor set up by a former **apprentice** (Yenidoğan in Bithynia, n.d.): *TAM* 132. Cf. *BE* (1976) 684 with references to papyrus apprenticeship contracts. A new example of the latter is provided by P. Pruneti, *MPL* 2 (1977) 43–48 (pl. on p.318; provenance unknown, 31/12/554), in which Theodora indentures her son Phoibammon to learn for eight years with τῷ εὐλαβεστάτῳ κληρικῷ καὶ βαρβαρικαρίῳ (5), 'the most reverend cleric and brocade-maker (name lost)'.

(l) **Romanization of Syria** from Pompey to Diocletian, a very useful discussion, by J.-P. Rey-Coquais, *JRS* 68 (1978) 44–73 (cf. *SEG* 1328). On this subject see also R. Tracey, *Preliminary Study for an Investigation of Romanization in Syria-Palestine. The Problems of Methodology and Evidence* (MA (Hons.) thesis, Macquarie University, 1981). *SEG* 1329 provides a concise summary of W. Liebeschuetz's not easily accessible article on the Christianization of Syria (noted at *New Docs 1977*, **120**).

(m) Ἀνήρ used of a child in a funerary epigram: *I.Bithynia* II.14 (Bilecik, later Imperial period); cf. *SEG* 981.

(n) Θεολόγος (dat. sing.) in a fragmentary funerary inscription: *TAM* 332 (near Nikomedeia, n.d.) — not Christian. On this word, for which MM provide an entry although it does not occur in the NT, note L. Robert, *R.Phil.* 17 (1943) 184ff. (*non vidi*).

(o) Φιλόλογος in two epitaphs for males aged 20 and 22: *TAM* 155, 232 (Nikomedeia, Roman period). For another instance, used of a person from Nikomedeia who died at Megara, aged 24, see *BE* (1976) 289. Cf. *New Docs 1976*, **74**, p.116.

(p) **Milestones in Judaea** from the time of Vespasian to Constantine surveyed: B. Isaac, *PEQ* 110 (1978) 47–60 (map of road system on p.48); cf. *SEG* 1621.

(q) Ἰησοῦς one of the dedicators of a synagogue mosaic (Gaza, VI): *SEG* 1407.

(r) Inscriptions on the **statue of St. Hippolytos** (Rome, c.233–35): *SEG* 802.

(s) Dedication ὑπὲρ σωτηρίας by Thanoum son of Aspas, **πρωτοπ(ρ)εσ|βύτερος** (Anazarbus in Cilicia, V/VI): *SEG* 1256. Almost certainly Christian in view of the title.

(t) Building inscription set by Theodoros, **διάκονος κὲ ἰατρός**, and his wife (Çemkale in Cilicia, VI(?)): *SEG* 1261.

(u) The abbreviation **ΧΜΓ**: a new interpretation is offered by A. Gostoli, *Stud.Pap.* 22 (1983) 9-14, Χριστὸς μάρτυς γένηται/γένοιτο (or possible some other form of γίνομαι). Cf. *New Docs 1977*, **104**.

(v) **Lent.** At *New Docs 1976*, **84**, J.R. Rea's re-edition of *PSI* 7 (1925) 831 was discussed, a letter (provenance unknown, IV) in which Lent is mentioned (*l.*9). Two other, doubtful, references to Lent were mentioned by Rea at *CE* 45(1970) 357, namely *P.Ant.* 2(1960) 92.26 (provenance unknown, IV/V) and *P.Flor.* 3(1915) 384.55-56 (Hermopolis Magna, V(?)). W. Brashear has kindly drawn to my attention (*per litt.*) a further example among 1976 publications, which escaped my notice: *CPR* V.2(1976)25.5 (Hermopolis, VII/VIII(?)), a business letter which includes instructions for work to be done 'during the above-mentioned fast', ἐν ταῖς προκειμέναις νηστείαις. On fasting before Easter in IVAD Egypt see R.S. Bagnall/K.A. Worp, *BASP* 15(1978) 239 with n.27. Their discussion (239-40) of the word παράλημψις as a term for the combined festival of Ascension/ Pentecost may also be noted here; cf. a reference to the Pentecost miracle in *P.Berl.* 13888.4, repr. at *New Docs 1977*, **93**, p.147.

109. Byzantine Dating Systems

R.S. Bagnall and K.A. Worp have established a very productive partnership for their fundamental re-examination of the dating formulae used in Byzantine papyrus documents in Greek. *CSBE* deals with the indiction system, with consular dating, and with the eras of Oxyrhynchos and of Diocletian. As a supplement to this they have also published *Regnal Formulas in Byzantine Egypt* (*BASP Suppl.*2; Missoula, 1979) which deals with the least problematic dating system, tabulating formulae used from Diocletian to Heraclius (284-641).

Their study of the indiction system is particularly useful (*CSBE* 1-35, with the relevant appendixes). It leads to the overturning of certain received views about this system, the date at which the indiction began and the reasons for the regular use of a 15-year cycle. They argue (15-16) that after 328 the indiction year began at a fixed date (Pachon 1) in early summer, by the harvest time; and though in certain regions of Egypt different dates were used for chronological reckoning of the indiction, this was due to scribal habits which do not conflict with the overall uniformity of the indiction system throughout the country. 'That Egypt had a different indiction [from the East, where the Constantinopolitan indiction began on Sept.1] is due ... to the unusual chronology of its agricultural cycle, a cycle which depended principally not on weather in Egypt but on the behaviour of the Nile' (*CSBE*, 27).

Regnal Formulas provides several pages (74-79) of addenda and corrigenda to *CSBE*, and both volumes need to be used in conjunction. In the course of this work Bagnall and Worp have had occasion to correct published readings of a considerable number of papyri. These 'footnotes' to their chronological investigations are appearing in a series of articles in *BASP*, beginning with 15 (1978) 233-46.

110. Corpus Inscriptionum Semiticarum IV

J. Pirenne and A.F.L. Beeston have collaborated in editing a *Corpus des inscriptions et antiquités sud-arabes* (3 vols; Louvain, 1977). It is intended to supplement the incomplete *CIS* IV (3 vols; 1889–1929), which was devoted to Sabaean and Himyarite texts. It is therefore largely beyond the scope of this Review, but some features of the new publication can be mentioned. The new work consists of editions with translations, dates and plates of inscriptions (vol. 1.1), and of non-epigraphic material, such as sculpture, altars, vases and statues (1.2). Vol. 3 consists of tables which classify the inscriptions by subject, and indexes S. Arabian words. The second volume provides a bibliography covering the period 1929-1975 for the pre-Islamic civilization of S. Arabia, focusing mainly upon the two Yemens, Saudi Arabia and Ethiopia. It may be useful to note here some of the sections in this bibliography.
— 'Sources épigraphiques et littéraires non sudarabiques' (103-28; especially 114-17 on Hebrew and Jewish sources, 119-26 on Greek and Latin literary sources);
— 'Épigraphie' (119-87);
— 'Religions' (215-43; especially 223-26 on monotheistic religions — Judaism, Christianity — in S. Arabia; 229-30 on penitence and purification);
— 'Histoire' (261-302; especially 294-97 on the crisis of VI).

111. Jewish and Christian entries in *BE*

BE 37 and 40 provide useful cross-references respectively to Jewish and Christian texts in Greek commented on in *BE* for 1978; two other publications on Christian inscriptions are treated at *BE* 38,39.

112.

The following Christian texts were encountered in 1978 publications and others listed in the Abbreviations section of the Introduction, but have not been treated at all in this Review. ('Christian' here is used very broadly to refer to a text which may be distinguished by its content, or merely by the presence of certain signs, e.g., a cross on an official document.) Nearly all of these are late Roman or Byzantine in date.

AE:	17(?), 18, 66, 95 *bis*, 422, 423, 424(?), 474, 476, 485, 486, 490, 492–94, 575, 821, 822 (= *I.Tyre* [1977] 28, repr. at *New Docs 1977*, **3**, p.26), 865–67, 869, 870, 873–83, 891;
Carthage 3:	p.169 no.3;
CPR:	9;
Fest. Dörner:	1.71 no.S16; 1.79 no.SR17;
IGA 2:	378;
IGA 5:	1, 11–14, 17–21, 23–27, 29–32, 34–47, 49, 50, 52, 53, 54 (? — 148AD), 55–68, 71–106, 108–20, 122, 125–88, 190, 192–223, 225–36, 238–82, 284–308, 310–41, 343–53, 355, 356, 358–79, 381–422, 424–61, 463, 464, 466–75, 477, 478, 480, 483, 484, 487–89, 491–93, 495–506, 508–14, 516–24, 527, 529–40, 542–56, 558, 559, 562–76, 578–86, 588, 589, 591–93, 595–607, 612, 614–18, 621–59, 661, 662, 664–740, 742–45, 747, 748, 750, 751, 754–61, 763–69, 771, 774–82, 784–808;
I.Bithynia:	II.3, 4, 16, 17 (= *SEG* 1058), 18, 19 (= *SEG* 1059), 21;
IGCB:	2a, 3, 4, 7, 8, 10, 11, 13, 14, 25, 30, 31, 32, 33–58, 58a, 59–64, 64a, 65, 66;
I.Lampsakos:	32;
NIP:	IV.50;
P.L.Bat.:	18, 19, 22, 23, 23 *bis*, 24;
P.Strasb.:	677, 678, 680;
SEG:	320, 360, 381 (= Wiseman, *Corinthians*, p.100), 388, 390 (= Wiseman, p.92), 406, 512, 540 (cf. *SEG* 26[1976/7] 725), 544, 548 (cf. *SEG* 26.732), 563–73, 575, 625, 642, 825 (to be treated in the next Review), 867, 876, 1047, 1057, 1062, 1068, 1069, 1260, 1262, 1265, 1283–88, 1294, 1308, 1344, 1347, 1354–57, 1377–80, 1393, 1397–1405, 1456, 1457, 1459–68, 1472, 1573–75, 1577, 1579–81, 1584, 1587, 1593;
TAM:	213(?), 353, 354, 356, 358–60, 362, 363, 365, 367, 370, 372a, 373;
Wiseman,*Corinthians*:	p.36, p.85, p.92 (= *SEG* 390), p.100 (= *SEG* 381).

113. Corrigenda to *New Docs 1976* and *1977*

The following corrigenda to *New Docs 1976* which affect clarity have been noticed (additional to those listed at *New Docs 1977*, **121**):

p.ii,   entry **60**: for 'Jn. 13.27' read 'Jn. 14.27'.
p.15,   item (vi): for 'see **35**' read 'see **11**'.
p.56,   Greek text, *l*.15: for 'ὀγίαν' read 'ὑγίαν.'
p.77,   last paragraph, *l*.3: for 'Keraklammon' read 'Heraklammon'.
p.99,   entry **60**, title: for 'Jn. 13.27' read 'Jn. 14.27'.
         three lines down: ditto.
p.147,   col. 1, *l*.1: for 'Jn. 13.27 — **60**' read 'Jn. 14.27 — **60**'.

The following corrigenda to *New Docs 1977* which affect clarity have been noticed:

p.3,   *l.*30: for 'Königshefte' read 'Königsfeste'.

p.9,   last line of first paragraph: for 'he' read 'she'.

p.10, last line: for 'Hermann' read 'Herrmann'.

p.34, entry **5**, *l.*23: for 'Gschnitzner' read 'Gschnitzer'.

p.35, second paragraph, *l.*3: for 'εἰς' read 'εἷς.'

p.93, entry **65**, first paragraph, second last line: for 'fr' read 'for'.

p.106, *l.*2: for '5 (1977)' read '3 (1977)'.

p.163, last paragraph, *ll.*1–2: K. Treu (*per litt.*) has kindly informed me that *P.Berl.*6788 and 6788A are *not* from the same codex. This affects the comments in the remainder of that paragraph, and the last sentence in the following one.

p.167, *l.*4: for 'Neve' read 'Nene'.

p.173, *l.*6 from the bottom: for '1980' read '1978'.

p.175, last paragraph, *l.*14: for 'thought' read 'though'.

p.181, first paragraph after translation, *l.*6: for '[1957]' read '[1947]'.

p.200, entry **113**: P.J. Sijpesteijn has kindly drawn to my attention (*per litt.*) the inaccurate punctuation of *ll.*6–8. They should read:

θεός. καὶ (μ)ήτις
τῶν λεκτικαρίων, διὰ τὰ γενόμενα
δι' ὑμᾶς ὧδε, κτλ.

p.207, *l.*6: for 'τῆκ.' read 'τῇ κ.'

p.214, entry **121**(!): for 'p.82' read 'p.83'.

p.217, index 2, col.1: add 'ἀθάνατος — 112, 116'.

INDEXES

1. Biblical passages

2. Words

This index does not register all occurrences of words in texts printed in this Review, but simply those words which receive some notice in an entry. Item numbers in bold type indicate more than a passing reference. An asterisk (*) indicates that comment is offered on the MM or BAGD entry, or occasionally on LSJ. New words are marked with a dagger (†).

A. Greek

ἀβάσκαντος — 52
ἀγαπάω — **2**
*ἄγγελος — *6,93
*ἄγρα — **4**
ἀειπάρθενος — 93,101
*αἱρετίζω — **6**
*ἀκοή — **22**
ἀκωλύτως — 4
*ἁλιεύς — 4
ἁμαρτία — 6
ἄμωμος — 11
*ἀνανεόομαι — 23
*ἀνανέωσις — 23
ἀνεγείρομαι — 93
ἀνήρ — 108
ἀνθρώπινος — 6
ἀντιστρέφω — 100
ἀπάθεια — 92
*ἀπαλλοτριόω — **24**
*ἁπλοῦς — **6**
*ἀπό (causal) — 100
*ἀπογίνομαι — **25**
*ἀποκαραδοκέω — 92
*ἀπόνοια — 101
*ἀποστερέω — 61
ἀποτακτικός — **104**
ἀπραγμοσύνη — **101**
ἁρπάζω — 101
*ἄρρωστος — **26**
ἀρχιδιάκονος — **27**
ἀρχιθιασίτης — 28
ἀρχιμύστης — **28**
ἀσκέω — **101**
ἀσκήτρια — 101
ἀσυλία — 68

ἀσφάλεια — 101
*ἀσφαλῶς — **1**
ἀτέλεια — 68
ἀφαρπάζω — 101
βαρβαρικάριος — 108
βαφεύς — 17
βίβλος — 29
βολ- words — 4
†βυβλίς — 29
γάρ — 100
γναφεύς — 17
*γυναικεῖος — 6
*δεκάτη — **30**
δέχομαι — 15
διακονέω τινί — 2
διάκων — 104
διαλογισμός — 2
διαρπάζω — 101
διασπάω — 101
διαστολεύς — 73
*διατηρέω — **31**,*32
διενοχλέω — 36
διϊσχυρίζομαι — 36
διόλου — 26
δοῦμος ἱερός — 9,80
δύναμις — 7
*δώρημα — 79
Ἑβραῖος — 94
*ἔγκλημα — **32**
εἴθε — 101
εἵλεως — 93
εἰμί
  μὴ εἴοιτο — **33**
εἷς θεός — 7
*ἐκκόπτω — **34**
ἐκλυτρόομαι — 46
*ἑκουσίως — 4

*ἐλαύνω — 15
ἐλευθέρα — **12**
ἐμβασιλεύω — 14
*ἐνδώμησις — **40**
ἐνέργεια — 92
*ἐνορκίζω — **35**
*ἐνοχλέω — **36**
ἐξελαύνω — 15
*ἐξιλάσκομαι — 6
*ἐξολεθρεύω — **64**
*ἔπαυλις — **45**
ἐπιδίδωμι — 100
ἐπικατάρατος — **96**
*ἐπικουρία — **37**
ἐπιπάλλω — **36**
ἐπίπνοια — **6**
ἐπίσκοπος — 104
ἐπιταγή
  κατ' ἐπιταγήν — **6,39**
ἐργάτης — 50
ἐριοργός — 17
ἑταῖρος — 75
*εὐαγγελ- words — **2**
εὐλογέω — 96
εὐλογία — 94
εὐνοῦς — 11
*εὐνοῦχος — **11**
*εὐποιΐα — **38**
εὐχαριστήριον — 22
εὐχή — **30**
ἐφίστημι — 101
ζωγράφημα — 93
ζωοποιΐα — 101
*θεῖον — **39**
θεῖος — 100
  θεία πρόνοια — **100**
*θεολόγος — 108

θεόπνευστος	— 6	*ὅλος	— 26	συμβίωσις/-ωτής	— 17,80,101
θεός	— 102	ὄναρ		συμμύστης	— 28
εἷς θεός	— 7	κατ' ὄναρ	— **6**	συμπαθ- words	— 80
θεοσεβής	— 17,96	ὀνικός	— 101	*συναγωγή	— *11,94
θεότοκος	— 102	ὄνομα		*συναγωνίζομαι	— **67**
θεραπευτής	— 108	κατ' ὄνομα	— 1,52,100	*συναντιλαμβάνομαι	— **68**
θλῖψις	— 98	*ὁπότε	— **2**	*συνείδησις	— **69**
θρεπτός	— 80,81	ὀρθόδοξος	— 91	συνεργασία	— 17
*θυμιατήριον	— **40**	*οὐρανός	— 7,*15	συνεργός	— **101**
θυρουρός	— 104	*πάμπολυς	— 53	*συνέρχομαι	— 70
ἴδιος	— 100	παντοκράτωρ	— **93**	συνζεύγνυμι	— 101
ἱερός	— 44	πάντοτε	— 76	σύνοδος	— 17
ἱερὰ βίβλος	— **29**	παραβοηθέω	— 100	*συνοικέω	— **71**
ἱερὸς δοῦμος	— 9,80	*παραιτέομαι	— **54**	*σύντροφος	— **9**
*ἱλάσκομαι	— **6**	†παρακαπηλεύω	— 108	*σωματικῶς	— **72**
ἱλασμός	— **6**	παράλημψις	— 108	σωτηρία	— 6
*ἱματισμός	— **41**	*παραλυτικός	— 55	†τεκνοθεσία	— **3**
ἵνα (imperatival)	— **100**	παράλυτος	— 55	τέκτων	— 17
†ἰνγένουος	— 11	*παραμυθία	— **56**	τιμάω	— 9
Ἰουδαῖοι, οἱ ποτὲ	— 17	*παραμύθιον	— 56	τράπεζα	— 6,40
ἰχθύς	— 4,7	παρανομία	— 101	τρόπος	— 101
*ἴχνος	— **39**	*παραπληξία	— 96	*τρυγάω	— 2
κάπηλος/-λεύω	— 108	*παραπλήσιος/-ίως	— **57**	ὕδωρ	— 100
*καταγινώσκω	— 2	παρασκευή	— **58**	*υἱοθεσία	— **3**
*καταρτισμός	— **42**	*πάραυτα	— 101	*ὑπεράνω	— **73**
*κατασκηνόω	— **89**	παραχρῆμα	— 31	ὑπηρεσία	— 1
*κατέχων, ὁ	— 6	πάσχω	— 92	ὕσγη/ὕσγινον	— 17
κέρμα	— 100	*πενθερά	— **9**	φαίνομαι	— 93
κεφάλαιον	— 43	*πενιχρός	— **59**	φιλαγαθία	— 11
*κεφαλή	— 12	*περιεργάζομαι	— **6**	φιλάδελφος	— 11,74
*κῆνσος	— **44**	*περιπίπτω εἰς	— **100**	*φιλανδρία/-ρος	— **11**
κοιμάομαι	— 80	*περιτέμνω	— 60	φιλέντολος	— **89**
κοίμησις	— 80	*περιτομή	— 60	φιλέω	— **2**
κοινωνέω	— 101	*πιέζω	— **61**	φιλόθεος	— 6
κοινωνία/-νός	— 4,101	πιλοποιός	— 17	φιλόκαισαρ	— 75
κολλύριον	— 17	πορφυροπώλης	— 17,104	φιλόλογος	— 108
*κολοβός	— 100	ποτήριον	— 100	φιλορώμαιος	— 75
κόλπος	— **89**	πραγματευτής	— 6	*φίλος	— *17,*75
*κράτιστος	— *2,9	πρεσβύτερος/-τέρα	— **98**,104	φιλοσέβαστος	— 75
*κυκλεύω	— **45**	προαίρεσις	— 92	*φιλοστοργία/-γος	— **11**
κυριακὴ ἡμέρα	— 58	προδικαία	— 68	*φιλοτεκνία/-νος	— **11**
*λάμπω	— 15	προεδρία	— 68	φιλόφιλος	— 11
λεινοργός	— 17	προευαγγελίζομαι	— 2	φράτρα	— 6
λιμώσσω	— 85	προμαντεία	— 68	φῶς	— **93**
*λούομαι	— 6	πρόνοια	— **100**	χμγ	— 108
*λύτρον	— **46**	προξενία/-νος	— 68	*χρῆσις	— 40
λυτρόω	— **46**	προσαμαρτάνω	— 6	χριστιανός	— **98**
λύτρωσις	— 46	προσευχή	— **94**	ψυχρός	— **100**
μακάριος	— 101	προσκύνημα	— **52**,81		
*μαρτυρέω	— 2	προσφωνέω	— 62		
μέλλω + aor. infin.	— **100**	*προχειρίζομαι	— **62**		
μένω	— 100	πρωτοπρεσβύτερος	— 108		
μέρος	— 23,**47**,100	*πρωτότοκος	— **63**		
μεστός	— **101**	ριζόσημος	— 17		
*μετασχηματίζω	— **48**	*ριψοκίνδυνος	— 101		
μισθαποδοσία	— 49	Σατανᾶς	— **64**	**B. Latin (selected)**	
*μισθαποδοτέω/-της	— **49**	*σβέννυμι	— 15		
μνηστεύω	— 101	σεβαστόγνωστος	— 75	*amicus Caesaris*	— **75**
μυστάρχης	— 28	σέβομαι	— 17,96	*custos*	— 8
μύστης	— 28	σεμνός	— 11	*familia Caesaris*	— **1**
μυστιάρχης	— 28	*σκάφη	— 4	*obsequium*	— 8
*νεομηνία/νουμηνία	— **50**	σκορπίζω	— 85	*officium*	— 1
*νουθετέω	— **51**	*σκωληκόβρωτος	— 65	*penicillus*	— 17
*νωθρεία	— **2**	*σκώληξ	— **65**	*praefectus*	— 95
οἰκιακός	— 1,75	σοφία	— 14	*societas*	— **4**
οἱοσδήποτε	— 72	†σοφοδιδάσκαλος	— 17	†*Tiberieum*	— 95
*ὁλοκληρία	— 6	*σπλάγχνον	— **66**		

3. Subjects

4. ECL, Patristic and Jewish Writers

5. Texts Discussed

Listed below are all texts new or old appearing in 1978 corpora and conspectus volumes and referred to in this work. Of other texts only those referred to in a more than passing manner are listed. Bold type indicates substantial discussion of a text at the item number given, or that a non-1978 text has been reprinted here. It is not the normal practice of this Review to suggest new readings or dates, but where they are offered an asterisk (*) beside the text in this index will indicate it.

357	89	374 (= *CIJ* 2.798)	⎫
361	23	375, 376	⎬ 94
364	94	377 (= *CIJ* 2.799)	⎭
366	23,91	Walbank, *Proxenies* (cf. *SEG* 11, 12, 48)	68
368	23	Wistrand (cf. *AE* 14)	**8**,11,14
369, 371	91	*ZPE* 27 (1977) 212 (cf. *BE* 369)	108

ORDER FORM

NEW DOCUMENTS ILLUSTRATING EARLY CHRISTIANITY

(Typewriting or Block Letters, please)

NAME_____

ADDRESS_____

CITY_____ COUNTRY_____ POSTCODE_____

☐ NEW DOCUMENTS 1976   ☐ NEW DOCUMENTS 1977   ☐ NEW DOCUMENTS 1978

Price for each volume (overseas orders: all prices refer to U.S. currency):

Hard cover
☐ $40.00 Institutions
☐ $32.00 Personal use

Soft cover
☐ $24.00 Institutions
☐ $19.00 Personal use

☐ Standing Order
   for continuation
   of series

For orders delivered outside Australia:

☐ $3.00 per volume surface postage, OR
☐ $10.00 per volume air postage.

☐ Official order enclosed, OR
☐ Cheque enclosed in favour of 'MACQUARIE UNIVERSITY NEW DOCUMENTS'

....
(Sign here if claiming rate for personal use)

Ancient History Documentary Research Centre, Macquarie University, North Ryde 2113, Australia

MACQUARIE UNIVERSITY, AUSTRALIA